Stepping stones

through the Bible day by day

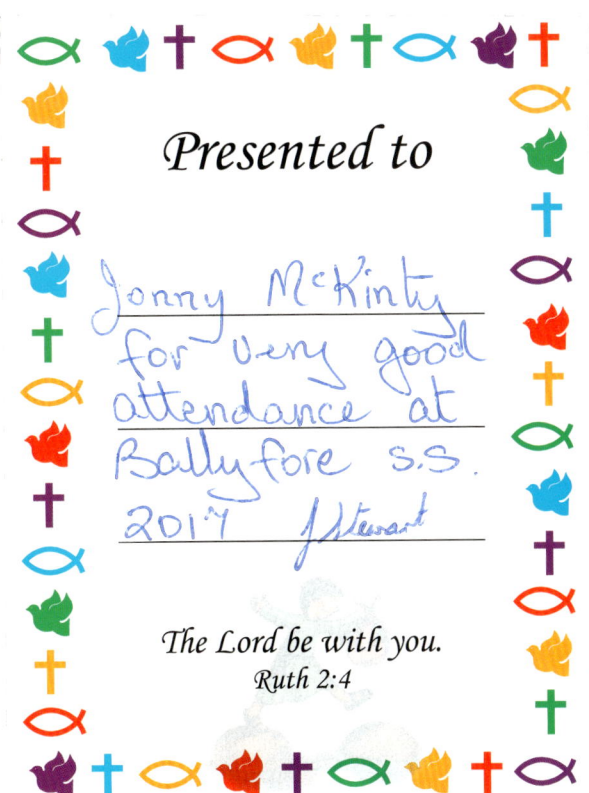

Presented to

Jonny McKinty
for very good
attendance at
Ballyfore S.S.
2017 J Stewart

The Lord be with you.
Ruth 2:4

Stepping stones
through the Bible day by day

Compiled and Edited by Ian Rees

Illustrated by Honor Ayers

Published by Precious Seed Publications

©Copyright Precious Seed Publications 2008

The Glebe House, Stanton Drew, Bristol BS39 4EH, UK

First published September 2008
Second Edition March 2010

ISBN 978-1-871642-24-7

Please note that the disk supplied with this book is free. It should not be copied. It has been tested on Windows Vista (SP1) and Windows XP (SP2) but it will not necessarily run on other versions of Windows or other operating systems. The disk is provided without any technical support but if it is broken or damaged a replacement can be ordered from the address above.

Printed in China

Contents

                Page

Foreword ix

Acknowledgements xi

The Contributors xiii

How to use this book xv

The Readings 2

Foreword

The Bible is the Word of God, written. That means that it is the best way we have, today, to know what God wants to teach us. The first thing He wants us to know is *what He is like*. We cannot see Him, so He has revealed Himself to us in the Bible, which often tells us His thoughts and intentions, and shows us through the ways in which He dealt with people years ago, what pleases Him and what displeases Him even today. The second thing He wants us to know is *what we are like*. As we read the Bible, we see people who were like us and we see what mankind as a whole is like. The Bible is like a mirror in which we can see ourselves. The third thing God wants us to know is *how to please Him*. So it is most important to read the Bible regularly, that we may begin to know God, know ourselves, and know God's will for us.

In years gone by God spoke to men directly, either with a voice they could hear from heaven, or through prophets who spoke His thoughts. Then His Son, whom men called Jesus of Nazareth, came into the world to reveal God to mankind. Now that He has returned to heaven, He has left us His word, written, for us to read. Preachers may use it to teach us; Sunday school teachers may be used of God to teach our children. But we should never neglect the reading of God's word for ourselves, either at home on our own, or with our families gathered around us. God's word *is* a lamp to our feet and a light to our path. Lift it up, then, so that it can shine on us.

This series of readings is designed to take us through the time-line of the Bible. The books of the Bible are not read in the order in which you will find them in the Bible; they are read in the order in which they took place. It is my hope that you will understand more fully how God dealt with the human race as a result of using this book and that it will draw you closer to God.

Ian Rees
September 2008

Acknowledgements

Scripture quotations are taken from the New King James Version.

Copyright © 1982 by Thomas Nelson, Inc.

Used by permission. All rights reserved.

The Contributors

It is no easy thing to write so that others can enjoy reading what you have written. It is hard enough to write for people of your own age; it is even harder to write for people who are much younger. The publishers of this book of Bible readings would like to thank the following people, who have spent a lot of time thinking and writing in these pages, so that you may learn about the Bible and the God they love. Some of them have been Sunday School teachers for many years, some are teachers in local schools, some teach children in Bible Clubs and some are experienced parents who have taught their own children about God and His Word. Their names are given in alphabetical order.

Stephen Baker, Stephen Buckeridge, Stan Burditt, Ian Campbell, Cyril Cann, Margaret Charles, David Coles, Janice Emerson, Adrian Ferguson, Sharon Grant, Mary King, Mark Lacey, Blair Martin, Paul McCauley, Gordon McCracken, Robert Plant, David Raggett, Ian Rees, Rebecca Rees, Della Rudge, Jeremy Singer, Gordon Stewart and Louise Stewart.

We are also very grateful to Honor Ayers who has brought her huge talent to this book and brightened its pages with her drawings. We are grateful to Barney Trevivian for his help in the design and layout of this book. Thanks are also due to the trustees of the Netherfield Trust who caught the vision for this book and made a major contribution to its printing costs. Now, all that remains is for you to use the book and learn more about God and yourself from it.

How to use this book

There are two ways in which this book can be used. Perhaps you have been given the book as a present, and hope to read it for yourself, on your own. The best way to do this is to keep it in the place where you hope to read it, and then use it every day. Take up the book, turn to the reading for the day, and look up the Bible passage in your own Bible, then read that part of the Bible first. If you don't have a Bible of your own, see if you can borrow one from a friend, a member of your family or someone who goes to your local church. Once you have read the verses for the day, think about the words that are highlighted at the top of the page in this reading book. They will give you a theme which will help you to understand what the reading is about. Read the rest of the page, and when you have finished, use the thought in the prayer bubble to help you to pray to God before you get on with the day.

This book of readings also comes with a CD-Rom which you will find tucked into a sleeve on the inside back cover. You can access all the readings from your computer if you wish to use the CD as well as the book.

Perhaps you have bought the book to read it with your family. We would encourage you to do this, if you are a father, mother or carer. You may find the best time to read to your family is over breakfast, though some families might find it more suitable to read it before bed-time. Whichever way is best for your family, take your responsibility seriously to teach your children the things of God. Read the Bible together and pray together. Someone has rightly said, 'the family that prays together, stays together'. The Bible gives us good advice and a strong hope that what we teach our children now will remain with them forever. It says, 'Train up a child in the way he should go and when he is old he will not depart from it', Proverbs 22. 6. Show your children, by your example how important it is to read the Bible every day.

Ian Rees

January 1

Reading: Genesis 1. 1-25

By faith we understand that the worlds were framed by the word of God, Hebrews 11. 3

How great God is! By His great power and wisdom He created our world. He made everything out of nothing. He spoke and it happened. God created light and He made life.

He made the sky and the land. How wonderful it is to go up in an aeroplane and look down at the clouds and see the fields, hills and rivers – all things that God made! We love to see the sun in the sky and the moon and stars on a clear night. King David said in Psalm 19 verse 1, 'The heavens declare the glory of God'. They tell us how great God is.

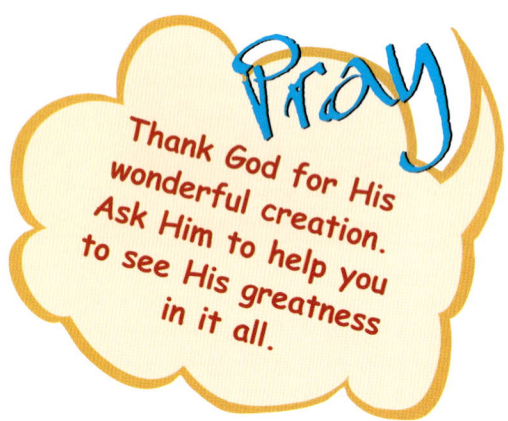

Pray: Thank God for His wonderful creation. Ask Him to help you to see His greatness in it all.

Look around outside and see all the plants and trees. God made some for food and others just for their beauty. Look closely at a flower and see its design and detail, its delicate colours. Each plant and flower is so beautiful.

Perhaps you have a pet – a dog or cat, a budgie or even a goldfish. But just think of all the different kinds of animals there are. Some move very quickly and others are very slow. Some are very big, like the elephant and others are so small, like the mouse. God made them all. Did you know that though there are many thousands of zebras their stripes are all different? If you visit an aquarium you can see some of the many kinds of fish that God made. Some are dull and some brightly coloured, some are long and thin and others are round and flat. What about the birds with their beauty and their own lovely song to sing?

Oh how great God is to make all these! God was pleased when He had finished and said His creation was very good – yes, and perfect too!

Stepping stones

Reading: **Genesis 1. 26-31**

God created man in His own image, Genesis 1. 27

On the sixth day of His creation God made man. He made man in His own image. This means God made man different to the rest of His creation. Apart from a body and a spirit, which all living creatures have, God gave man a soul so that we could get to know Him.

This is the main reason why God made us. He really wants us to know His presence with us and to enjoy His friendship day by day. God also gave man a will so he could choose to serve Him. That is a very important choice we all have to make. God gave man emotions too. These are the things we feel, like love, fear, joy and happiness. God gave us emotions so we could love Him from our hearts.

God wanted man to be His manager in the world, to look after all the animals, birds and fish He had made. Some people look after animals in zoos. Others work in aquariums where there are many different kinds of fish, or in aviaries where we can see so many beautiful birds. Maybe you would love to work in places like these when you are older.

When the first man was given the privilege of looking after God's animal kingdom, everything was different to what it is today. There were no wild or dangerous animals as there are now. The first man was not afraid of the lion, the bear or the crocodile. God had made everything beautiful and perfect.

God gave fruit, vegetables and herbs to both man and animals to eat. This was a very healthy diet. God knew what was best for them. He still wants the best for us today. What a caring God we have! Let's thank Him for that.

Pray

Ask God to help you to get to know Him personally and to love and serve Him in the way He would like.

... through the Bible day by day

January 3

READING: Genesis 2. 4-17

I have set before you life and death, blessing and cursing; therefore choose life, that both you and your descendants may live, Deuteronomy 30. 19

Imagine living in a place where it never rained and having no need for an umbrella. That is how it was when God first made the world. God watered the earth by dew. Some mornings we still see dew on the grass.

God made the first man, Adam, out of the dust then He breathed life into him. Man became a living soul, able to experience fellowship with God and, later, enjoy friendship with other people. God made a beautiful garden in Eden with all kinds of trees in it. There were ordinary trees like the oak and beech which are beautiful to look at and there was every kind of fruit tree for man to eat. God's garden was big and had a river flowing through it, which became four main rivers. Take time to look at God's wonderful creation around you.

Pray

Ask God to help you to make the right choices to obey and not to disobey Him.

God put the man in this lovely garden to look after it and keep it. What an easy job he had! No weeds grew then so he could just enjoy its beauty. He was able to eat as much fruit and vegetables as he liked. God had put it all there for his food.

But there were two special trees in the garden. One was called the tree of life, which was in the middle of the garden. The other was called the tree of the knowledge of good and evil. God told Adam very clearly that he must not eat of the fruit of that tree or he would die. The man understood completely what God had said but he was going to be tested. What would he do? Obey God or disobey Him? There are many times when we have to make that same choice. It is always best to obey God.

Stepping stones

Reading: **Genesis 2. 18-25**

January 4

The LORD God said, 'It is not good that man should be alone; I will make him a helper comparable to him', Genesis 2. 18

God had made all the animals and birds and brought them to Adam so he could give them their names. What fun he must have had! He was no doubt given intelligence and wisdom by God. Imagine him saying, 'I think I will call this one a rhinoceros, that one a donkey, this one I will name elephant and that little one over there, mouse' – in his own language, of course. Perhaps we would have given them different names. It must have taken Adam quite a long time because there are so many species of animals and birds.

Adam had plenty of animals around him for company but there was no one he could talk to as his friend. Do you like being alone? Sometimes it is nice to have some peace and quiet but not all the time. Adam was alone in the garden, so God said, 'I will make him a helper, a companion who will be good for him'.

God put Adam to sleep and then performed an operation on him. He took a rib out of his side and then closed the skin over again. Adam didn't need stitches or any time to recover. God is so great He is able to do anything! With the rib God made a woman and brought her to Adam. She became his wife. She must have been very beautiful, just like the rest of God's creation. This was the first wedding in the Bible.

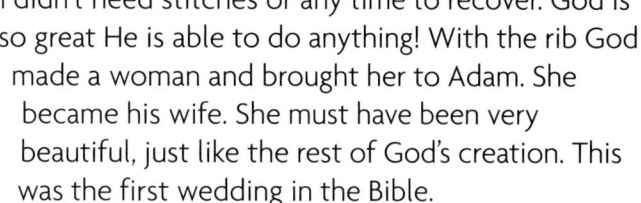

Pray
Thank God for your parents and ask Him to continue to give them help, wisdom and love for each other.

God knew what was best for man and so He gave man instructions about marriage. Marriage was not man's idea. God designed it. He said that He wanted a man to leave his parents and to live with his wife and they would be one. This is still God's ideal. Marriage is good for men and women.

. . . through the Bible day by day

January 5

Reading: Genesis 3. 1-24

Through one man sin entered the world, and death through sin, Romans 5. 12

Why is it that God created a perfect world and yet today there are natural disasters like earthquakes and volcanoes? There are wars and violence and crime on our streets. Millions of people are poor and have little or nothing to eat. The answer is found right at the beginning of time.

Adam and Eve lived in the beautiful Garden of Eden in harmony with God's creation. God gave them everything good to enjoy and especially His friendship. But all this was going to change. The devil, disguised as a snake, came and tempted Eve. He questioned and even denied what God had said. Adam and Eve knew they must not eat of the tree of the knowledge of good and evil or they would die but Eve was tempted. This means she was encouraged to do something wrong. We all know what it is like to be tempted. If we give in to temptation we sin against God.

Pray
Ask God to help you not to give in to temptation today and to keep you from sinning against Him.

Eve saw the fruit on that tree looked good and thought it would make her wise. The devil had deceived her. She took it, ate it then gave some to Adam to eat. Their consciences immediately told them they had done wrong. They tried to hide from God but He knew what they had done. Adam blamed Eve, she blamed the serpent, but their sin was serious. God punished them. He cursed the ground, too, so that from then on thorns and weeds began to grow. God's wonderful creation was affected by sin. This is why we have famines and floods and why there is so much suffering and evil in our world.

Adam and Eve were sent out of the garden so they could not eat of the tree of life and live forever in sin. Sadly they had lost their friendship with God. Sin always spoils things. Be careful not to sin today.

Stepping stones

Reading: Genesis 4. 1-7

January 6

Let brotherly love continue, Hebrews 13. 1

Eve was delighted when her first son Cain was born. She believed he was a gift from the Lord. Then Abel was born. The two brothers were quite different. When they were older they had different interests. Cain was a farmer but Abel became a shepherd.

Adam and Eve would have told their sons what life had been like when they were younger, just as parents do today. Both boys were taught the way to come to God because they both brought Him an offering. An offering is something we give to God. God had always wanted men and women to enjoy a relationship and friendship with Him. Sin had spoiled that friendship for Adam and Eve. Yet God had shown them the way to come back to Him.

Pray

Ask God to help you to obey Him and to show love to all in your family.

The time came for Cain and Abel to bring their offerings to God. The sad thing is that Cain refused to come near to God in the right way. He wanted to make his own kind of sacrifice and offered to God some of the vegetables he had grown. God had made it clear that a life had to be given and blood had to be shed before He could accept the sacrifice. This is what Abel did when he offered a lamb. That lamb was a lovely picture of what the Lord Jesus was going to be as a sacrifice on the cross. God was pleased with Abel and his offering but not with Cain's.

Cain became very jealous of his brother. He was angry and miserable because he was disobeying God and wanting his own way. God spoke to Cain about his attitude and gave him the opportunity of putting things right. He warned him of the danger of disobedience. Sadly Cain did not listen. Are our own attitudes to God right or wrong?

. . . through the Bible day by day

January 7

Reading: Genesis 4. 8-16

You shall not murder, Exodus 20. 13

How sad it was that Cain would not listen to God! He was stubborn and rebellious and wanted to do things his way and refused to change. He would not come to God in the right way. He became jealous of his brother Abel, who approached God properly by sacrificing a lamb. Cain's jealousy led to hatred and hatred led to murder. As they were talking in a field Cain became so angry that he killed his brother Abel. How this must have made God very sad! To think that the first man to be born became a murderer!

The Lord asked Cain where his brother was. Cain replied he didn't know and was not responsible for him. One sin often leads to another and makes a person try to cover up his wickedness and tell lies about it.

Pray

Pray that God will keep you from jealousy and help you to do as He says, so that you can enjoy His friendship.

God knew where Abel was and had seen all that had happened. He has not changed and still today He sees and knows all we do and say and even think. Cain was guilty before God. God put a curse on him and told him that he would no longer be successful as a farmer and he would wander around from place to place in the earth. Cain realized that he had lost the opportunity and privilege of having contact and friendship with God forever. This was the result of his disobedience and terrible sin. God put a special mark on Cain so that no one would take revenge for Abel and kill Cain too.

The Lord Jesus warns us that if we hate someone it is like murdering them in our hearts. Let's be careful not to hate other people, even those who are different to us. Hate may lead us to do wicked things.

Stepping stones

Reading: **Genesis 4. 17-24**

Whatever a man sows, that he will also reap, Galatians 6. 7

The book of Genesis is the book of beginnings. It tells us when and how so many things began. Cain built a city and named it after his son Enoch. Sadly he was living without God in his life because of his awful sin and rebellion against Him.

> **Pray**
> Ask God to help you not to argue and fight. Pray that He will help you to be a good example to others.

We can see that his attitude and rebellion towards God had a bad effect on his family. His great, great grandson, Lamech, sinned against God by marrying two wives. Their children each followed a different pathway in their lives. We read that Jabal began living in a tent. Perhaps he found it difficult to settle in any one place and so wandered from place to place like his ancestor Cain had done. He looked after cattle. His brother Jubal became an inventor of musical instruments and played the harp and the flute. He wanted to find pleasure playing music. Their cousin Tubal-Cain showed skill in metal-work and taught others too. We don't read that any of them enjoyed friendship with God.

Lamech spoke to his two wives and made a confession. He must have been in an argument with another man who started fighting with him. Lamech was wounded in the fight and he killed the man. It is sad to see Lamech boasting about his violence. Sin was now increasing, affecting people's lives and spoiling the society in which they lived. There is great danger in arguing and fighting. Even though Lamech may have been defending himself from this man, he had done what Cain had done before him. Cain had failed to set a good example to his family and so he influenced the behaviour of others. We need to remember that what we do affects others, for bad as well as for good.

. . . through the Bible day by day

January 9

Reading: Genesis 5. 21-27

Without faith it is impossible to please Him, for he who comes to God must believe that He is, and that He is a rewarder of those who diligently seek Him, Hebrews 11. 6

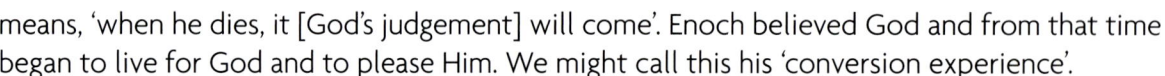

At the age of sixty-five Enoch must have had a special experience of God. God warned him of the judgment coming upon the world because of its wickedness. We know this had a real impact upon his life because he named his son Methuselah, which means, 'when he dies, it [God's judgement] will come'. Enoch believed God and from that time began to live for God and to please Him. We might call this his 'conversion experience'.

After this experience Enoch walked with God. This means that from morning until night he lived every day in fellowship with God, enjoying His presence and friendship. His life was so different to others around him. God received such pleasure from Enoch's life. This is really what God wants from all of our lives – that we should please Him. We can only do this when we turn from the wrong and sin in our lives and give ourselves to Him. This seems to be just what Enoch did. He enjoyed the warmth of God's nearness and presence for three hundred years until God took him to heaven - without dying! This is what every true believer hopes for today. God has promised that all who are saved and are still alive when the Lord Jesus returns to the clouds will be taken to heaven without dying. Do you have that wonderful hope?

It is amazing to notice that Methuselah died when he was nine hundred and sixty-nine. He is the oldest person we read of in the Bible. It seems as if God delayed sending the judgment of the flood to give people as much opportunity as possible to turn from their sin, for the flood came in the year that Methuselah died, as Enoch had said. God is so gracious, patient and kind.

Pray

Ask God to help you to please Him so that you can enjoy His presence and nearness.

Stepping stones

Reading: Genesis 6. 5 - 22

By faith Noah . . . prepared an ark for the saving of his household, Hebrews 11. 7

Sin had spoiled God's creation and ruined mankind. God saw that the people living at the same time as Noah had become violent and were living wicked and sinful lives. God is holy and hates sin. He was sorry He had made man. He decided He would destroy the world and everything in it.

Noah, however, was a good man and was warned by God that a flood was coming. He believed God was going to judge the world with a flood even though there had never yet been any rain on the earth. He had a real faith and respect for God. He walked with God as Enoch had done and God was gracious to him.

Noah obeyed God and did exactly what He had told him to do. He built the ark so that God could save him, and all who would believe, from the flood. He preached to the people, telling them to turn from their wickedness. But they wouldn't listen. God wanted to save them but they refused to believe God and so would die in their sin. By building the ark, Noah was condemning the people around him for their unbelief.

God wanted to preserve each of the animal species that He had made. The ark was big enough to hold every kind of animal and bird. It had three stories in it, with a window at the top and a door in the side. There was to be enough food in it to feed all. What great faith Noah had to build it! No doubt the people around made fun of him but he still obeyed God. We, too, must obey God and trust in the Lord Jesus who, by His death on the cross, can be our Saviour from the coming judgement.

Pray

Thank God that He sends preachers to warn us about His judgement on sin. Pray for those around who are still rejecting Him.

. . . through the Bible day by day

January 11

Reading: Genesis 7- 8. 1

Those that entered, male and female of all flesh, went in as God had commanded him; and the LORD shut him in, Genesis 7. 16

Pray

Thank God for His goodness, kindness and love in providing the Lord Jesus as the only saviour from the coming judgement.

Noah heard God's invitation to go into the ark that he and his family had worked hard for so many years to build. It was to be his place of safety. It was the way by which God would save him from His judgement of wicked people. Noah had obeyed God, following carefully the design that God had given him. Chapter 7 verse 1 tells us that Noah was righteous. This means that his faith and trust in God had made him right with God.

God had said that in just seven days it would start to rain. For all the people around it was going to be too late to respond to God's voice through Noah. He had preached and warned them but they would not listen. By building the ark, Noah had been a constant witness to them all those years. Soon the people would see that God was right. Noah had to take into the ark seven pairs of the clean animals – like sheep and cows – and two pairs of all unclean – like the pigs. Seven pairs of each type of bird were also preserved in the ark.

When Noah and all the animals and birds were safely inside the ark, God shut the door. They were completely safe inside, but those who had rejected Noah's preaching were unable to get in. It was too late. They should have believed God while there was still time.

After this it rained for forty days and everywhere was flooded. The water covered even the highest mountains. Every person and animal left outside the ark died. God had warned them but they had not listened. We need to listen to preachers today, too, while there is still time. Do we?

Stepping stones

Reading: **Genesis 8. 15 - 21**

January 12

Give to the LORD the glory due His name; bring an offering, and come before Him. Oh, worship the LORD in the beauty of holiness! 1 Chronicles 16. 29

After about a year in the ark, the flood waters had finally gone down and the earth was dry again. God spoke once more to Noah. He had been used to hearing the voice of God – he walked with God. He spent every day listening to God and living close to Him. God told Noah and his family to go out of the ark with all the animals, birds and creeping things. God said they should breed and multiply so they would fill the earth again. They all left the ark, no doubt glad to be free.

Noah built an altar so he could sacrifice to God. He wanted to show how grateful and glad he was that the Lord had saved him from the judgement of the flood. God had told Noah to take seven pairs of the clean animals into the ark. This was done so that he would be able to offer sacrifices to God. God had always wanted to enjoy man's fellowship and this was made possible through a sacrifice being made, a life being taken. It is through the sacrifice of the Lord Jesus on the cross that we, too, can approach God to enjoy His friendship.

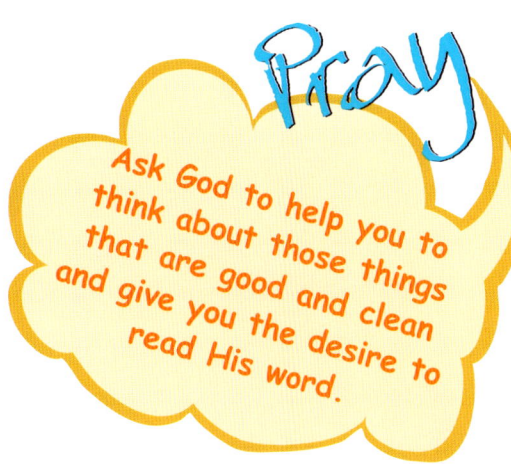

Pray

Ask God to help you to think about those things that are good and clean and give you the desire to read His word.

God was pleased with Noah's sacrifice and He made a promise. He said that He wouldn't curse the ground any more or destroy every living thing again with a flood as He had just done. God again has to tell us how evil people had become. Even from their youth people can only think of evil, God said. This is still sadly true today and God is grieved, for He hates sin. We all have to be very careful what we think about and guard our minds from evil and sinful thoughts. Are we careful?

... through the Bible day by day

January 13

Reading: Genesis 8. 21 - 9. 17

You have set a boundary that they [the seas] may not pass over, that they may not return to cover the earth, Psalm 104. 9

Noah continued to listen to the voice of God and to enjoy His presence. God told him that he could now eat meat as well as vegetables and the animals would be afraid of him. They were to be for man's food from now on. We are superior to animals because we have a soul and are made in the image of God. That is why human life is so precious and murdering people is so wrong. God said that those who murder other people should be executed. Noah was now encouraged to repopulate the earth. God sees human life as special and we are precious to Him.

In the Bible we read of many wonderful promises that God has made. He has promised that as long as the earth remains, the seasons will continue. There will be summer and winter, cold and heat and day and night. He will bring out new life in the spring and give us harvests in the summer. He is such a great God and is in control of everything.

God made another promise to Noah, a promise that He will never fail to keep. He said that He would never bring a world-wide flood again that would destroy all life. The flood from which Noah had been saved had not given God any pleasure at all. He told Noah that He would put a rainbow in the sky as a sign of this promise. So when we see a rainbow it should remind us of that wonderful promise that God has made. We must not forget that God said that He, too, will see the rainbow and will remember to keep His promise. God always keeps His promises and we can trust and rely upon them. Do we keep ours?

Pray

Thank God for His wonderful promises. Ask Him to help you to believe and trust in them and to claim them for yourself.

Stepping stones

Reading: Genesis 11. 1-9

January 14

The eyes of the LORD are in every place, keeping watch on the evil and the good,
Proverbs 15. 3

Have you ever wondered where all the different languages in the world came from? Well here we have the answer. Originally everyone spoke the same language and could easily talk to other people.

One day people became very proud. These people wanted to be great, to please themselves and not God. Pride is sin. God had told Noah to repopulate and fill the earth but these people wanted to live together in a big city where they could enjoy themselves and live as they liked.

Pray for those Christians who are learning a foreign language so that they can tell other people the good news of the gospel.

They wanted to build a big tower to reach high into heaven. They were very foolish. They wanted to show how big and powerful they were but they were really rebelling against what God had said. Today we can see that big cities across the world are very wicked places and many areas in these cities are dangerous to live in. This is what it would have been like in those days, as the people wanted to go their own way and not God's. God knew what was best for them and He still does today. He wants us to enjoy His creation and to please Him.

God saw what they were doing. He sees and knows everything we do. He knew what they were thinking and what it would lead to. So God decided to cause confusion. That is what 'Babel' means. He confused their languages so that the people couldn't understand each other and would divide up and separate from each other to fill the earth as God had intended.

Today we talk about language barriers and spend much time and effort in learning other languages so that we can talk with people of other nationalities. How different it would have been if these people had not been so rebellious and proud!

. . . through the Bible day by day

January 15

Reading: Job 1. 6-12

Preserve me, O God, for in You I put my trust, Psalm 16. 1

What would God say about our lives? Could He say that we have a respect for Him and we hate evil? That is what God said about Job. Of course, God knew Job through and through and saw Job was still a sinner. Yet what a testimony he had! I wonder what God would say about you and me?

When the angels came to stand before God, Satan came too. He is opposed to God and to all who belong to Him. He goes around the earth looking for those he can attack and trip up. He wants to see our downfall. He is called 'the accuser' and is always looking for opportunity to accuse God's people. He wants to stop them from living to please God. We need to be very much aware of his desires and tactics. He is our great enemy.

God said to Satan, 'Have you thought about Job and how good a man he is?' Satan then accused God of protecting Job. He thought that God was extra kind to Job. But, he said, if God put Job under pressure and gave him some trials and difficulties then the story would be different. If God wasn't so caring towards him, thought Satan, Job would fail and curse God.

God gave Satan permission to attack Job and his family and even take away his possessions, only he was not to harm him. God knew that Job would not curse Him. He knew that Job would remain faithful to Him even when put under great pressure and while experiencing real difficulty, pain and sorrow. Job had already brought pleasure to God by his upright life. Now he would bring pleasure to God by his unfailing faith. How we react when difficulties come our way can also bring pleasure God.

Pray

Ask God to help you to react in the right way when you experience problems and difficulties. Pray for His strength and help so that you can please Him.

Stepping stones

Reading: **Job 1. 13-22**

January 16

The LORD gave, and the LORD has taken away; Blessed be the name of the LORD, Job 1. 21

Job was one of the richest people of his time. He had many of life's treasures to enjoy. He had a family, a home, livestock and plenty to eat. But when God let Satan attack Job his most important possession of all, his faith, was tested to the limit.

In one day, messengers came to tell Job that he had lost all his oxen, donkeys, sheep and camels. His servants had been killed. Even his own children had died in some kind of tornado. What a day! Job was devastated. He tore his clothes and shaved his head to show his sorrow.

Although he was very upset, Job showed great faith and trust in God. He knew that he had brought nothing into the world and that when he died he could take nothing out of it with him. How wonderful is Job's response! He fell to the ground and worshipped. Rather than blame God for his troubles, he showed that his greatest possession was his faith. He believed God was still worthy of praise and worship.

Pray

Thank God for all the blessings that you have to enjoy. Thank Him even more for His gift of eternal life that can never be taken away.

One great thing that we can possess now is 'the gift of God' which is eternal life, Romans 6. 23. Whatever else God gives, or takes away, from us, eternal life is the only thing we will never lose and which we can take with us when we die. Paul tells us not to 'trust in uncertain riches but in the living God, who gives us richly all things to enjoy', 1 Timothy 6. 17.

How often we take for granted the blessings that God gives! How would we feel if God were to allow our possessions to be taken away from us? We may have clothing, food, housing, family and possessions but we must not make these the most important things in our lives.

... through the Bible day by day

January 17

Reading: Job 2

Though He slay me, yet will I trust Him,
Job 13. 15

We might have thought that things could not get any worse for Job but what a reputation he still had! God thought that he was still blameless and upright. Even Satan must have been impressed and challenged God to test Job even more. In fact, Satan himself sends Job painful boils that seem to have appeared all over his body. Job has lost everything and now even his own body is being attacked.

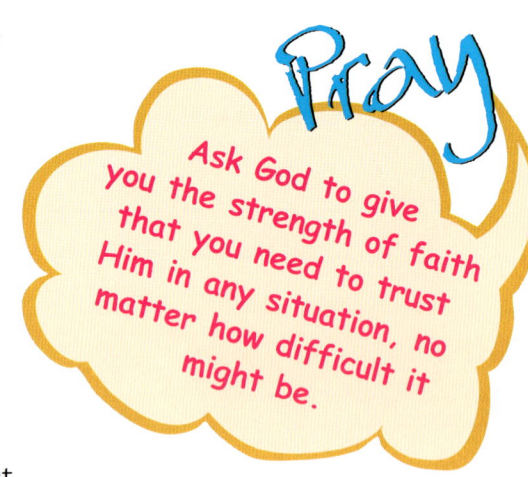

Pray

Ask God to give you the strength of faith that you need to trust Him in any situation, no matter how difficult it might be.

Job's wife thinks she has the answer to his problems. 'Curse God and die', she says. This might have seemed the only way out. After all, what did Job have left to live for? Job's friends too, when they came, could only see someone in a hopeless situation. They could not even think of anything to say to comfort him.

Despite all this, Job's faith remained strong. He rebukes his wife and rejects her ideas completely. 'Is it right for us to accept good things from God and not accept bad things?' he asks in verse 10. Job knows that we should not just trust in God when things are going well. We need Him even more when things are tough.

Think of a time when you have faced a real difficulty. Did your faith remain strong? Did you ask God to help you overcome the problem? Next time you face such a difficulty, remember Job and follow his example. Paul reminds us that, 'God is faithful, who will not allow you to be tempted beyond what you are able, but with the temptation will also make the way of escape, that you may be able to bear it', 1 Corinthians 10. 13. Let's not be like many people who only love God when things are fine. Let's be like Job and love Him whatever happens.

Stepping stones

Reading: Job 38. 1-3; 42. 1-6

January 18

'For My thoughts are not your thoughts, nor are your ways My ways', says the Lord, Isaiah 55. 8

Job's friends eventually came up with many things to say to him. They gave him all sorts of advice and told him how they thought he should react to the problems he faced. However, they did not think about most of what they said. It would have been better if they had kept quiet. God was quite angry with some of the comments they made.

Now that Job's friends have finished what they had to say, Job is going to meet God Himself. What an amazing experience that must have been! The Lord tells him to prepare himself and to be ready to listen to what He is going to say. God then reminds Job that He is the great Creator; the One who sees and knows everything and that He is the Almighty. He reminds Job how very small he is compared to God. Do we really appreciate the greatness of God?

When Job eventually answers God he says, 'I know that You can do everything and that nothing can stop You from doing what You want', Job 42. 2. Job also realizes that God saw him as sinful and that he needed to repent. He begins to understand that the ways of God are wonderful and beyond anything Job could ever have come up with himself.

If we ever try to work our lives out for ourselves, we will get into all kinds of difficulties. God has said, 'I know the thoughts that I think toward you . . . thoughts of peace and not of evil, to give you a future and a hope', Jeremiah 29. 11. We must recognize our own sin and weakness, as Job did, and ask God to guide us in His ways. Only then can we be sure that we are living our lives as we ought.

Pray
Give thanks to God for His greatness. Recognize that there is no one as wonderful as Him. Humbly admit that you need Him to guide you.

. . . through the Bible day by day

January 19

Reading: Job 42. 7-12

Bless those who curse you, and pray for those who spitefully use you, Luke 6. 28

As we reach the end of the story of Job we learn three things. First of all, Job's friends needed to make themselves right with God. Then Job was encouraged to pray for these friends, even though they had not helped him properly. Finally, Job was blessed by God more than ever before.

Pray

Is there someone with whom you find it really hard to get on? Pray for that person now and ask the Lord to help you show kindness towards them.

Job's friends had tried to do the right thing. They had tried to give him good advice but they had failed. They had not recognized God as they should have done and used their own wisdom to try and solve Job's problems. They were told to offer sacrifices to God if they were to avoid God's judgement. In the same way, we need to recognize that we cannot use our own intelligence to understand God. We need to come to Him and accept the sacrifice of the Lord Jesus upon the cross if we are to avoid His judgement.

Job prayed for these three friends, although they had not been very helpful to him, in the hope that they would not be judged. God heard Job's prayer and answered it. There may be people in our lives who are not very helpful to us. Perhaps they are deliberately unkind. We should pray for them, ask God to save them from their sins and ask Him to help us show them kindness.

After all he had been through God blessed Job with twice as much as he had had before. What a wonderful lesson to learn! If our faith and trust are in God, no matter how tough life may be, and if we show kindness to those around us, then God will bless us. It may take time as we learn to depend upon Him. How good it would be if we learned the lesson sooner rather than later!

Stepping stones

Reading: Genesis 12. 1-9

January 20

By faith Abraham obeyed when he was called to go out, Hebrews 11. 8

Imagine the shock for Abraham. He had been living very happily with his wife and family in Ur and the last thing they wanted to do was leave. Suddenly, though, the Lord speaks to him and says, 'Get out of your country'. What would we have done? Some might have made excuses; others would have refused outright. Not Abraham!

'Abram departed as the Lord had spoken to him', verse 4. He was completely obedient to God's word and did exactly as he was asked. Abraham had no idea where God was taking him but he was still prepared to go. Although we may not understand all that it means to be a Christian, we can still have the faith to start out on the journey that will lead us to heaven. Do we obey God's word? When we hear the Lord Jesus say, 'Come to Me', how do we respond? Matthew 11. 28. Some make excuses, others refuse outright. Are we prepared to be completely obedient to the Lord Jesus?

When Abraham obeyed, God made very clear promises to him. He promised to bless him and give him a land. God still makes wonderful promises to those who are prepared to obey Him today. He does not promise us a land but He promises to give us forgiveness and salvation. He promises that we will be received into heaven to be with the Lord Jesus forever. Will we obey?

Abraham built an altar to the Lord. This was to show how much he appreciated what God had done for him. We, too, should give thanks to God for all He has done for us and for all the wonderful promises we have if we trust the Lord Jesus as our Saviour.

Pray

God calls each one of us to obey Him and to accept His Son the Lord Jesus. Ask God to help you be obedient to His word.

. . . through the Bible day by day

January 21

READING: Genesis 13. 1-13

Let each of you look out not only for his own interests, but also for the interests of others, Philippians 2. 4

Every day we are faced with many choices. Some things will be appealing to us, others will not. Abraham and Lot had to decide where they were going to live because there was no longer enough room for them to be together. They had so many flocks of sheep and goats there was no room for them all. Abraham was older and should really have been given the first choice about where to go. He wasn't selfish, however, and gave Lot the chance to choose first.

When Lot looked out over the land, his eyes were attracted to the plain of Jordan. He saw that it was fertile and green and to him it seemed like Paradise. This was certainly the place where he wanted to go as he was bound to become rich there. It was far more attractive than the alternative, which was the land of Canaan. Abraham did not complain at Lot's choice and let Lot go on his way.

So what was wrong with the choice that Lot made? His decision was based on his selfish thoughts. He was attracted by the beauty of what he saw. What he did not realize was that it was a place that would be no good for him at all. It was a place that was 'exceedingly wicked and sinful against the Lord'.

Can we think of a time when we made selfish choices rather than thinking of others and of what God would want us to do? Perhaps today we can begin to think more carefully about what choices God wants us to make. Lot was to get into many problems because he chose selfishly and without thinking of God. Abraham was much less selfish, made the right choice and God eventually blessed him greatly.

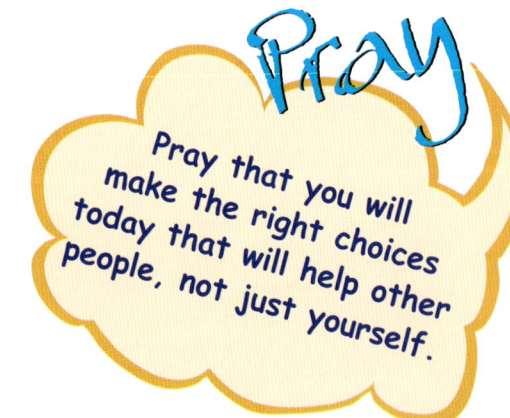

Pray

Pray that you will make the right choices today that will help other people, not just yourself.

Stepping stones

Reading: Genesis 14. 14 – 15. 1

January 22

Do not be afraid, Abram. I am your shield, your exceedingly great reward,
Genesis 15. 1

Abraham had come to Lot's rescue and had freed Lot, his possessions and many other people from the kings who had just captured them. Now Melchizedek, the priest of God, came out and blessed Abraham. The King of Sodom also wanted to reward Abraham for what he had done but Abraham was having none of it. He knew that God had helped him. It was God Himself who deserved the praise and the credit for what had happened. Abraham also wanted to be independent of other people and would not take a reward from anyone.

God was very pleased with this response. He showed this to Abraham by telling him that He would be his 'very great reward'. It was God Most High who had protected him and now He would reward him. Abraham was about to discover how God would reward him for being obedient to Him in his life.

Although he was getting old and had no children, God promised Abraham that his descendants would be like the stars of heaven in number. What a blessing! But what a response from Abraham too, for we read that he 'believed God'! Well, why not? God had brought him this far; he had proved God in so many ways. Now he would continue to put God first in everything that he did.

Pray

Tell God that you want to put Him first in your life, if you really mean it. Then ask Him to be with you in everything that you do.

It is so easy to let things take a grip of our lives. Friends, family, work or entertainment can all take over before we know it. Will we give God the first place in our lives? If we believe His word, and obey it He will bless us. As Hebrews chapter 11 and verse 6 tells us, 'he who comes to God must believe that He is, and that He is the rewarder of those who diligently seek Him'.

. . . through the Bible day by day

January 23

Reading: Genesis 16. 1-16

A sound heart is life to the body, but envy is rottenness to the bones,
Proverbs 14. 30

Abraham and Sarah were two great characters. They did amazing things for God and became the father and mother of the nation of Israel. What happens now, however, shows how even the most devoted and obedient people can sin and displease God.

Abraham knew that God had promised to make his children into a great nation but now that he is over eighty years old, he and Sarah begin to doubt whether it will ever happen. They still have no children. So Sarah came up with a plan. Her servant, Hagar, should marry Abraham and have his child. Then from this child God would build a great nation and Abraham would be a father after all.

Pray

Ask God to help you recognize when you are feeling jealous. Pray that you will have the strength to deal with those feelings.

The danger of this plan is all too obvious to us. This was certainly not what God would have wanted. Once Hagar becomes pregnant, all the problems we might have predicted begin. Hagar despises Sarah and is then forced to run away after Sarah becomes jealous and angry. Hagar eventually comes back and Ishmael is born. But a great deal of trouble followed from Ishmael's birth, and still does. No wonder we are told envy is rottenness to the bones – there is nothing good about it at all.

So often when our faith in God is weak, we can fall into sin. We quickly become envious and angry, forgetting to trust everything to God. The effects of jealousy and hatred can last a long time so we need to be careful to keep these feelings away. In the end God had to come and take control of things in Abraham and Sarah's lives. What a pity that they had not left Him to control things earlier on. 'In all your ways acknowledge Him, and He shall direct your paths', Proverbs 3. 6

Reading: Genesis 18. 1-15

January 24

Do not forget to entertain strangers, for by so doing some have unwittingly entertained angels, Hebrews 13. 2

This strange story became a really important occasion in Abraham's life. God actually came down from heaven to talk to Abraham. Abraham thought he was talking to an ordinary man, but it was really God Himself.

Abraham was resting in his tent when the three strangers appeared. He could have ignored them and let them pass by. Instead of doing that, though, he jumped up and ran to meet them. Quickly, he provided them with water, somewhere to rest and something to eat. He made sure that he gave them the very best that he had. Abraham was actually entertaining the living God of heaven! What a good job it was that he treated these strangers so well.

How important it is for Christian families to be hospitable – to show kindness, generosity and love to others in our homes. Sometimes it is easier just to ignore their needs and get on with our own lives. However, this is not the way that we should behave. We should be prepared to give of the very best that we have for the good of others. We should be prepared to do for them what we would like them to do for us. Our verse in Hebrews makes it clear that we should do this not just to those we know but also to those who are 'strangers' – to people we don't know.

After that lovely meal God blessed Abraham and Sarah in an incredible way by promising them a son. Sarah could hardly believe it! Although God may not promise us children, we can be sure that if we show kindness, generosity and hospitality to others, as if they were angels or even God Himself, we will be blessed by God. And we may be surprised at what He can do!

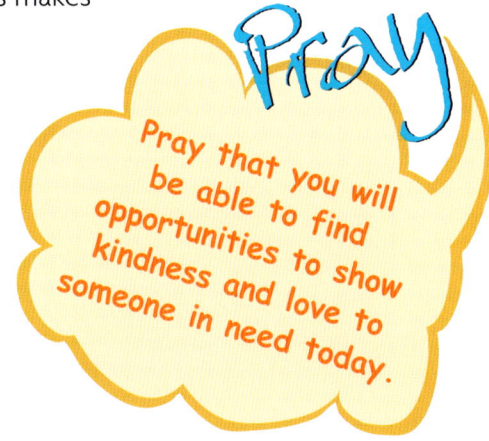

Pray

Pray that you will be able to find opportunities to show kindness and love to someone in need today.

. . . through the Bible day by day

January 25

READING: Genesis 18. 16-33

I exhort . . . that . . . prayers . . . and giving of thanks be made for all men, 1 Timothy 2. 1

God tells Abraham that He is going to judge Sodom and Gomorrah because of their sin. God must judge sin because He is righteous and holy. 'I will know', God says, verse 21. God sees and knows everything. No one can escape His judgement.

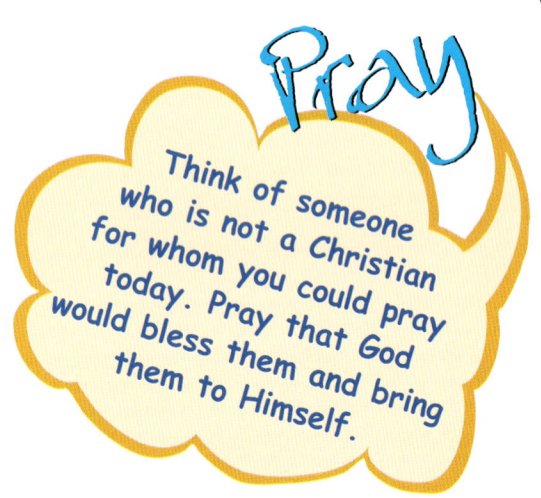

Pray

Think of someone who is not a Christian for whom you could pray today. Pray that God would bless them and bring them to Himself.

When he hears this Abraham is deeply concerned. He knows that his nephew Lot and his own family are in Sodom. He does not want them to pass through this judgement that God has spoken of. So he begins to plead with God for them. Abraham acknowledges that God is the 'Judge of all the earth' and that He must punish wicked people. He also understands, though, that God would not want to punish righteous people with wicked people.

We might think that Abraham is trying to bargain with God, or that he is speaking out of turn. Abraham is speaking openly with his God, however. He is praying to Him out of a genuine concern and longing that his own family might be saved from God's judgement. We know that Abraham realizes his own smallness before God because he says, 'I who am but dust and ashes'. So he recognizes how great God is. Yet he also knows that he can speak to God about anything.

How do we feel about those we know who are facing God's judgement on their sin? Are we concerned about them? Would we like to see them saved? We can learn a lot from Abraham here. We need to come before God in prayer, acknowledge His greatness and pray that He will save those who need Him so much. God answered Abraham's prayer. Perhaps He will save some of our friends as a result of our prayers. Do we pray for them?

Stepping stones

Reading: Genesis 19. 1-4, 12-14

January 26

Whoever walks blamelessly will be saved, but he who is perverse in his ways will suddenly fall, Proverbs 28. 18

When the two angels arrive in Sodom, they discover a wicked place. People are living lives that are far from what God would expect. Sin, selfishness and immorality are everywhere. However, they also discover one man who wants to show them kindness, and that man is Abraham's nephew Lot. Just as Abraham had done, Lot invites them into his home.

The men tell Lot that they have been sent by God to perform a special task – to destroy the city of Sodom. They know that Lot is a righteous man and they want to rescue him from God's judgement. So they give him and his family an opportunity to escape.

Lot realizes that what they are saying is very serious so he hurries out to inform his family. He respects God and knows he needs to take action. Sadly, others in his family do not take it so seriously. In fact his sons-in-law just think that he is joking. What a tragic response that is going to be!

We can be sure that God still works in the same way today. We have already seen that God must judge sin. However, He has provided a way to escape. We can be made righteous, we can be right with God, because of what the Lord Jesus Christ has done for us. Through faith in Him we can be delivered from the judgement of God.

Sadly again, many people in the world today do not realize they need to take these things seriously. They treat God's word as if it were a joke and do not see the need to respond to it. How important it is for us to make sure that we are right with God through faith in the Lord Jesus, so that we can be delivered from sin and judgement.

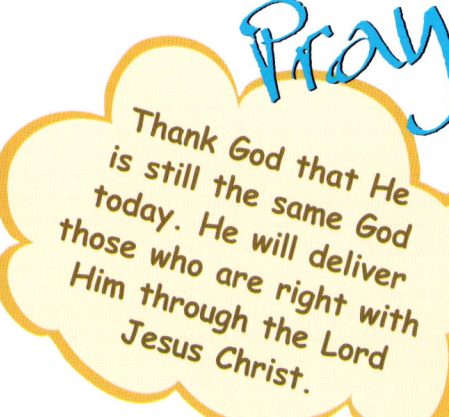

Pray

Thank God that He is still the same God today. He will deliver those who are right with Him through the Lord Jesus Christ.

. . . through the Bible day by day

January 27

Reading: Genesis 19. 15-28

Remember Lot's wife, Luke 17. 32

At last the terrible judgement falls as God had warned it would. He was also true to His word in saving Lot and his family. Lot understood this. 'You have increased your mercy which you have shown me by saving my life', he says.

We should remember that it is only by God's kindness and compassion, that any of us can ever be saved. He has proved to us through the story of Lot that He does not want any of the godly to perish. He knows how to save them, 2 Peter 2. 9. What a merciful God we have!

This story does not have a happy ending, because there was punishment for Lot's wife. So serious is this, that when the Lord Jesus spoke to people about the judgement that is to come upon this world, He said, 'Remember Lot's wife', Luke 17. 32.

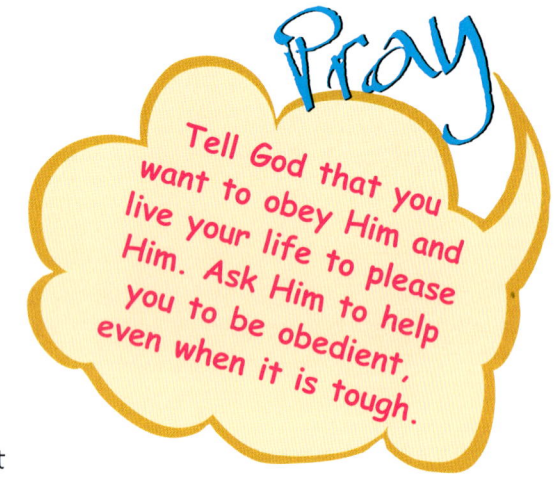

Pray

Tell God that you want to obey Him and live your life to please Him. Ask Him to help you to be obedient, even when it is tough.

God had given clear instructions to the family of Lot. 'Do not look behind you'. If they did, the result would be the same as it was for the city – they would be destroyed. Quite why Lot's wife decided to look back as they were fleeing, we do not know. Perhaps she was curious, or longed to be back in the city, or did not really believe what God had said. The fact is that she did look back and she was turned into a pillar of salt! What a terrible thing to happen to someone who could have been safe.

We can be sure that there is no escape from God's judgement on our sin unless we are totally obedient to His word. We cannot do our own thing to save ourselves. We simply need to be obedient to Him through believing in the Lord Jesus Christ as our Saviour. Are we?

Stepping stones

Reading: *Genesis 21. 1-8*

January 28

Children are a heritage from the Lord,
Psalm 127. 3

Abraham and Sarah had waited, and waited, and waited for God to fulfil His promise to give them a child. There were times when their faith struggled to believe it, but now, when Abraham is 100 years old and Sarah is 90, the promise comes true. By a miracle, Isaac is born.

Very often in the Bible names have important meanings. The name Isaac means 'laughter'. The name reminded Sarah of the time when she had laughed at the promise made by the three visitors. It must also have shown the real joy that she now had in her heart at the birth of this child. What a blessing Isaac was to her and to Abraham!

Abraham, too, was delighted at the birth of his son. He held a feast to celebrate the growth of Isaac probably at the time when Isaac could feed himself. He and his wife knew what a blessing children are. Isaac really was a 'heritage from the Lord'.

The family is a very precious thing and each member is incredibly important. Children are a blessing from the Lord and are something to be extremely thankful to God for. In the same way, children should thank God for their parents and ask for God's help to be obedient to them. A family that is determined to serve God together is a very precious thing. It brings great pleasure to God.

Abraham and Sarah had waited a long time for a family, which probably made them even more grateful once their son was born. Do we ever take our families for granted? Parents and children should do their very best, with God's help, to value and love each other more every day. Do we?

Pray

Give thanks to God for your family. Think about something that you could pray about for each member of your family.

. . . through the Bible day by day

January 29

Reading: Genesis 22. 1-14

By faith Abraham, when he was tested . . . offered up his only begotten son,
Hebrews 11. 17

Although we have learned families are very important, no matter how important something is, it should never come between us and God. He should always have the most important place in our lives.

It seems unbelievable that, having finally given Abraham and Sarah a son, God would ask Abraham to take Isaac and offer him as a human sacrifice. What a test of faith this was going to be! It is amazing to read through this story and see the faith that Abraham had as he took his son up the mountain and as he took the wood and laid his son onto the altar ready to sacrifice him. It is wonderful as well to see the obedience and faith of Isaac as he allowed his father to do all this.

'Abraham stretched out his hand and took the knife to kill his son'. He was prepared to go through with what God had asked him to do because his faith said that he must. He must surely have expected God to do something amazing to save Isaac when he said, 'God will provide for Himself the lamb for a burnt offering'. And so God did just that. Abraham had proved his faith was strong and he had shown that God was number one in his life after all.

This story also reminds us of the sacrifice of the Lord Jesus Christ upon the cross. God 'did not spare His own Son, but delivered Him up for us all', Romans 8. 32. This was done so that we could have our sins forgiven and be made ready for heaven. After such a sacrifice, shouldn't we be prepared to give the Lord Jesus the first place in our lives? He gave Himself for us. We should be ready to give ourselves for Him.

Pray

Pray that nothing in your life would become so precious to you that it would become more important to you than God and the Lord Jesus.

Stepping stones

Reading: Genesis 24. 1-8

January 30

He who finds a wife finds a good thing, and obtains favour from the Lord,
Proverbs 18. 22

Abraham was determined to see that Isaac married a suitable wife. Marriage is one of the biggest commitments that people ever enter into and so it was important that Isaac married the right person. In Isaac's time parents would have had a big say in choosing a wife or a husband for their children. Even though that may not be true for many people today, there are important lessons for us to learn from this story.

Abraham's servant was sent to look for a wife for Isaac from Abraham's own people, not from the Canaanites. This is because the Canaanites did not believe in God. It is so important for us today that Christians should only marry other Christians. The Bible teaches us clearly that a believer should not be married to an unbeliever. How can there be real unity when one person loves the Lord and the other does not?

The servant was worried about whether any girl he found would be willing to return with him to Isaac. Abraham insisted that it needed to be someone who was prepared to live in the land that God had promised to his son. When two believers marry they should be prepared to live together in the place where God wants them.

Abraham took all of this very seriously. In today's world, people often do not take marriage and relationships seriously. Some have lots of different girlfriends and boyfriends. Many people live together without being married and young people get involved in immoral things that are unacceptable to God. Parents should guide their children to do what is right. Young people should wait patiently for the Lord to guide and direct them to the right person at the right time. Marriage is such an important step, it is vital to get it right!

Pray

Pray that you might have the right relationships with your friends and that God would guide you and your family in the future.

. . . through the Bible day by day

January 31

Reading: Genesis 24. 15-28

Wait on the Lord; be of good courage, and He shall strengthen your heart,
Psalm 27. 14

Abraham's servant was determined to get this right. He knew he would not be able to find a wife for Isaac in his own strength, so he prayed that God would help him. 'O Lord God of my master Abraham, please give me success this day', he asked. He needed God's help if he was to be successful.

How wonderfully God answered his prayer! Before he had even finished praying, God brought Rebekah to the well and it became obvious that this was the woman Isaac should marry. She was everything that the servant had prayed for and it seemed clear that God was working things out perfectly.

As the servant realized that God was bringing everything together beautifully, he had to bow his head in worship and thanksgiving to God. He recognized the mercy of God in helping him to succeed in his task.

Pray

Thank God that He shows us His will for our lives in every situation. Ask for His help to remember this every day and to find out the right way.

It is wonderful to know God's hand leading and directing our lives. Things do not always work out as well and as quickly as they did for Abraham's servant. But we can be sure that, when we wait for God to show us what He wants for us, He will. This applies to marriage, as it does in this story. It is also true in many other decisions we need to make - which subjects we should study, how to tell our friends about the Lord Jesus, what job we might have one day or how we can serve the Lord. We will only make a mess of things when we try to work these things out for ourselves. When we wait for God to show us the way, however, He will give us the courage, strength and patience we need and, finally, success in knowing His perfect will for our lives. Are we prepared to wait?

Stepping stones

Reading: Genesis 24. 58-67

February 1

In all your ways acknowledge Him, and He shall direct your paths, Proverbs 3. 6

Rebekah was a great girl. She was so pretty. Her beauty was one of the first things the servant noticed about her. We know that she was kind because she offered to get a drink for Abraham's servant. We also know that she was very hard-working because she offered to get enough water from the well for all the thirsty camels to drink! She was polite as she spoke to the servant about her family. But one of the nicest things about Rebekah's character is this – she was committed. She had fallen in love with a man whom she had never seen.

Pray
Ask God to help you to trust in the Lord Jesus Christ and follow Him, even though you can't see Him.

The servant might have described Isaac to Rebekah but they didn't have photographs, webcams or mobile phones in those days. She could only guess what he looked like or what type of person he was. Despite all this, as soon as she was given the opportunity she was ready to leave her family and her home. She wanted to begin travelling through the desert with the servant, to meet the man she was going to marry.

We have never seen the Lord Jesus either but we need to trust in Him. He told Thomas that people who believe in Him without seeing Him will be blessed, John 20. 29. We also have to love Him without seeing Him, 1 Peter 1. 8. If we have trusted Him as our Saviour, then in the same way as Rebekah travelled to see Isaac, our lives have already become a spiritual journey to His home, which is heaven. And in the same way as Rebekah travelled a long way before she met Isaac, we shall see the Lord Jesus there in heaven for the first time and be with Him for ever. We have so much to look forward to. It's so exciting being a Christian!

... through the Bible day by day

February 2

Reading: Genesis 25. 24-34

Esau . . . for one morsel of food sold his birthright, Hebrews 12. 16

How often do we take God's gifts for granted? He is good to us in so many different ways. We should be thankful to God for mum, dad or whoever it is who looks after us. We should be glad we have brothers, sisters or friends to play with. God makes sure we have clothes to wear and food to eat. He knows just what we need and gives it to us. Yet so often we forget to say 'thank you'. Just imagine for a moment what it would be like if we didn't have all these blessings from God. Life would be horrible.

The best gift that Esau had was his birthright. Because he was the oldest son, he would have the right to become the head of the family. Then he could expect to know God, work for God and enjoy God's help in a special way. Sadly Esau did not understand what this birthright meant – maybe his dad had not explained it to him. So when tricky Jacob offered to swap it for some tasty food, Esau said, 'Yes!' Esau missed out on so much in his later life, all because of that one mistake he made when he was young.

If we have trusted in the Lord Jesus Christ to save us then we are born again. We have a birthright too. We can know God as our Father. We should do things that please Him. We can ask God to help us in our lives. We have lots to look forward to as well with an 'inheritance incorruptible' kept for us in heaven. Do we value this spiritual birthright more than anything else? Or would we sell it for something of much less value? Many do. Let's make sure we don't.

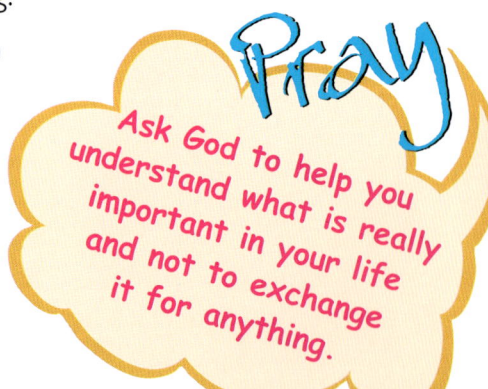

Pray

Ask God to help you understand what is really important in your life and not to exchange it for anything.

Stepping stones

Reading: Genesis 27. 1-19

February 3

Do not lie to one to another,
Colossians 3. 9

Cheats always lose! Jacob cheated his brother Esau when he told lies so that he could steal a blessing from their father. Jacob lost so much on that sad day when he dressed in his brother's clothes and even pretended to have hairy hands and a hairy neck like his brother. First he lost his brother's friendship. Afterwards Esau hated Jacob and wanted to kill him. Then he lost his mother's care. He never saw her again after he had to leave home to escape from angry Esau. Jacob also lost his father's respect. Isaac knew he could not trust his lying younger son after he had done such a deceitful thing.

We must learn that whenever we cheat or lie about something we are going to miss out in some way or other. God has a better plan for us, even if we don't understand what it is straight away. He promises 'those who honour me I will honour', 1 Samuel 2. 30. But people who cheat are bound to get into trouble. Ananias and Sapphira were a couple who tried to deceive God in the New Testament. They lied about how much money they were giving to God. They were badly punished.

Let's think about someone who is quite unlike Jacob. Tricky Jacob robbed his brother of his father's blessing because he wanted it for himself. The Lord Jesus 'did not consider it robbery to be equal with God', Philippians 2. 6. He left His Father's side and all the glories of heaven even though they all belonged to Him. He chose to come into the world and die at Calvary to save sinners like us. He gave up everything so we might have the greatest blessing of forgiveness when we trust in Him. He did not take – He gave. So should we.

Pray

Ask God to help you to be honest and humble today. Thank God for the great example of the Lord Jesus Christ.

. . . through the Bible day by day

February 4

Reading: Genesis 27. 41-45

Love as brothers, be tenderhearted, be courteous; not returning evil for evil,
1 Peter 3. 8-9

We read about the first murder in the Bible in Genesis chapter 4. Cain kills his brother Abel. Cain thinks it is a secret but God knows exactly what he has done. Similarly in today's story Esau is planning to murder his brother Jacob. Esau hates Jacob for stealing his blessing from their father Isaac. Esau's anger and hatred are so strong that they lead to thoughts of murder.

The Lord Jesus explained to His followers that hatred is just as much a sin as murder, Matthew 5. 21-23. In the same way that God knew what Cain had done when he killed his brother God knows our thoughts when we hate people. It's true that family members, and others, can get on our nerves and upset us, sometimes accidentally and sometimes on purpose. But we must not repay evil with evil. To love our brothers is a clear sign that we love God. This is the message of 1 John, which was written by a man who was once full of anger and was known as a 'son of thunder'. John was transformed into a loving and caring person when he followed the Lord Jesus. God changed men like John. He can change our lives too.

Just as we should not hate people when they do us wrong, we should also try not to do things that cause offence and make other people hate us. Peter tells us that we might suffer for being Christians but we should not suffer for wrong-doing, 1 Peter 2. 19-20. Again, our good witness is a clear sign that we belong to God.

Are we good to others even when they are not good to us? Do we reward evil for evil? That is not God's way. It should not be ours either.

Pray
Thank God for your family and friends. Ask God to help you to get on with them, and to keep you from upsetting them.

Reading: **Genesis 28. 10-19**

February 5

Surely the Lord is in this place, and I did not know it, Genesis 28. 16

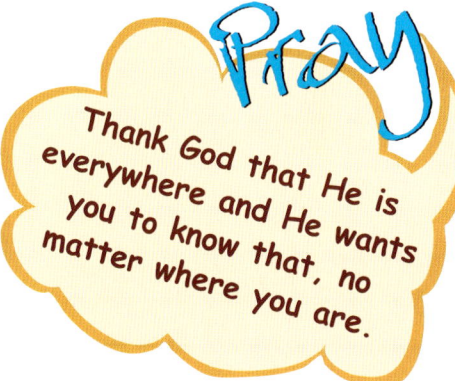

Pray

Thank God that He is everywhere and He wants you to know that, no matter where you are.

Jacob is running away from home. He finds out that he will never be able to run away from God. This is just what David says in Psalm 139 verse 7. God is everywhere. We can't escape Him!

It's late and Jacob is tired so he goes to sleep. He rests his head on some stones. What a funny pillow! He has a strange dream about a ladder but this is a message from God. What's the world record for the longest ever ladder? This one wins because it stretches all the way from earth to heaven.

God wants Jacob to know that He will look after him. Jacob needs to learn to trust in God. The angels going up the ladder remind us that we can bring all our worries and problems to God because 'He cares for you', 1 Peter 5. 7. Even though Jacob was in big trouble, God promised to look after him. The angels coming down the ladder remind us that God has so many good things to give us. 'Every good gift and every perfect gift is from above, from the Father', James 1. 17. Even though Jacob had run away from home, God promised to give him much more than he had left behind.

But what is best of all is that God promises to be with Jacob wherever he goes. In the morning when Jacob wakes up, God is still with him. Even though Jacob can't see the ladder any more, he is still at the 'gate of heaven'. If we have trusted in God as our Saviour then we can be sure that He will be with us and help us today and every day! He is with us now. The trouble is that, like Jacob, we don't always know that.

. . . through the Bible day by day

February 6

Reading: Genesis 29. 15-28

Whatever a man sows, that shall he also reap, Galatians 6. 7

Imagine you want to marry Cinderella but you end up with the ugly sister. What a disappointment! What a horrible trick! This is exactly what happened to Jacob. He fell in love with pretty Rachel the first time he saw her by the well. She was so beautiful! But Jacob needed to learn a lesson. God thinks our insides are more important than our outsides. Look up 1 Samuel 16. 7. God taught Jacob this lesson the hard way.

Uncle Laban tricked Jacob by making him marry Leah, his oldest daughter, when he had promised that Jacob could marry Rachel, the youngest. This must have reminded Jacob of the time when he deceived his own father by pretending to be his older brother. Sometimes, when we do bad things, God lets bad things happen to us in return. We need to be sorry and confess our sins to Him. 'If we confess our sins, He is faithful and just to forgive us our sins', 1 John 1. 9.

However, it's not all disappointing. God can bring good out of our bad situations. Jacob was allowed to marry Rachel, the woman he really loved. He had to work hard, for 14 long years, to earn this reward. When we trust in God and try to live to please Him, He takes notice and blesses us in ways that we would never expect – both now and in heaven to come. In the meantime, let us not cheat or deceive other people. We may be cheated or deceived in return, just as Jacob was. It is so much better to be honest.

Pray
Ask God to keep you from sinning because the consequences can be serious. Sometimes what you do comes back to you.

Reading: **Genesis 30. 1-2, 22-24**

February 7

Love suffers long and is kind,
1 Corinthians 13. 4

No wonder it was hard work living in this family! There were too many people in it. Jacob had two official wives and two extra unofficial wives by the end of today's chapter. God expects one husband and one wife in the ideal family – just like Adam and Eve in the beginning.

Rachel wanted to have Jacob's children. She did not understand that God gives children to people. Children are a 'heritage from the Lord', Psalm 127. 3. Hannah knew this, which is why she prayed to God for Samuel. Mums and dads should remember how much their children are worth. They are God's gift to you. Girls and boys, don't get annoyed when your parents protect you so carefully. You are extremely precious to them.

Rachel was jealous of her sister Leah. Rachel did not have any children but Leah had several. We should not be jealous of other people. It's so easy to envy someone else's good looks, money, family, possessions or Christian testimony. But this is sinful. Instead we should thank God for such people and love them. Paul's attitude to Apollos was that they were fellow companions, not fierce competitors, 1 Corinthians 3. 5-9. He did not get jealous of him.

At last God remembered Rachel and she had a very special baby boy called Joseph. Rachel had tried hard to have children without God's help earlier on but she could not do God's job for Him. Despite her impatience and frustration, God was kind to her in His own time. Rachel had a lot to learn about true love which is patient and never jealous. God can do the impossible for us. We must just learn to wait for the right time.

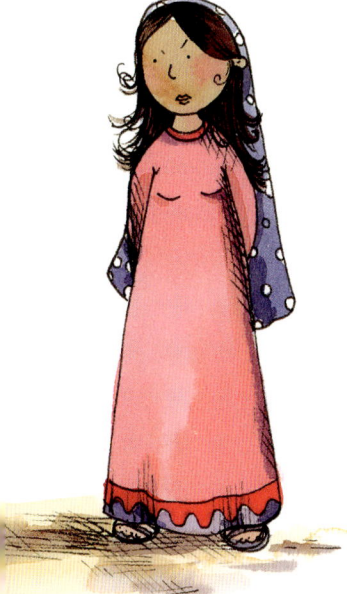

Pray

Thank God for His love to you. Ask God to help you love other people and to be more patient with them.

... through the Bible day by day

February 8

Reading: Genesis 32. 1-13

Let there be no strife between you and me . . . for we are brothers, Genesis 13. 8

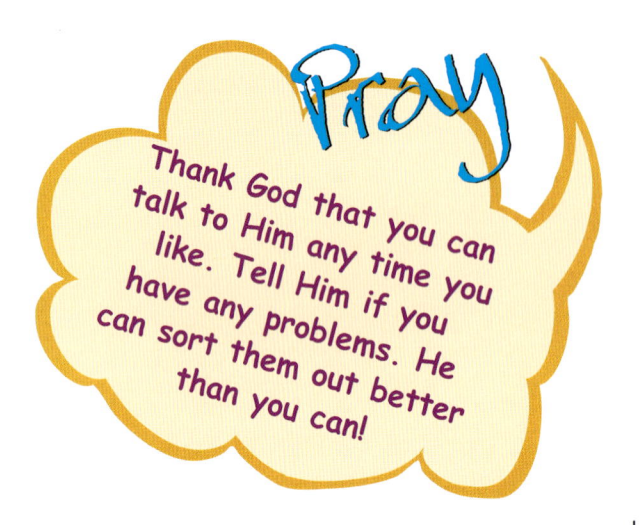

Pray

Thank God that you can talk to Him any time you like. Tell Him if you have any problems. He can sort them out better than you can!

When I was in Sunday School my teacher used to give us colouring competitions. Once he told us the story of the prodigal son, Luke 15. After the story he gave us a picture of the father running to give his homecoming son a big bear hug. We had to colour the picture in and also do some extra homework. The teacher asked us to think about stories in the Bible that might teach the same thing – two people who were very glad to see each other. I thought hard all week but I could not find another good story. The teacher told us the answers the following Sunday. One of the possible stories about people being glad to see each other is where Jacob meets Esau again after so many years apart.

In the picture the teacher gave us both Jacob and Esau (if that's who they were!) were smiling happily. But I think Jacob's smile was probably quite forced. Inside he was extremely worried. He thought Esau still hated him and wanted revenge for Jacob's trick all those years before. Look at the three things Jacob did to try to please Esau.

First he gave *presents* to Esau. Jacob sent lots of different animals trotting off to Esau as a gift. Secondly Jacob was *polite* to Esau. He bowed down to his older brother and called him 'lord'. Thirdly Jacob *prayed* to God. At the end of the day prayer is what really counts. Jacob asked God to keep His promise and protect his family. If God wanted Jacob to come back home, God would have to look after him.

Jacob did not need to be scared when he faced Esau. He had prayed so he could have confidence in God. We must do the same.

Reading: **Genesis 37. 1-11**

February 9

Wrath is cruel and anger a torrent, but who is able to stand before jealousy?
Proverbs 27. 4

Everyone in Jacob's family made mistakes. Jacob showed his favouritism to Joseph by giving him a special coat. It's unfair for mums and dads to love their children unequally like this. Fathers must respect their children and care for them all properly, Colossians 3. 21. Joseph's mistake was that he boasted to his brothers about his amazing dreams. We should not be proud about anything we have, even if it comes straight from heaven like Joseph's dream. Pride was the devil's first sin. We must make sure we don't fall into that trap. All Joseph's brothers made the same mistake as each other. They hated Joseph! They were jealous because of the special attention he got from his dad and also because of his amazing dreams. Brothers and sisters should love one another, especially when they are surrounded by unfriendly neighbours. Remember what Abraham said to Lot, Genesis 13. 8.

Pray
Tell God that you find it easy to make mistakes and cause problems. Thank God He can fix your mistakes and make things better.

God forgave the sins of the family and, although it took years, He changed their characters to overcome their mistakes. Jacob had a blessing for each of his sons before he died. He was not unfair any more. Joseph learned how to be humble in Egypt. He spent years as a slave and a prisoner before his promotion to the palace. He found out that God was in control. His pride disappeared. Joseph's brothers eventually did not resent what God had done for him and them. They were really sorry for being cruel and jealous and made friends with Joseph again.

It's exactly the same for us. We all make mistakes, but when we come to God and say we're sorry, He forgives us, will help us to put things right, and is working to change us for the better.

. . . through the Bible day by day

February 10

Reading: Genesis 37. 12-30

You meant evil against me; but God meant it for good,
Genesis 50. 20

How often do our good ideas turn out to be wrong? Jacob had the good idea of sending Joseph to check on his other sons but what terrible things happened to Joseph as a result! Mums and dads must be careful to protect their children from harm and danger but they can't anticipate everything.

Reuben had a good idea too. He knew his brothers wanted to hurt Joseph or even kill him. So Reuben pretended to go along with them but he was secretly planning to rescue Joseph when his brothers had gone home. Was this a good idea? No, not really. Reuben was too weak to stand up to his brothers who were wicked. If we get caught in the 'way of sinners' today, then we must not pretend to agree with them. Make sure they know that we are different because we love the Lord! Reuben's good idea did not work out. He was not able to rescue Joseph in the end.

Judah had another good idea. He decided it would be better to sell Joseph than to kill him. This was not Judah being kind. He thought that the only thing he would gain from killing Joseph would be a guilty conscience. He would get some pocket money if he sold his brother instead. How mean and heartless was Judah! Some people will do anything for money. We must remember that 'the love of money is a root of all kinds of evil', 1 Timothy 6. 10.

So all their good ideas were really bad ones. But behind the scenes God was in control and carrying out His plans, although no one realized it there and then. Let us spend time with God and see if we can spot Him working out His plans in our lives.

Pray

Help me to remember that despite my successes and failures, You are in control and You want the best for me.

Stepping stones

Reading: **Genesis 37. 31-35**

February 11

Whatever you want men to do to you, do also to them, Matthew 7. 12

A dead goat, a stolen coat, an absent son, a tricked father. Haven't we heard all this before? Of course we have! Genesis 37 is an action replay of Genesis 29. The main difference is that Jacob cheated others before, but now he is being cheated. He should have expected this. God makes sure that we get back what we deserve, Galatians 6. 7. Other people treat us like we treat them. So tricky Jacob gets tricked!

> **Pray**
> Thank God that He is always fair. He can help you to be fair to other people too.

Let's think about Joseph's brothers. They were *liars*. They deliberately put animal blood on Joseph's coat to make their father think he had been killed. There were no DNA tests in those days, so it looked like Joseph's own blood on his clothes. The colour of blood turned that beautiful coat into something ugly and sinister. Joseph's father sees it and thinks that Joseph is dead. The other brothers say nothing to change Jacob's mind. See how easy it is to lie? Sometimes we lie by saying what we shouldn't. But sometimes we lie by keeping quiet when we ought to say something. Joseph's brothers lied by their actions rather than their words on this terrible day. Their sin was just as serious in God's sight.

Joseph's brothers were also *cruel*. They ignored Joseph's tears of fright and rejection in the pit. Now they ignore Jacob's tears of sorrow and disappointment when he discovers the bad news. We should not be like those brothers. We should try to be like the Lord Jesus, who was always ready to 'heal the brokenhearted', Luke 4. 18. Are we truthful and kind? If we want people to tell us the truth and be kind to us, we need to do the same to them – first!

. . . through the Bible day by day

February 12

Reading: Genesis 39. 1-4, 7-20

Flee also youthful lusts, 2 Timothy 2. 22

Joseph is now a slave in Egypt. He is so far away from home. Maybe he thinks that no one will know if he does something bad. Joseph's father will not be disappointed. Joseph's brothers will not be able to criticize. They are all too far away to see. But Joseph knows that God will be upset if he sins. Potiphar will not know if Joseph betrays him because Potiphar trusts Joseph. But Joseph knows that to do wrong would be to 'sin against God' which is 'great wickedness'.

We often wonder whether we might be able to get away with doing something wrong. We suppose that our family and friends will never see or find out. We get ourselves into temptation like Joseph in the house, David in the palace or Peter in the courtyard. However, God is watching over us. He knows when we disobey Him. We must remember that God sees us and we must 'be sure your sin will find you out'.

Pray
Ask God to help you to do the right thing, even if it means upsetting other people.

Joseph does the right thing and he gets into trouble for it. Because he runs away from Potiphar's wife, she tells lies about him and makes sure he is sent to prison. Joseph loses his job, his home and his good reputation. Despite all this, there is one thing that Joseph does not lose. He does not lose touch with God. 'The Lord was with Joseph'. Staying close to God should be the top priority in our lives. It is only possible if we behave like Joseph – run away from sins and 'walk in the light as He is in the light', 1 John 1. 7. Shall we try to do that today? God will help us, if we are serious about it.

Stepping stones

Reading: **Genesis 39. 20 – 40. 23**

FEBRUARY 13

Be kind to one another, Ephesians 4. 32

Joseph has another change of clothes! First the smart coat of many colours in his father's house was ripped from him by his brothers and dipped in animal blood. Then the slave's uniform in Potiphar's house was snatched away by Potiphar's wife. Now Joseph is wearing prison clothes as he is in an Egyptian jail.

Even if Joseph's address and clothes have changed, he still has the same character. Whenever we read about Joseph, he is always helpful and kind to everyone he meets. The prison guard notices how helpful Joseph is. He may even have noticed that God was with Joseph. So he puts Joseph in charge of looking after all the prisoners. We should be helpful too, so people notice. Who can we help? Perhaps our teachers at school, our parents at home, or our neighbours in the street. Think about how we might be able to help others today.

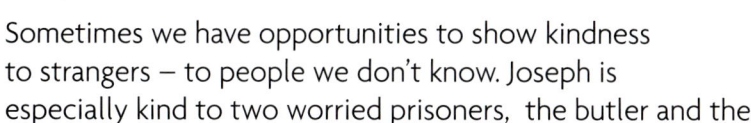

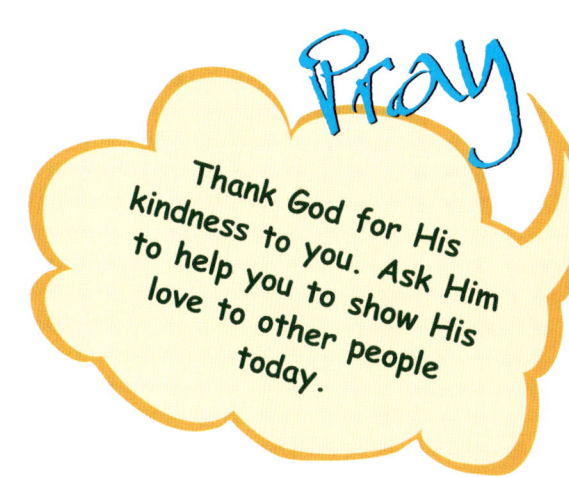

Sometimes we have opportunities to show kindness to strangers – to people we don't know. Joseph is especially kind to two worried prisoners, the butler and the baker. They must have looked very anxious as Joseph came to see them one day at breakfast time. He was kind enough to ask them about their problems. They told him about their strange dreams. Joseph was able to help them because he was in touch with God. We will be most able to help people if we are trusting in Him. Then God can use us to sort out other people's problems. Joseph didn't tell them what their dreams meant because he was clever, but because God was with him. If we are saved, then God is with us too. So let's go out and be kind to people today.

Pray

Thank God for His kindness to you. Ask Him to help you to show His love to other people today.

... through the Bible day by day

February 14

Reading: Genesis 41

He who promised is faithful, Hebrews 10. 23

Some people call special days 'red letter days'. Our reading today describes an amazing day in the life of Joseph. He woke up as a prisoner but he fell asleep as the prime minister of Egypt. What a change! He still has the same character throughout the day. He is just as kind and helpful to Pharaoh in the palace as he was to the butler and baker in the prison. He is still brave enough to tell other people about the power of God.

Can we remember the best ever day in our lives? If we have been saved, then that should be a very special day for us. The day we were saved is the day when we changed from being a child of disobedience to becoming a child of God. You might have woken up today with your sins unforgiven but it would be wonderful to be saved by God's grace before you fall asleep. Could today be that special day for you?

Pray
Thank God that He always keeps His promises and that you can trust in Him.

God certainly keeps His promises. Once Joseph had dreamed that he would be an important ruler and now he is. His dream has come true. God has also promised in His word that one day the Lord Jesus Christ will be king over all the world. Do we believe this will come true?

Are we looking forward to the day when the Lord Jesus comes back? Everyone who has trusted Him will be invited to share in His kingdom with Him. Today could be that special day when He returns. Are we ready and waiting for Him?

Reading: Genesis 42. 3-14, 21-22

February 15

Be sure your sin will find you out,
Numbers 32. 23

Conscience, the quiet voice put in us all by God our Creator, which whispers, 'that is wrong' when we do bad things, can be dreadful. We can try to silence it, but it keeps speaking to us. It can go on speaking for years, as Jacob's sons found out.

Ten foreigners bowed to the ground before Joseph, who was now governor of Egypt. Joseph's mind went back to when he dreamed that his brothers would do just this. He recognized them, but they did not recognize him! He longed to hear news of his father and Benjamin. For twenty-three years what they had done to Joseph had been on his brothers' consciences. Had they been successful in trying to silence them?

Pray

Ask God to help you to keep a clear conscience. When you do wrong ask God to forgive you and put it right.

'You are spies', Joseph accuses them. They reply, 'We are honest men. We are all brothers, the sons of one man. He is in Canaan'. How could they say they were 'honest men'? Joseph knew what they were really like – they had lied to their father and treated him dreadfully. Didn't their consciences prick them?

Joseph puts them in prison for three days. As they have time to think and talk together, their consciences work and they have to admit, 'We are guilty of what we did to our brother. We saw his distress; now distress has come to us'.

It is said that 'a guilty conscience is a bad companion'. It makes us feel uncomfortable and spoils our link with God. We can try to push the thoughts to the back of our mind but they will come back. Look what happened with Joseph's brothers. Like Paul in Acts chapter 24 verse 16, we should always try to have a clear conscience before God and before men.

... through the Bible day by day

FEBRUARY 16

Reading: Genesis 45. 1-9

Be kind to one another, tenderhearted, forgiving one another, even as God in Christ forgave you, Ephesians 4. 32

'I am Joseph!' The hearts of the ten brothers stopped – now what would happen to them? Would he pay them back?

The brothers are back in Egypt again to buy corn. This time, Benjamin is with them. Jacob was not happy about this but he had no choice. The brothers sat down to feast with Joseph and then set off for home but they were soon taken back to Egypt accused of stealing. Joseph's silver cup had been found in Benjamin's sack of corn! Judah pleads with Joseph on Benjamin's behalf and offers to take his punishment.

Joseph sends everyone else out of the room so as not to make his brothers embarrassed and so that other people did not hear how badly they had treated him. Look at his reaction! He cries out loud and forgives his brothers. 'Love covers a multitude of sins'. Joseph did not blame them nor bear a grudge against them. He had every right to, but no! He saw God's hand in what had happened – he saw the bigger picture. 'God sent me before you to save life', he said, verse 6. 'You meant evil against me, but God meant it for good', 50. 20.

Has your brother or sister or friend been unkind to you? Are you plotting revenge? Take Joseph as your example and don't bear a grudge. But better still, look at the Lord Jesus and what He suffered to deal with our sins so that we could be forgiven. Did He bear a grudge? Of course not! When He was reviled He did not revile in return; when He suffered, He did not threaten, 1 Peter 2. 23. We should show the same forgiveness to others as Joseph and the Lord did. Do we?

Pray

Ask God to help you to be prepared to forgive people who wrong you and not to bear a grudge against them.

Stepping stones

Reading: **Genesis 45. 21-28**

February 17

God sent me before you to preserve life,
Genesis 45. 5

'Joseph is still alive and he is governor of Egypt!' What wonderful news! No wonder Jacob's heart stood still. It took all the messages Joseph had sent plus all the gifts and the carts to take Jacob into Egypt to convince him it was true, verse 27. But it was all in God's plan. Joseph had been taken from him. Both men had suffered, Joseph in a pit and in a prison, whilst Jacob had never got over the loss of his son. But God is able to bring good out of evil. Look at Joseph's position in Egypt, his wealth, his influence with Pharaoh. He could use all this to help Jacob in his last years and particularly in the last five years of the famine. No wonder Jacob said, 'Joseph my son is still alive. I will go and see him before I die', verse 28.

This was quite a big thing for a man of 130 years old to do, but what a wonderful reunion with Joseph! The son he thought he had lost forever is found. For seventeen more years Jacob lived in Goshen, one of the most fertile parts of Egypt. He enjoyed being surrounded by all twelve of his sons and their families. They were a united family once more.

Are you feeling sad at what is happening to you at the moment? If you belong to the Lord Jesus take heart. God has a plan for your life and He is working it out just as He did for Jacob and Joseph. It will not be easy all the time but God is in control.

'I know the plans that I have for you, declares the Lord, plans for welfare and not for calamity to give you a future and a hope', Jeremiah 29. 11 (NASB).

Pray
Ask God to show you His plan for your life and ask Him to help you to follow it.

. . . through the Bible day by day

February 18

Reading: **Exodus 1. 8-22**

Now there arose a new king over Egypt, who did not know Joseph, Exodus 1. 8

'Look, the people of the children of Israel are more and stronger than we are'. This was how the new king of Egypt saw it. Seventy people had left Canaan with Jacob but now they were a huge number.

Joseph had died, aged 110, having been in Egypt for 93 years. He had been called 'the saviour of Egypt'. He was known world-wide for his skilful organisation during the seven years of plenty and seven of famine. Now, 400 years later, the sons of Israel were looked upon by the new king as a threat to him. He had not known Joseph and had obviously not read the history books. Time had passed and Joseph's fame wasn't even a memory. How good it is to know that God does not forget! He knows all we have done for Him and keeps a record.

Pray

Ask God to help you to do His work faithfully even if no one remembers or appreciates what you have done.

The king dreamed up a dreadful plan to stop the Israelites increasing. For adults he had a scheme of hard labour; for new-born boys, it was death by drowning. Herod had a similar plan when he tried to destroy the Lord Jesus, Matthew chapter 2.

But look at verses 12 and 21 – the more the children of Israel were persecuted, the more they grew. God was watching and looking after them. He particularly noted the faithfulness of the midwives and rewarded them, verses 19-21.

Over a thousand years later, God was watching another faithful group of people. 'Those who feared the Lord spoke to one another, and the Lord listened and heard them; so a book of remembrance was written before Him', Malachi 3. 16. Today Christians are still being persecuted, in Pakistan, Indonesia, and many other countries. But the church keeps growing. Other people may not remember what we have done or suffered for Him, but God does.

Stepping stones

Reading: **Exodus 2. 1-10**

February 19

By faith Moses, when he was born, was hidden … by his parents, because they … were not afraid of the king's command,
Hebrews 11. 23

'When she opened it, she saw the child and behold, the baby wept,' verse 6. Few people can resist a crying baby, not even an Egyptian princess! What should she do? She recognized the baby as 'one of the Hebrews' children'. She ought to throw him into the river Nile as her father had ordered but she just couldn't. Miriam was watching nearby, *but* so was God. He had a plan for Moses and not even Pharaoh could stop it.

Amram and Jochabed had two children, Miriam and Aaron, and then another boy was born right in the middle of Pharaoh's dreadful massacre of baby boys. They trusted God, believing their beautiful son was special. For three months they managed to keep him hidden but babies grow and get noisy, so Jochabed made a plan to save his life. Was she surprised when Miriam came running with news that Pharaoh's daughter wanted to speak to her? Surely not. Her faith in God told her all would be well. How thankful to God she was as she carried her son home to bring him up for the princess. Jochabed and Amram gladly taught him about the true God who had cared for his ancestors and now cared for them. They told him how God had preserved his life despite Pharaoh's order. Moses must have seen their personal faith in God. In spite of Pharaoh's plans to weaken the Israelites, his own daughter brought into the palace one of their children to be brought up as her son, *his grandson!*

Pray
Thank God that His plans cannot be altered by anything that man can do.

We may wonder why some Christians have big problems, why things are not going the way we expect. We must keep trusting. God is always in control and He is working out His purpose. 'Have faith in God', Mark 11. 22

… through the Bible day by day

February 20

Reading: Exodus 2. 11-15

There is no creature hidden from His sight, but all things are naked and open to the eyes of Him to whom we must give account, Hebrews 4. 13

'He looked this way and that'. Then Moses did a dreadful thing. He killed a man!

For about thirty years Moses was being prepared to be the next pharaoh. He was the heir-apparent. He was taught everything about Egypt, its culture, its learning, its army. Stephen says Moses 'was mighty in words and deeds', Acts 7. Moses was a good student but he also never forgot what his parents had taught him when he was a child. Now he was distressed to see how badly his fellow-Hebrews were being treated. Moses saw an Egyptian beating a Hebrew and took the law into his own hands. He acted without God. Why did he 'look this way and that'? He knew that what he was going to do was wrong. If we have to look around to see who is watching before we do anything, it must be wrong.

Pray
Ask God to help you not to act on your own but always to ask for His help.

'He supposed that his brethren would have understood that God would deliver them by his hand, but they did not understand', Acts 7. 25. Moses knew he was to be the deliverer but this was not the way to do it. The time was not right and God had a lot more to teach Moses. His next school was to be the desert. How different to the palace!

The next day Moses tried to intervene in a fight between two Hebrews and realized that what he had done the day before was known. Pharaoh would threaten to kill him. What does Moses do now? Little does he know, as he runs for his life to Midian, that this is exactly where God wants him. God still has many lessons to teach Moses before he delivers the people from Egypt. Your ways are not My ways, says the Lord, Isaiah 55. 8.

Stepping stones

Reading: **Exodus 3. 1-10**

February 21

The Lord said: 'I have surely seen the oppression of My people who are in Egypt, and have heard their cry because of their taskmasters, for I know their sorrows', Exodus 3. 7

'I will now turn aside and see this great sight, why the bush does not burn'. A burning bush is not unusual in hot deserts but a bush on fire without being burnt up is a miracle! Moses had been in Midian for 40 years. He was now 80, with a wife and two sons. He had spent the time working as a shepherd for his father-in-law, Jethro. In Egypt he had relied on himself, but in the desert he learned to rely on God. God was preparing Moses for his future work. Today was the day this education was finished.

Pray

Pray today for people who are suffering because they are Christians. Ask God to strengthen their faith and give them courage to continue to witness for Him.

Moses had taken the sheep near Mount Horeb when he saw the amazing sight. This was not all, for *God* spoke to him from the middle of the bush. There was no doubt that He was speaking to Moses, verse 4. Moses immediately sensed the holiness of God and took off his sandals. God's message was that He had seen His people's troubles and felt for them in their distress. The time had come for them to be set free. Moses had got the timing wrong 40 years ago, but now God's time had come, Gen. 15. 13-14. God's timing is always right. He was going to lead them somewhere far better than Egypt, to 'a land flowing with milk and honey' – a large country full of plenty.

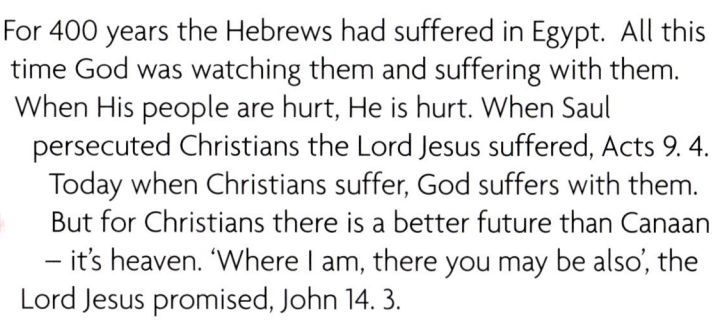

For 400 years the Hebrews had suffered in Egypt. All this time God was watching them and suffering with them. When His people are hurt, He is hurt. When Saul persecuted Christians the Lord Jesus suffered, Acts 9. 4. Today when Christians suffer, God suffers with them. But for Christians there is a better future than Canaan – it's heaven. 'Where I am, there you may be also', the Lord Jesus promised, John 14. 3.

. . . through the Bible day by day

February 22

Reading: Exodus 7. 1-13

Pharaoh said, 'Who is the Lord, that I should obey His voice to let Israel go? I do not know the Lord, nor will I let Israel go', Exodus 5. 2

Pray

Ask God to give you a heart that listens to Him and does what He says.

'Pharaoh's heart grew hard' and he did not listen to them. When Moses and Aaron went to face Pharaoh with God's message, 'Let my people go!' Pharaoh questioned who God was and why he should obey Him. This Pharaoh, who may have been Rameses Sesostris, was important. We can read about him in history books and see statues of him in museums. He could not imagine anyone greater than himself and certainly not the God of the Hebrews. As a result of this attitude God was going to show him who was great and powerful.

God instructed Moses and Aaron to face Pharaoh again. This would not be the last time because Pharaoh's heart would become hard so he would keep refusing them. God was going to have to show him by 'signs and wonders' His own great superiority and His glory and majesty. How did Pharaoh's heart become hard? At the first visit of Moses and Aaron he was stubborn and refused God's request – and the more he refused, the more stubborn he became.

We can be the same as Pharaoh, stubborn and proud. We want to go our own way and 'do our own thing'. God may be asking us to do something and we don't want to do it. The more we refuse the more stubborn we get. God may send difficulties into our lives to bring us to Him. Don't be like Pharaoh, proud and stubborn. Be humble and do as God asks.

It's interesting to see the difference between Pharaoh and Moses and Aaron. Pharaoh refused to obey God but Moses and Aaron did 'just as the Lord commanded them', verses 6, 10. What a good example for us to follow! Let's humble ourselves 'under the mighty hand of God', 1 Peter 5. 6.

Reading: Exodus 7. 14, 19; 8. 1-2, 16, 20-21; 9. 1-3, 8-9, 13-15, 22; 10. 12, 21

FEBRUARY 23

Egypt was glad when they departed, for the fear of them had fallen upon them,
Psalm 105. 38

'The Egyptians shall know that I am the Lord'. During the following months Moses and Aaron met Pharaoh nine times with God's message, 'Let My people go!' Each time Pharaoh refused. As a result God sent nine plagues which fell on things the Egyptians worshipped, like the sacred River Nile, the frog-head god, sacred oxen, etc. The aim was to show God's power and make Pharaoh change his mind.

The plagues came in groups of three. In the first two of each group God gave Pharaoh warning. But in the last, when lice, boils, and darkness came, He gave no warning. When we look at the trail of destruction left behind it's no wonder the Egyptians were glad when the Israelites had gone.

The magicians tried their best to do the same plagues and were allowed success in the first two. After that they had to admit, 'This is the finger of God'. If they were so clever why did they imitate the plagues and make more destruction? Why did they not remove them?

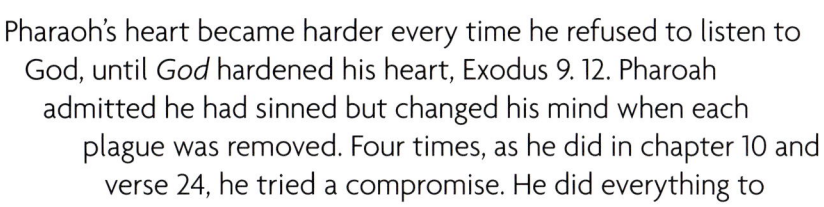

> **Pray**
> Speak to God using the words of the hymn, 'Take my will, and make it Thine; it shall be no longer mine'.

Pharaoh's heart became harder every time he refused to listen to God, until *God* hardened his heart, Exodus 9. 12. Pharaoh admitted he had sinned but changed his mind when each plague was removed. Four times, as he did in chapter 10 and verse 24, he tried a compromise. He did everything to keep the Israelites in Egypt or to make sure they had to return. But God's people were going to leave Egypt whatever Pharaoh said. He would soon learn that Jehovah is the Lord. Moses had said, 'Not a hoof shall be left behind', Exodus 10. 26. With God there is no room for negotiation. To call him *Lord* means we must obey Him fully. If He is not Lord of all He is not Lord at all!

... through the Bible day by day

February 24

Reading: Exodus 11

You hide your face, they are troubled; You take away their breath, they die and return to their dust, Psalm 104. 29

'I will bring one more plague upon Pharaoh'. It was to be the last and most terrible of all the plagues. As a result Pharaoh would *drive* the people of God out of Egypt.

Up till now the Israelites had not been paid a penny for their years of hard labour, but God was going to see that they did not leave empty-handed. They would have their wages. The Egyptians, including Pharaoh's servants, thought well of the Hebrews and greatly respected Moses. They gave willingly the silver and gold articles they asked for.

Pray

Ask God to help you to listen to Him and not to have a hard heart which turns right away from Him.

Moses had to face Pharaoh with the details of the final plague. It was not a pleasant task! Pharaoh's heart was still stubborn. He had refused time and time again to do as God commanded but this would be the last time. No family would escape, whether it was Pharaoh's family or that of a very lowly worker in his kitchens. Even the animals would not be excluded. The first-born in the whole land was going to die.

Yet again God would show Pharaoh the difference between Israel and Egypt. Among the Egyptians there would be a great wail of sorrow but in Goshen, where the Israelites lived, there would be no sound. Not even the barking of a dog.

It is very sad to read that God hardened Pharaoh's heart, v. 10. Previously Pharaoh had hardened his own heart, but now, because of his attitude, *God* hardened his heart. God is patient and forgiving but He does not wait forever, as we see with Pharaoh. We too can refuse to do as God asks us once too often. Then God stops asking and we are left on our own. The Lord is patient, and wants that 'all should come to repentance', 2 Peter 3. 9.

Reading: **Exodus 12. 1-14**

FEBRUARY 25

When I see the blood, I will pass over you, Exodus 12. 13

'When I see the blood'. 'Why are you doing that, Dad?'

'God told us we must or the first-born in every house will die'. 'But, Dad, the first-born – that's me! Will I die?' 'No son, this blood will shelter you'.

You can imagine this conversation in many of the Hebrews' homes. They had chosen a lamb, kept it for four days and now the time had come to kill it. God had given Moses detailed instructions about what kind of animal had to be taken, when it was to be killed, what to do with the blood, how to cook the meat and when to eat it. Nothing was left out. These were God's instructions to be carried out to the letter. The blood had to be painted on the door-posts and the lintel of the house and then they had to stay indoors. Only if they were inside, with the blood outside, would the angel spare them.

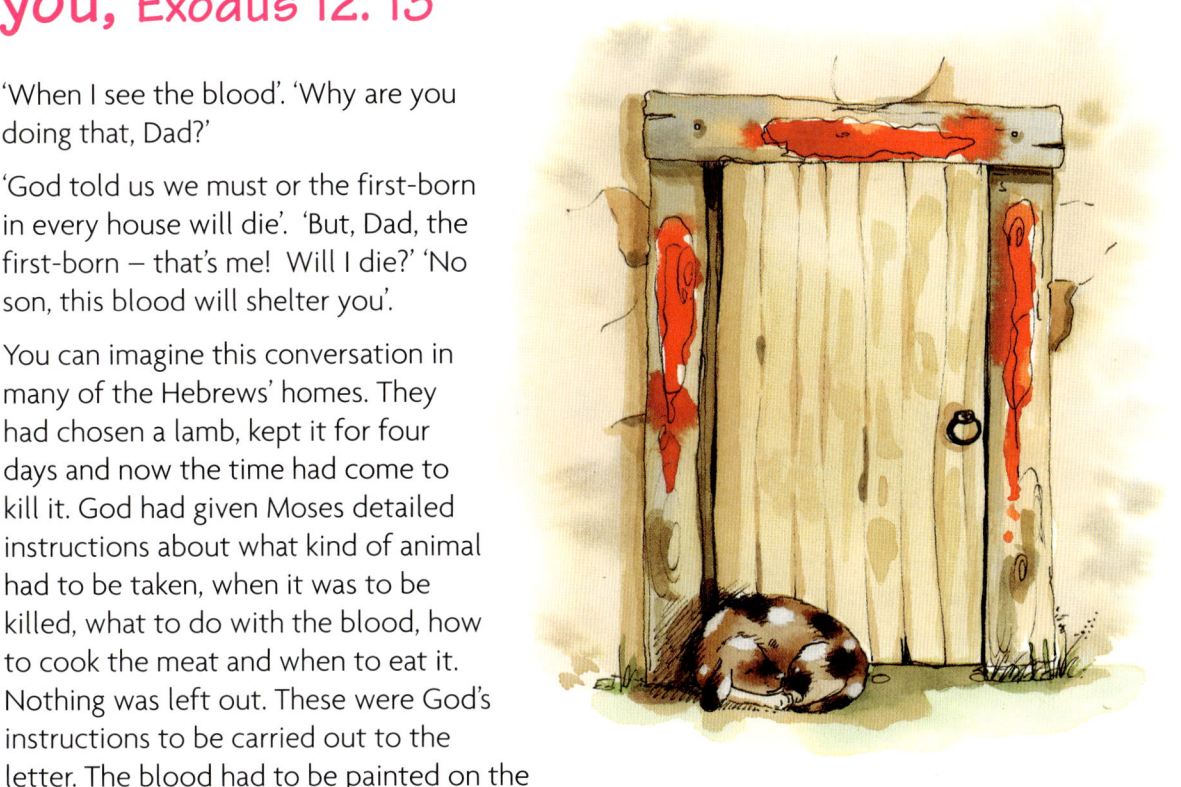

At midnight the angel passed through the land. Where there was no blood on the outside the first-born inside died but where God saw the blood, the first-born was spared. This applied to both the Hebrews and Egyptians. The blood was a sign of protection.

The blood is still important in God's eyes for salvation, our salvation. Not the blood of a lamb but the blood of the Son of God, *the* Lamb. The Lord Jesus was the perfect sacrifice. He shed His blood so that God would pass over us and not judge us. Jesus 'our Passover, was sacrificed for us', 1 Corinthians 5. 7. As the Hebrews had to apply the blood on their doors to be saved, we must apply His blood by faith to our hearts. Have we done that?

Pray
Thank God for the Lord Jesus, the Lamb of God who shed His blood so that you can have salvation from your sins.

. . . through the Bible day by day

February 26

Reading: Exodus 13. 17-22

You led them by day with a cloudy pillar, and by night with a pillar of fire, to give them light on the road which they should travel, Nehemiah 9. 12

Pray

Thank God for His care and protection over you and your family. Ask Him to guide you today in all that you do.

'The Lord went before them'. There could have been as many as two-and-a-half million people led out of Egypt by God, a vast company in orderly ranks under the direction of Moses. It was carefully organized. Each family had made preparations before they ate their final meal in Egypt. They took with them all they needed for their journey including their bread dough! Moses made sure that the promise made to Joseph some 400 years ago was carried out. His bones were taken with them to be buried in Canaan.

God knew what His people were like when He chose the route to Canaan. He did not direct them by the shortest route through the land of the Philistines because the Philistines were fierce and if the Israelites had to fight them they might change their minds and go back. Their first camping place was Etham on the edge of the wilderness.

How were they going to find their way to the Promised Land? There was no GPS, no 'sat. nav.', no map. Not even a signpost saying, 'Promised Land, this way'! They had to rely totally on God.

God led them in two ways, with a pillar of cloud during the day and of fire by night. This meant that if they had to travel at night they could see the way. God took care of everything. All they had to do was follow. There is no pillar, or column, for us today, so how does God lead us? By His Word, the Bible. This wonderful book is a map, a compass and a lamp, Psalm 119. 105. It contains all we need to guide us on our journey through life. We must read it and ask God to show us the way.

Reading: **Exodus 14. 5-31**

FEBRUARY 27

I will sing unto the Lord, for He has triumphed gloriously! The horse and its rider He has thrown into the sea, Exodus 15. 1

Pray

Ask God to help you rely on Him and wait for Him to show you the way to go. Thank Him for His help to you in the past.

'Stand still and see the salvation of the Lord'. The Israelites had marched boldly out of Egypt. Pharaoh had told Moses to go. Now, when he realized they really had gone, he changed his mind. He gave orders for a large army to be mustered and to pursue them. The Israelites did not know this until they were nearly on top of them! They panicked.

Now begins a pattern of complaining. This is the first time and there will be many more. Whenever anything goes wrong in their eyes they blame Moses and want to go back to Egypt. Slavery becomes more desirable than God's way. Moses' answer is, 'Stand still'. They had nothing to do. God was going to do everything. 'He will fight for you'.

God told Moses to lift up his rod. The rod which had brought nine plagues on Egypt was to be used for the salvation of God's people. This was carried out in four stages. The pillar of cloud moved behind the people. Then a strong east wind divided the sea making a dry path through the middle. The Israelites walked safely through to the other side. All two-and-a-half million of them! Finally the Egyptians followed them and were drowned as the waters flowed back. God had worked a miracle for them!

How easy it is for us to panic when difficulties come and how hard it is to stand still and let God take control. Naturally we want to be doing something but we need to wait for God to give us the instruction to 'go forward'. He will show us the way. It is an important, but sometimes a hard lesson, for us to learn. 'Rest in the Lord, and wait patiently for Him', Psalm 37. 7.

. . . through the Bible day by day

February 28

Reading: **Exodus 16. 2-15**

Jesus said to them, 'I am the bread of life. He who comes to Me shall never hunger, and he who believes in Me shall never thirst', John 6. 35

'The children of Israel complained'. This is the third time that the children of Israel have grumbled against Moses and Aaron and so against God! Again they have short memories. The food in Egypt, they said, was plentiful – when they were slaves without wages. God, in His love for them, was going to provide food – bread in the morning and meat at night. How was he going to do this in the desert! By another miracle.

God's instructions were very clear. The food would be provided, as much as they could eat for that day. The people had to gather it at dawn, daily, because as soon as the sun rose it would go rotten. There was no provision for a 'weekly shop' and a 'lie-in' for the rest of the week. Yesterday's manna would not do for today. The meat came in the evening in the form of flocks of quails which they could easily catch and cook.

God provided all that the Israelites needed and today He has provided all that we need. The Lord Jesus said, 'I am the bread of life'. He is the food for our souls. How do we get it? From the Bible. His word is the source, but we have to gather it for ourselves. That means we have to read it regularly and carefully and think about it. If we follow the pattern God gave to Israel, it will be in the morning and it will keep us going during the day.

God is faithful. He gave the manna to the Israelites fresh every day. And He will give us new thoughts about Himself every day. We had breakfast this morning for our bodies. Did we have any breakfast for our souls? Have we read the Bible today?

The Lord's mercies are new every morning. His faithfulness is great, Lamentations 3. 23.

Pray

Thank God for all the good things He gives you daily, such as a family, food, and a home. Ask Him to help you read and learn from your Bible every day.

Stepping stones

Reading: **Exodus 17. 8-16**

FEBRUARY 29

The Lord's hand is not shortened that it cannot save; nor His ear heavy that it cannot hear, Isaiah 59. 1

'Now Amalek came and fought with Israel'. Amalek was a grandson of Esau. His people were a nomadic tribe who throughout history were a major enemy of Israel. The Israelites had been led southwards down the western side of the Sinai Peninsula and arrived at Rephidim where they encountered the enemy.

Joshua was the commander of the army and had been sent by Moses to do battle with Amalek. Moses, with Aaron and Hur, went to watch the battle from a nearby hill. Moses assured Joshua that he would have the rod of God with him. Moses had used this rod to perform many miracles.

While Moses was holding up his hands the Israelites were winning the battle but when he became tired his hands dropped and the Amalekites began to win. Moses clearly needed help.

Aaron and Hur proved to be true friends and they supported Moses. They found a stone for Moses to sit on, and, one on each side, held up his hands until the battle was won.

We may not be like Joshua fighting God's enemies on the front line, but just as Aaron and Hur held up Moses' hands, we can do our part. Evangelists who are preaching the gospel to grown-ups and children here at home or in other countries need us to pray for them regularly. This is how we can do our part – a most important part – by praying and supporting God's servants. 'Continue earnestly in prayer . . . praying also for us, that God would open to us a door for the word', Colossians 4. 2-3.

We may have to face the enemy ourselves, one day, but we can be sure that God will fight for us and give us the victory, just as He did for Israel. Have we prayed for others today?

Pray

Ask God to help you to be a faithful 'prayer soldier'. Pray today for someone you know who is taking God's good news to people who have never heard it.

. . . through the Bible day by day

March 1

Reading: Exodus 20. 1-17

The law was our tutor to bring us to Christ, that we might be justified by faith, Galatians 3. 24

Up Mount Sinai trudged Moses until he reached the top. Normally there would have been a fantastic view across the wilderness plains, but not today. God was present! The mountain smoked like a furnace, there was thundering and lightning and the noise of a trumpet. Far away the children of Israel looked on this dramatic scene to see what would become of their leader, Moses.

It was a very special day for the nation of Israel. It was a day when God would give them ten commandments to keep so that He could enjoy fellowship with them. God wrote them on the back and front of two huge, flat stones. They can be summarized like this:

1. Love the Lord your God more than anyone else.
2. Love the Lord your God more than anything else.
3. Do not use God's name irreverently.
4. Keep the Sabbath Day special.
5. Be respectful to your parents.
6. Do not kill.
7. Be faithful to your wife or husband.
8. Do not steal.
9. Do not tell lies.
10. Do not desire things that are not yours to have.

Pray: Thank God that your salvation doesn't depend on you keeping the commandments. Remember that when you break them your only hope is in Christ.

After these commandments had been read to them the people said, 'All the words which the Lord has said we will do', Exodus 24. 3. Sadly, they did not manage, for time and again the people broke these commandments and so disobeyed God. What a sorry state they found themselves in! The law only showed them how sinful they really were.

When we read these commandments we realize how sinful we are too. Thankfully, though we break the law of God, God sent His Son to die for us. Galatians chapter 3 verse 13 says, 'Christ has redeemed us from the curse of the law, having become a curse for us'.

Reading: Exodus 32

March 2

Take up the whole armour of God, that you may be able to withstand in the evil day, and having done all, to stand,
Ephesians 6. 13

For forty days and forty nights Moses stayed up the mountain as God had commanded him. Some of the people grew impatient and ordered Aaron to do something. 'There is no sign of Moses. Make us gods to lead us, instead of this Moses who brought us out of Egypt', they said. Aaron obliged, took all their golden ear-rings, melted them down in a fire and moulded a beautiful shining golden calf. 'These are your gods!' said Aaron. The people worshipped the golden calf and in doing so broke the very first commandment. They became unfaithful to God and to each other.

Moses, of course, was high up in the mountain and knew nothing about this until God told Him. 'Go down, the people have sinned and made a golden calf and worshipped it instead of me'. God was very angry with the people and threatened to destroy them. Moses was angry, too, when he saw their terrible worship. In horror he smashed the commandments of stone upon the ground.

'Let my anger fall upon them', said God. But Moses cared for the people and pleaded with God not to destroy them. 'What would the Egyptians say?', he asked. 'Please forgive them'.

Pray
Help me not to fall into sin even when others around are sinning. Help me to stand for God.

Three thousand wicked people died that day. But God in grace gave Israel another chance and Moses was allowed to go back up the mountain to get another set of stones. Not all the people wanted to worship the golden calf. The tribe of Levi remained faithful to God and stood faithful for Him. They wanted to worship only the Lord. This is a great lesson to us. When everyone else around is moving away from the truth of God, we should remain firm to His word and make a stand for Him. Do we?

...through the Bible day by day

March 3

Reading: Numbers 12. 1-15

Let nothing be done through selfish ambition or conceit, but in lowliness of mind let each esteem others better than himself, Philippians 2. 3

Pray

Help me not be jealous of others. Help me to treat other people better than I treat myself.

It was a sad day when Miriam and Aaron began to complain about Moses. They accused him of marrying the wrong woman and also said, 'Why should God always speak through Moses to the children of Israel and not use us?' Moses was very humble. In fact, he was the meekest man on earth. In spite of these hurtful words, he kept quiet and trusted in God.

But the Lord was not happy! Suddenly the voice of God was heard. 'Come over to the tabernacle, I want to speak to you'. Moses, Aaron and Miriam quickly went to the tabernacle and God came down to them in a pillar of cloud. It must have been a terrifying experience.

Much to the embarrassment of Miriam and Aaron the Lord told them how great His servant Moses was. He told them how faithful he was and that there were many prophets whom God spoke to in dreams but to Moses God spoke in a special way – face to face. The Lord was angry with Aaron and Miriam for daring to speak against His servant. Miriam was the one who took the lead in the criticism. When the pillar of cloud left the tabernacle Miriam was left totally white, covered in leprosy. Imagine the horror on her face as she looked at herself!

Moses had every right to say, 'That will teach you'. But he didn't. Instead he prayed that God would remove the leprosy. The Lord responded and healed her. Miriam had learnt her lesson! It is a lesson to us that we should not be jealous of others, especially if we are good at leading or doing certain things. Let us learn to encourage each other and also learn to pray for each other, like Moses who prayed for Miriam.

Reading: Numbers 13. 17-33

March 4

If the Lord delights in us, then He will bring us into this land and give it to us, 'a land which flows with milk and honey',
Numbers 14. 8

It was about a year before this that God had spoken to Moses from a burning bush at Horeb. The Israelites had not yet left Egypt and God promised to bring them out of their troubles. In Exodus chapter 3 God promised Moses that He would bring them into Canaan, a land full of good things to eat. It was an exciting promise and one that Moses often thought about. As soon as he was able, Moses gathered a representative from each tribe to go and search out the promised land.

Pray: Help me to be an encouragement to others and to trust and believe in God when things ahead look difficult.

The twelve spies went up from the wilderness, into the land, and searched the land for forty days. Sure enough, God was true to His word and they saw some exciting things. To show the Israelites, they brought some of the fruit back. Pomegranates and figs and a cluster of grapes so big that it took two men to carry!

The camp was all abuzz when they returned. The Israelites were keen to find out about the land. Joshua and Caleb and the other spies showed them the delicious fruit they had brought. 'It really is a land that flows with milk and honey', they said. Caleb stood up boldly and said, 'Let us go up at once and take possession, for we are well able to overcome it', verse 30.

Sadly, not all the spies believed God or were as brave as Joshua and Caleb. They began to discourage the people by saying things like, 'The land is very difficult to live in. There are giants there. We are like grasshoppers in comparison'. The people became very discouraged. What a sad ending to what had promised to be a happy day! They doubted because they looked at the problems, not at God. Let's not do the same thing.

... through the Bible day by day

March 5

Reading: Numbers 14

But the men who had gone up with him said, 'We are not able to go up against the people, for they are stronger than we', Numbers 13. 31

The ten spies who did not have faith made the Israelites cry all night. Morning came and their weeping turned to anger. They began to speak against Moses and Aaron. 'We might as well have died in Egypt or in the wilderness', they said. They even questioned why God had brought them out of Egypt to die in battle. They had forgotten that God was looking after them and that He was far bigger than any enemy.

The people decided to appoint a new leader and make their way back to Egypt. Moses and Aaron, anxious to stop the tide of rebellion, fell on their faces before the people. Joshua and Caleb came and told the Israelites how good the land was. 'If the Lord is pleased with us, He will bring us into the land and give it to us', they said. There was no calming the people though and they planned to stone Joshua and Caleb to death!

Suddenly the glory of the Lord appeared in the tabernacle and God was very angry. 'How long do I have to put up with these wicked people?' He asked Moses. 'I will destroy them and make a new and better nation. Ten times they have tempted me'. Once again Moses pleaded with God to save the people.

The Lord agreed but said two things would happen. No one over twenty would be allowed to enter the land apart from Joshua and Caleb, the two believing spies. And the Israelites would have to wander around the wilderness for forty years until everyone over twenty had died.

The people should have listened to Joshua and Caleb and believed God. It is good for us to remember that God is in control of our lives and we should trust Him for guidance in everything.

Pray

Help me to remember that God is in control and can overcome things in my life that seem impossible.

Stepping stones

Reading: **Numbers 20**

March 6

Be angry and do not sin: do not let the sun go down on your wrath, Ephesians 4. 26

Pray

Help me not to lose my temper and not to speak badly to others. Help me to say sorry to others if I offend them.

The sun was beating down, the desert was dry and there was no water. 'Why do we have to die like this?' the people snapped at Moses. 'This place is evil. Why did you bring us up out of Egypt?' This was a rather unfair question considering all the suffering that Pharaoh had made them go through. Once again, Moses and Aaron came to the tabernacle and fell on their faces before the Lord. The glory of the Lord came down and God spoke. He told Moses to take his rod and speak to a certain rock. 'When you do that', said the Lord, 'water will gush out of the rock'.

Moses took the rod and gathered all the people in front of the rock. But then Moses did a very sad thing. Numbers chapter 12 tells us that Moses was the meekest man on all the earth but on this day he lost his cool. 'Listen now you rebels', he said and without a word of warning he hit the rock twice. Water gushed out. But God hadn't told him to *hit* the rock. Moses had disobeyed and the Lord had to punish him. 'Because you have not believed me and have been unholy in front of the people, I cannot allow you to take the people into the land', He said. If only Moses had not lost his temper! One lapse of self control affected the rest of his life.

Sometimes we may be guilty of losing our tempers. People may upset us and make us angry. That still doesn't mean that we have the right to speak badly towards them. Remember that many people spoke badly of the Lord Jesus but He never replied in bitterness to them. He really is the greatest example to us.

. . . through the Bible day by day

March 7

Reading: Numbers 21. 4-9

As Moses lifted up the serpent in the wilderness, even so must the Son of Man be lifted up, John 3. 14

The people in the wilderness were often murmuring and provoking God. Today was no exception. It had been a long journey from Mount Hor to the land of Edom. They were tired, hungry, thirsty and fed up! To cap it all the only food they did have was the manna, small rolls of bread, which they had grown tired of. It wasn't long before they began to complain bitterly to God and Moses again. As a punishment God sent poisonous snakes into the camp. They began to bite the people and many died.

Soon the Israelites began to realize that they had no right to complain about God and that actually God had been very good to them. He had delivered them from Egypt and kept them safe, giving them food and water for forty years. 'We have sinned', the people said to Moses. 'Pray to God that He will send the snakes away'. Moses prayed and God told him to make a snake out of brass and set it upon a pole in the middle of the camp. 'Everyone who looks on the serpent (snake) will live', said the Lord. And this is exactly what happened. All who looked in faith upon the brass snake were healed from the poison and lived.

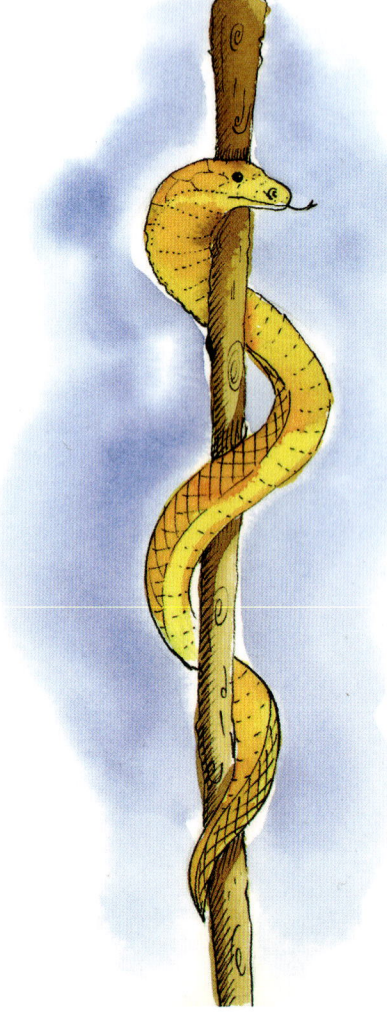

The Lord Jesus used this story to teach Nicodemus that one day He would be lifted up on a cross. The Lord Jesus meant that all guilty sinners who look to Him and believe on Him will be saved from punishment just as the people were saved when they looked to the snake. The Lord Jesus also said, 'This is the will of Him who sent Me, that everyone who sees (looks upon) the Son and believes in Him may have everlasting life', John 6. 40. Have we ever made that look of faith?

Pray

Help me to turn away from sin, to look by faith on the Lord Jesus and to believe that He was lifted up on a cross for sinners.

Stepping stones

Reading: **Numbers 22**

March 8

The Lord opened the mouth of the donkey, and she said to Balaam, 'What have I done to you?' Numbers 22. 28

The children of Israel pitched camp in the plains of Moab near to Jericho. Balak the king of Moab was very worried. 'The Israelites are so many and they will destroy us like an ox licking up grass!' he said. Balak's servants came to Balaam and invited him, 'Come with us and meet Balak to curse the Israelites and he will make you very rich'. But God told Balaam not to go because the Israelites were His special and blessed people.

It is often said, 'Money talks', and this was true with Balaam. He knew that he shouldn't go to Balak but the thought of getting his hands on a large sum of money was just too much and after some thought he disobeyed God and went off to meet the king.

God was very angry. At a narrow part of the path on the journey the Angel of the Lord stood in the way of Balaam who was riding on his donkey. The donkey refused to move, seeing the Angel, but Balaam didn't see it. Three times Balaam beat the donkey with his stick. It was at this point that the donkey spoke to Balaam. It must have been a very strange thing to hear! Then the Angel of the Lord revealed himself to Balaam and said, 'Why have you beaten the donkey three times? I came here to stop your disobedience and by refusing to move, she has saved your life'.

Peter tells us that the dumb donkey spoke with a man's voice and stopped the madness of the prophet, 2 Peter 2. 16 . God does not need us to do His will. He can use someone else. He can even use a donkey! But He wants to use spiritually obedient people. Let us make sure we are just that.

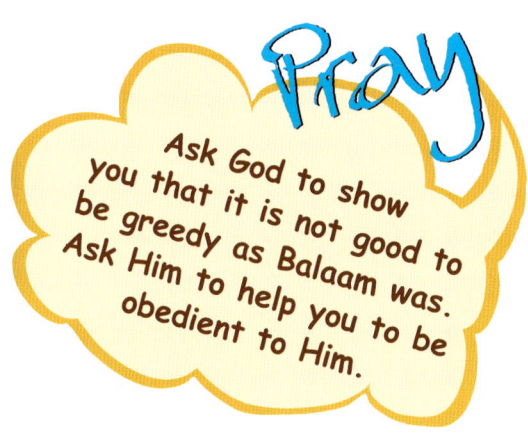

Pray

Ask God to show you that it is not good to be greedy as Balaam was. Ask Him to help you to be obedient to Him.

. . . through the Bible day by day

MARCH 9

Reading: **Joshua 2**

By faith the harlot Rahab did not perish with those who did not believe, Hebrews 11. 31

Joshua's two spies were on a mission to investigate Jericho. This great city stood between the Israelites and the promised land. They arrived at Jericho and lodged with a woman called Rahab. Unfortunately the king of Jericho was very wary of the Israelites and with good reason. The intelligence soon came back to him that two Israelites were in the house of Rahab.

His servants came quickly to arrest them but Rahab was clever. She took the two spies on to her roof and hid them in a large pile of flax. 'There were men here earlier', she said to the king's servants, 'but they have left and gone in the direction of the Jordan'.

As soon as the men left the house, Rahab ran up to the roof and spoke about her faith. 'I know all that the Lord has done for you, the drying up of the Red Sea, the kings that have been destroyed and the fear that has come upon all the land. I know that the Lord your God is the God of heaven and earth. I have shown you kindness, so please save me and my family when you come to destroy this city'. The spies agreed and she let them down the city wall with a rope to escape into a nearby mountain. 'Tie this red cord in your window and gather your family into the house', the men told her. 'All who are in your house will be kept safe when we attack'.

Rahab had become a true convert and had proved her faith in the living God by hiding the spies. May the Lord help us to live faithfully in obedience to Him no matter what it may cost us.

> **Pray**
> Give me the courage to stand for God in such a powerful way that it might influence unbelievers and make them turn to the one and only true God.

Stepping stones

Reading: **Joshua 6. 1-25**

March 10

By faith the walls of Jericho fell down after they were encircled for seven days,
Hebrews 11. 30

Jericho was a strong city with walls as wide as a house. The king of Jericho looked smug as he thought about his defences. Large walls, strong wooden gates barred and locked and enough supplies to last for months. 'Only a fool would attack us!' he thought.

When Joshua and the people arrived at the city the Lord told them to do something rather strange. For six days they walked around the city in silence, once a day. Soldiers, seven priests with seven trumpets, more priests with the ark of the covenant and the Israelites all marched around without saying a word! God was reminding the people that He fought their battles and that they should trust in Him even when the mighty walls looked impossible to breach. The ark was in the middle of them to remind them of this very fact.

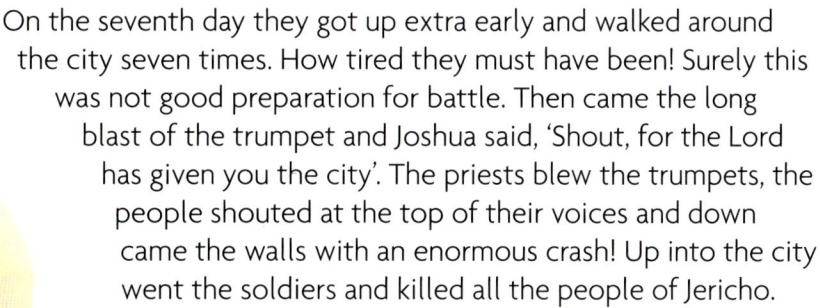

On the seventh day they got up extra early and walked around the city seven times. How tired they must have been! Surely this was not good preparation for battle. Then came the long blast of the trumpet and Joshua said, 'Shout, for the Lord has given you the city'. The priests blew the trumpets, the people shouted at the top of their voices and down came the walls with an enormous crash! Up into the city went the soldiers and killed all the people of Jericho.

Well, nearly all. All except Rahab and her family who obeyed the two spies and remained in her house. God chose not to destroy her house and they were all saved. The story shows us that God is a righteous judge. He must judge wicked men and women. But it also shows us He is full of mercy to those who faithfully trust in Him. Would that include us?

Pray

Teach me to allow You to fight my battles and to trust in You even when things look impossible.

... through the Bible day by day

March 11

Reading: Joshua 7. 1-21

Take heed, and beware of covetousness, for one's life does not consist in the abundance of the things he possesses,

Luke 12. 15

Pray

Teach me to want the things that please God so that I influence others in a good way. Remind me that my sin can affect other people.

Now that Jericho was destroyed, fighting against other cities would be easy. At least that's what the Israelites thought. The next city to destroy was Ai and Joshua said, 'There's no need for all of us to go and fight. Let's just send two or three thousand soldiers'. They were in for a shock. In the first battle the men of Ai chased the Israelites away and killed thirty-six of them!

'How could this be?' The people were dismayed. Joshua threw himself to the ground before God. 'Lord, what is wrong with us? Why is this happening? Our enemies will hear about our defeat and come after us', he said. The Lord told Joshua to get up. 'Someone in Israel has sinned badly. They have stolen forbidden things out of Jericho'.

It would be difficult for Joshua to find out on his own who had done this wicked thing so God helped him. The following morning God identified the man who was wrong by choosing the tribe of Judah, then out of them the Zarhites. He then narrowed the choice down to Zabdi's family. Finally Zabdi brought his household forward and Achan was picked out. 'Tell me what wicked thing you have done?' said Joshua. Achan admitted that he had taken beautiful clothing, silver and gold for himself.

The Lord told Joshua and all Israel to take Achan and his possessions to the valley of Achor. There they stoned him and burned his body. The New Testament teaches us that, just as the wickedness of Achan affected the lives of others and caused the death of thirty-six men, so our sin can affect other Christians badly, 1 Corinthians 5. 6. We need to live godly lives and be very careful not to disobey God. Do we?

Stepping stones

Reading: **Joshua 10. 1-28**

March 12

There has been no day like that, before it or after it, that the Lord heeded the voice of a man; for the Lord fought for Israel,
Joshua 10. 14.

Joshua and his army were sweeping through the cities of the promised land. The kings of the remaining cities were running out of ideas to stop them. Five kings of the Amorites joined forces and decided to attack the city of Gibeon, which had surrendered to Israel and agreed to serve them.

Pray

Pray for courage to do things for God and ask God to help you get through difficult days.

The kings gathered their armies together, marched to Gibeon and made a large camp, right outside the city. The Gibeonites looked out in fear on this enormous army. They hurriedly sent a message to Joshua who was at Gilgal. 'Come quickly and help us'.

Joshua immediately gathered his army and marched through the night to Gibeon. He knew it was going to be a difficult battle but the Lord encouraged him. 'Don't worry. I am going to help you fight the battle and not even one man will be able to stand before you', He said.

The following day the battle began. God's promises are always true and sure enough, the Lord fought with them. He even dropped mighty hailstones upon the Amorites so that more died because of the hailstones than the sword. Then Joshua, encouraged by the presence of God and wanting to finish the battle before darkness, said, 'Sun and moon stand still'. To the amazement of everyone that's exactly what happened! For a whole day the sun remained high in the sky and Israel were able to win the battle.

The story shows us how mighty God is and what amazing things He can do for us if we only have the faith to ask Him. He wants us to be willing to have faith and courage like Joshua. How wonderful to know that He is able to be with us, even when we have difficult things to do.

. . . through the Bible day by day

March 13

Reading: Joshua 24. 14-28

Choose for yourselves this day whom you will serve . . . But as for me and my house, we will serve the Lord, Joshua 24. 15

Joshua was worried about the children of Israel. It appeared that they might be in danger of not serving God. Some of them were already worshipping idols. So he arranged for all the leaders and tribes to meet him at Shechem. There they worshipped the Lord.

Joshua then gave them a history lesson and reminded them how God had delivered their nation from idolatry and from their enemies for five hundred years. He emphasized God's faithfulness in bringing Abraham out of a wicked land and how He had eventually brought the Israelites into the promised land.

'You've got to make a choice. Either you serve the Lord or the gods of the Amorites. But one thing is sure', he said, 'My family and I are going to serve the Lord'.

It was decision time and the people wholeheartedly chose to serve the Lord. Joshua wanted to impress upon them that they should be very serious about their decision. 'If you really mean what you say, then put away your false gods and turn to the Lord with all your heart. Don't change your minds, otherwise the Lord will come down upon you with a mighty judgement', he said. Again the people replied that they would serve and obey the Lord.

Joshua made a special agreement that day between the people and God. He placed a huge stone under an oak tree near the house of God at Shechem. He engraved on it their promise to serve the Lord and also wrote their promise in a book. We also need to be very serious about our christian faith and our commitment to serve the Lord Jesus. Anything that takes the place of God in our lives should be thrown out!

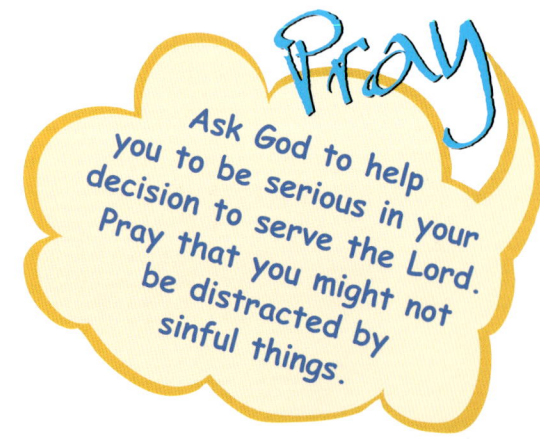

Pray

Ask God to help you to be serious in your decision to serve the Lord. Pray that you might not be distracted by sinful things.

Stepping stones

Reading: **Judges 2. 6-23**

March 14

'In those days there was no king in Israel; everyone did what was right in his own eyes', Judges 17. 6

Pray
Ask God to show you if you are stubborn and keep on sinning. It is important to be really sorry if you do.

The Israelites eventually settled and built houses in the promised land. The people served the Lord faithfully while Joshua was alive but it was a sad day when, at the age of one hundred and ten, Joshua died. They remembered all the remarkable miracles that the Lord had done – the manna and quails He had given them to eat, the help that they had had to win their battles, and the Lord's mighty presence in the tabernacle. But eventually these people also died.

Their sons and daughters grew up and did not remember the wonderful things the Lord had done. They began to do evil things. They chose not to love the Lord, they refused to obey His commandments and they served other gods. The promise that the whole nation of Israel had made to God in Shechem when Joshua was their leader had been broken.

The Lord was very angry with them because of their wickedness. So He allowed their enemies to beat them in battle and to rule over them at times. Their sin made the people very unhappy, but they could not blame anybody but themselves.

God showed how gracious He is and sent special men and women called 'judges' to deliver them from their enemies. But the people still refused to serve the Lord. They were interested in themselves and stubbornly refused to change.

God is holy and must punish sin. So He punished the children of Israel by allowing many of their enemies to live nearby. It would mean strife and wars for centuries to come. God doesn't want us to be stubborn like the children of Israel. He wants us to serve Him alone. When we sin and need correcting He doesn't expect us to carry on living a sinful life like they did. We must listen to Him.

. . . through the Bible day by day

Stepping stones

March 15

Reading: Judges 3. 12-26

When the children of Israel cried out to the Lord, the Lord raised up a deliverer for them, Judges 3. 15

Eglon, the king of Moab, ruled over the Israelites. Israel had sinned and served an idol called Baal. Eglon, with some help from the Amorites and Amalekites, defeated them in battle. Eighteen years later the miserable Israelites cried to the Lord for help.

The Lord brought to them a special man called Ehud. God gave him the difficult task of delivering Israel from King Eglon. Ehud made a dagger that was very sharp on both edges. One day he took the dagger and walked to the house of Eglon. What was special about Ehud was that he was left-handed. This meant that, when the guards searched him for a weapon and looked on his left side, they didn't find one – it was hidden on his right side! He brought a present to Eglon, pretending to be friendly with him.

After he had given the present, Ehud walked boldly up to Eglon who was sitting in his summer house surrounded by servants and all sorts of luxuries. He whispered into his ear, 'I have a secret to tell you Eglon'. Eglon was very excited about this. What could it be? He ordered everyone out and shut the door. 'What do you want to tell me?' 'I have a message from the Lord', said Ehud. And with that he took out his dagger and stabbed Eglon! Eglon was a very fat man and the dagger disappeared right into his belly so that Ehud couldn't pull it out again. Eglon fell down dead.

God helped Ehud that day and later he gathered all Israel together to fight against Moab who were defeated. The story of Ehud shows us that God is able to use anyone to do special things for Him. Being different to others does not mean we cannot do things for God.

Pray

Thank God that, though we are all different, you can each serve God in your own way. Ask Him to help you appreciate people and their different gifts.

Stepping stones

Reading: **Judges 4. 4-24**

March 16

Deborah arose, a mother in Israel,
Judges 5. 7

The Lord used one man and two women to save His people from Jabin's power. Jabin's army of Canaanites was cruel so God told Barak to gather together an army that would do what God said. But Barak needed help because his faith wasn't quite strong enough. It would be quite scary leading the people into flat land by the river, without any spears to throw, when the enemy had nine hundred iron chariots and lots of weapons.

Deborah was a woman of great faith and wisdom. People went to her for help, like children go to their mothers. Deborah helped Barak and the people to obey the Lord. However, she was careful not to be the leader. That was Barak's role. She would support him. So she *called* Barak to her, *asked* if God had spoken to him, then *explained* how the victory would happen. She was *invited* into battle and *reminded* him of the Lord's instructions all the way along. Their faith was rewarded for the Lord sent a huge thunderstorm so the enemy's chariot wheels stuck in the mud. Then God's people fought with their swords.

Sisera, the enemy's general, ran away to Jael's tent because her husband had made peace with Jabin. He thought he would be safe there. But Jael still honoured the Lord. She bravely hammered a tent peg right through Sisera's head while he was asleep, and killed him. So the Lord used wise Deborah and brave Jael. The victory was finally won.

Pray
Ask the Lord to give you the faith to do what He asks you to do. Then pray for the courage to do it.

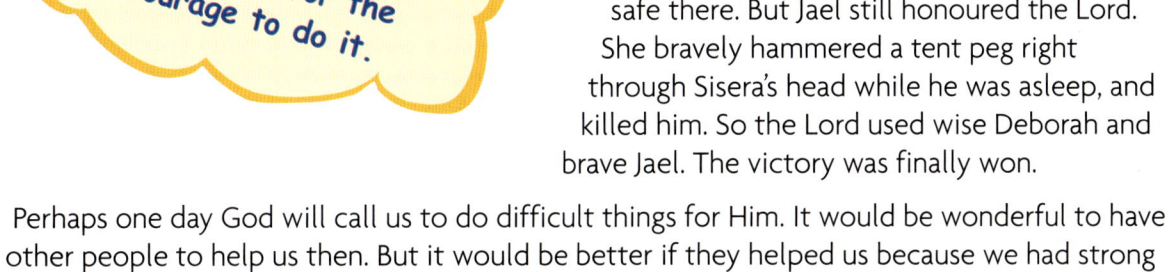

Perhaps one day God will call us to do difficult things for Him. It would be wonderful to have other people to help us then. But it would be better if they helped us because we had strong faith rather than because they had to strengthen our weak faith. Do we always believe and trust in God?

. . . through the Bible day by day

March 17

Reading: Judges 6. 11-24

I am the least in my father's house,
Judges 6. 15

Gradually the Israelites turned away from the Lord and worshipped made-up gods like Baal instead. So the Lord stopped looking after them and it wasn't long before the Midianites attacked, stole their crops and drove them out of their homes. They had to live in caves in the mountains. 'Midian' means 'strife'. This shows what happens when Christians value the gods of this world, like money, sport or entertainment, more than the Lord. Trouble comes in and destroys the peace of our homes and spiritual fruit in our lives.

The Lord chose humble Gideon to lead the people back to Him. Gideon thought he was too young, poor and unimportant to make any difference, but the Angel called him a 'mighty man of valour' and said God was with him. Gideon thought God had forsaken the whole nation. He knew the only way to survive a visit from this Angel was to bring an offering, so he did. When Gideon saw the fire leap out of the Angel's rod and burn up his offerings he was afraid and thought he would die. But God accepted his offering and Gideon was reminded that there is only one true God. He is almighty and powerful and must be feared. After that Gideon worshipped the Lord and felt brave enough to obey Him by destroying his father's altar to Baal.

The Lord is the same powerful God today and loves us, even though we don't deserve it. That is why we must be humble, like Gideon and always put the Lord first in our life. We must be careful not to let things that only last in this world become more important than worshipping and obeying Him.

Pray

Thank the almighty, holy God that He is able to use the humblest. Ask for help to put Him always first in your life.

Stepping stones

Reading: **Judges 6. 36-40**

March 18

He knows our frame; He remembers that we are dust, Psalm 103. 14

After Gideon destroyed the altars of Baal the Midianites wanted to kill him and the Israelites. They joined forces with neighbouring countries and gathered huge armies. Helped by the Holy Spirit, Gideon gathered thirty-two thousand men in defence. It was a big responsibility. Gideon wanted to be absolutely sure that God would save Israel and that he was His chosen leader. So he asked God for a sign. He took a fleece, which is the thick woolly skin of a sheep, and put it on the ground. He asked God to make the fleece wet with dew, but not the ground around it. In the morning, sure enough, the ground was dry and the fleece wet – very wet. Gideon squeezed enough water from it to fill a bowl.

Still Gideon was not certain. Perhaps the fleece was wet because it hadn't dried out as quickly as the ground. He asked the Lord to perform the miracle the other way round – keeping the fleece dry, whilst the ground around was wet. Patiently the Lord reassured him. Then Gideon knew the Lord was with them and He would give the Israelite army power to fight while keeping it safe from the battle around. They were serving the living God who holds even the dew drops in His hand.

If we want to show the power of the living God to other people, we need to prove it first in our own lives. When the Lord answers our prayers we feel stronger in our faith. We might ask Him for strength or protection, to do or not to do something. Either way, the Lord will hear us, giving us the confidence to follow His instructions. What could you pray for today to strengthen your faith in the Lord?

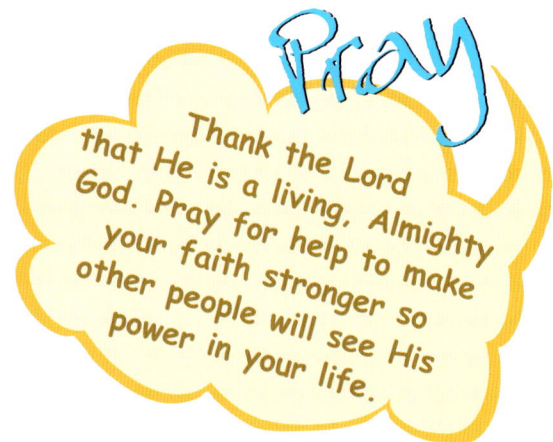

Pray

Thank the Lord that He is a living, Almighty God. Pray for help to make your faith stronger so other people will see His power in your life.

. . . through the Bible day by day

March 19

Reading: Judges 7. 15-23

Be strong in the Lord and in the power of His might, Ephesians 6. 10

Pray

Ask the Lord Jesus to help you know how and when to warn others about God's judgement and do things that will show them God's love.

The army that Gideon finally led into battle had only three hundred men in it. They had all passed God's special entry test first. It proved they were fearless and humble and would therefore trust and obey all the Lord's commandments. Gideon's tiny army looked ridiculous beside the Midianites' mighty forces. But they knew they had the Almighty God with them, who had power, not only over the dew drops of Gideon's fleece, but also over the thoughts and dreams of the enemy.

The battle plan that the Lord gave Gideon began with a surprise attack on the enemy by night. Gideon did not give his soldiers heavy weapons to carry. Instead he gave them a trumpet in one hand and, in the other, an earthenware pot with a burning lamp inside. He arranged them into three smaller bands and positioned them around the enemy camp. Their instructions were very simple – watch Gideon and copy him. When he blew his trumpet they had to blow theirs, break their pots so the light inside shone out and shout, 'The sword of the Lord and of Gideon!' Everyone obeyed loud and clear. The trumpets rang out, and the burning lights burst in upon the dark, sleeping, enemy camp. The Lord made the panicking Midianites fight each other and run away terrified.

As Christians we need to be fearless, united together as local churches in witness to the sinful world around us. We must watch the Lord Jesus and humbly do everything He says. That includes telling people about the judgement that is coming and letting the light of God's love shine out through our lives. Then God's Holy Spirit will help us to resist temptations and strengthen us to do good things in the name of Jesus Christ our Saviour.

Reading: Judges 13

March 20

Before I formed you in the womb I knew you, Jeremiah 1. 5

Manoah's wife had the wonderful experience of meeting the Angel of God. Awestruck, she listened as He told her that she would give birth to a baby boy. When grown up, he would begin to win Israel's freedom from the Philistines' rule. She must dedicate her son to the Lord from the moment he was born and was to teach him that lasting happiness comes only from obeying God's word. She and her son were to take a Nazirite vow. This meant they were to avoid drinking alcohol and eating food that God's law said was unclean. Also, her son's hair must never be cut, so everyone would know his life was set apart for the Lord.

When his wife told him the astonishing news, Manoah pleaded with the Lord to send His Angel again to tell them how to bring up the child. His prayers were answered. The Angel told Manoah to help his wife do all the Lord had said and honour Him by offering thanks and worship to God. They saw the Angel go up to heaven in the flame of their offering, because the Angel was God's sinless Son who would one day be sent into the world to deliver mankind from Satan's rule. Manoah did not need to be afraid of dying. He had offered an offering acceptable to God. Now God wanted them to do His will.

The Lord wants us to dedicate our lives to Him when we are 'born again' so we can fulfil His plans for us and bring others to know Him too. We must pray and read God's word every day, and avoid getting tangled up in the thinking and behaviour of this world. Then we will be free to do His will, giving thanks and honour to God through the Lord Jesus, our Deliverer.

Pray: Ask the Lord to help you say 'No' to things that dishonour His name and guide you into the special plans He has for your life.

...through the Bible day by day

March 21

Reading: Judges 15. 1-8

Do not be unequally yoked together with unbelievers, 2 Corinthians 6. 14

The Israelites had become used to being ruled by the Philistines. But the Philistines had never been covered by the passover blood of the lamb nor had they been led through the divided waters of the Red Sea. They had not known God's deliverance or been given the commandments of the Lord to obey. They did not worship God. Yet the Israelites feared them rather than the Lord.

Despite his God-fearing upbringing Samson wanted the Philistines' friendship. He ate, drank and joked with them and insisted on marrying a Philistine woman. He learnt through his own bitter experience that the Philistines did not make good company. They lived by a different set of rules, threatened him with violence and betrayed his trust and marriage vows.

So, one night the Philistines woke to find the fields all around them burning in huge flames. Olive groves, vineyards and grain stores were all on fire. Angrily, they asked who was to blame. It was the long-haired, Nazirite Samson! He had paired up three hundred foxes, tied their tails together, put burning grass between their tails then let them loose amongst the Philistines' crops. The Philistines reacted by burning Samson's wife, and father-in-law to death, thinking it would scare him. But Samson used his God-given strength against them. He killed, single-handedly, all the Philistines around him, before taking refuge upon the rock Etam.

Pray
Ask the Lord to help you recognize when people or situations are leading you away from Him and His loving commandments. Pray for the strength to turn back.

People in the world today offer lots of entertainment and appear to be good company. However, they follow a different set of rules that oppose the commandments of God. They may eventually suffer the fire of God's mighty judgement. That is why we must not get tangled up in their enjoyment or be tied to them by partnerships of any kind. It can only lead to sadness and destruction in the end.

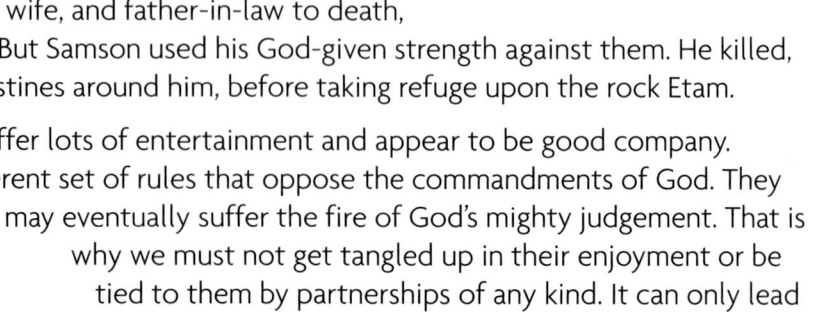

Stepping stones

Reading: Judges 16. 4-22

March 22

I can do all things through Christ who strengthens me, Philippians 4. 13

Samson judged Israel for twenty years until his weakness for Philistine women surfaced again. Rather than marry an Israelite woman, who would have had a beautiful character, who shared his faith and could help him in his responsibilities toward God, Samson set his heart upon worldly Delilah. He spent so much time in her company that the Philistine rulers noticed his love for her. They had tried unsuccessfully to overcome Samson's great strength many times before and saw, at last, their chance to weaken him. So they offered Delilah vast sums of money to help them. Delilah had no scruples about betraying Samson's trust and willingly agreed. She began to ask Samson openly how his strength could be restrained to make him just like any other man.

Instead of telling her about God's delivering power in his life Samson tried to impress her. He tantalized Delilah with lies and walked away from the Philistines each time, showing off his own strength, not the Lord's. Enticed by her apparent love Delilah crept closer to his secret and stepped up her campaign of daily interrogation. Finally, Samson gave in and he told her of the vow made by his parents to the Angel of God. Then he fell asleep upon crafty Delilah's lap. Gleefully she called for a razor, with the Philistines' jingling silver ringing in her ears.

Giving in to temptation is a gradual process and begins when we take our eyes off the Lord Jesus and begin to use our God-given personality for our own glory rather than the Lord's. That's why proving God's strength in our lives is all about will-power, not muscle power. It's about being willing to be different, obediently living each day through God's strength, not our own. Samson didn't manage to do it. Can we?

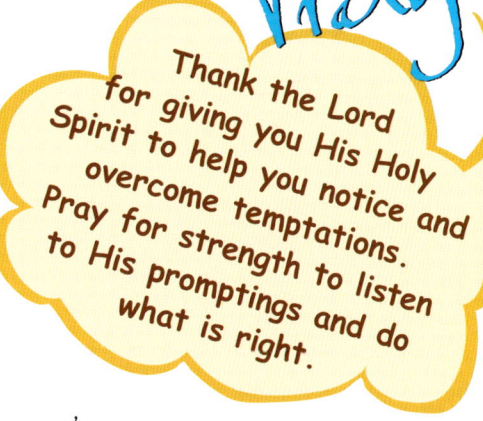

Pray

Thank the Lord for giving you His Holy Spirit to help you notice and overcome temptations. Pray for strength to listen to His promptings and do what is right.

... through the Bible day by day

March 23

Reading: Judges 16. 23-31

The dead that he killed at his death were more than he had killed in his life,
Judges 16. 30

One day the Philistine rulers were having a riotous party, praising their god for delivering Samson into their hands. They got drunk and decided to have some fun at Samson's expense. They thought he couldn't fight back now that he was blind, bound with chains and worn out from pushing a heavy grinding stone. But they forgot his hair had begun to grow back. Although they had captured his body, they could never capture his soul or his faith.

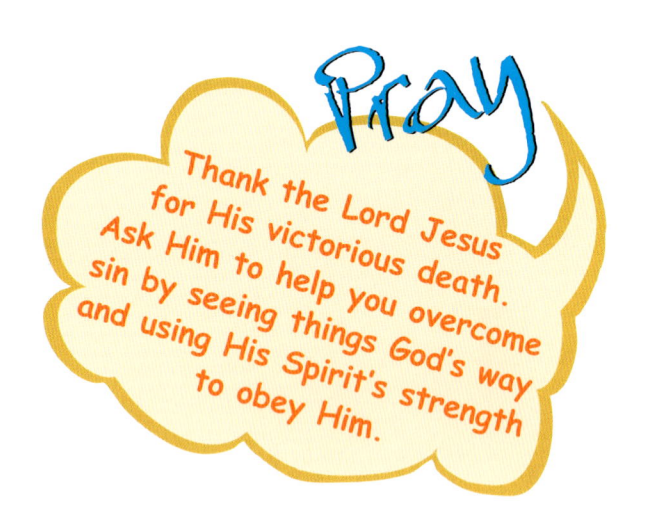

Pray

Thank the Lord Jesus for His victorious death. Ask Him to help you overcome sin by seeing things God's way and using His Spirit's strength to obey Him.

While they taunted him Samson was praying. He asked the lad guiding him to let him lean against the pillars that held up the roof of the temple. Samson knew the whole house rested upon them. Then he called upon the Lord from the bottom of his repentant heart and put his body and soul into using the strength God's Spirit gave him. Bowing with all his might he brought the enormous pillars crashing to the floor, burying the drunken Philistines above and around him in the thunderous collapse of their glorious temple. So in his death, Samson was dramatically victorious. His life had been a mixture of weakness and strength but he died knowing God had forgiven him and showing the power of the one true God who must be feared and obeyed.

Like Samson, we are captives too – not under the Philistines but to Satan's rule. He has made us blind to God's will, chained to sin and slaves to it. But we can be freed through the death of the Lord Jesus. If we ask Him for forgiveness, His Spirit will live within us, opening our eyes to see things from God's viewpoint and strengthening us to overcome sin. Then the grinding routines of every day can be filled with hope and the pain of death replaced with the joy of living for ever in heaven.

Stepping stones

Reading: **Ruth 1. 1-15**

March 24

Your people shall be my people, and your God, my God, Ruth 1. 16

When fierce famine burnt its way into Israel's history during the time of the judges, Elimelech took his family out of Israel to live in Moab hoping to keep them all alive. Instead he died there. Later his two sons, who had married Moabite wives, died too. Elimelech's wife, Naomi, and her two daughters-in-law, Orpah and Ruth were left without husbands. Naomi knew the only place to find happiness was with the Lord so she decided to return to the promised land.

As the three women travelled toward the borders of Moab, Naomi said farewell to her daughters-in-law. Orpah and Ruth had only known sadness since marrying her sons, so they had no reason to stay with her. She encouraged them to return to their own families and to the gods they had been brought up with. Orpah kissed Naomi and turned back to her people. But not Ruth. She clung to Naomi. Throughout all their sorrow Ruth had grown to love Naomi and wanted to know more about her land, her people, and her God. She did not think she would have more happiness back with the hollow gods of Moab. She wanted to get to know the living, true God that Naomi spoke about. Ruth's beautiful answer to Naomi is a wonderful description of love and loyalty that is often used to express dedication today. Ruth decided to follow Naomi and her God.

As we get older in life we reach important turning points. Our decisions will affect not only our lives but the lives of others too. If we make mistakes it is never too late to return to the pathway of blessing. We must cling to the Lord and to those who follow Him. Then we will find happiness in the end and lead others to find it too.

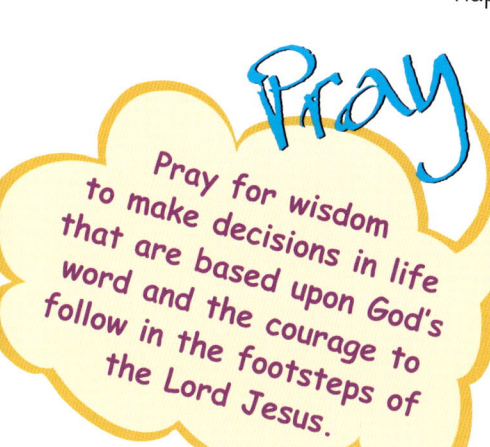

Pray

Pray for wisdom to make decisions in life that are based upon God's word and the courage to follow in the footsteps of the Lord Jesus.

. . . through the Bible day by day

MARCH 25

Reading: Ruth 2. 1- 23

Where have you gleaned today? Ruth 2. 19

Arriving in Israel as a penniless foreigner, Ruth wanted to provide for herself and her mother-in-law. With Naomi's loving consent, she set out to find a field where she would be allowed to gather the left-over corn. She 'happened' to find the field of a man called Boaz and worked hard under the hot sun, hardly stopping to rest all day.

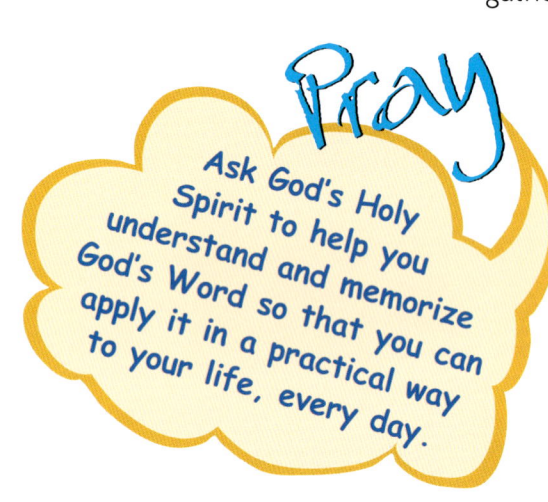

During the afternoon Boaz came and greeted the reapers. He noticed Ruth, and his servant explained who she was and how hard she had worked. To Ruth's amazement, Boaz spoke to her, saying he had heard of her loyal devotion to Naomi and her wish to trust in the God of Israel. He told her to glean in his field always, to stay by his servants and to drink the water his young men drew from the well. He assured her she would be safe because he had ordered his servants to protect her.

Pray
Ask God's Holy Spirit to help you understand and memorize God's Word so that you can apply it in a practical way to your life, every day.

When Ruth humbly thanked him he invited her to eat with him. When she went back to glean he told his servants to drop corn deliberately for her to find. By the time evening came Ruth had gathered plenty. When she told Naomi about Boaz and his invitation to glean only in his fields, Naomi praised the Lord. She explained Boaz was a close relative and therefore responsible for her. It was good that Ruth had accepted his offer.

Just as Ruth met Boaz by gleaning in his field so a person finds the Lord by reading the Bible, helped by His Holy Spirit. He wants us to stay close beside His people working together in service for Him. Then we will find protection and be satisfied, certain of a happy future united with our kinsman-redeemer, the Lord Jesus Himself.

Stepping stones

Reading: Ruth 3. 1-18

March 26

The Lord repay your work, and a full reward be given you by the Lord God of Israel, under whose wings you have come for refuge, Ruth 2. 12

Naomi watched Ruth's growing faith in God. She knew that if an Israelite man died before he had children, then his nearest, unmarried relative had first right to buy back his land and marry his widow. This was important so that the dead man's inheritance could be kept and the family name continued. Now that harvest was over, Naomi felt it was time to help Ruth put that law into effect and enjoy the security of marriage again.

Boaz was asleep on the threshing floor, tired but satisfied after a long evening beating the corn so that the breeze would blow the husks away. At midnight he woke up, startled, to find a young woman lying at his feet. It was Ruth, who had gleaned in his field all harvest. The sweat of her laborious day had been washed away and replaced by sweet-smelling perfume and instead of her work-worn clothes, she was dressed beautifully. Privately and respectfully, Ruth was asking him for protection according to her rights as his relative. Boaz acknowledged her suitability to be his wife but pointed out that there was an even closer relative who must be asked first. It turned out that he did not want that right, so Boaz willingly bought back Naomi's land and married Ruth. Their son, Obed, became the grandfather of King David. How gracious and kind God is! Someone so poor, and who was not an Israelite was brought into the family into which the Lord Jesus was eventually born.

Through following Naomi's godly example and obeying her wise guidance, Ruth learnt to trust the one true God and apply His word to her life. Whose example and guidance could we follow to help us find the Lord and apply God's Word to our lives too?

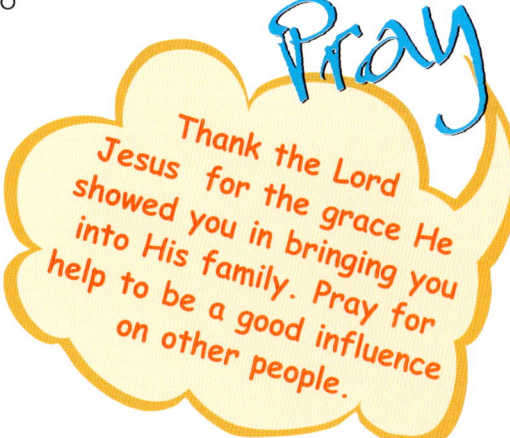

Pray

Thank the Lord Jesus for the grace He showed you in bringing you into His family. Pray for help to be a good influence on other people.

... through the Bible day by day

March 27

Reading: 1 Samuel 1. 1-10

Her rival also provoked her severely, to make her miserable, 1 Samuel 1. 6

Even though Elkanah was from the tribe of Levi he had not kept God's pattern for marriage. Instead he followed the customs of the people around him which allowed a man to have more than one wife so he could have lots of children to carry on the family name. By having two wives, however, Elkanah brought division and rivalry into his home. We should be careful to follow God's plan for our lives, and not do what unbelievers do.

Every year Elkanah took his family to Shiloh, where the tabernacle was, to offer sacrifices to the Lord. Peninah, who had many children, teased Hannah because she had none. But Elkanah gave Hannah twice as many gifts because he loved her so much. Each year Hannah remained childless, her distress grew, until eventually she cried and refused to eat. Elkanah couldn't understand it. Surely his love for her was better than ten sons! But Hannah didn't want ten sons – just one, who could be trained to serve the Lord as a Levite should. So Hannah made a very serious promise. If God would give her a son, she would dedicate him to the Lord right from the time of his birth and she would give him back to God to serve God in the tabernacle.

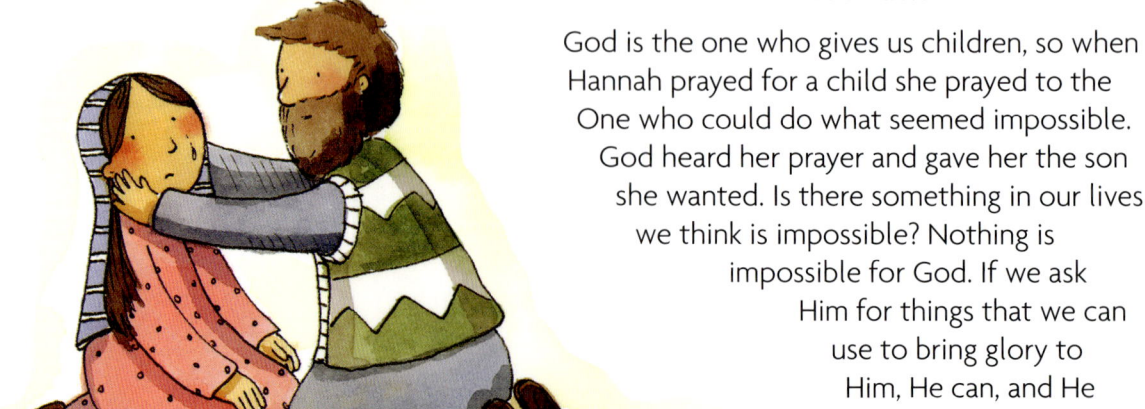

God is the one who gives us children, so when Hannah prayed for a child she prayed to the One who could do what seemed impossible. God heard her prayer and gave her the son she wanted. Is there something in our lives we think is impossible? Nothing is impossible for God. If we ask Him for things that we can use to bring glory to Him, He can, and He might, give them to us. What can we pray for today that will bring glory to His name?

Pray

Thank the Lord for giving you new life through His death and resurrection. Pray for a desire to have children 'in the faith' who are dedicated to His service.

Stepping stones

Reading: **1 Samuel 1. 11-23**

March 28

For this child I prayed, 1 Samuel 1. 27

Eli had been a priest for many years and was now old and tired. He sat watching from his seat behind one of the pillars of the tabernacle as people came in to pray. He watched Hannah pray but he couldn't hear a word she was saying and thought she was drunk! But God heard her. In her prayer she called God the 'Lord of Hosts' who ruled over all the armies of angels in heaven. She knew the answer to her prayer did not depend upon God's power but upon His will. So Hannah pleaded with Him, tears streaming down her face, to allow her barren body to have a baby boy. In return she would dedicate him to the Lord's service from the time of his birth.

Hannah's silent, agonized prayer went on for ages. Becoming impatient, Eli asked her how long she would stay there drunk and told her to give up alcohol! Hannah explained why she was so upset. Then Eli blessed her, praying that the God of Israel would answer her prayer. Within the next year, Elkanah and Hannah had a baby boy and called him 'Samuel', which means 'asked of God'.

But Hannah couldn't forget her vow. Rather than take him to the tabernacle to give thanks for him, she waited. She would take him up only when he was weaned and then leave him in Eli's care before the Lord for the rest of his life.

Imagine how difficult it must have been to say good-bye to that little boy for whom Hannah had prayed and waited so long. Have you ever promised God you would do something for Him if He did something for you? Let's not forget to keep our promises.

Pray

Thank the Lord for all the prayers other people have prayed for you. Ask Him to show you someone that you can pray for.

...through the Bible day by day

MARCH 29

Reading: 1 Samuel 1. 24 - 2. 11

As long as he lives he shall be lent to the Lord, 1 Samuel 1. 28

Hannah breast-fed Samuel through his first few years. As he grew older she taught him not to eat food which God said was unclean, and when his hair grew long Hannah did not cut it. She knew she would soon have to say goodbye to her special first-born son. He belonged to God and to His service.

When he was weaned, Elkanah and Hannah prepared their offering and went up to the tabernacle again. Samuel put his little hand into Hannah's and together they went to Eli the priest. Hannah reminded Eli of her silent, agonized prayer and humbly presented him with its answer – Samuel. Looking down upon the tender young boy standing before him with his long, Nazirite hair and hearing Hannah's selfless, humble faith, Eli worshipped the Lord. His own sons, Hophni and Phinehas, were grown up and although they worked in the temple, they were not following God's commandments. They greedily took for themselves what should have been offered to God. Little Samuel gave Eli hope. Then Hannah prayed, overflowing with thanks to the Almighty God who had rewarded her faith. He had given her life and strength according to His plans.

God blessed Elkanah and Hannah with three more sons and two daughters but Hannah never forgot Samuel. Every year she made him a new coat to wear and came up to see him. God rewarded Hannah for giving Him her little boy. God will always look after us if we give Him anything. He gives us more in return. That does not mean we should give to God so that we can get more. That would be selfish. But we can be sure He will always be more generous to us than we can ever be to Him. What can we give to Him?

Pray

Thank the Lord that you can give things to Him. Ask Him for help to think of what you can give Him today.

Stepping stones

Reading: **1 Samuel 3. 1-10**

March 30

Speak, for Your servant hears,
1 Samuel 3. 10

Pray

Thank the Lord that He is near you through His Holy Spirit. Pray for help to listen like a willing servant so that you will obediently hear when He calls.

Growing up in the temple, Samuel obediently learnt the responsibilities of priestly work from old, tired Eli, who could hardly see. Eli's sons disobeyed God's laws and instead of giving spiritual help encouraged people to do wicked things. So the Lord did not reveal His word through them. But Samuel was different. Dressed in the priest's linen tunic and his mother's special coat, he grew bigger and stronger, doing jobs around the tabernacle that a little boy could.

One night Eli was woken from a deep sleep by Samuel standing beside him asking why he had called. Eli was surprised. He hadn't called Samuel at all! Thinking Samuel was dreaming, Eli sent him back to bed. But Samuel came a second time and then a third. Eli was puzzled. Samuel was so insistent. Could the Lord be calling him? Samuel was still young, but he served God with unquestioning faith and obedience. Perhaps the Lord wanted to speak directly to him. So Eli told Samuel that if his name was called again he must answer, 'Speak Lord, for your servant is listening'.

Obediently, Samuel went back to bed and the Lord patiently called again – 'Samuel! Samuel!' Then Samuel replied as Eli had told him, and listened carefully to what the Lord said to him. It was a solemn message about the importance of obeying the Lord's commandments and honouring His holy house. Samuel's work as a prophet had begun and he knew it depended completely upon listening to and obeying God's word.

The Lord is close to us today and calls us each one through His Holy Spirit. It doesn't matter how old we are. The important thing is to answer when He calls us and then to listen to what He wants us to do. Have we ever heard Him call?

. . . through the Bible day by day

March 31

Reading: **1 Samuel 3. 15-21**

It is the Lord. Let Him do what seems good to Him, 1 Samuel 3. 18

Samuel lay awake. The awesome memory of being visited and spoken to by the Lord was mixed with the fear of telling Eli God's terrible message of judgement. He knew Eli was bound to ask him about it, but how could he, Samuel, so young and inexperienced, tell him God's stern words? How could he tell him that God had seen the way his sons had corrupted the house of God and deceived the people and tell him that He held Eli accountable for it? It wasn't enough to tell his sons that they grieved the Lord. Eli should have stopped it from happening. How could Samuel tell the old man that the Lord was going to judge him and his sons for their behaviour?

The hours slowly slipped by until it was time for Samuel to open the doors of God's house as usual so the people could come in. Sure enough, Eli called him and asked him to tell him truthfully everything God had said. Fearfully, Samuel told him every word – nothing added, nothing taken away. But Eli didn't get angry or jealous or make excuses. Eli knew the Lord is the only true judge and He sees all we do and knows even the thoughts and motives behind what we do. His punishments are always based upon perfect knowledge and truth.

Today, we serve the same Lord and He will hold us all responsible for how we respond to His commandments. Like Samuel, we should not let our fear about how people will react stop us from respectfully telling them everything God says. We, too, must always be honest in everything we do. The Lord is watching and will hold us to account for how we do, or don't, obey His Word.

> **Pray**
> Pray for help to be respectful of other people's feelings, brave enough always to tell the truth and wise enough to know when to speak it.

Stepping stones

Reading: 1 Samuel 4. 1-11

April 1

The ark of God was captured; and the two sons of Eli, Hophni and Phinehas, died, 1 Samuel 4. 11

The army of Israel was not having a good day. It had been defeated by the Philistines and four thousand soldiers lay dead.

In desperation the elders of Israel decided to take the ark of the covenant from Shiloh. This was a special box that symbolized the power and presence of the Lord. The elders foolishly thought that if they took it into battle it would help them win. What they were really doing was treating it like a 'good luck' charm!

It looked as if their idea might work for a short time, as the Philistines were afraid when they saw the ark. It made the Philistines fight with all their might, though, and by the end of the day thirty thousand Israelite foot soldiers were killed and the ark of the Lord was captured. What the people of God learned that day, to their horror, was that God wasn't actually with them at all. The ark was nothing without God.

Do you think God is with you? Maybe we think that because we have a Bible and go to church or Sunday School that means God is with us. Perhaps we go out into the day to face difficult situations and God actually isn't with us. Maybe we live every day in our own strength.

If we want to know that God is with us then first of all we have to get to know Him. We must speak to Him in prayer and listen to Him when we read the Bible. The more time we spend with Him, and the more we get to know Him, the more we will feel His presence and power with us. Let's try to live our lives knowing God's not in a box but by our sides helping us win every battle.

Pray

Thank God that He has said He will be with you. Ask Him to be near you so that you can live each day in His power.

... through the Bible day by day

April 2

Reading: **1 Samuel 4. 19-22**

She named the child Ichabod, saying, 'The glory has departed from Israel!' because the ark of God had been captured, 1 Samuel 4. 21

Have you ever read such a sad story? The Israelites had been beaten by the Philistines and the ark had been stolen. In the battle the two sons of Eli had died. When Eli heard the news he fell backwards from his chair and died. Do you think this story could get any worse? Well it did! When Phinehas' pregnant wife heard the news she went into labour and died in childbirth! As she was dying she gave her new son the name Ichabod, saying, 'The glory has departed from Israel'.

Pray

Confess any disobedience in your life to God. Ask Him to help you turn away from sin and stay near to Him.

Well, we didn't read that story to cheer us up, but hopefully it will teach us a very important lesson. The lesson we learn is found in the meaning of the name given to the newborn child. 'Ichabod' means 'Where is the glory?' or 'No glory'. To an Israelite the word 'glory' was associated with God, so the name means 'Where is God?' The word 'departed' means 'gone into exile'. Because the ark was gone they thought God had gone into exile and would no longer be with them!

The story goes on to show that, in His amazing grace, God did still care for them, but at this point Israel did not know that. They had been so disobedient that they were far away from God.

Have you ever felt like this? Maybe you have been disobedient to God and do not feel Him near anymore. Maybe 'Ichabod' could be written over your life and you feel God has left you. Let's all examine our lives to see whether our disobedience has put a distance between us and God. Let's put the wrong things right. Let's get back into fellowship with our God and know and feel once again that He is with us.

Reading: **1 Samuel 5. 1-9**

April 3

They have no knowledge, who carry the wood of their carved image, and pray to a god that cannot save, Isaiah 45. 20

Do you study R.E. at school? I would guess in your Religious Education classes you have to learn about lots of different 'world religions' and lots of different 'gods'. Perhaps, if you are a Christian, you find it all very confusing and may even begin to wonder how we know our God is the one true God. Today's Bible reading gives us a wonderful story which reassures us that our God is God alone and He is all-powerful.

The Philistines had stolen the ark and had placed it in the house of their 'god' Dagon. Dagon was a false god, a god people had made-up, who had the lower body of a fish and the upper body of a man. He was the leader of the Philistines' false gods and may even have been the father of Baal. By putting the ark in Dagon's house they thought they were showing his power over the power of the God of Israel.

Yet it was our God who overturned the supposed power of Dagon and the next day the idol lay on its face before the ark. In a second display of God's power the head and hands of the idol were cut off, displaying that this idol had no power and was just a dead god. Instead, 'the hand of the Lord' was very powerful against the Philistines in judgement, causing them to be terrified and making them realize that the God of Israel was great and awful in power.

Keep this event in your mind the next time you have to study R.E. Remember the 'gods' of man-made religions are only idols which cannot see, hear, speak or save us. Remember our God is greater than all 'gods' and He alone is mighty in power and able to save!

Pray

Thank God that He alone is God and He is mighty in power. Ask Him to help you never to doubt this, no matter what others may say.

. . . through the Bible day by day

April 4

Reading: 1 Samuel 7. 3-13

God has chosen the foolish things of the world to put to shame the wise, and God has chosen the weak things of the world to put to shame the things which are mighty, 1 Corinthians 1. 27

Do you ever feel like a very weak Christian? You are still young and you may not have been saved for long. Every day you have to go in to school and perhaps you are the only believer in your class. Maybe you have regrets that your behaviour is not always what it should be. This sense of loneliness or failure can leave us feeling very weak.

Pray

Thank God that He has chosen you, even though you are weak. Ask Him to help you be a strong Christian as you live for Him at school.

The children of Israel knew what this felt like. They had neglected God and had been serving false gods for 20 years. Now they were miserable and they were sad about their sin and lack of loyalty to Him. It was time for them to change. With the help of Samuel they confessed their sin and poured out water before the Lord as a sign of true repentance. Now things would be different!

But soon they were under attack as the Philistines found out where they were and came to fight. This time, instead of using their own methods, the Israelites, through Samuel, called out to the Lord. And what an answer they got! The Lord 'thundered with a great thunder' which so confused the Philistines that the Israelites were easily able to chase them and win the battle!

If you're feeling weak, take heart from this story. Maybe confide in an older person you trust, who could help you stay closer to God and live better for Him. Ask that person to pray for you as Samuel did for the army of Israel when it was in trouble.

Let's learn today's verse so that when we feel weak we can be assured that God has chosen weak people. Remember that we can win the 'battles' of everyday life because God is on our side.

Reading: **1 Samuel 8**

April 5

You are old, and your sons do not walk in your ways. Now make us a king to judge us like all the nations, 1 Samuel 8. 5

Do you ever feel like you stick out like a 'sore thumb'? Maybe you think, speak and look differently to everyone else at school. Monday morning is the worst because everyone else is talking about their weekend activities that you did not take part in. Being the odd-one-out all the time is difficult.

Maybe you are embarrassed about this and are now trying to become more like everyone else. Perhaps you have started to speak like your friends and dress like them and you really wish you could go to the places they go to. Trying to be the same as everyone else is a big mistake.

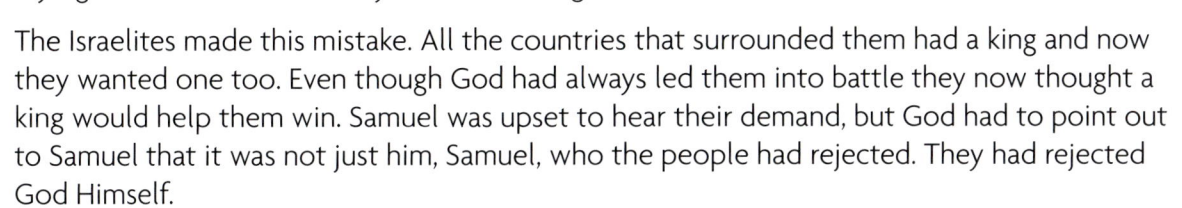

The Israelites made this mistake. All the countries that surrounded them had a king and now they wanted one too. Even though God had always led them into battle they now thought a king would help them win. Samuel was upset to hear their demand, but God had to point out to Samuel that it was not just him, Samuel, who the people had rejected. They had rejected God Himself.

God gave them a king, but the sad history of Israel shows that their desire to be like everyone else eventually led to disaster.

Do you think we could learn a lesson from them? Being like everyone else will be a disaster for us too. Living like an unbeliever is the same as rejecting God. That is a serious thing. Let's be brave enough to be different to those around us today. God has called us to be different, so if it means sticking out like a 'sore thumb' then that's OK! Other people may not think much of us, but God will. And isn't what God thinks of us more important than anything else?

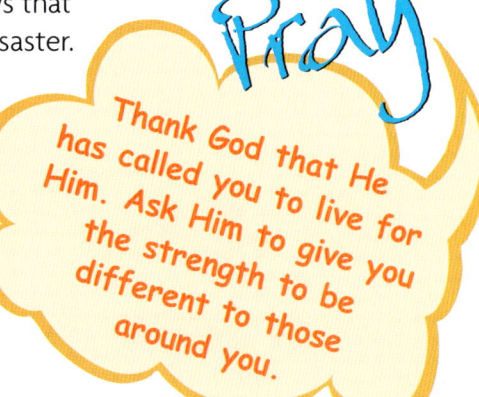

Pray

Thank God that He has called you to live for Him. Ask Him to give you the strength to be different to those around you.

. . . through the Bible day by day

April 6

Reading: 1 Samuel 9. 15-22

He gave them their request, but sent leanness into their soul, Psalm 106. 15

'I'll thcream and thcream 'till I'm thick. I can, you know!' So screamed Violet Elizabeth Bott the lisping spoiled daughter of the local millionaire found in the *Just William* books. It worked every time. If she screamed long enough and loud enough she would get her own way! Does this sound familiar? Do you know anyone like that? Are YOU like that? If you want something, do you go on and on to your mum and dad till you get it?

This is what the Israelites did. They demanded that God give them a king. It was a very bad idea but eventually God gave them their wish. Soon they regretted having a king. They had got what they wanted but it hadn't done them any good. It had been the same when the children of Israel were in the wilderness. They moaned about the food God had given them and asked for meat. So God sent them quails to eat but as they ate the quails a terrible plague came upon them. They had got what they wanted but it hadn't done them any good.

The next time you really, really want something, remember this. If your parents say, 'No', it's for your own good. Also be very careful what you ask God for. Make sure you are not making selfish requests hoping to use God to get your own way. He might give you what you want and it may not be for your good.

Let's not be like Violet Elizabeth Bott and scream to get our own way. God knows what's best for us, and our parents act on God's behalf when they bring us up. So respect their decisions and learn that 'No means No'! And when God says that, there's always a good reason.

Pray

Thank God for parents or carers who try to do what's best for you. Ask for God's help to respect them and not to be selfish in your demands.

Stepping stones

Reading: 1 Samuel 13. 8-16

April 7

Your kingdom shall not continue. The Lord has sought for Himself a man after His own heart, and the Lord has commanded him to be commander over His people, 1 Samuel 13. 14

'I saw', said Saul, when asked by Samuel why he had offered a burnt offering. 'I saw that the people were scattered from me'. Saul had used his eyes to look at the people around him instead of using his faith to trust in God.

Jonathan, Saul's son, had attacked a garrison of the Philistines and now the army of Israel was terrified of retaliation. Saul was waiting for Samuel at Gilgal as he had been told to do, 1 Samuel 10. 8. When Samuel did not turn up, the people who were with Saul began to drift away in fear. So, in an attempt to regain the confidence of the people, and to appear in control, Saul offered a burnt offering. He should never have done this. It was Samuel's responsibility to be the priest. Saul acted because of what he *saw* in other people. As a result of what he did, God decided to remove Saul as king and choose 'a man after His own heart' to be the next king. Saul's foolishness, impatience and disobedience caused him to lose his throne.

Sometimes we fall into the trap of looking at those around us and worrying about what they think of us. This can lead us to do foolish things to impress others. It can also make us impatiently rush into things as we try to explain ourselves. It may even make us do something that is disobedient to God's word. This all happens when we look at others instead of relying in faith on God. Let's remember the awful consequences of this behaviour for Saul.

Keep other people and their opinions in perspective. What they think of us does not matter as long as we are walking in God's ways and doing what He wants.

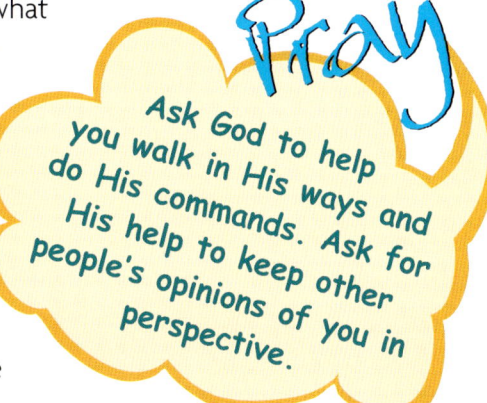

Pray

Ask God to help you walk in His ways and do His commands. Ask for His help to keep other people's opinions of you in perspective.

. . . through the Bible day by day

April 8

Reading: **1 Samuel 15. 1-14**

To obey is better than sacrifice, and to heed than the fat of rams, 1 Samuel 15. 22

Pray

Thank God for the Bible which tells you what He wants you to do. Ask for help to be obedient to it so that your sacrifice is not worthless.

When I was young I often went to a Gospel Hall which had today's text above the platform. I didn't have a clue what it meant! As the preacher spoke I would study the text above him trying to puzzle out its meaning. Then one day I read 1 Samuel chapter 15 and all became clear. The words come in a story about king Saul. He had been told by God to go to war against the Amalekites and destroy *all* of them and *all* their animals. God was going to use Saul to punish the Amalekites because they had attacked His people when they came out of Egypt.

God may have been giving Saul an opportunity to put things right and be obedient. Would he pass the test and do as he was asked? Sadly he did not. Saul did fight the Amalekites, but his obedience was incomplete. He let Agag, the king, live and he selfishly kept all the best animals. He even pretended he had kept the animals to sacrifice to God. Put simply, Saul was disobedient again. As I read this story the meaning of the words became clear. I realized that God says some things are good but others are better. He says it is good to sacrifice to Him, but to be obedient to Him is best.

Do you take pride in sacrifices you make for God? Are you pleased that you give up time and energy to serve God? Do you even give up your money for Him? These things are good but they are of no value if you are not being obedient. Let's look at our lives today and get our priorities right. Let's keep on sacrificing to God but make sure our lives are lived in obedience to Him. As He says, that is best.

Stepping stones

Reading: 1 Samuel 15. 15-23

April 9

I have sinned; yet honour me now, please, before the elders of my people and before Israel, and return with me, that I may worship the Lord your God, 1 Samuel 15. 30

'Keeping Up Appearances' was a 1990's BBC comedy about a woman who did everything she could to make herself seem smarter, richer and 'posher' than she really was. She looked down her nose at others and always tried to present herself as a wonderful, sophisticated person. In fact, she was just a fake! Whether you have seen the sitcom. or not is beside the point. The title is interesting. Many people are, just like her, 'keeping up appearances'.

Saul was doing just this. He knew he was messing things up badly and his time as king was coming to an end. Instead of being genuinely sorry and repenting to God for what he had done, Saul was content with 'putting on a face'. He pleaded with Samuel to come with him so he could worship the Lord, but he just wanted Samuel to make him look good in front of the people.

If we are honest we have to admit we can all be like this. We often live our lives pretending to be something we are not. We are content to look good to other people and worry little about how we look to God. If we are caught doing wrong our default reaction is to find an excuse or cover up our actions.

Let's take this very seriously. How we look to others means nothing compared to how we look to God. He sees right into what we really are and knows if we are covering up with a 'false face'. Let's try to live honestly before God and, if we sin, be willing to admit it and genuinely turn from it. Let's not be content with 'keeping up appearances' but live openly and honestly before God who knows the reality of our hearts.

Pray

Sincerely ask God to help you be an honest person who cares about what He thinks and not just about the image you present to others.

. . . through the Bible day by day

April 10

Reading: **1 Samuel 16. 1-13**

The Lord does not see as man sees; for man looks at the outward appearance, but the Lord looks at the heart, 1 Samuel 16. 7

Pray

Thank God that He knows what goes on in your heart. Ask Him to help you to be beautiful from the inside out!

How long does it take you to get ready in the morning? If you are very young it probably won't be very long. Maybe just a hairbrush dragged through your hair and a quick wash of your face. Clothes don't matter too much as long as you are comfortable. As you get older this will change. You will become more aware of how you look and be conscious of what others think. You will take longer to make sure you look and smell good and your clothes will be chosen carefully.

For older children and teenagers it takes more time. What does the Bible say about appearances to help us? Interestingly, it does not emphasize how we look on the outside at all. The teaching of the word of God about what is attractive deals with what goes on *inside* us. Our personality, character and subsequent behaviour are more important than how pretty or handsome we are.

Samuel had to learn this lesson when he chose a new king. As David's tall and handsome brothers passed before him, God made clear the choice would not be based on their looks. In fact, David, the youngest, was chosen because God had looked right into his heart and seen there what he needed in a king. It's true David *was* handsome, with a good complexion and nice eyes. Perhaps his appearance was enhanced by his genuine faith and joy in his God. What was inside David was reflected on his face.

If you want to be a lovely person it's not what you put on your face that matters but what you are inside. So let's try focussing on beautifying that. Let's aim to be more like Christ and display Him in our lives. Then we will be attractive from the inside out!

102

Stepping stones

Reading: **1 Samuel 17. 12-27**

April 11

Honour your father and your mother, that your days may be long upon the land which the LORD your God is giving you, Exodus 20. 12

Many years ago, in Africa, a father watched as his young son played under a tree. Suddenly the father shouted to the son, 'Get down, now!' The boy, who had always been taught to obey his parents, immediately ducked down and lay flat on the ground. The crack of a gunshot rang out as the father raised his weapon and aimed it right at a venomous snake that hung from the tree. That day, his son's instant obedience saved his life.

God expects us to show instant obedience to our parents. These days many children selfishly think that only their opinions matter. They think they have freedom of thought and therefore do not need to obey anyone. The Bible says otherwise. Your parents have been appointed by God to do His work on earth. They are bringing you up on behalf of God. This makes what your parents say very important. It is not for you to argue or try to change their minds but to do what they say – immediately! David did this. His dad asked him to take food to his brothers on the battlefield and he got up 'early in the morning . . . and went as Jesse had commanded him'. He honoured his father and did not object or waste time, but willingly did what he was asked to do. David's obedience eventually led to the deliverance of a whole nation as he went on to defeat Goliath.

The next time your parents ask you to do something, or tell you not do something, obey them instantly. Today, do everything your parents say without arguing. This will lead to a happier home and even better, you will know that you are pleasing God!

Pray

Thank God for your parents who have your best interests at heart. Ask God for help to obey them at all times.

April 12

Reading: 1 Samuel 17. 28-37

Why did you come down here? And with whom have you left those few sheep in the wilderness? I know your pride and the insolence of your heart, 1 Samuel 17. 28

In Scotland there are two brothers, Andy and Jamie Murray, who both play tennis. Andy decided to miss an important match because of an injury and Jamie didn't agree with his decision. He publicly said he was disappointed in his brother. Andy was very hurt and felt Jamie had misjudged him. I'm sure it took them a long time to work through their differences. Try to imagine how David felt when his brother turned on him with unfair accusations. He was an obedient son, a loving brother and now prepared to be a brave fighter. I'm sure he was extremely hurt and angry.

Perhaps Eliab was jealous of David because God had picked him to be the next king of Israel. He decided to bring David down a peg or two in front of the other soldiers. I hope you never do that to anyone. It is unkind and most definitely not Christ-like.

Eliab accused David of being careless, proud, insolent and nosy. David didn't argue, shout or retaliate in kind. He calmly explained he was only asking a question and turned away from his brother. It's good to remember, no matter how wrong someone is about you, always keep yourself right. Even if you're angry, never lose control of your temper. Think of how the Lord Jesus acted when He was falsely accused before Pilate. He didn't even answer back. He asked God to forgive those who wronged Him.

In the end, David disproved everything Eliab said about him by his actions. David told how he had once protected his sheep from a lion and a bear. Saul believed in him. David went out to defeat Goliath. I'm sure Eliab was the one who felt small in the end. God will always honour those who do right and 'behave wisely'.

Pray

Ask God to help you always to behave properly – even when you are being judged and misunderstood. Thank Him for those who believe in you.

Stepping stones

Reading: **1 Samuel 17. 38-50**

April 13

The Lord does not save with sword and spear; for the battle is the Lord's, and He will give you into our hands,

1 Samuel 17. 47

Pray

Pray that God will show you what He wants you to do for Him. Thank Him that He has promised to be with you.

A few years ago I read an article in a newspaper about a small business taking a much larger one to court to sort out an unfair business deal. The newspaper called it a 'David and Goliath' case! What they meant was that a weaker person was willing to stand up to a stronger person.

That is exactly what happened when David volunteered to fight the giant, Goliath. David was a shepherd boy and Goliath was a giant of a man, nearly ten feet tall. Some people said David was being rash and foolish but he knew exactly why he couldn't let the giant torment the Israelites any more. They were God's people. How dare this Philistine make a fool of them! There may be times when you hear people mock Christians or even mock the Lord Himself. It is important to be as brave as David and stand up to them. After all, they are laughing at the people Christ died for.

Why do you think David was so courageous? It wasn't because he was a good fighter or quick witted. He was brave because he had faith in God. He knew what he was doing was for God and that God would be with Him. He said to Goliath, 'the Lord will deliver you into my hand'. A man and his weapons were no competition for a boy and His God.

Although you are young, like David, you have the same God as he had – One who has promised to be with you. When the Lord Jesus commanded His disciples to spread the gospel He told them, 'I am with you always'. When the apostle Paul was on trial before being killed for his faith he said, 'the Lord stood with me'. He is with us too and we can be brave because of that.

... through the Bible day by day

April 14

Reading: 1 Samuel 18. 1-4

Then Jonathan, Saul's son, arose and went to David in the woods and strengthened his hand in God,

1 Samuel 23. 16

I find it interesting to watch how young children interact with each other. One minute they are 'best friends', and the next they are telling tales. One minute it's all love and hugs and the next it's, 'She hit me!' My 5-year-old daughter gets a new 'best' friend every day! Hopefully, as she gets older she will come to know what true friendship is.

So, what is true friendship? There's a lot more to it than sleepovers and sharing secrets. Jonathan and David's friendship teaches us a lot. Jonathan loved David as much as he loved himself. He showed this in a couple of ways. He gave to David what was precious to him. It's very important to 'give' in a friendship. I don't mean that giving presents will buy you good friends. I mean giving your time and energy. If you are a good friend you will make time for others. You will speak to them when you can't be bothered and listen to them talk about things that are important to them – even if it bores you! Jonathan also treated David as an equal even though he was the king's son and David was just a shepherd. Never think yourself superior to your friends.

A good basis for friendship is shared interests. As a Christian your main interest should be the things of God. Surely it should be obvious, then, that your best friends are also Christians. Of course you must be friendly to everyone but that doesn't mean you compromise your beliefs for anyone. It is safer to surround yourself with Christian friends.

The Bible tells us that, 'a man who has friends must himself be friendly, but there is a friend who sticks closer than a brother', Proverbs 18. 24. Remember, the very best friend to have is the Lord Jesus.

Pray

Thank God for the good friends you have. Ask Him to keep you all close to Him and to each other.

Reading: **1 Samuel 18. 5-9**

April 15

A sound heart is life to the body, but envy is rottenness to the bones,
Proverbs 14. 30

When I was younger there was a cartoon character that changed dramatically when he was angry. He was an easy-going chap until he exploded into a huge green monster that terrorized everyone! Something would annoy him, then something else and something else until he couldn't control himself and the anger took over. It turned him into a monster. It was very scary!

When Saul became jealous of David a change came over him. Saul noticed that David was more popular than he was and he hated David for it. Saul had once been the one that everyone sang about and he didn't like that someone else was sharing the praise. King Saul let this feeling grow and soon became completely taken over by envy. Before too long it led to deep anger and he wanted to kill David.

Is there someone more popular than you at school? Someone with nicer clothes, more money or is better looking than you? Do you feel jealous? It's hard not to, but it's how you deal with the feeling of jealousy that's important. You can be completely taken over by it too quickly and you can turn into someone who is not nice and not Christ-like. Like Saul, your envy can turn to anger and then you find yourself wishing harm on the person you're jealous of. Maybe you don't try to kill them but it is easy to tell a few tales and kill someone's character instead.

If we feel pangs of envy how should we deal with it? The best way is to thank God for the blessings we do have. We should also pray for the person we feel jealous of. It's impossible to pray for someone and hate them! Let's not allow the monster of envy to destroy us. Crush it before it can grow!

Pray
Thank God for the times you have managed to be happy for people and not envious of them. Pray that God will always keep you this way.

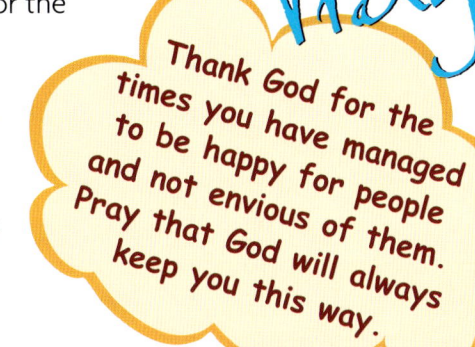

. . . through the Bible day by day

April 16

Reading: 1 Samuel 18. 10-14

You are more righteous than I; for you have rewarded me with good, whereas I have rewarded you with evil, 1 Samuel 24. 17

Have you ever been so jealous that you couldn't think straight? That's what happened when King Saul thought that he was better than anyone else. Along came David, a shepherd boy from the country. Suddenly everyone was talking about him. In fact people were writing songs about him. Saul couldn't take it any more.

King Saul thought, 'I have been really generous to this "country boy". I allowed him to be friends with my son, Jonathan. I gave him a top job in my army. And for what? All this "strip of a boy" has done in return is to go off and make himself popular. Now everyone is ignoring poor old me'.

David was actually very talented. He was a good shepherd and he was a good shot which must have helped him as a soldier. He had a great personality and was a brilliant musician. At first, when Saul had liked David, he had given him access to the royal palace. Some time later David was playing the harp for Saul when suddenly Saul tried to murder him with a javelin. He tried it twice but on each occasion David saw the javelin coming and ducked. It looked like God had left Saul and was now protecting David and this was a really scary thought to Saul. To belittle David, Saul changed his job from being in charge of the best fighters in the army to looking after the 'footsoldiers'.

How would you have reacted if you had been treated so badly? David just kept on trusting God and was very sensible and wise about how he behaved. He understood that the most important thing in life is to live to please God. Do we understand that?

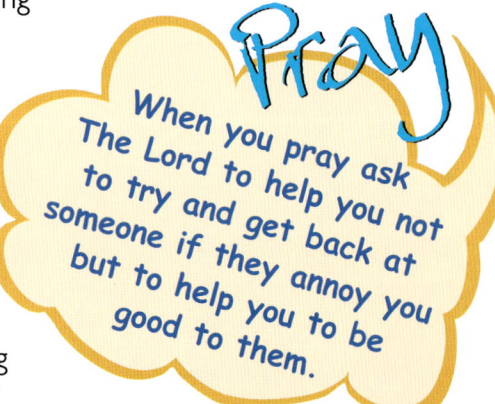

Pray

When you pray ask The Lord to help you not to try and get back at someone if they annoy you but to help you to be good to them.

Stepping stones

Reading: **1 Samuel 20**

April 17

He was grieved for David, because his father had treated him shamefully,
1 Samuel 20. 34

David was a bit mixed up! He couldn't work out what he had done wrong. He had tried to live to please God. He hadn't gone out of his way to offend the king but whatever he did, it just wasn't enough. Have you ever felt like that? I don't mean just feeling fed up. I'm asking if you have ever been falsely accused of something you did not do. If so, you will understand David's feelings.

What made it worse was that David's best friend was the king's son. David could take the pain himself but he didn't want his friend to suffer. And to top it all Jonathan, the king's son, could not see that David's life was in danger.

David thought that his only option was to run away. This would mean that he wouldn't see his friend any more. He really did not want to do this but it seemed like his only choice. David stayed away from some important palace dinners to see if Saul was still angry with him. The plan was for Jonathan to tell his father why David had missed two evening feasts. If Saul 'blew a fuse' then David would know that his time was up.

The night came. David's seat was empty and Jonathan was asked where David was. When he explained that David had gone to a family function, Saul exploded. For the first time Jonathan realized that his Dad really hated David.

When he could, he got away from the dinner and warned David to leave the area. It was a sad day for them both. As they said 'goodbye', they promised each other always to be friends. Jonathan had learned a hard lesson. Standing with your friends when they are in the right can cost a lot.

> **Pray**
> Ask God to help you stand up for what is right every day.

. . . through the Bible day by day

April 18

Reading: 1 Samuel 22

You shall not go about as a talebearer among your people, Leviticus 19. 16

When I was a boy we used to sing a little song. It went like this, 'Sticks and stones may break your bones, but words can never hurt you'. I grew up to learn that, even though I liked the song and it was a cool reply when someone was making a fool of me, it really wasn't true.

Doeg is what you might call a 'tell-tale'. A 'tell-tale' is someone who does not mind their own business but instead goes about telling people things that will damage others. What they say may not be lies but they know that it will make things difficult for people.

David had visited the town of Nob to get some food and a weapon, in case Saul attacked him. Ahimelech the priest helped him out as he had no idea that David was on the run, though he was surprised to see him. In the shadows was a shady character called Doeg. He worked for King Saul and had a good job. He just listened and watched but said nothing. If he had wanted to, he could have stopped the priest from giving David food and a sword but he just watched. Doeg kept what he knew 'up his sleeve' and at the right moment he told Saul and – and added a little bit to the story as well.

When Saul heard what had happened, he didn't ask any questions but immediately sent for the priest and his family. After questioning him he told his palace footmen to kill them all. The footmen refused because they would not hurt these men of God. So Saul commanded Doeg to kill them.

The book of Proverbs tells us 'the words of a talebearer are as wounds' – they really were in this story!

> **Pray**
> Lord, help me not to tell tales about anyone today. Help me only to say the things that would help people.

Reading: **1 Samuel 24**

April 19

The Lord delivered you into my hand today, 1 Samuel 26. 23

Imagine that someone has been giving you a really hard time. They never miss an opportunity to make you feel bad, they never give up. Then one day you get the chance to get even with them. What would you do?

David is having a tough time with Saul. He can't go home or the king's men will get him. He can't relax, he is in hiding with his followers and life is really difficult for him. Saul has three thousand men searching for David in the EnGedi Desert.

David had discovered a cave which was really deep and had a number of tunnels. They thought that no one would find them hiding in there. Suddenly they heard somebody coming. As they look out, to their amazement they see it is Saul, on his own, coming in for a moment of privacy. I imagine they moved back down the cave and whispered to David. 'Look you have him now. The Lord has led him to you. Kill him and all your problems are over. God said you would be king one day and he has given you the chance to take Saul's life'.

David crept forward, not making a sound. Not a rustle, not a cough, no quick movements just quietly creeping towards Saul and 'the throne of Israel'.

Then his men couldn't believe their eyes. Instead of cutting his throat, David cut a bit of cloth off Saul's clothes! Has he gone mad? When he returned David whispered, 'I feel really guilty for doing that'. Saul is the Lord's king. Why should I even damage his clothes? I'll trust God to give me the throne when He is ready'. Let's trust God like David did. He will work out His plans for us.

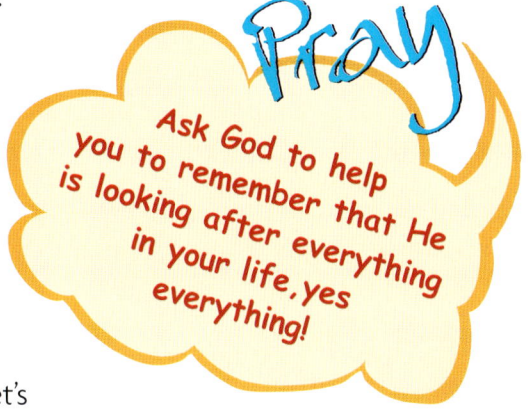

Pray

Ask God to help you to remember that He is looking after everything in your life, yes everything!

... through the Bible day by day

April 20

Reading: **1 Samuel 28**

Should not a people seek their God?
Isaiah 8. 19

Israel's prophet, Samuel, had died. He had brought them God's message for over one hundred years. He was really respected and sometimes people had even been frightened of him. There were not many people who could tell King Saul what to do. Samuel had been one of them. Saul had got rid of wizards and witches because Samuel had told him to.

The Philistines were one of the nations that were Israel's enemies. They were fierce fighters and brought a large army to fight him. Saul was scared. He had always asked Samuel. He did not know what to do. There was a time when Saul had prayed to God and He had guided him. Who could he ask for advice? God used to answer through a prophet, by a dream or through one of the priests. Saul asked God again for help but he got more and more frustrated because he was not getting any answers. What could Saul do?

Sadly he made another bad choice. He visited a witch, though God had told him that contact with wizards and witches would always end in trouble. He knew it was wrong but he disguised himself. Once the witch started to speak, however, she knew who he was and got very upset.

Saul asked her to bring Samuel back from the dead to speak to him. The message Saul got was very real and frightened him. He was told that the Lord had left him and that by the next day he and his sons would be dead. This is exactly what happened.

It is a very harmful thing to play about with anything to do with the devil. Horoscopes, tarot cards and all such things should be left alone. Keep away from the devil.

Pray

Help me, Lord, never to play about with things that are bad and from the devil.

Stepping stones

Reading: **2 Samuel 5. 1-7**

April 21

As for God, His way is perfect,
2 Samuel 22. 31

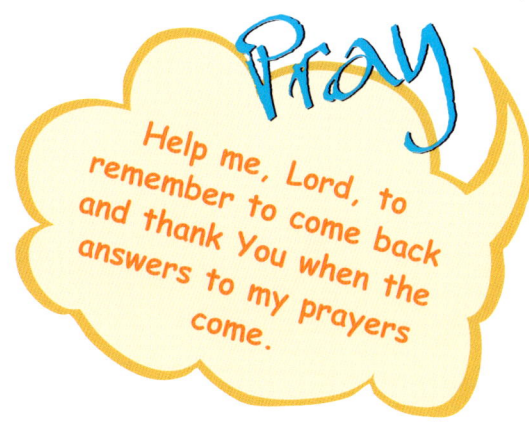

Pray

Help me, Lord, to remember to come back and thank You when the answers to my prayers come.

Most of us find it really hard to be patient. The new bike, the new clothes, the latest game or DVD! It is hard to wait, especially in a society where all the advertising invites us to get what we want now.

In real life most things don't just appear. It takes time and the more valuable the thing the longer it takes. Babies normally take nine months to grow before they are born, new computer games take time to develop, houses have to be built, and food has to be grown. Diamonds have to be mined and trees have to be grown to produce good timber.

There were people in the Bible who had to wait for God to keep his promises. Abraham was promised a son but it was twenty-five years before he was born. David was a teenager when the prophet Samuel came to tell him that one day he would be king. It was around fifteen years later before it happened.

So what about you? Do you keep praying and asking God to answer your prayers? Don't give up. God will answer you when the time is right. Do you feel that God has made promises to you and that He hasn't kept them yet? Keep trusting Him, He will keep His promises. He always does.

I am sure that David could not imagine being king when he was being chased by Saul and sleeping rough in the desert. All his boyhood dreams must have seemed so far away when he couldn't even go home to his own house. 'But God'. That's the key phrase to remember. It is God we trust. He is not like us; He does not break His promises. We can really trust Him.

. . . through the Bible day by day

April 22

Reading: 2 Samuel 6. 1-5

David offered burnt offerings and peace offerings before the Lord, 2 Samuel 6. 17

When David was young there had been a disaster in his nation. Israel had been in battle with the Philistines and had been beaten. Now if it was bad to be beaten in a fight it was even worse to have the 'ark of God' stolen by your worst enemy.

The 'ark of God' was a beautiful box made of strong, light wood and covered in gold. It was worth a fortune but its value was not measured in money but by the fact that it reminded the people that God lived among them. It is strange to us to think about a box meaning so much but when God gave Moses instructions to build the tabernacle He had told him to make a number of pieces of special furniture. All the furniture reminded the priests and the people about God in some way. The box we are talking about was extra special as it was placed in the room called the 'Holiest of all', which was where God lived among His people.

When David became king he remembered that the 'ark of God' was still a long way from where it should be and he decided that it must be brought back. This was because David knew that it was important to have God's presence with him and he wanted the people in his country to understand this as well.

Do you want to know God's presence like David did? If you do you will need to do something to bring His presence into your life. If you are not saved you will need to repent and trust the Lord Jesus as your Saviour. If you are saved you will need to keep in touch with God by reading your Bible every day and by praying to Him.

Pray

Please help me to be full of wonder when I am in the presence of the Lord.

Reading: 2 Samuel 9. 1-13

April 23

Do not fear: for I will surely show you kindness for Jonathan your father's sake, 2 Samuel 9. 7

It makes us feel good when we promise someone that we will never let them down or forget them. Maybe you have done this when you have been changing school or moving to a new house.

But it is also very easy to forget what we said especially when we are busy and thinking about lots of other things.

David and his best friend, Jonathan, had made a promise. It was a big promise but they both really meant it. They had promised that, whatever happened to either of them, the one who lived the longest would look after the other one's family. I think Jonathan knew that he would probably die before David and he knew that his family would be safe if David was looking after them.

When David eventually became king, Jonathan's family had left their houses and gone into hiding. In those days it was normal for a new king to execute all the relatives of the previous king. If they could, the old king's family would run and hide.

David had been king for a long time when he remembered his promise to Jonathan. David searched hard and found that Jonathan had one living son, Mephibosheth, who was disabled. He sent for him. Can you imagine how Mephibosheth felt? He must have been scared stiff!

When he arrived at the palace, however, he was in for a big shock. David was not going to kill him, as he had feared. David wanted to be kind to him and invited him to live with him in the palace. David was kind to Mephibosheth because of his promise.

God is just as kind to everyone who trusts in the Lord Jesus. He blesses us forever because He promised Jesus, His Son, that He would. God always keeps His promises!

Pray: Please show me some way today that I can be kind to someone who is not expecting it.

... through the Bible day by day

April 24

READING: 2 Samuel 11. 1-5

How then can I do this great wickedness, and sin against God?
Genesis 39. 9

People sometimes say that when people are bored 'the devil finds things for idle hands to do'. That means that if you have nothing to do the devil will make sure you have plenty of wrong things to think about or to do. Maybe if someone had said this to King David we would not have this sad story to tell today.

David should have been out fighting with his army. It was the time of the year when his enemies attacked the armies of Israel. One of David's jobs was to lead his troops into battle. For some reason David decided not to go this year. Was he bored, was he frightened, were the enemies scary, was he too proud? We really don't know but what we do know is that he stayed at home in his comfortable palace and got into big trouble.

One evening the king went for a walk on the palace roof. While there he saw a very pretty lady. David then made the biggest mistake of his life. Instead of going back into the palace to his own family, he told his servants to bring the lady to him. When he did this he disobeyed God, stole another man's wife and eventually had her husband murdered so that he could marry her. This was all very wrong and it brought a lot of sadness into his life, into his family's life and into the life and family of Bathsheba, the lady.

It is always better to obey God even if it does not seem as much fun as doing what we feel like doing. We might never steal or murder but when we disobey God we hurt Him, ourselves and everyone else who is involved. Let's always be careful.

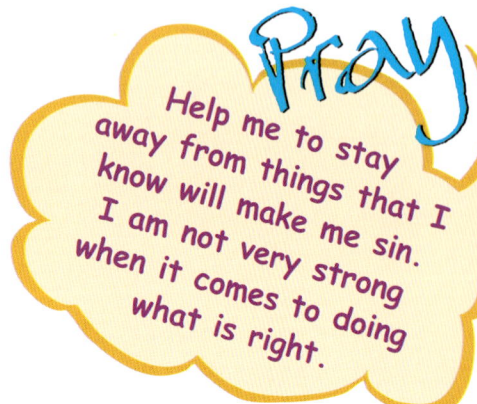

Pray
Help me to stay away from things that I know will make me sin. I am not very strong when it comes to doing what is right.

Reading: **2 Samuel 11. 6-27**

April 25

Be sure your sin will find you out,
Numbers 32. 23

It seems like no one had found out about the night that King David had spent with the beautiful Bathsheba. He had sinned and got away with it. Sometimes we, too, seem to get away with doing wrong things. Sadly this can make us think that we can keep on sinning because as long as we don't get caught it's OK. But it's not OK. Wrong is wrong even if we don't get caught.

One day a message came to David in the palace. Maybe it was a note saying 'Private and Personal' on it and David sneaked away to read it alone. If he thought it was a love letter from Bathsheba he was mistaken. It read, 'I'm having a baby'. 'It can't be true', David thought. Now everyone will get to know about my bad behaviour.

Being a quick thinker and a 'smart Alec', he thought, 'I have a plan'. Let's get Bathsheba's husband, Uriah, back from the battlefield. When he comes home he will have missed his wife so much that he will sleep with her. Everyone will think it's his baby. No one will know.

So he put his plan into action but Uriah did not play the game the way David wanted. Uriah was a thoughtful man. He wouldn't go home while the other soldiers were on the battlefield. He slept at the palace. So David prepared a meal in Uriah's honour, hoping to make him drunk. Maybe then Uriah would go home. But he didn't. He slept with the servants. So finally David sent a letter to his general telling him to let Uriah die in battle. It worked. Uriah died but now David was a murderer as well as a wife stealer. Doing one wrong thing sometimes makes us do another. It's best not to start.

Pray

Help me, Lord, to see my sin and to say sorry before it gets me into trouble.

. . . through the Bible day by day

April 26

Reading: **2 Samuel 12**

You are the man! 2 Samuel 12. 7

Pray

If someone shows me where I did something wrong, Lord, help me to accept their advice.

We all like a good story. Some stories make us sad, some make us laugh but sometimes we hear a story and it really makes us angry. Even though it's just a story we get caught up in it and react as if it were true.

This is what happened one day to King David. Nathan the prophet came to speak to David. God had sent Nathan with a story about two men. One had a farm with lots of sheep and cattle; the other was poor and had only one little lamb. One day the man with the big farm had an unexpected visitor. Instead of taking one of his own sheep or cattle to cook for dinner, however, he went next door and took the poor man's only lamb. When Nathan came to this part of the story David became very angry and shouted at him – 'this man must die'! His behaviour is totally out of order but before he dies he must pay back four times as much as he stole'.

Nathan replied, 'David, God says that you are that man. God told me to tell you that He made you king. He saved your life from Saul and He gave you more than one wife. But that was not enough for you. You killed a man to get his only wife. You have despised God by doing these things'.

So much for David's sin being a secret! God knew about it all along. Remember God knows everything. Nothing we do is hidden from Him. We may do things when we are on our own and think no one is looking and we can get away with it. Someone else, who was alone in the desert, once said, 'You, God, see me'. Never forget – God is always looking. Be careful.

Reading: **2 Samuel 13. 23-29**

April 27

Do not grumble against one another,
James 5. 9

You may remember that when David killed Bathsheba's husband Nathan the prophet had told him that 'the sword would never leave his house'. In other words, people in David's family would keep on being killed. Sadly we are reading today about the first one.

Amnon was a half-brother of Absalom. Both of them had David as a father but a different mother. Amnon had behaved very badly towards Absalom's sister Tamar. As a result Absalom wanted revenge and had stored his anger for two full years. He was waiting for an opportunity to get back at Amnon.

One day Absalom persuaded his father to allow his brothers to join him and his men when he was shearing his sheep. It would be a time of celebration. Once they were all together Absalom got his half-brother drunk and, when he gave his servants the signal, they murdered Amnon.

It was a very sad day for David. His family were behaving the way he had once behaved. His sins were being copied by his sons. One of them had misbehaved with a girl and the other had killed to get away with what he wanted.

Pray
Help me, Lord, not to remember when someone has done me wrong. Help me to forgive and forget.

We need to be very careful about what we do. Sin is a very strong thing. It drives us to do things that we never thought we could do. Hating someone hurts us and we could end up hurting someone else. The word of God tells us that we should put away from us all ways of being angry. If someone has done something wrong, try to sort it out with them. But pray first and ask God to help you to deal with it the way the Lord Jesus would have done. He is the best example of how to behave.

. . . through the Bible day by day

April 28

Reading: 2 Samuel 15. 1-6

He shall never permit the righteous to be moved, Psalm 55. 22

Things just seem to go from bad to worse in King David's family. The last episode we read about ended with Absalom running away to his grand-dad's home. His grand-dad probably lived in a palace as he was king of Geshur. Absalom stayed there for three years. David longed to see his son Absalom again, despite his wicked behaviour. Eventually, after some gentle persuasion, David allowed Absalom to come back and live in Jerusalem but he still did not actually meet up with him. This went on for two more years.

By the time Absalom was reunited with David it would seem that he had decided to go for the 'top job' and replace his father as king. For a while he drove about Jerusalem in his chariot with fifty men running in front of him. It was quite a sight. Every day he could be found standing outside the government's offices. He spoke to everyone who came to the king for advice. He told them that there was no one from the king's office appointed to see them, but he would see them instead. So day by day he became more popular. He was creepy and flattered the people to get them to like him.

It is so sad when someone is determined to get their own way especially if they end up fighting against their own family. As Christians we are all in the family of God. Ephesians chapter 4 teaches us to be 'kind one to another, tenderhearted, forgiving one another'. After all, God for Christ's sake has forgiven us. What a difference it would have made in David's family if they had behaved like that!

Pray

Help me Lord, to obey my parents and to love my family.

Reading: **2 Samuel 15. 10-15**

April 29

Even my own familiar friend in whom I trusted, who ate my bread, has lifted up his heel against me, Psalm 41. 9

Things began to turn really nasty after a while in Jerusalem. Not that you would have known anything until the last minute. Absalom had come to his father and asked if he could go to Hebron to keep a promise he had made to God. David let him go telling him to 'go in peace'. But Absalom was up to no good.

Once he got to Hebron, which is where David was first crowned king, Absalom secretly sent his men throughout the whole country with an order. 'When you hear the trumpet sound you must announce to everyone that Absalom has been crowned king in Hebron', he said. It was a well organized plot and everything went according to plan.

There was another major surprise for everyone who worked in the palace. One of King David's main advisors deserted him and went over to support Absalom. What a shock! This man had worked for David for years and was well respected and trusted. What could have made him betray David? Think back. Who was Bathsheba's grandfather? Yes you are right. It was Ahithophel, the palace advisor. Why did he desert David? Was it to get back at him for stealing his grand-daughter from Uriah and for killing his son-in-law? Are David's past mistakes still haunting him?

I want you to think of someone else who experienced the same feelings when a close friend deserted him. It was the Lord Jesus. Judas had walked with Him, eaten with Him and been closely involved with Him for three years. But he also became a deserter, though in his case it was for the sake of making some money. This grieved the Lord Jesus as we find recorded in our scripture text today. May the Lord help us never to let Him down!

Pray

Help me to cope when someone I trusted lets me down.

...through the Bible day by day

April 30

Reading: 2 Samuel 17. 1-14

If the Lord wills, we shall live and do this or that, James 4. 15

Today we come to the end of this sad part of David's life. He is still hiding from his son, Absalom. He cannot go back to the palace but God is working out His plan. Absalom thought that he could control everything and that he had won the fight against his father. But he was about to lose everything including his own life. We have to be careful how we live our lives. God allows us to make choices and we have to accept what happens as a result.

Ahithophel, David's old friend and advisor, told Absalom that he would get twelve thousand men and chase David. He thought that by the time he caught him David would be exhausted and alone. His plan was to kill David. Before making a final decision, however, Absalom sent for Hushai. Hushai was also a friend of David, and Absalom did not know Hushai was one of David's secret agents. Absalom asked Hushai what he thought about Ahithophel's plan.

Hushai advised Absalom to do something completely different. In the end Ahithophel's advice was ignored. The Bible says that God was working behind the scenes to 'bring evil upon Absalom'. Absalom was eventually defeated, David became king again and Absalom was killed by one of David's men.

Absalom disobeyed lots of God's laws. He did not honour his parents, he wanted what didn't belong to him, he lied and he misused God's name. It's a very sad story which reminds us that God will catch up with us if we disobey Him. Thankfully God does not punish us every time we do something wrong. It is even more amazing to think that God punished His 'well beloved Son', the Lord Jesus, so that we could be forgiven for all our wrongs.

Pray

Help me to remember Lord that You control every day and that even my breath is in Your hand.

Reading: 1 Kings 1. 22-40

May 1

He has chosen my son Solomon to sit on the throne of the kingdom of the Lord over Israel, 1 Chronicles 28. 5

Why is it that things can become seriously complicated in families? Jealousy is often the problem. It affects the 'haves' and the 'have nots'. From the monarch on the throne to the beggar in the gutter, human nature, being what it is, will always bring trouble. 'Man who is born of woman is of few days and full of trouble', Job 14. 1.

King David's life was coming to an end. He was old and soon to die. His fourth son, Adonijah, was aware of this and decided to take matters into his own hands. He wanted to make himself king. A selfish spirit made Adonijah want to take the throne for himself. He certainly did not live up to his name, which means 'My lord is Jehovah'. It was not God's will but his own that made him do this. He said, 'I will be king', although his father had said to Bathsheba that Solomon would be king. The prophet Nathan had heard him say that.

Old age can creep up on us, sometimes bringing health problems. At such times we can take our eye off the ball and not notice what is going on around us. David had reached that stage but he had a good prophet named Nathan who kept him informed of what Adonijah was doing. It is good to listen to the advice of a man of God.

Adonijah's treachery led to the ultimate downfall of others too! Some important men like Joab and Abiathar the priest became involved in his revolt and, as a result, Joab died. Through all this time, however, Solomon was quietly waiting. Then, David suddenly announced that Solomon was the new king. How sad that was for Adonijah! Selfishness will always get us into trouble. It's better to let God have His way.

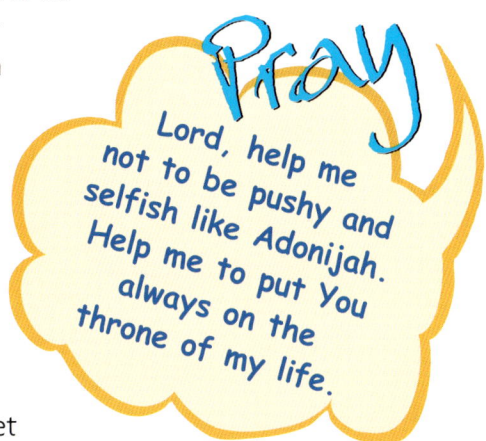

Pray

Lord, help me not to be pushy and selfish like Adonijah. Help me to put You always on the throne of my life.

... through the Bible day by day

May 2

Reading: **1 Kings 3. 5-15**

I have also given you what you have not asked, both riches, and honour: so that there shall not be any one like you among the kings all your days,

1 Kings 3. 13

Pray

Lord, I know that I am not up to what you want me to be and do. Please make me that person.

To be thrown into the deep end of a swimming pool before you can swim must be really frightening. Solomon must have felt he was out of his depth when he suddenly became king. He did not feel able to be the ruler and leader of the great nation of Israel.

We too can feel that we are not up to anything that God wants us to do, but God can change us.

Harry Trueman was once President of the United States of America and he recognized the huge responsibility upon him. He had on his desk these words, 'The buck stops here'. I don't know if Trueman was a Christian, or whether he ever prayed to God, but Solomon did know God and prayed to Him. God was pleased with how Solomon prayed. He said, 'I am but a little child'. This meant he was willing for God to teach him. We all need to be taught by God, and we can be by reading the Bible.

God was also pleased with what Solomon prayed for. He asked God to give him an understanding heart so that he could judge the people wisely. Solomon did not ask God for riches or for a long life, for power over his enemies, or to be famous. These are the things that most people want. He asked for God's help to do his job well.

His prayer was answered. God gave him more wisdom than any other man has ever had, other than Jesus Himself. God also made Solomon rich and gave him the things that he did not ask for. We never know what God will do in our lives until we give everything to Him. What a blessing we can be to others when God helps us.

Stepping stones

Reading: 1 Kings 3. 16-28

May 3

So King Solomon surpassed all the kings of the earth in riches and wisdom,
1 Kings 10. 23

Girls usually like to play with dolls. They dress and undress them, pretend to give them a bottle to drink and take them for walks in a pushchair. Boys usually have no time for such things. All they want to do is kick a ball around or use dad's computer!

Playing with dolls is one thing; to be responsible for a living baby is another. Solomon had to deal with two women one day who were the type of women he had warned his son about when he said, 'My son, if sinners entice you, do not consent', Proverbs 1. 10. These were bad women. One was worse than the other.

They both had babies. One of them was careless and rolled over on top of her baby while she was sleeping and the baby died. When she woke up, she saw that her baby was dead. She went to where the other mother was sleeping, gave the other woman her dead baby and took back to her bed the living one! When she woke up, the mother of the living baby realized straight away what had happened. An argument began between them. To solve the problem they brought the matter to the king.

How would anyone be able to decide whose baby had died? Solomon called for a sword and ordered that the living baby should be cut in half and that the women should be given half a baby each. He knew that the real mother would do anything to keep her baby alive. The natural love which a real mother has for her baby would not want her child to die. The other woman didn't care. So Solomon soon saw who was lying and who was telling the truth. He gave the baby to the right mother. How wise was that!

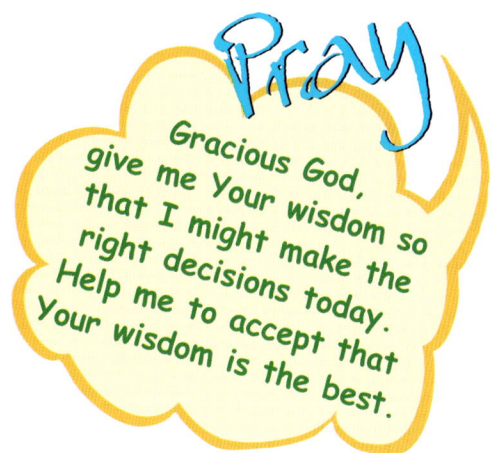

Pray

Gracious God, give me Your wisdom so that I might make the right decisions today. Help me to accept that Your wisdom is the best.

... through the Bible day by day

May 4

Reading: 1 Kings 8. 1-29

Will God indeed dwell on the earth? Behold, heaven and the heaven of heavens cannot contain You. How much less this temple which I have built! 1 Kings 8. 27

Some village houses, in India or Africa for instance, are very poor, made of mud or grass only. This is true in many parts of the world. The house that Solomon built for God was a grand building of massive stones and beautiful carved wood. Lots of gold was used. 'Solomon overlaid the inside of the temple with pure gold', 1 Kings 6. 21. It was a very beautiful and expensive building. The king wanted only the best for God and when it was finished he ordered that two weeks should be set aside for thanking God by offering thousands of sacrifices upon the altar. He wanted the God who had made heaven and earth, to dwell in the house he had made for Him. Yet Solomon knew that God was too 'big' to live in even the grandest temple. God is everywhere. He fills heaven and earth. He is just awesome. He cannot be kept in one building, no matter how grand the building.

Pray
I feel so small when I am in Your presence. Make me realize the privilege I have when You live in my heart.

Some people build big houses and they look upon their house as a showpiece. There is no feeling of 'home' about them, no feeling of the house being lived in. Perhaps there is no sound of children playing there, no music, no laughter. Who would want to live in a house that is like a museum?

Solomon wanted the house that he built for God to be a place where prayer was made. C. F. BUTLER wrote, 'What matters where on earth we dwell? On mountain top, or in the dell? In cottage or in mansion fair? Where Jesus is, 'tis heaven there'.

God does not live in temples or churches today. He lives in our hearts when we believe in Him. The Babylonians came and destroyed Solomon's wonderful temple. No one can destroy the temple of God which is in our hearts.

Reading: **1 Kings 9. 1-9**

May 5

If you walk before Me . . . and if you keep My statutes and My judgments, then I will establish the throne of your kingdom over Israel forever, 1 Kings 9. 4-5

What football managers expect from referees is consistency. They want the referee to interpret the laws properly and apply them fairly to both teams. Some referees are 'homers'. They listen to the crowd, with their biased chants and appeals, and make decisions in favour of the home team. Away managers get angry at such unfairness.

Pontius Pilate was a 'homer' and listened to the crowd when they cried out for the crucifixion of Christ. He had declared three times that he found no fault in Jesus but he delivered Him up to die on the cross. That was totally inconsistent!

Solomon was privileged to have David as a father because David set a good example for his son. To have a father who lives and walks close with God is great. However, God wants us to walk with Him for ourselves and not live on the merits of dad or granddad. What Solomon had done in building the temple, and the prayer that he had made, pleased God. It showed that Solomon had learned from his father, who had wanted to build a house for God but was not allowed to do so. David's son accomplished more in this respect, than his father. We do not have to live in the shadow of a good, or great man. God wants each of us, even rulers, to be our own man and do exploits for Him.

Every encouragement was given to Solomon by the Lord's promise that if he and Israel went on with God, walking in His ways, then Solomon's children would sit on the throne of Israel for ever. History tells us that some did and some did not. In the future, the Lord Jesus will reign in Jerusalem – and He is one of Solomon's family – so God does keep His promises.

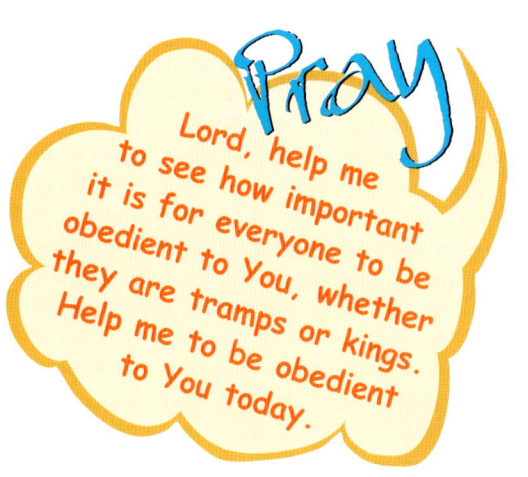

Pray

Lord, help me to see how important it is for everyone to be obedient to You, whether they are tramps or kings. Help me to be obedient to You today.

. . . through the Bible day by day

May 6

Reading: 1 Kings 10. 1-10

The queen of the South will rise up in the judgment with this generation and condemn it, for she came from the ends of the earth to hear the wisdom of Solomon; and, indeed a greater than Solomon is here, Matthew 12. 42

Just to grab your attention and get the brain-box working, Bible charts tell us that one talent is equal to about seventy pounds weight. The Queen of Sheba gave Solomon one hundred and twenty talents of pure gold which is around three and three-quarter tons. At today's value, that's about £44,000,000! And that was only one of the gifts she brought to Solomon. We are talking 'Fort Knox' value treasures that she gave the king. This was not 'slush fund' money to buy favour. This was a genuine gift from one very wealthy monarch to a king whose wealth was greater than her own. The weight of gold that came to Solomon yearly was 666 talents of gold, verse 14. That was serious money!

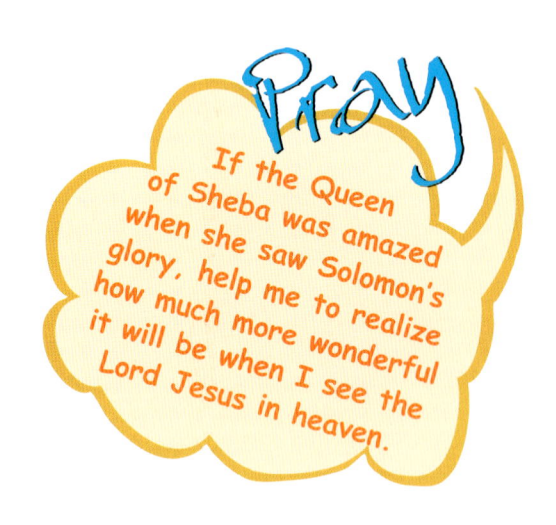

Pray

If the Queen of Sheba was amazed when she saw Solomon's glory, help me to realize how much more wonderful it will be when I see the Lord Jesus in heaven.

What interested the queen in taking this 1400 mile journey to see Solomon was to ask him hard questions and hear for herself his wisdom. When she heard his instruction and saw all that was in his kingdom, it took her breath away. She was amazed and said, 'the half was not told me. Your wisdom and prosperity exceed the fame of which I heard', verse 7.

We know how she felt because when we try to understand the wonderful things about our Saviour, who is greater than Solomon, we too realize that we know so little about Him, or about heaven where He now is. The glory of heaven, and of the Lord Jesus, is far beyond our imagination. And here's a thought about heaven: Revelation chapter 21 and verse 21 says, 'The street of the city was pure gold'. Our council can't even afford a bit of tarmac for our street!

Reading: 1 Kings 11. 9-13

May 7

When Solomon was old, his wives turned his heart after other gods; and his heart was not loyal to the Lord his God,

1 Kings 11. 4

When a man, or a woman, has lots of money they become targets for people who want to help them spend it. A Christian has three enemies, the world, the flesh and the devil. As a general rule it is the flesh that is the problem for men, and the world is a problem for women. Advertising people often use scantily dressed, beautiful women to sell products to men and glossy shopping catalogues display goods for women with a 'buy me' appeal.

At this stage of his life, Solomon could not sing, 'O for a thousand tongues to sing my great redeemer's praise'. He had accumulated a thousand tongues – seven hundred wives and three hundred concubines – that did not sing the praises of the true and living God. Their tongues whinged and whined to him to build temples or shrines to their gods and they wanted him to go with them to worship the gods of their own making.

We lose every advantage of being brought up in a godly home when we go after people or things that we know will take us away from God. Our example can also affect others, either for good or bad. How sad it would be if the devil used us, as he used Solomon's many wives, to stumble others.

God says, 'the heart is deceitful above all things, and desperately wicked', Jeremiah 17. 9. That may be why the hymn-writer wrote, 'Prone to wander, Lord, I feel it, prone to leave the God I love'. Solomon started well by loving the Lord. But strange women turned his affections towards them and away from the Lord. This can still happen today, and it does not take a thousand wrong companions to turn our hearts. Only one will do! Let's choose our friends carefully.

> **Pray**
> Father, may my friends be those who will help and not hinder me from pleasing You. May I help others to walk with You.

. . . through the Bible day by day

May 8

Reading: 1 Kings 12. 1-15

The king answered the people roughly, and rejected the advice which the elders had given him; and he spoke to them according to the advice of the young men, 1 Kings 12. 13-14

How often do you hear someone say that another man or woman is 'past their sell-by date'? This usually means they think the older person is no longer of any use. Sometimes that assessment is valid, but sometimes it is not. When employees get over fifty years of age, they are targeted for redundancy. It is true that the energy of youth begins to fade as old age advances; stamina is the first casualty and memory loss is not far behind. Priests in Israel began with ten years of training when they were twenty years old. At thirty the man began to do his full priestly service and he continued until he was fifty years old. The best years to get prepared and committed to serve God are in that period. But that does not mean that older men have no wisdom and experience.

Solomon's son, Rehoboam, was unwise not to listen to the advice given to him by his father's old advisors. Jeroboam and the people had asked the new king to lighten the burden that his father had put on them. The wise old men said, 'Speak good words to them, then they will be your servants forever'. His young friends advised him to increase the burdens and to beat the people with scorpions instead of whips. They probably thought Jeroboam was being cheeky. Rehoboam took their advice and told Jeroboam he would be harder than his father. This made Jeroboam and his followers think they did not want to stay in Rehoboam's kingdom. So they rebelled and divided the nation.

Pray

Lord, I pray for older Christians today, that they might be a good example to me and that I might follow them and respect their advice.

Many local churches have been divided in the same way, when young people disregard the godly counsel of older people. We should listen to what the old grey heads have got to say. They might not be past their sell-by date.

Stepping stones

Reading: 1 Kings 16. 30 – 17. 5

May 9

I have commanded the ravens to feed you there, 1 Kings 17. 4

Some cyclists ignore a red light at the traffic lights. They look left and right and then decide to chance it across the junction. This is a silly thing to do. It spells danger and disaster for the rider.

King Ahab was like that. No, not on a bike, but he ignored the warnings of God's word and of his conscience that told him he should not marry Jezebel the Zidonian! She was a scheming woman who diverted Ahab from serving the true and living God to serve Baal, a dumb idol. Ahab must have been dumb to fall for that one!

Elijah, however, obeyed the green light from God to go and tell Ahab that there would be no rain for three-and-a-half years because of his wickedness. He waited again for the green light from God to direct him to the little stream, Cherith, where God would provide him with water and food. What God promises He always does. He told Elijah that the brook would meet his thirst and that ravens would bring him food. Every morning these black-coated waiters brought Elijah his breakfast and every evening they brought his dinner. These must have been the first in-flight meals known to man, long before British Airways caught on to the idea.

It is not natural for a greedy raven to share its food, let alone deliver food for someone else. This just shows us how God can do wonderful things, even with His creatures. God can make a donkey to speak to Balaam, a fish to swallow Jonah and spit him out later. God can do anything, and He will do anything, to look after those who love Him. Isn't God just wonderful!

Pray

Father, help me to remember You always look after Your people. I pray for Your protection and provision today.

. . . through the Bible day by day

May 10

Reading: **1 Kings 17. 7-24**

My God shall supply all your need according to His riches, Philippians 4. 19

Elijah told Ahab that there would be no rain for three-and-a-half years. It did not rain, so eventually the brook Cherith dried up and it was time for Elijah to move on. God told Elijah to go to Zarephath where He had told a widow woman to provide for him. When he got to Zarephath he found the lady in a very poor state. Her barrel of flour was almost empty. There was only a handful left in it, not even enough to make one small loaf of bread. There was only a little drop of olive oil in her jug, too, only enough to make one last little cake.

When Elijah met her she was out looking for some firewood to make a fire to cook the cake. Two sticks would be enough for a little fire to cook with. Her two small ingredients and her two small sticks meant that she had a big problem. When they were finished she and her little boy would die.

Then came problem number two! A strange man came to her with a word from God that tested her faith. The word said, 'Make My servant a little cake first and the barrel of flour and jug of oil will never again be empty'. She obeyed and she proved that God keeps His word. Elijah and her son lived for many days eating the good food. Problem solved!

Problem number three, when it came, was massive. Her little boy fell sick and died. Her husband had already died and now her son had died too. But Elijah took the dead child into his room and prayed that his soul might return to his body. God heard him, the boy lived again. When we look after God's people, He looks after us.

Pray

Father, You are a giving God. You gave Your Son to die so that I might have eternal life. Thank You too for all Your other gifts.

Stepping stones

Reading: 1 Kings 18 *May 11*

The effective, fervent prayer of a righteous man avails much, James 5.16

Three-and-a-half years of drought were coming to an end and God told Elijah to find King Ahab. When Elijah met Ahab the king was still not sorry for sinning against God by committing idolatry. Elijah told Ahab to gather the prophets of Baal on Mount Carmel for a contest.

Four hundred and fifty prophets of Baal and all the people came. Elijah told them to prepare a sacrifice but not to light the fire to burn it. They were to pray to their god to send fire from heaven. So the prophets of Baal prepared their bullock to sacrifice to Baal. They cried to their god all day long – and nothing happened. At mid-day Elijah started to mock them. 'Baal is probably talking to someone or he's on a journey, or perhaps he is asleep and needs to be wakened', he said. This annoyed the prophets who cut themselves and shouted aloud to attract the attention of their dumb idol.

When the time came for God's priests to offer up an evening sacrifice Elijah built an altar with twelve stones, one for each of the tribes of Israel. He dug a trench around it, and put the wood and the pieces of the bullock on top. Then, he did something strange. He did not pour oil on the wood to encourage burning. He poured twelve barrels of water over it, soaking the wood and the sacrifice until the water filled the trench. Then, he prayed and asked God to show these people who had turned their back upon Him that He is the living and true God. Fire came down from heaven and burnt up the bullock and the wood. It even licked up the water and burnt the stones into dust. What amazing faith Elijah had! What an amazing God!

Pray

Lord, help me to be like Elijah, so that when I pray, I really do believe that You will hear and answer my prayers.

. . . through the Bible day by day

May 12

Reading: 1 Kings 19. 1-15

After the fire a still small voice,
1 Kings 19. 12

Ahab was a weak-willed man. He behaved like a spoilt child when he could not get his own way. He relied on his wife to do his dirty work. Jezebel sent a message to Elijah saying that by the next day he would be dead, because he had killed all her prophets,

Elijah fled from her threats into the wilderness and asked God to let him die. Tiredness took over and he slept. An angel woke him up with water to drink and a freshly baked cake to eat. He ate the food, drank the water and slept again. Eventually, the angel told him he had a long journey to take. Elijah went to Mount Horeb and found a cave to live in.

> **Pray**
> Loving Father, I know that You are all powerful and yet You don't always speak to me in amazing ways. Help me to listen to You when You speak to me quietly.

While he was in the cave God asked him what he was doing there. It's a fact we cannot hide from God. He knows where we are and He knows what we are thinking. Poor Elijah was really down in the dumps and he poured out his complaint to God, finishing with the words, 'I'm the last prophet alive and they want to kill me'.

The Lord told Elijah to stand in the entrance of the cave. As he stood there, God caused three dramatic things to happen. A fierce wind passed by that smashed big rocks, an earthquake shook the mountain and then there was a fire. Each thing was frightening, but Elijah realized that God was not in any of those things. Then he heard a still, small voice. God spoke to Elijah to tell him that He still had things for him to do. He was not finished with Elijah. God does not give up on us so easily, either. And Elijah learned that, although God can speak through amazing things, He can also speak in very ordinary ways. Are we listening?

Stepping stones

Reading: 1 Kings 19. 15-21

May 13

There is no one who has left house or brothers or sisters or father or mother or wife or children or lands, for My sake, and the gospel's, who shall not receive a hundredfold now in this time . . . and in the age to come, eternal life,

Mark 10. 28-30

It is said that you can't put an old head on young shoulders. But the experience of an 'old head' can be passed on to a young person that may help that young person to do more for God than the older one ever did. Elijah did seven miracles but Elisha did fourteen!

Elijah's work for God was ending though it was not yet finished. Elisha's work for God was about to begin and it was Elijah's responsibility to prepare Elisha for the work.

Pray

Father, help me to be obedient, to do what You want me to do and go where You want me to go.

God told Elijah to anoint Elisha, which meant that Elisha was being marked out for the service of God. Elisha was to take Elijah's place when the older man went to heaven. Elijah was encouraged to find Elisha ploughing in a field with twelve yoke of oxen. He saw him start the first pair off, ploughing a straight furrow, and then the next pair do exactly the same. He did this with all eleven pairs and then he took the last pair and started ploughing. The first pair was out in front and a diagonal line of oxen was busy ploughing the earth. Elisha was in control in the field. That is what Elijah wanted to see. So Elijah threw his coat over the young man. That told Elisha that the prophet Elijah wanted him to follow him.

Elisha wanted to say goodbye to his family and friends. To show that he really meant it he made a feast, killed and cooked his best pair of oxen, using the wooden plough to make a fire to cook the beef. We sometimes sing, 'I have decided to follow Jesus, No turning back, No turning back!' Elisha was prepared to leave all to serve God and he was never disappointed with that decision. Neither should we be.

. . . through the Bible day by day

May 14

Reading: **1 Kings 21**

You shall not covet your neighbour's house, Exodus 20. 17

Some people are never satisfied. They never grow out of their childhood 'gimmee' tantrums, or the 'I want that!' phase of life. The prodigal son, in Luke chapter 15, said, 'Give me!' He wanted his inheritance before his dad died and when he got it he wasted it.

Naboth had received an inheritance from his father. It was a vineyard located next to Ahab's palace. Ahab must have looked often at his neighbour's vineyard and began to have thoughts as to how he could turn it into a herb garden, a nice add-on to his palace where he could walk and breathe the pleasant smell of the herbs. But, when he asked Naboth to sell it to him or to exchange it for another vineyard, Naboth said, 'No'. He could not do that, he said, because the vineyard was to stay in the family. God had provided it for them.

Pray

Lord, thank You for everything that I have. Please keep me from wanting things that belong to others.

Ahab started to sulk. Jezebel soon saw his miserable face and asked him what was the matter. He told her about Naboth not parting with his vineyard and straight away Jezebel's devious mind thought of a plan to kill Naboth and steal the vineyard from his family. She told some of her thugs to make a feast, invite Naboth as a special guest, get him drunk and then accuse him of blaspheming God and the king. Then they were to stone him so that he died.

The men did just as she said. So Ahab was able to go and take possession of the vineyard. But he did not reckon that God knew what he had done. God sent Elijah to tell Ahab He had seen his wickedness. Elijah was to tell Ahab how both he and Jezebel would die. Even kings and queens are not above God's law. We all have to obey God.

Reading: 2 Kings 2

May 15

For so an entrance will be supplied to you abundantly into the everlasting kingdom of our Lord, 2 Peter 1. 11

Shetlanders call the Northern Lights, 'The Merry Dancers'. The proper name is Aurora Borealis. The University of Alaska displays photographs of this spectacular sight on their website. Scientifically, it is God's method of disposing of the small magnetic particles of copper, cobalt and other minerals that are from explosions on the sun. Clouds of these particles are attracted either to the North or South Pole and, as they enter the Earth's atmosphere, they are burned up, giving a beautiful display of light and colour.

Elijah was taken to heaven in a whirlwind. That was something special too! However, before that happened Elijah had some important things to do to teach Elisha. They started at Gilgal, the place where the children of Israel were circumcized when they came out of Egypt. Elijah showed Elisha that a servant of God must be a separated man. Then, he took him to Bethel and taught him about the house of God. From Bethel they went to Jericho and he showed the younger man things to expect in a cursed city. Finally, they came to Jordan, the river of death, where later John baptized people. Jordan teaches us we must put an end to the self-life.

Elisha knew his master was going to be taken away from him that day but he did not know how. Elijah did something miraculous. He wrapped his cloak up and struck the waters and the river Jordan parted to allow them across. As they talked, a chariot of fire and a whirlwind came and took Elijah to heaven without dying. His cloak fell on Elisha, God's new servant. He took it, struck the river in the same way and went across, beginning where Elijah left off. Wasn't God good to take Elijah to heaven in such a wonderful way! Some of us may go to heaven without dying, if we are still alive when Jesus comes back.

Pray

Thank You that Heaven is real and those that love You will soon go to be with You Lord.

... through the Bible day by day

May 16

Reading: 2 Kings 4. 1-7

The Lord watches over the strangers; He relieves the fatherless and widow,
Psalm 146. 9

It's Bristol, in the United Kingdom, November 1840. A huge number of mouths need feeding, but there's no bread, milk or money. Mr Muller, a great man of faith and prayer, is once again depending on God to meet the needs of his orphanage. Then, just before the milkman is due to call, £10 is received from a lady. Once more God has met the need and shown that He is 'a father of the fatherless', Psalm 68. 5.

A man who had served God with Elisha died. This left his wife as a widow and his sons fatherless, and they had a big problem. Someone was going to take her sons to be slaves as payment for a debt if she could not pay. God wonderfully provided for their need. In Bible times widows and orphans, or those who were fatherless, were often poor and despised. However, God cared for them and the Bible encourages us to give them the help they need.

There were quite a few widows connected to the Lord Jesus. Ruth, in the Old Testament, became one of His ancestors. Anna was one of the first to see Him when He was a baby, He saw a widow in the temple giving her offering to God and He raised a widow's son to life again. Joseph had probably died before the Lord Jesus was thirty years old. If so, we see His care for His mother, Mary, as a widow, John 19. 25-27. Therefore, even He experienced being 'fatherless', as far as an earthly father was concerned.

God meets the need of those who, in dire straights, trust themselves to Him when they want to be saved. This is true of the way God takes care of the fatherless and widows. Do we care for them too?

Pray

Ask God to help you find those who really need help today, especially those who may be lonely or ignored by others.

Stepping stones

Reading: 2 Kings 5. 1-14

May 17

Go therefore and make disciples of all the nations, Matthew 28. 19

Have you ever been in a really dark place with just a torch to give you some light? If you've taken a torch apart (not a good idea if you are still in the dark!) you'll know the bulb that gives the light is actually quite small. Can you imagine the bulb thinking to itself, 'I'm only small. I can't be much use in this big, dark place'?

There was a young girl who could have given a long list of reasons for not telling her master's wife about what God could do for him.

She was only young.

She was only a slave.

She was probably frightened, living a long way from home.

The Syrians were, after all, the enemies of the Israelites.

It would have been almost unheard of for anyone to be cured of leprosy.

But no, she still spoke up! Whatever reasons we may think of for not telling others about the gospel, there is one reason for witnessing that beats them all. The verse for today reminds us that the Lord Jesus commanded His disciples to tell others the gospel.

Of course, we must make sure we know the Lord Jesus as our Saviour first. How strange, to be telling others the good news but not believing it ourselves!

I don't suppose we would ever have read Naaman's name in the Bible if he hadn't been cured of his leprosy. And it is all because that young girl simply said what she knew to be true. And, perhaps, there is someone whose name will be written in the book of life because God used you to tell them about Him. Who could you speak to about the Lord Jesus today or tomorrow?

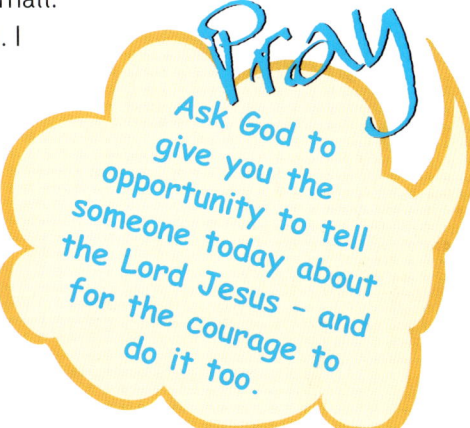

Pray

Ask God to give you the opportunity to tell someone today about the Lord Jesus – and for the courage to do it too.

. . . through the Bible day by day

May 18

Reading: **2 Kings 5. 13-27**

For the love of money is a root of all kinds of evil, 1 Timothy 6. 10

There was an uncle I used to like visiting. When it was time to leave, he would hold a large tin full of money just above my head. I was allowed to put my hand in to grab as much money as I could hold in one hand! I would quickly count how much I had got and if I did really well, I would have just over a pound (the tin was full of 1p and 2p coins!). Many people today are trying to get as much money as they can, too. They don't realize that, as they try to get rich, things may not be as good as they seem. Gehazi was given money and nice clothes, but he had told lies to get it. He ended up with leprosy. He is a classic example of those 'who desire to be rich' and 'fall into temptation and a snare', 1 Timothy 6. 9.

Pray

Thank the Lord Jesus for becoming so poor that he had to borrow a penny. Ask for help to 'be content with such things as ye have'.

Having money – even a lot of money – is not necessarily wrong. In the Old Testament it was a sign of God's blessing to be rich. However, the *love* of money is wrong. If wanting to be rich becomes too important to us we will have major problems. In many of His parables the Lord Jesus shows us the right attitude towards money. And He is the one who, 'though He was rich, yet for your sakes He became poor', 2 Corinthians 8. 9.

It is right to think about the cost when spending our money. But what about the cost of getting, or holding on to, money in the wrong way? Try to get the right principles. Money should be gained properly and morally. We should have the right priorities and the right perspective. Put God first. There is no money in heaven. Treasure, up there, is something spiritual.

Reading: **2 Kings 6. 8-17**

May 19

Do not fear, for those who are with us are more than those who are with them,
2 Kings 6. 16

People have been fighting wars for hundreds of years. However, one thing has been different during the last few decades. A British army general said to his troops, on the eve of World War 1, 'I hope none of you gentlemen is so foolish as to think that aeroplanes will be usefully employed for reconnaissance from the air'. Yet aircraft have since formed an essential part of many countries' military strategies. Today helicopters, cargo planes and fighter jets are there to support ground forces as they go into battle. The modern soldier has to fight well, but he also looks up for essential help.

Elisha was aware of help and protection coming from somewhere that was even higher than aircraft – from heaven itself. The king of Syria had been trying to attack Israel but Elisha kept telling the king of Israel where to avoid the attack. So one night the Syrian king sent some of his army to surround the city where Elisha was. When Elisha's servant saw it he panicked. 'What shall we do?' Elisha asked God to open his eyes to see the great divine forces that were there to protect him.

One day the Lord Jesus will come back from heaven and destroy the armies of the world. It's a challenge, because no one will be able to stand and fight against Him in that day. How foolish it is to oppose what God wants to do in our lives. It is also a comfort because in the battle against sin, difficulties, opposition and fear, we are on God's side. It's no wonder our verse for today is one of over fifty where the Bible says, 'Don't be afraid'. There's no need to be afraid if we are on God's side.

Pray
Thank God for His amazing glory, His awesome majesty and greatness and His unlimited power. But don't be afraid to speak to Him about something that's troubling you.

... through the Bible day by day

May 20

READING: **2 Kings 7. 1-20**

But without faith it is impossible to please Him, Hebrews 11. 6

Have you ever seen, or perhaps even tried, bungee jumping? It is not for the faint-hearted. The 'jumper' is attached by his ankles to 'elastic' ropes and jumps from a platform up to 200m high. He plunges head-first towards the ground until the elastic is at full stretch and is then catapulted back into the air and bounces up and down until the bungee cord energy is used up.

There is one thing the person jumping needs, other than perhaps a little insanity, and that is complete confidence in the bungee cord. Without fully trusting what he is attached to there is no way he can have the excitement of a jump.

It is a simple truth, but God cannot bless us if we do not trust Him. A man once died for saying he did not believe it was possible for God to do what He promised, 2 Kings 7. The fact that the man had an important position in society and what God had said went against human logic did not matter. No belief meant no blessing.

We may not see such dramatic examples today but the results of refusing to believe can be very serious. Firstly, we must believe to be saved, because a person is 'condemned already, because he has not believed in the name of the only begotten Son of God', John 3. 18. 'He who does not believe . . . shall not see life', verse 36. Secondly, Thomas missed out on the joy of believing the Lord was alive on the day of His resurrection because he said, 'I will not believe', John 20. 25. The Israelites did not enter into the promised land because of their unbelief either, Hebrews 3. 19.

It is understandable, then, that the Saviour gave the simple but essential instruction, 'Have faith in God', Mark 11. 22.

Pray
Lord, teach me how necessary it is to have faith in God. Help me to believe.

Stepping stones

Reading: **2 Chronicles 26. 1- 4, 16-22**

May 21

Pride goes before destruction, and a haughty spirit before a fall, Proverbs 16. 18

I once had a great, shiny, red bike. Better still, I thought it had a great rider – me! I could pedal fast and knew where all the bumps were in the road to swerve round. In fact, I was so good that I knew my three-year-old little brother would just love a ride sitting on the back of my bike. Mum said, No! but I thought I was a good enough rider, so off I went. Sure enough, it wasn't long before I found out I had the wrong opinion of myself. My little brother's foot got stuck in the back wheel and he had to go to hospital!

King Uzziah also had too high an opinion of himself, and that pride got him into a lot of trouble. He was still a teenager when he became king and for 52 years he was a good king, v 3. Sadly, in the end, he thought he could do as he liked and went into a part of the temple that God had said only the priests could enter. His punishment was horrible. God sent him what was then the incurable disease of leprosy.

Pray

Thank God for the Lord Jesus who is the perfect example of humility. Ask for help to imitate Him.

God doesn't normally judge us today in the same way and that's just as well, isn't it? But pride is still something God absolutely hates. What starts as a thought of inward pride can lead to far greater consequences than we imagined, Proverbs 16. 18.

Every day we take time to get dressed and the clothes we put on are seen by others. The Bible tells us to 'be clothed with humility', 1 Peter 5. 5. Each day we need to make a deliberate effort to have a heart that is free from pride. In this way we will live a life that will show humility towards others.

... through the Bible day by day

May 22

Reading: Isaiah 6. 1-8

These things Isaiah said when he saw His glory and spoke of Him, John 12. 41

Pray

Praise God for His greatness and glory. Ask forgiveness for any unconfessed sin. Ask what God wants you to do for Him today.

An important event in Judah's history in the year 740 BC was the death of King Uzziah. However, Isaiah does not give any more details about this. Instead, we read about something else that happened in the same year, something that would be one of the greatest experiences in Isaiah's life.

Isaiah was given an amazing insight into the supreme glory of God. He was awestruck as he saw the glory of God. John tells us that it was the Lord Jesus that Isaiah actually saw, John 12. 41. Indeed, the three persons of God were there, for God asks 'who will go for *us*', verse 8. That may be why the seraphim say, 'Holy!' three times, verse 3. To be holy means to be set apart from sin, to be pure. Isaiah was immediately aware in the holy presence of God of how different God is. How glad he must have been that God provided a way for his sin to be dealt with!

Isaiah showed his appreciation of the greatness of God and what He had done for him by being willing to be sent by God. He did not place conditions on where or when or to whom God could send him. He simply said, 'Here am I, send me', verse 8.

This amazing sight had two effects on Isaiah. He became very aware of his sin, verses 5-7, and he was willing to be sent in the service of God, verse 8. We must notice the order. God did a work *in* Isaiah, purifying him before He could work *through* him. Centuries later, Paul speaks of Christians who are sanctified, made holy, set apart to be pure, and therefore able to be used in the service of God, 2 Timothy 2. 21. Are we like that?

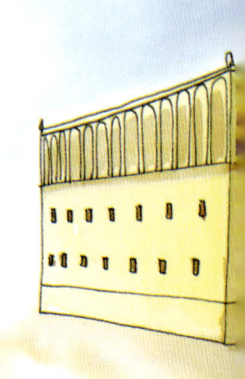

Stepping stones

Reading: **2 Chronicles 29. 1-11**

May 23

Seek first the kingdom of God and His righteousness, and all these things shall be added to you, Matthew 6. 33

Lots of people wish that they were rich or famous, but if you were, what would be the first thing you would do? Hezekiah had many options open to him as king but his priority was to put God first. Did you notice it was in the first month of his first year that he repaired the house of God?

The Lord Jesus doesn't want us to wait until we have certain things. Instead, in whatever circumstances we are in, He wants us to put Him first with our time, interests, money, decisions and ambitions. That may sound like a big sacrifice. But everything we have comes from God, so He has the right for it to be given back. The Lord Jesus did not hold back His life at the cross, so what right have we to hold anything back from Him?

God also promises that those that give to Him will not lose out. He says, 'those who honour me, I will honour', 1 Samuel 2. 30. Those who, in faith, take Him at His word find the reward is great. Significantly, the most often-quoted statement of the Lord Jesus is regarding this subject. Six times He says, 'Whoever will lose his life for my sake shall find it', Matthew 16. 25.

Jim Elliot was one of five missionaries who were martyred in 1956 while spreading the gospel in South America. He once wrote, 'He is no fool who gives what he cannot keep to gain what he cannot lose'. Let's be like Hezekiah today and 'seek first the kingdom of God'.

Pray

Thank God that the Lord Jesus gave everything when He died on the cross. Ask for help to be like Hezekiah and seek first the things of God.

...through the Bible day by day

May 24

Reading: 2 Kings 19. 1-21

Casting all your care upon Him, for He cares for you, 1 Peter 5. 7

Pray

Speak to God about a problem or concern that you have today. Ask Him not only for the solution, but also for peace in trusting Him.

Would you like to be a bit taller than you are? Then try this! Close your eyes . . . think about it really hard. Now check the mirror . . . have you grown? No change? Well the Lord Jesus said if we can't even use our thoughts to make ourselves half a metre taller then why do we use our thoughts to worry about things? Matthew 6. 25-34.

Hezekiah had the right idea. A big problem came his way. The land of Judah, in the southern part of the promised land, was being threatened by a man called Rabshakeh. Many of the surrounding nations had already been defeated by the Assyrians.

Did you notice the first thing he did? Hezekiah took the threatening letter he had received from Rabshekah and prayed to God about it. Did you notice too that he didn't focus on how big the problem was? Instead, he started by thinking about how great God is. He also didn't want the problem to go away so he could have an easier life instead. What he was asking for was that God's name would be honoured.

It is interesting that God used a fisherman to write the words 'Casting all your care'. Peter would have remembered well how he used to cast, or throw, his net into the sea. It made no difference whether it was a big net or a small one. The net was thrown overboard. It was thrown over completely. There's no point keeping half of it in the boat.

In the same way, our problems and concerns, whether we think they are large or small, need to be thrown completely out of our 'worry boat'. Not because the problems don't matter or will immediately disappear but because 'He cares for you'. When we are seeking to live for Him, God's love can be trusted to meet our need and work things out for our best and His glory.

Stepping stones

Reading: **2 Kings 20**

May 25

For with God nothing will be impossible,
Luke 1. 37

If you have a watch and want to move the time back by an hour you can probably do so easily just by turning the hands of the clock or pressing a few buttons. In fact, each October we have to do this when the clocks go back. In the days of Hezekiah people used a sundial to tell the time. Perhaps you have seen a sundial which has a flat metal plate and an indicating piece pointing upwards. When the sun shines the upright piece makes a shadow fall on the metal plate, and as the sun moves during the day so the shadow moves, telling us the time.

Whatever the sundial that Hezekiah had looked like, it was rather more limited than a watch. For a start, it would have been impossible to carry around on your wrist. It was no use at night, couldn't be used in the rain, and it was impossible to change the time it showed. Impossible, that is, for a human being. But, as Luke chapter 1 verse 37 says, nothing is impossible with God and the books of the Bible, as well as the lives of many Christians, are full of examples of how God is the God of the impossible. How many 'impossible' miracles can you think of?

Although it is not always as dramatic as the shadow on the sundial moving back for Hezekiah, every time someone is saved it is a wonderful miracle that shows the great power of God. Considering that God is able to save us and remembering the great miracles recorded in the Bible, we should confidently come to Him in prayer to ask for what we consider to be the big and impossible things. And we should believe He can do them.

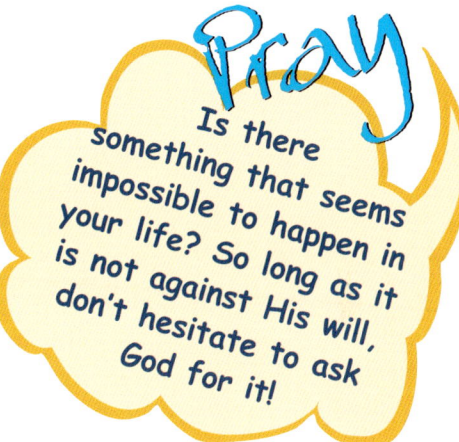

Pray
Is there something that seems impossible to happen in your life? So long as it is not against His will, don't hesitate to ask God for it!

. . . through the Bible day by day

May 26

Reading: Jonah 1. 1-3

I know that You are a gracious and merciful God, slow to anger and abundant in lovingkindness, Jonah 4. 2

Have you noticed that, whatever your favourite sport may be, there is one thing that is the same regardless of what you play? Where you play, the length of time it takes and the size of team all vary between sports. One thing all sports have in common, however, is that there is someone to check the rules are being obeyed. This person may be called an umpire, a referee or a judge but his job is to check that the rules are kept. Some rules are there for safety, others for fairness and they are generally for the enjoyment of those involved. How do you feel when you are playing and someone breaks the rules and gets away with it? None of us likes a cheat.

If we are willing to obey rules when we play sport – and we know that there will be consequences if we disobey the rules – shouldn't we be willing to obey God? After all, we owe God so much. He created the human race, gives us air to breathe and sent His Son to die for us.

Jonah was a great prophet but he still chose to disobey God. The Bible is full of commands from God, but He doesn't force us to obey Him. Instead, He wants us to obey Him out of love for Him, believing His will for us is best. The consequences of Jonah's disobedience were more serious than he imagined, both for him and the sailors. The results of sin in our lives can be serious for us and for others. Think about how we feel when others cheat when we are playing sport. If for no other reason, we should obey God so as not to displease Him.

Remember, as Jonah found, in the long run it doesn't pay to disobey.

Pray

Is there a time when you have disobeyed God for which you need to ask His forgiveness? Will you ask for help to be willingly obedient in the future?

Stepping stones

Reading: Jonah 1. 4-17

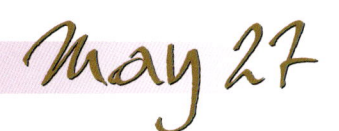

May 27

Where can I go from Your Spirit? Or where can I flee from Your presence?
Psalm 139. 7

One day a young lady decided enough was enough and she would run away from home. She was living a long way away from where she had grown up, she had been badly treated and was now hated because she was pregnant. To her surprise someone knew where she was, found her, spoke to her, knew what was happening in her life and told her to go back. That person was none other than God Himself and the experience had such an effect on her she called the place 'The well of the God who lives and sees'. The young lady's name was Hagar, Genesis 16.

Jonah learnt a similar lesson. Despite going in the opposite direction to which God had sent him and being on a boat, one of the fastest forms of transport they had in those days, he could not get away from God. Trying to run away cost him the price of his ticket and almost his life as well.

Wherever we are God sees us and knows what we are thinking, saying and doing. How important it is that we do not try to run away and go our own way! The Bible asks the question, 'How shall we escape if we neglect so great salvation?', Hebrews 2. 3. When it comes to trusting the Lord Jesus as our Saviour there is no escaping for those who run away from God's way.

Are you trying to run from trusting the Lord Jesus as Saviour? I hope not. On the other hand, if you are already a Christian, remember that Jonah was one of God's people who mistakenly thought he could run from God. Are you running away from something God wants you to do?

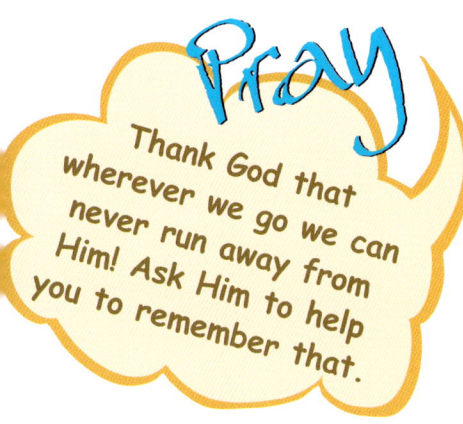

Pray
Thank God that wherever we go we can never run away from Him! Ask Him to help you to remember that.

... through the Bible day by day

May 28

Reading: **Jonah 3**

He has not dealt with us according to our sins; nor punished us according to our iniquities, Psalm 103. 10

If you have ever been ice skating you will probably know that falling over can be a painful and even wet experience! The advice leaflet given out the last time I went included suggestions for how not to fall over and what to do if it was about to happen. What particularly caught my attention was the advice given if I did fall over. As there is a risk of being hit by others or getting cold, it recommended getting up as quickly as possible. Not easy if our body, or pride, has been hurt, but better than lying there feeling sorry!

The devil would like us to think that once we have failed and disobeyed God then that is it — we're finished. Sometimes we are so taken up with the consequences of our failure, or our regrets over it that we don't do what we need to do. Jonah, however, went back to where he had gone wrong when he disobeyed God and with God's help started obeying.

The command from the Lord had not changed. Jonah chapter 3 and verse 2 is practically identical to Jonah chapter 1 and verse 2. Perhaps you know that you should trust the Lord Jesus to be your Saviour and you have put it off before. Maybe there is another command of God you are not obeying. Never use the longsuffering of God as an excuse for disobedience. It should rather be a reason to be gratefully obedient to His word.

God's patience with us should also stop us thinking that others who have failed are no longer able to be something for God. We should try to show the patient, forgiving attitude of the Lord. It will help us to get up and start again, and help others that have to do the same.

Pray

Thank God for the Lord Jesus who never needed a 'second chance'. Thank God for His patience and forgiveness in not giving you what you deserve.

Stepping stones

Reading: Jonah 4

May 29

God said to Jonah, 'Is it right for you to be angry about the plant?' Jonah 4. 9

Some Scottish £10 notes show a picture of the missionary Mary Slessor from Dundee. She served God in Nigeria for nearly 40 years, living a lot of the time alone with blood-thirsty, fierce natives. She was horrified by the terrible cruelty these people showed to each other. Wives would be killed when their husbands died and any twins born were considered evil and were left in the jungle to be eaten. The first thing she saw in one place she went to spread the gospel was a human skull swinging on a pole!

One day the chief's son died and the witchdoctor blamed a neighbouring village. Some of the villagers were captured and were about to be killed. In these circumstances the grave would always be covered with human blood. Relying on God's help, Mary Slessor spoke with the chief and eventually he was persuaded to let the people free.

This courageous lady missionary wanted the love of God to reach a people like this, rightly believing that no one is too bad for the mercy of God. Nineveh was also an evil place. However, Jonah forgot how recently he had needed forgiveness for his own failings. He was fuming at the longsuffering of God. God wanted to save even the people of Nineveh if they would only repent. He wants to save you, too, if you are not yet trusting the Lord Jesus. If God has this pity for those lost in sin how much more pity does He have for His own children bought by the death of His Son.

In contrast to Jonah's anger, Psalm 103 tells us 'the LORD is merciful and gracious, slow to anger, and abounding in mercy', verse 8, because 'as a father pities his children, so the LORD pities those who fear Him', verse 13.

Pray: Ask God for help so that when you are cross you will think of the cross, and, instead of being too heated, you will be tender hearted.

...through the Bible day by day

May 30

Reading: 2 Kings 22. 1-2, 8-20

Remember now your Creator in the days of your youth, Ecclesiastes 12. 1

In 1555 a teenager called William Hunter was tied to a wooden stake and given a last chance to say that what he had done was wrong. When he refused, the fire was lit and the young man burnt to death. What do you think he had done? He had entered a church building, gone to a Bible on the desk – and read it! Wicked people hated the idea of 'common people' reading the Bible for themselves. His memorial in Brentwood, Essex, in the UK, reads, 'WILLIAM HUNTER. MARTYR. Committed to the Flames, March 26th MDLV. Christian Reader, learn from his example to value the privilege of an open Bible. And be careful to maintain it'. Josiah was a young man who was trying to do what was right, even when what there was of his Bible was lost. But, as soon as it was found, he read it and he immediately obeyed it.

Pray

'Your Word have I hid in my heart that I might not sin against You'. Teach me to see wonderful things in Your law.

There are six important things to do with the Bible, which can easily be remembered on your hand. Your thumb tells you the most important thing is to read it. Then, on your other fingers, think about it, learn it by heart, study it and listen to others explaining it. For the sixth, use your wrist, where there is a vein going to your heart, to remember to apply it by putting it into practice in your life.

You may know that Psalm 119 is the longest 'chapter' in the Bible but do you know what it is about? Almost every verse speaks about the Word of God – its preciousness, importance and the need to obey it.

How many Bibles are there in our homes? Are we as desperate to read them as William Hunter? Are we as quick to obey them as Josiah?

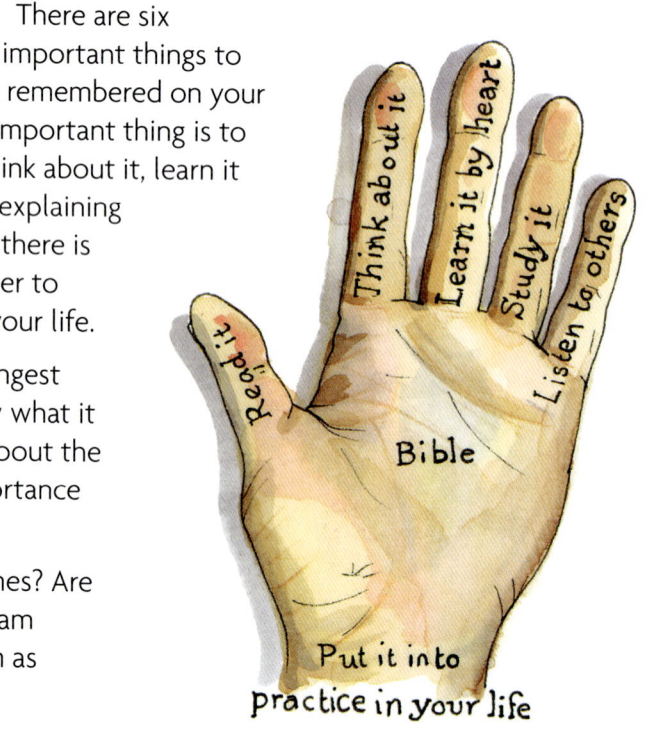

Reading: Jeremiah 1. 1-10

May 31

The Lord said to me, 'Do not say, "I am a youth", for you shall go to all to whom I send you and whatever I command you, you shall speak', Jeremiah 1. 7

Young Jeremiah was a busy man. He was a priest, and had an important job to do helping people to worship God in the temple. He was sure he was doing all he could to serve His God. Then one day God said to him, 'Before you were born I intended you to become a prophet'.

'Oh! No!' thought Jeremiah. 'That's one job I don't want to do.' He remembered that God had once said if someone claimed to be a prophet, and said he spoke in God's name, the people were to listen and remember. If what the prophet had said would happen did happen, they were to respect him because God had obviously spoken to him and he was special. He really did speak for God. If it didn't happen, however, they were to take the false prophet outside and kill him. 'No thank-you!' thought Jeremiah. 'I can do without all that pressure'.

'Can't do it, Lord', he said. 'I'm too young!' 'No you're not,' replied God. 'It doesn't matter how old you are, if you come from Me. In fact, I'll even tell you exactly what you are to say and tell you who you should go to. And don't be afraid of what other people think. Just do what I say. That's all I ask'.

Jeremiah did exactly what God told him. I am sure he was pleased to think that God had known about him even before he was born. God knew all about us, too, before we were born. Perhaps God has something special for us to do for Him. He wants us to go into the whole world to tell other people about Him, but perhaps He has a special place for some of us to go. Let's ask God to show us what He wants us to do.

Pray

Lord, show me what plan You have for my life. Show me what You want me to do.

... through the Bible day by day

June 1

Reading: Jeremiah 18. 1-6

The vessel that he made of clay was marred in the hand of the potter; so he made it again, Jeremiah 18. 4

Have you been to a pottery where people were actually making the pots in front of you? It is quite something to see how a lump of clay can be thrown into the shape the potter wants with just a little pressure from the potter's thumb or hand as the wheel spins around. The potter has total control over the clay. If he makes a shape he doesn't like he just changes it or starts all over again.

God wanted to teach Jeremiah that He can do what He wants with people. After all, He has made us all. The Israelites were especially His. He had chosen them to be His nation. 'I will be your God and you will be My people'. He promised to bless them if they would obey Him. But they didn't. So God said, 'Remember, I can do what I like with you'.

It is the same with us. If we know Jesus as our Saviour He is also our Lord. That means He can send us wherever He wants and tell us to do whatever He wants. Paul knew this, which is why he sometimes tells us he is a 'slave' of Jesus Christ. A slave had no rights. Clay has no rights. Believers have no rights, apart from the right to be like the Lord Jesus one day and be forever with God. This right is a gift of God to all true believers.

But God may have to work on us to make us fit for His presence. There are all sorts of bumps and dents in us at the moment. Things like anger and pride spoil us. The Potter will sort all that out. But if we are in His hands, we couldn't be in any better or kinder hands, could we?

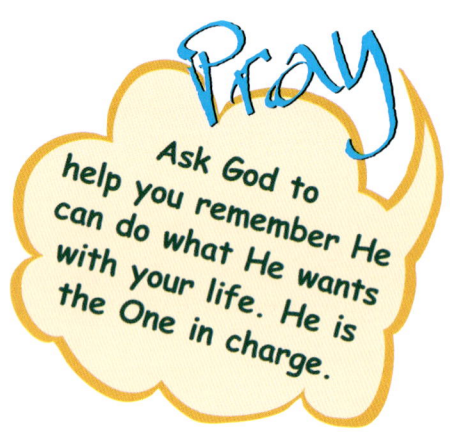

Pray

Ask God to help you remember He can do what He wants with your life. He is the One in charge.

Reading: **Jeremiah 36. 9-30**

June 2

On this one will I look: on him who is poor and of a contrite spirit, and who trembles at My word, Isaiah 66. 2

Have you ever had a letter that made you so angry you wanted to tear it up? Or perhaps you received a letter from someone you didn't want to hear from so you just threw it away. Either way, it shows you did not have much respect for the writer or for what was written. If the person who wrote it knew what you had done he would have been quite upset. Perhaps it's just as well he didn't know.

God told His prophet Jeremiah to write down on a scroll what He was going to do to His people who were so disobedient and disrespectful. Jeremiah's helper went into the Temple and read the message to the people. The princes also heard it and were worried about it. They thought it was important enough to read to the king. They knew the king did not respect God. So they told Baruch and Jeremiah to hide in case the king tried to kill them. But the message didn't make the king angry. He just showed what he thought of it by cutting it into pieces and throwing it into the fire! He had no respect for God or His word at all. He wasn't the only one. God sent another prophet, Malachi, to speak to the people, but they argued over everything God said.

Today God sends us preachers rather than prophets. He uses the Bible to speak to us rather than write special messages to us. I doubt if anyone of us would cut up the Bible and burn it. We can show disrespect for God's word in other ways, though – dreaming during the meetings, laughing at the message or just simply ignoring it. God will bless those who hear His word, respect it and put it into practice. Are we up for that?

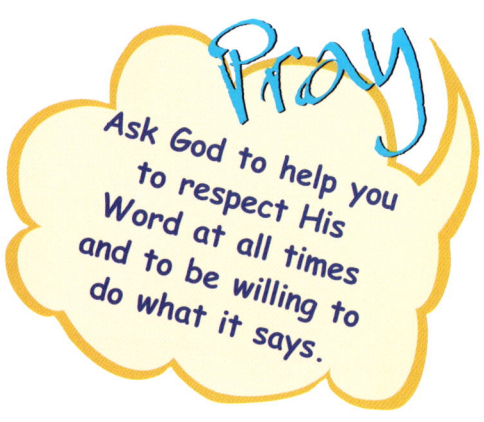

Pray

Ask God to help you to respect His Word at all times and to be willing to do what it says.

... through the Bible day by day

June 3

Reading: 2 Kings 25. 8-15

Judah has gone into captivity,
Lamentations 1. 3

Jeremiah could not believe it! The terrible day of God's judgement had at last come and Jerusalem was being smashed to pieces.

When he had first heard God call him to become a prophet God had told him not to be afraid of other people. 'They will not listen to you', God said, 'But I will keep you safe'. Sure enough, the people had not listened to what Jeremiah had said. God had told him he would punish them but they still had not listened.

Now the awful day had come. Armies that had camped around Jerusalem had finally broken down the walls and were inside killing men, women and children, and taking some away to be slaves. Houses were burning, gardens and trees were being up-rooted. The king's palace was on fire. Even the beautiful temple of God was ruined.

People had said for years that it would never happen. 'God loves this place too much to allow people to do that'. 'You tell us God will punish us, destroy our city and take us away? Never! We are His people. It's all hot air'.

Where was the hot air now? Over the burning temple and the smoking city! God does keep His word. Oh, He may be a long time in doing it, so that people have every opportunity possible to change their minds. But it will come.

People's hearts were broken that day but it was too late. Jeremiah cried for months but it was too late. God was very sad too. But it was too late.

Is God speaking to us and telling us to obey Him? How long has He been telling us that? He will not be patient for ever. He will punish us one day. That is why we should be obedient to Him now.

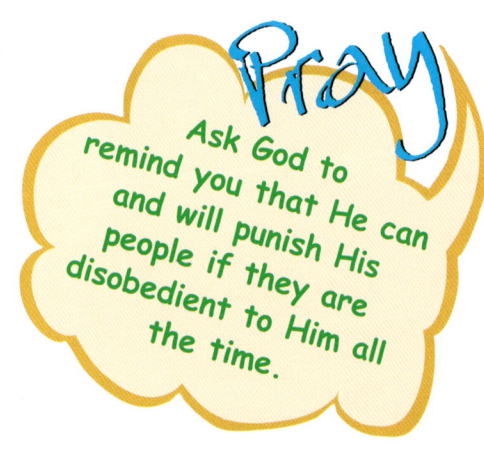

Pray
Ask God to remind you that He can and will punish His people if they are disobedient to Him all the time.

Stepping stones

Reading: **Lamentations 3. 22-33**

June 4

His compassions fail not. They are new every morning; Great is Your faithfulness, Lamentations 3. 22-23

Jeremiah's heart was broken. He had loved this city of Jerusalem, and the people who lived in it. He had preached to them, prayed for them, and cried over them. He had known God would eventually punish them for their disobedience. God had said so. How hard it was to see it when it came! How much it upset him to see all these enemy soldiers in that lovely city, and to see so much suffering around him!

God does not promise us all an easy life. There may be times when He will bring great sadness upon us. Some preachers see great results from their preaching – Jonah did, but Jeremiah didn't. Some people live to old age; some people don't. Some are always healthy; others seem to be always sick. Some seem to suffer more than others. God has different experiences for each of us.

Yet the wonderful thing that Jeremiah had to hold on to was that God would always be faithful to His people. Even when things were hard to bear God still loved them. Jeremiah could sit in a burning, broken, beaten city, and remember God always does what is best. 'God is merciful to us even when He is hard on us', Jeremiah said. 'He will never punish us completely. His kindness is fresh and new. Every morning it is new. God is always faithful'.

If things should ever get too much for us, let us always remember God is faithful and will always care for us, and be with us through every heartache. Although things may be hard at school, at home, and, when we get to it, at work or at college, with every new morning we can see again God's kindness. We can be sure of that.

Pray

Thank God that He will always forgive you if you turn back to Him. He will never be unfairly hard on you.

. . . through the Bible day by day

June 5

Reading: **Hosea 11. 1- 12**

I will return again to My place till they acknowledge their offense. Then they will seek My face, Hosea 5. 15

One day God told a man to go out and marry a woman who would not be faithful to him and who would leave him. Hosea did just that. He married a woman called Gomer even though he knew she would let him down. They had three children and then Gomer left Hosea and went after other men. That was hard! But God had an even harder thing for Hosea to do. He told him to find Gomer and take her back as his wife.

What incredible kindness Hosea showed to Gomer! But Hosea's kindness to her is nothing compared to the kindness and goodness of God to His disobedient people, the Jews. Through the words of Hosea God shows us the deep love that He had for them. He reminds us of the time when He first decided to bless the Israelites. He brought them out of Egypt and gave them their own land. God describes His relationship with them as being like a parent feeding a child or teaching a toddler how to walk. Yet His child, Israel, had left Him, disobeyed and forgotten Him. But God could not punish His people for ever. 'How can I give you up?', He cries, just as a loving father or mother would cry over a rebellious child. God promised He would welcome His people back and love them again.

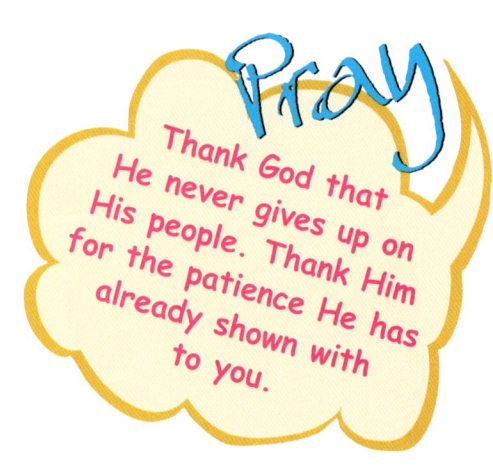

Hosea shows God's love for His people, not just by telling His story but also by being a living example. God loves us, too, we who are His spiritual people. Despite all that we do to disappoint our God, and even should we leave Him or let Him down, He still wants us back. Have we left Him? Let's come back to Him now!

Pray
Thank God that He never gives up on His people. Thank Him for the patience He has already shown with to you.

Reading: Daniel 1

June 6

Daniel purposed in his heart that he would not defile himself with the portion of the king's delicacies, Daniel 1. 8

Nebuchadnezzar took King Zedekiah away after destroying Jerusalem. Several years before this he had also taken captive into Babylon many young men from the rich and ruling families of Jerusalem. Nebuchadnezzar wanted to turn these young men into leaders in his own country so he brought them to live in his palaces and provided food and education for them. He gave them new names so that they would forget their loyalty to their old nation and to their God.

Daniel and three of his friends did not want to give up their loyalty to God. They believed in their God so much that they did not want to disobey Him even though they were now living in a far away land. God had forbidden His people to eat food offered to idols so Daniel made up his mind he would not do this. How could he do so without appearing to be difficult?

He asked the man in charge of the captive Israelites to try an experiment. 'Please let us eat only vegetables and fruit and drink only water', said Daniel. 'Give us a ten-day trial and see what we look like. If we are pale and sickly then you can feed us with the meat and wine from the king's table'. The man agreed. God honoured the four friends for their refusal to compromise their faith although the food from the king's table looked very tasty. At the end of the trial Daniel and his friends looked fitter and healthier than any of the others.

This does not mean that we all have to have a vegetarian diet to be healthy. But it does teach us the importance of standing for our principles and leaving the result to God. God will always honour those who honour Him – even when they are far from home!

Pray
Thank God that He can help you to stand for Him at all times, even if you are away from home.

...through the Bible day by day

June 7

Reading: Daniel 2

There is a God in heaven who reveals secrets, Daniel 2. 28

Daniel had shown he was willing to stand for God. God had blessed him and had given him good health and great wisdom. Now God wanted to prove him faithful in public.

So, God made Nebuchadnezzar dream. It was not a happy dream. The king woke the next morning and was very anxious but he could not remember what he had dreamt. The king believed that his astrologers and magicians, who had always been able to tell him what his dreams had meant in the past, would also be able to tell him what he had dreamt. But they could not. In fact, they seemed to think the king was being unreasonable in asking them to. 'Tell us what your dream was and we will tell you what it means', they said. But the king said, 'No. Unless you can tell me what I dreamt and what it means, I will kill you all. You magicians claim to be able to tell the future so you must also be able to tell the past'.

Daniel and his friends were also arrested and taken to be executed. When Daniel heard why, he went in to the king. 'Give me some time, and I will tell you what you dreamt', he said. So the king gave him some time. Daniel went to his three friends. 'Pray hard', he said. That night God told Daniel what dream He had sent to the king and what it meant. The following day Daniel told the king everything. He was promoted to a position of great authority.

Daniel trusted in God again and God responded. But Daniel was also humble enough to say, 'I cannot reveal dreams but God can'. Let us always remember to give God the glory and not to take it to ourselves.

Pray

Each one of God's children has a spiritual gift. Ask God to keep you humble when you use what He has given you.

Stepping stones

Reading: Daniel 3

June 8

Our God whom we serve is able to deliver us... but if not... we do not serve your gods, Daniel 3. 17-18

King Nebuchadnezzar had declared that Daniel's God was 'the God of gods'. Yet he was still so vain he wanted people to bow down to a statue of himself. Everyone in Babylon was told, 'When you hear the music play you must bow down to the ground and worship my statue'. Anyone who refused would be burned alive.

Most people quite happily believed that there were many gods. Nebuchadnezzar was only one more that they had to add to their list. But Shadrach, Meshach and Abednego had a problem. They believed there is only one true God. God had punished their nation because their own people had worshipped other gods. How could they now bow down to this image? They would be as bad as their own people and God would judge them.

The band began to play. Only three people in the huge crowd remained standing. Every one else bowed down to the ground. The three friends were arrested, brought before the king and sentenced to death. The fire had been heated up seven times hotter than before because the three young men had annoyed the king at their trial. He had told them that no god could save them from death and they had replied that their God could, if He wanted to. But, they said, 'If He does not save us, we would rather die than bow down to your image!'

The vain king and all his court stood around the furnace. But when the three friends were thrown in, they did not die, but the soldiers who threw them in did. God spared them in a wonderful way. He can rescue us from any danger if He wants to. But if He does not want to rescue us, let us never forget that He knows what is best.

Pray

Sometimes God rescues His children and sometimes He doesn't. Pray that He will give you courage to stand for Him whatever happens.

June 9

Reading: Daniel 4. 29-37

Whoever exalts himself will be humbled, and he who humbles himself will be exalted, Matthew 23. 12

The other day I was amazed to hear a woman say, 'If there is a God He should show His power now by striking me dead!' I was afraid for her just in case God did do as she said. But He kindly didn't. He does not always do what we want as soon as we ask Him, which is just as well for her!

He doesn't always respond to us as quickly as He responded to King Nebuchadnezzar. The king was proud of himself and boasted about the wonderful things he had done. While he was still boasting God said to him, 'I will humble you and show you who is the greatest. You will become so ill that you will behave as though you were an animal until you recognize that I am the Most High'. Sure enough, before very long Nebuchadnezzar started making animal noises, and wanted to go outside the palace. When he was let out he began to eat grass! He would not let anyone go near him, so his nails became like bird claws and his hair was all tangled up. He had gone mad.

After a long while he grew better. But though he had lost his mind he had not lost his memory. He remembered what God had said. He then told everyone that God is the great ruler, not man.

God hates pride. He hates it when people think too much of themselves. After all, His own Son, the Lord Jesus, was never proud. He humbled Himself and was born man which meant He was lower than the angels. He humbled Himself even more and became a servant, washing His disciples' feet. And then He humbled Himself even more and died a criminal's death for us. That's who God wants us to be like.

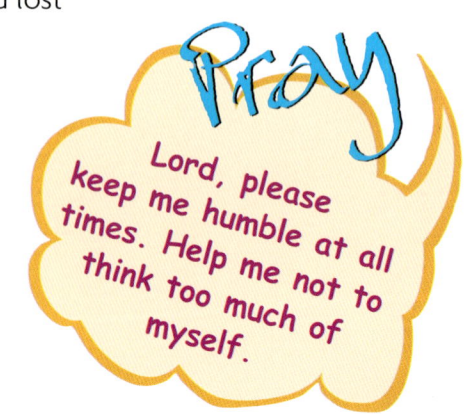

Pray

Lord, please keep me humble at all times. Help me not to think too much of myself.

Reading: **Daniel 5**

June 10

You have been weighed in the balances, and found wanting, Daniel 5. 27

Some people tell us they can see ghosts. I don't know if that is true or not, but I am sure if I saw one I would turn white with fear. King Belshazzar turned white one night and his knees knocked together but it wasn't because he saw a ghost. It was because he saw a hand writing on his wall – but there was no arm and no body connected to it! Just a hand, writing words on the wall that he could not understand.

Pray
Lord, help me to remember You see and know everything I do. Help me to think Your opinion of me is more important than anyone else's.

He called for his wise men but none of them knew what the words meant. But Daniel knew and told the king that God was angry with him. Belshazzar had become proud. He had decided to show everyone that he despised the God of the Israelites. So he called for the special cups that had been used to worship God in the temple in Jerusalem – and then used them at his party!

The three words written on the wall told him that God was going to take the throne from him, that God had thought about Belshazzar and decided he was no good, and had even decided to whom He was going to give his kingdom. And it was all true. While Belshazzar was drinking out of God's cups, the armies surrounded his city, broke through the walls and then killed him and his party-goers.

Some people think there is no God because they cannot see Him. They think that because they cannot see Him He cannot see them. He sees everything and knows everything. He weighs everyone up, just as a cook weighs things up in her scales. And all who despise God will get a real shock one day when they meet Him. Respect God. He is watching.

. . . through the Bible day by day

June 11

Reading: Daniel 6

With God nothing will be impossible,
Luke 1. 37

Some animals are very clever. Not only can they do what is in their natures to do, they can even learn to do what others want. Dogs can be amazingly well trained by people, as can elephants, lions, dolphins and monkeys. I haven't seen anyone train a cat yet, but that doesn't mean a cat isn't very intelligent in its own way.

Years ago, zoos and circuses used to be more popular than they are now. Children and their parents used to get excited about seeing the animals and their trainers go through dance routines and play with balls and hoops. Sheepdog trials show us what an amazing bond there can be between a man and a dog. Dogs can also learn how to walk, how to stand, how to show themselves off in dog shows like Crufts. Hours and hours are spent teaching these animals tricks. Yet God can control wild and hungry lions without having to train them. Daniel was thrown into a pit full of very hungry lions. Yet God would not allow them to eat him. He shut their mouths! You can be sure, however, that when Daniel's enemies were thrown in, God opened the lions' mouths. In fact, the men were torn to pieces before they had even landed at the bottom of the pit.

King Darius had been tricked into putting Daniel in the lion pit. Yet he knew Daniel's God was a great God. He encouraged Daniel. 'Your God, whom you serve continually, will deliver you', he said. And he was right. God could and did deliver Daniel. You and I may never be thrown to lions. But God can deliver us from any problem or danger if He wants to. And that is simply because He is God. Trust Him.

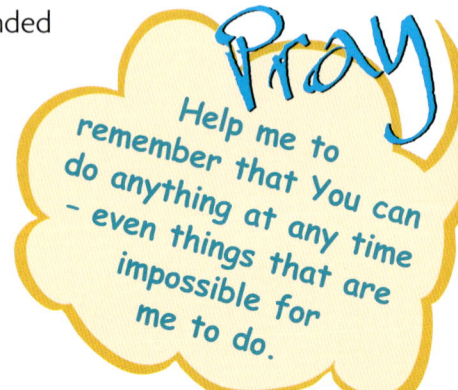

Pray
Help me to remember that You can do anything at any time – even things that are impossible for me to do.

164   Stepping stones

Reading: *Ezra 1. 1-11*

June 12

The king's heart is in the hand of the Lord, like the rivers of water; He turns it wherever He wishes, Proverbs 21. 1

God had warned the Israelites that they would be taken away from their own land if they worshipped other gods. They did not believe He would do it but He did. Most of them ended up living far away in a land where they could not worship God in their usual way. They had no temple so they built synagogues, places where they could read God's word together. As they read, some of them noticed that God had promised to bring His people back to Jerusalem after seventy years. Would He keep this promise as well? But how could He do it?

Nothing is too hard for God. King Cyrus did not trust in the God of the Israelites. He believed there were many gods and there were many people living in his kingdom who had been taken away from their own countries. Yet one day everyone was amazed to hear the town crier shout out, 'Hear ye! Hear ye! The Lord God of heaven has commanded me to build Him a house in Jerusalem'. 'What was that?', they asked. 'Could you say that again?' 'Jerusalem? Why Jerusalem?'

Pray: You are the great God who can do whatever You wish. You can even make unbelievers do Your will. Help me to worship You for Your greatness.

The town crier carried on. 'King Cyrus commands all God's people either to go back to Jerusalem or to give donations to those who are going back to build the house of the Lord God in Jerusalem'. God had done it. He had kept His promise. The seventy years were up and He had arranged for the people not just to go back but to be sent back with the king's permission.

God can make believers do His will. He can make animals, birds and fish to do His will. He can even make people who don't believe in Him to do His will. Now that's power! Do we do His will?

... through the Bible day by day

June 13

Reading: Ezra 3

If my people who are called by My name will humble themselves . . . then I will . . . forgive their sin and heal their land,
2 Chronicles 7. 14

The long caravan of horses, donkeys and camels carrying over forty-two thousand people wound its way through the dust to Jerusalem. The leader of the expedition, Zerubabbel, was taking some of the Israelites back to the land to re-build the temple. Those who could not return, or who did not want to, donated gold, silver and jewels. It was going to be a very expensive building project. What was even more exciting was that they were carrying with them the special plates and cups that had been reserved for use in God's temple only. These had been taken away by Nebuchadnezzar when he had destroyed the temple and Jerusalem. King Cyrus was now sending them back and the people were thrilled.

Pray
Help me to put Your interests before mine at all times.

When they got back to Jerusalem, however, they had a shock. Many of the people had never seen Jerusalem before. The city walls were ruined, the beautiful houses were burnt-out shells and there was almost nothing left of the wonderful temple. But they got to work. They rebuilt the altar and started to offer sacrifices to God once again. They bought beautiful timber and paid people to cut new blocks of stone to rebuild the foundations. And then they celebrated! The foundation of the temple had been relaid. The walls were next.

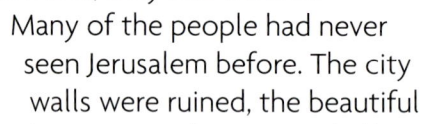

As they celebrated some sang but some of the older ones cried. Did they cry because they were happy that the work had begun? Or did they cry because they remembered how beautiful Solomon's temple had been and they realized this new one would never be so good? Yet it was still a wonderful day. God's temple was being used again. The people had learned their lesson. Putting God first is the best thing anyone can do in his life. Have we learned that lesson?

Reading: **Ezra 4. 1-7, 13-24**

June 14

Satan hindered us, 1 Thessalonians 2. 18

God had promised He would bring His people back when they had shown they were sorry that they had disobeyed Him. He had made King Cyrus send them back and He had kept them safe. The Jews were excited that they had begun to rebuild the temple but the people living round about them were not. They tried to stop the work by offering to help. When the Jews said, 'No thanks!' they bothered and troubled them until King Cyrus died. Then they wrote letters to the new king. 'Do you know what is going on in Jerusalem?' they asked. 'The Jews are rebuilding the temple and the city. But these Jews are trouble makers. You had better look at your history books to find out'.

So King Darius did just that. Then he sent a reply to them. 'You are quite right,' he said. 'These people have always been a nuisance. I give you permission to go up to Jerusalem and to stop the work.' You can imagine how quickly the enemies of God's people went up to stop the rebuilding and how they laughed that they had got their own way.

The devil was behind this. He has always tried to stop God's work from being done. He even caused trouble in the garden of Eden, right in the very beginning of the history of this world. You can be sure he was going to do his best to stop God from being worshipped in Jerusalem again.

The Jews stopped building. Instead of trusting God to look after them and keep them safe they gave up. Many people around us today do not want God's work to be done. But let us trust in God to keep us safe and get on with doing His work.

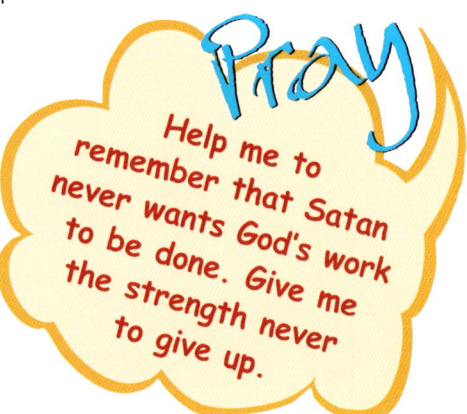

Pray
Help me to remember that Satan never wants God's work to be done. Give me the strength never to give up.

. . . through the Bible day by day

June 15

Reading: Ezra 5. 1; Haggai 1

Is it time for you yourselves to dwell in your panelled houses and this temple to lie in ruins? Haggai 1. 4

God had to do something to shake His people up. They had given up re-building the temple and had settled down. Perhaps during the first year or so as they passed the half-finished temple they felt guilty about it. 'Didn't God send us back to rebuild this?' 'Yes, but its dangerous work, you know. We could get killed for doing that. Besides, it's against the law'. So God sent Haggai and Zechariah to speak to them. 'What right have you to live in your smart houses, when my house is ruined?' asked God.

The people felt guilty. So they wrote another letter to the king and started the work again. Their enemies were not happy and tried to stop them. But this time they could not. The king even sent another letter to the enemies of the Jews saying this time they had to help them. God had looked after His people. Perhaps, if they had allowed Him to, this would have happened in the first place.

It is easy for any of us to put our own interests before God's. It is easy for us all to get used to things. Perhaps your local church is not doing very well. Instead of praying about it and trying to do our best to strengthen it, we just get used to it. School, play, hobbies, friends even houses become more important to us. The lesson we should learn from Haggai is that we should always put the things of God first. Then He will bless us in amazing ways.

Some tell us that we can find joy by putting **J**esus first, **O**thers second, **Y**ou last. They are quite right. Let's always do that.

Pray

Help me not to be discouraged when I find it hard to work for You. Give me strength to do Your will even though others may be against me.

Reading: **Nehemiah 1-2**

June 16

I told them of the hand of my God which had been good upon me, Nehemiah 2.18

The story of Nehemiah is quite amazing. We learn that he was good at praying because when he hears that the city of Jerusalem is in a dreadful state with the walls all tumbled down and the gates burned he sits down and cries, doesn't eat for days and then prays. What would we do if we received any bad news?

Nehemiah worked for the king of Persia. He had a very special job. He was responsible for the king's wine. He was serving the king when the king noticed that Nehemiah looked sad. The king thought something was wrong and demanded to know what was up. Nehemiah remembered how God had rescued His people in the past and that made him feel that God would help him now. So, with a quick prayer to God, he told the king about the state of his city. To his great surprise the king said, 'How can I help?' God answered Nehemiah's prayers that day. The king gave him permission to go to Jerusalem, soldiers for a safe journey and materials for the re-building of Jerusalem.

Nehemiah knew that the Lord's hand was helping him. When he arrived in Jerusalem he toured the walls alone and found things were worse than he had been told. However, he only talked to God about the matter. When he had seen for himself the condition of things he told the leaders and officials he had come to rebuild the city walls. Some were glad but others laughed, so he told them how God had guided his way and how the king had helped him. When they heard this they were all keen to start the work. We, too, can trust God to guide us in every problem, if we ask Him.

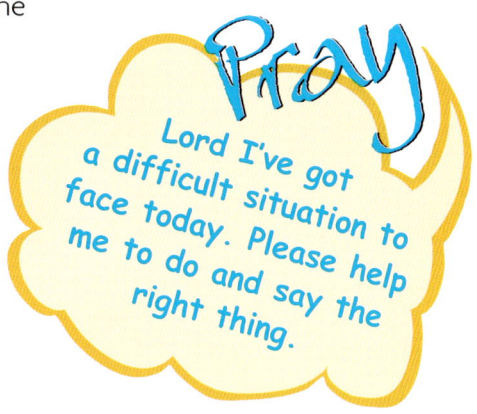

Pray

Lord I've got a difficult situation to face today. Please help me to do and say the right thing.

...through the Bible day by day

June 17

Reading: **Nehemiah 4**

Do not be afraid of them. Remember the Lord, great and awesome, Nehemiah 4. 14

Pray
Lord, I want to do something for You. I am willing, so please use me. Help me to stand up for what is right.

So the walls of Jerusalem were rebuilt. It is amazing to see how all sorts of people helped rebuild the walls and repair the gates. There were priests, goldsmiths, merchants, and rulers as well as ordinary people, men, women, young and old. All played their part. There will always be something for us to do for Him if we are willing.

God uses all kinds of people to fulfil His plans but there is always someone who will turn against us. Sanballat, a local leader, heard what was happening and laughed at the people as they worked. Tobiah, his friend, jokingly said that if a fox walked over the walls they would collapse!

Others were so angry they planned to frighten the workers by attacking them and so stopping them work.

What could Nehemiah do? He prayed first and then set a guard around the city to stop any attack. Remember that, though we ask God for help, we may need to do something ourselves and not expect Him to do everything for us. Nehemiah thought about the situation and then told the people not to be afraid of the enemy. 'Remember the Lord who is great and glorious', he said. Nehemiah was a good leader, dedicated and determined. So armed guards took watch in turns while others worked at building. They worked from sunrise to sunset. They didn't even take off their clothes to go to sleep and they carried their weapons ready at all times. This is how determined they were to see the building completed.

It is good to be committed when we do things for God. Let's give it all our hearts and minds. Put on His armour of faith and truth. God's word is also a great sharp sword that we can use against all foes.

Stepping stones

Reading: **Nehemiah 6. 1-9**

June 18

Now therefore, O God, strengthen my hands, Nehemiah 6. 9

Nehemiah had finished rebuilding the walls and was busy putting in the gates when suddenly the people had a problem. With the end in sight and everyone so happy, Nehemiah's enemies seemed determined to cause trouble. Out of the blue, they asked him if he would meet them to talk. Nehemiah was wise enough to realize that they didn't have anything good in mind. So, he said he couldn't possibly stop, as he was 'doing a great work'. Often, when we are serving God, there is someone or something that will try to distract us. If we know we are doing what God wants us to do then we need to watch that we are not side-tracked.

Pray
Lord, help me to tell the truth even if friends tell lies about me.

Sanballat, Tobiah and Geshem sent four times, asking the same thing. Nehemiah didn't respond. The fifth time they sent him a letter. In it they accused him of plotting a rebellion and intending to make himself a king. They said Nehemiah's prophets had been paid to tell lies and prophesy to make the people believe things would come true. They also said that if reports got back to the king about these things then Nehemiah would be in very great trouble indeed.

All these accusations were, of course, lies and Nehemiah knew that they were only trying to frighten him and to stop the work. Whatever Nehemiah was doing, whether he was under pressure, sad, or frightened, he always seemed to know he could turn to God for help. Once again, he prayed.

We too will find it the same no matter what others may say against us or twist things around to make it look as if we are in the wrong. If we are doing God's work we need to carry on and do the right thing. This always wins in the end.

. . . through the Bible day by day

June 19

Reading: **Nehemiah 8**

They read distinctly from the book, in the Law of God; and they gave the sense, and helped them to understand the reading, Nehemiah 8. 8

What an incredible man Nehemiah was! Despite all the opposition he so encouraged the people that the walls of Jerusalem were repaired and the gates hung in only a few months. His enemies lied and tried to turn him aside from his work but he kept his eye on the goal and, with God's help, succeeded. This done, he appointed men to govern the city. They were good men and known to fear God. Guards stood on duty at the gates but everyone was on the watch for their enemies. It is good to be successful but we should always be on our guard for the things which may trip us up and cause us to sin.

When everyone had settled into their towns again, Nehemiah called all the people together to listen to the book of the Law of Moses being read by Ezra the scribe. Ezra stood on a platform specially prepared for the occasion and read every morning. The Levites, Ezra's helpers, explained things for those who didn't understand. Everyone listened very carefully and cried when they heard the words. 'Don't be sad', said Nehemiah, 'Be happy and celebrate. Share what you have with those who have nothing. Rejoice, for we have heard God's words and will do what He says'.

So they made a feast and the resulting festival was called 'Shelters' because the people built little tents from tree branches and camped outside their houses. Everyone carried out the instructions and they were all full of happiness and praised God for His goodness to them.

Let us learn how important it is to read God's word and to listen to His voice and obey. Then we will be filled with great happiness as all the people at Jerusalem were on that day.

Pray

Lord, help me as I read Your word, to listen to Your voice, and obey so that I will be truly happy in Your love.

Stepping stones

Reading: **Esther 3. 1-11**

June 20

Who knows whether you have come to the kingdom for such a time as this? Esther 4. 14

Although the name of God isn't mentioned in the book of Esther it is clear that God is working behind the events. He is watching over His people, who were the Jews at this time, although it looks at the beginning of the story as if they are going to suffer terribly.

Pray

Lord, help me to obey my parents even though I may find it hard at the time.

Esther and her uncle Mordecai, who were Jews, lived in the land of Persia where Ahasuherus was king. One day the king gave a banquet to show off to his subjects. It lasted six months! He also wanted to show off his beautiful Queen, Vashti, but she refused to be put on show. The king was angry and asked advice from his councillors. They suggested that Vashti should be banished, sent out of the country never to return, as an example to other women. The king should find a new queen.

Mordecai was like a father to Esther and suggested that his beautiful niece be put forward as a possible queen. First, he told her to keep it secret that she was a Jew. Esther did what Mordecai said. Amazingly, she was chosen and became Queen. The king also promoted Haman, his favourite courtier, to be his Prime Minister.

Everyone bowed to Haman to show respect but Mordecai refused to do so. His reason was that, being a Jew, he bowed only before God. Haman was furious and decided that somehow he would kill all the Jews and Mordecai with them. He told the king about this race of people, the Jews, who had their own laws and didn't obey the king's laws. He suggested that they should be destroyed. The king agreed, gave Haman his ring and said, 'Go ahead, do what you like with these people'. Was God still in control do you think?

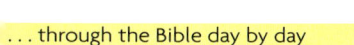

. . . through the Bible day by day

June 21

Reading: **Esther 6. 1-11**

Our God is in heaven; He does whatever He pleases, Psalm 115. 3

At the end of Esther chapter 2 we read that Mordecai was loyal to the king. He discovered that the guards to the king's private quarters were plotting to assassinate him. Mordecai passed this information on to Queen Esther and the plot was foiled. It was all recorded in the king's official diary but nothing more was done about it.

One night the king couldn't sleep so he asked for this official diary to be read to him. What do we do when we can't sleep? The king used his time wisely. We, too, could read or talk to the Lord, couldn't we? That night the king discovered that Mordecai had never been rewarded for his loyalty. 'We must do something about this', he said and the next day he sought the advice of Haman, his Prime Minister.

Now Haman was a very proud man and had big ideas about himself. It is never a good idea to think too much of yourself. He immediately thought that the king was going to reward him for something. He dreamt up the best reward he could think of and what could be better than wearing the king's robe, riding the king's horse and wearing the royal emblem on his head? That's almost as good as being the king himself. So he suggested this to the king, and it was immediately received with enthusiasm. 'Ideal', said the king. 'Go and do exactly as you have said to Mordecai the Jew!' So Haman was forced to lead Mordecai through the streets shouting, 'This is what happens to the man the king delights to honour'. Haman must have felt dreadfully humiliated. Be careful, because pride always brings a fall!

Pray

Lord, help me to leave things in Your hands rather than try to arrange matters myself.

Stepping stones

Reading: Esther 7

June 22

By transgression an evil man is snared, but the righteous sings and rejoices,
Proverbs 29. 6

Don't get worried. Haman won't win. God is still looking after His people. Esther's place in the palace was part of God's plan to save her people.

Have you ever wondered why Esther prepared a banquet for the king *and* Haman? She wanted to ask the king to save her people but did not know how he would answer. Was she trying to lull Haman into a false sense of security? She knew the king loved her, so possibly a banquet wouldn't make much difference to him and he had promised her half of his kingdom.

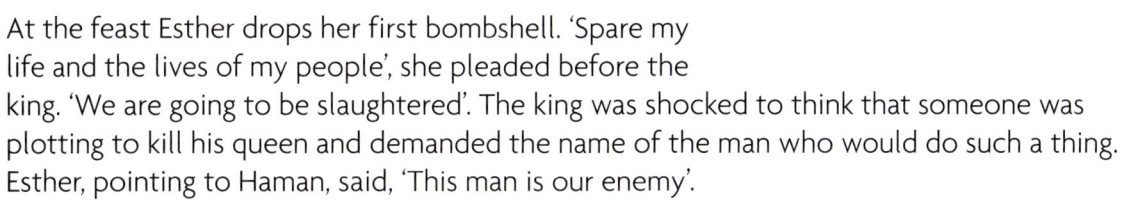

At the feast Esther drops her first bombshell. 'Spare my life and the lives of my people', she pleaded before the king. 'We are going to be slaughtered'. The king was shocked to think that someone was plotting to kill his queen and demanded the name of the man who would do such a thing. Esther, pointing to Haman, said, 'This man is our enemy'.

The king was in such a rage that he went into the garden to calm down. Inside the palace, a frightened Haman knew he was doomed, but pleaded for his life to the queen. He fell on to the couch where Queen Esther was lying. The king, returning just at that moment, believed Haman was assaulting the queen. Things could not have looked worse for Haman.

One of the king's men had already told the king that Haman had prepared some gallows for Mordecai the Jew, the very same man the king had just honoured for saving him from assassination. 'Hang Haman on his own gallows', orders the king. So they did and the king's anger was satisfied and the Jews were saved.

Haman received his just deserts for God has said, 'Be sure your sins will find you out'.

Pray

Lord, help me to trust in Your word and remember that all things work together for my good.

. . . through the Bible day by day

June 23

Reading: Malachi 3. 1-3

I am the LORD, I do not change, Malachi 3. 6

It seems so sad. After the Jews had rebuilt the temple and the priests were serving God properly things began to go backwards. It can be the same for us. When all is going well we can become self-satisfied, forget God and go our own way again.

Pray

Lord, I want to come back to You. I am sorry for all the wrong things I have done.

The Jews forgot God's way and goodness in the past. God was not pleased with the priests. They offered sick and crippled animals for sacrifice, turned aside from God's clear instructions saying, 'Anything will do'. They failed to give Him what they should. The people married heathen wives and wondered why God didn't hear their prayers. They tired God by constantly saying prayers that meant nothing and refusing to bring any gifts to Him. They even argued with Him and His messenger. Malachi openly complained at their failure.

Although things were bad God had some good news for them. He was going to send a messenger who would announce the arrival of the Messiah. He promised, in the meantime, that if they returned to Him He would open heaven's windows and pour out on them such blessing that there wouldn't be room enough to take it all in.

Even though they failed God, He still loved them. God is waiting to bless us too if we return to Him. Some of the people did respond and these met together to talk about their Lord and His promises. God was so pleased that He wrote their names down in a book and called them His own special treasure. Just as Malachi told the people in his times, so we need to turn to God and admit we have sinned before He will forgive. We can do the wrong things, too, but as for God He never stops loving us.

Stepping stones

Reading: **Psalm 1**

June 24

He shall be like a tree planted by the rivers of water, that brings forth fruit in his season, Psalm 1. 3

If you want to do something for God and please Him in your life, if you want to get the best out of your life here and not care what people think about you, then you need to become a Psalm One Person! This is because Psalm 1 tells us exactly how to get this. We should read God's word everyday and think about it all the time. This is not easy and it takes practice. If we take just one verse with us through the day and think about it when we have a spare moment, it will give us great joy. This will help us do what God wants and we will really feel good about life.

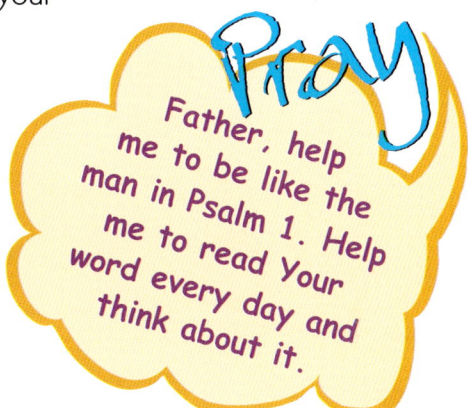

Pray

Father, help me to be like the man in Psalm 1. Help me to read Your word every day and think about it.

The word *'man'* means anyone - boy, girl, man or woman. A Psalm One Person doesn't follow the advice of those who don't know God nor stand around with those who do wrong or those who mock at God. God will judge and condemn these people one day. They are heading for destruction. Instead, we should make friends with God's children. We will stand out and be different but we can encourage and help each other. It is difficult to realize it, but it is not the road we travel along that is the most important, it is where that road leads to that is!

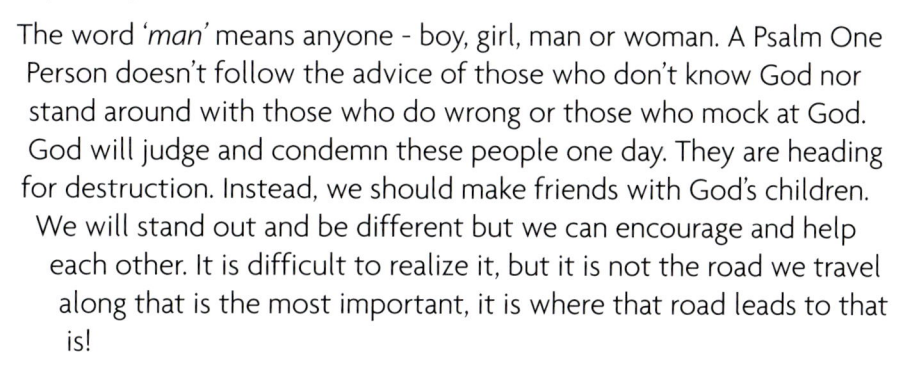

It's lovely to think that God is watching over everything we do if we belong to Him. What a pleasure it is to bring joy to God's heart day by day as we follow the path He wants us to go by, listen to His word and think about it. Psalm One People make God every thing and He is so very happy when we do. What can be better than that?

...through the Bible day by day

June 25

Reading: **Psalm 8**

O LORD, our Lord, how excellent is Your name in all the earth, Psalm 8. 9

This is a Psalm that really makes us say, 'Thank You' to God for all His wonderful creation. However young you are you can't help marvelling at God's colour box or His variety seen in the animals and plants that live on our planet. How we wonder at the frightening power of a storm, too. This is God's earth and our home. Surely even people who don't believe in God must ask, 'Who made this?' We look at the night sky and see the moon and the stars that were made by God's fingers and we feel their cold majesty. It makes us say to ourselves, 'Why should God think of me? Why should God care for me? I am so small and minute compared to His creation.'

God spoke to Job about our smallness. He said, 'Can you hold back the movement of the stars? Are you able to restrain Pleiades or Orion? Can you guarantee the proper sequence of the seasons or guide the constellation of the Bear with her cubs across the heavens? Do you know the laws of the universe and how God rules the earth?' Job 3. 8. Of course we can't but God does every moment.

It just makes us bow and worship Him to think that He cares for us far more than anything else He has made. We are so different to all else that He put us in charge of everything He has made. We have charge over everything, sheep, cattle, the wild animals, birds in the sky, fish in the sea and all things in the ocean. We should take great care of all He has given us and say, 'Thank you, Lord for trusting us with Your wonderful world.'

Pray

Thank You, Lord for all the wonderful things that You have made. Help me never to stop being amazed by it all.

Stepping stones

Reading: Psalm 19

June 26

Your words were found, and I ate them, and Your Word was to me the joy and rejoicing of my heart, Jeremiah 15. 16

God has different ways of talking to us. This psalm tells us how God's creation, although silent, is still one way He uses to tell people everywhere about Himself. The message the heavens and the skies tell us is of God's marvellous craftsmanship. All men in the world see it every day. Look at the sun. It remains where God put it yet it travels across the sky, daily rising and setting, as we see it. It is like a bridegroom greeting his bride on their wedding day or like an athlete running a race. Nothing can hide from its warmth. It tells us of God's unchanging faithfulness.

Pray

Help me to say and think the things that will please You. Help me to remember that You hear everything I say.

David, who wrote this psalm, also tells us why we should read God's word, which is another way God speaks to us. He calls it by different names – laws, decrees and commands – to show us how varied it is. He says God's words are complete, to be trusted without doubting, always right, simple to be understood, clean, true, fair and desirable. There's no other book like it!

But what does God's word do for us? Well it makes us wise when we need advice, if we're down it lifts us up, and it brings joy into our hearts. His word lasts forever, so God's words are much better than lots of money and bring us into the best things in life! These words will warm us and reward us.

What do we do about sin in our life? His word will show us even our hidden faults as well as our deliberate sins. It tells us what we can do about our guilt by asking God to wash it away. It will teach us how to bring pleasure to God. God's creation is a treasure, but so is His Word.

. . . through the Bible day by day

June 27

Reading: **Psalm 23**

I am the good shepherd; and I know My sheep, and am known by My own, John 10. 14

Psalm 23 is perhaps the best known of all the psalms. Many people have heard it read at special occasions. Most churches quote it often and a lot of people have learnt it off by heart.

David who wrote it was a shepherd himself so he had first-hand experience of how a shepherd would care for his sheep. If we belong to the Lord, He is our Shepherd and looks after us. What else do we need if we have Him? As a shepherd will rest his flock in the green meadows and by peaceful streams, so we too can rest quietly in the care of the Lord Jesus. Our Shepherd will guide us along the right paths and even when we face death or unhappy times, there is no reason to be afraid. Our Shepherd is close beside us. He will look after us and protect us from those things that would harm us.

The shepherd would provide a safe place for his sheep to feed, looking out for the best grass and keeping watch for dangerous wild animals. He used oil to heal their wounds, scratches and bruises. He would carefully examine the condition of sheep and refreshes and restores them when they need it.

As the Lord is our Shepherd, we can rest in the fact that He keeps just as careful a watch over us. He binds up our wounds when we are hurt, He makes us feel good and keeps us under His protection all the days of our lives. We need to remain close to the Shepherd and listen out for His voice. To know God in this way is to be safe and satisfied.

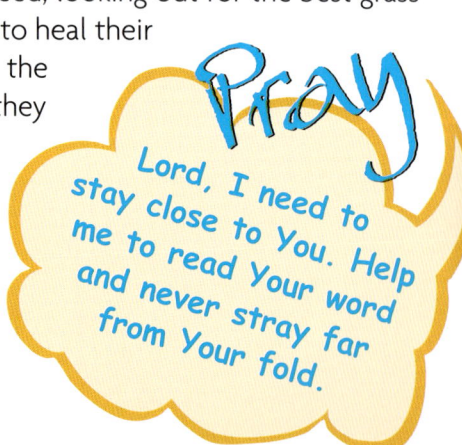

Pray

Lord, I need to stay close to You. Help me to read Your word and never stray far from Your fold.

Reading: Psalm 34

June 28

Taste and see that the Lord is good,
Psalm 34. 8

Have you ever been really scared about something? It isn't a comfortable feeling, is it?

David wrote this psalm at a time when he was running away from King Saul who wanted to kill him. David went to see Abimelech the priest for help. This man gave David and his friends bread to eat and he also gave them giant Goliath's sword. David then took shelter with king Achish of Gath but, realizing that the king had recognized him and he was in great danger, he pretended to be mad. When King Achish saw David behaving so stupidly he decided he didn't want a mad man as a guest so David was able to escape to a cave. This is when he wrote this 'Thank You' psalm to God for answering his prayers, freeing him from his fears and saving his life. Although he was anxious and worried David never forgot how great God was, remembered how He rescued him and thanked Him for being there when he needed Him.

We too can be sure God will help us when we need Him. That is what David encourages us to believe in this psalm.

In the second half of the psalm David teaches us how to live for God. Do you want to live a long and good life? Here's the way to do it. Watch what you say, don't tell lies, turn away from evil, do good whenever you can and work hard at living peacefully. Then you will be blessed in so many ways. The eyes of the Lord do watch over us and He hears when we cry to Him for help. He does rescue us from trouble and protect us from harm. He cares for the broken-hearted!

Pray

Father, hear me when I cry to You for help. Help me to trust You whatever is happening to me, for I know You love me very dearly.

... through the Bible day by day

June 29

Reading: Psalm 51

Blessed is he whose transgression is forgiven, whose sin is covered, Psalm 32.1

Pray

Father, I want to ask forgiveness for all the wrong things I have done. I believe Jesus took my punishment in my place. Help me to live for You day by day.

David pours out his heart to God. He is asking for forgiveness for some terrible things he had done. He had sinned by loving another man's wife, called Bathsheba, and he had plotted the murder of her husband. We can hear his agony in the words of the psalm and sense how distressed he feels at the terrible weight of his crimes. He knows God's love never fails and His care for him was great, so he begs for mercy.

He wants the stain of his sin blotted out and his guilt washed away. He tells God how bad he has been and that he can't sleep at night. He knows that he has sinned against other people but most importantly he has sinned against God. He knows that God sees everything and that he should be punished for what he has done. He wants to feel clean and to be happy again with his relationship with God put back on track.

We can learn so many valuable lessons from David's actions in this psalm. Like David we need to confess our sins for God is willing to forgive us. Romans chapter 3 verse 25 says that God sent Jesus to take the punishment for our sins and to die in our place. We are made right with God when we take the Lord Jesus as our Saviour. Daily from then on we can ask, like David did, for wisdom and for joy. The Holy Spirit will help us to keep away from sinning as we live lives obedient to God's Word and tell others about our Saviour. God doesn't want sacrifices and burnt offerings but a heart that is broken and deeply sorry about sin. Are we ever that sorry?

Stepping stones

Reading: Psalm 91

June 30

He is my refuge and my fortress; my God, in Him I will trust, Psalm 91. 2

This is a lovely psalm that encourages us to trust in God. It is only when we do this that we can be kept in peace and away from harm.

Moses probably wrote it at the beginning of the 38 years the Israelites spent wandering in the wilderness. Moses was their leader and if ever there was a man who needed God's protecting care it was him. To lead thousands of people through the unknown desert while they continually moaned and groaned at him because of their difficulties was a great undertaking. Moses needed all the help he could get.

The promises in this psalm, whether for Moses or for us, are amazing. As we make the Lord our hiding place and rest in Him, we can enjoy these promises. God becomes our refuge from danger so we don't need to be afraid of whatever is happening around us or fear any disaster, even though it surrounds us. No evil will touch us as God guarantees our safety.

Pray

Lord, help me to trust You in everything I do. I do love You and I want to claim Your protection.

The promises of God are like armour. They shield, shelter and protect us. Those who love Me, says the Lord, 'I will protect and rescue. When they call, I will answer. When they are in trouble, I will be with them. They will be satisfied with a long life'. We will not escape the trials of life but if we trust the Lord and make Him our shelter in the storms we will know He will not leave us. He is there for us all the time. He promised He would be.

What else do we need? What more do we want? In His love and providing, we are safe from everything. He does take care of His people as we make Him our first priority.

. . . through the Bible day by day

July 1

Reading: Psalm 103

He has not dealt with us according to our sins, nor punished us according to our iniquities, Psalm 103. 10

What a great and merciful God we have! A God who shows mercy is a God who doesn't give us what we deserve. In this wonderful psalm King David takes us on a journey to heaven and around the world to show us how good and kind our God is.

Have you ever travelled right around the world? Probably not. If you were to travel around the world at its widest point – that's the equator – you would cover a distance of 24,902 miles. That's a very long way. In fact if you boarded a Jumbo Jet and travelled at 600 mph it would take you nearly two days to cover the whole distance. David tells us that God has removed our sins as far as the east is from the west, verse 12. That's further than travelling round the world because if you set off east you will always be travelling east and never begin to travel west. You could go round the world millions of times and still never have gone west. In other words God has removed our sins so far away that the distance cannot be measured!

When does God take our sins so far away? The very moment we repent – turn away from them – and trust the Lord Jesus to be our Saviour. Our memory verse tells us that God does not want to punish us for our sins. God is a merciful God and wants to rescue and save us. To do this He sent His Son the Lord Jesus down from heaven to take the punishment we deserved and make it possible for us to be in heaven. Once we trust Him, no matter how many times we travel around the earth we will never be able to find our sins again!

Pray

Thank God for His great mercy in removing your sins so far away that they can never come back to trouble you.

184   Stepping stones

Reading: Psalm 119. 1-40

July 2

How can a young man cleanse his way? By taking heed according to Your word, Psalm 119. 9

Are you wholehearted in everything that you do? Sportsmen or women who are totally committed to their sport are wholehearted. They put all their time and effort into what they love and like to do best. The Lord wants us to be just the same when it comes to His word and work. He longs for us to be wholehearted for Him.

> **Pray**
> Ask the Lord to help you find the time to read the Bible every day.

This wonderful psalm, which is all about God's Word, tells us that there are real blessings available from the Lord for those who seek Him with their whole heart! Take a look at verse 2. 'Blessed are those who keep His testimonies, who seek Him with the whole heart'. The Lord says that those who obey His word and follow Him with their whole heart will be blessed! It would be good each day to know the Lord's blessing upon our lives in school, at home, when we meet with other Christians and in everything else we do. Again in verse 10, the writer says, 'With my whole heart I have sought You'. He longs for the blessing of God in his life. Read through the rest of these verses and you will discover that the secret of real blessing from God is to spend time carefully reading His Word, the Bible, every day.

'God's Word is a lamp to my feet and a light to my path', verse 105. As we read it, God will show us wonderful things to help us in our everyday life.

However, we need to do more than read it daily. We must try to remember what we have read and put it into practice on a daily basis. Should we not decide now to be wholehearted in finding time to read the Bible every day? We should also be wholehearted in trying to put into practice what we have read. Real commitment to God will bring us real blessing from God.

...through the Bible day by day

July 3

Reading: Psalm 119. 41-64

Your word is a lamp to my feet and a light to my path, Psalm 119. 105

How often do you read the Bible for yourself? Perhaps you have a time with your family when your parents read the Bible to you and pray with you. If you do that is great, but you really need to read the Bible for yourself if you are going to make progress as a Christian. In Psalm 119 verse 42 the writer says, 'I trust in Your word'. God's word meant everything to him.

Not only does he trust God's word but in verse 47 he says, 'I will delight myself in Your commandments, which I love'. That means that he was far more interested in God's word than anything else. Do we love the Bible above everything else? More than sport, entertainment, even our friends and family?

Only by reading the Bible daily can God continually lead us and guide us in our lives down here. Our memory verse describes God's word as being like a 'lamp to my feet'. An old-fashioned oil lamp would give just enough light for us to take one step at a time. So the Bible gives us just enough light to guide us as we walk daily with the Lord. But the psalmist goes on to describe God's word as being a 'light to my path'. This describes a light that shines out into the distance lighting up the way ahead. God's word not only guides us on a daily basis but shines light out into the distance and gives us a little look at what could happen in the future.

Do we read the Bible daily and love it above anything else? It is the main way that God uses to guide us in our Christian lives.

Pray: Ask the Lord to show you from the Bible what He wants you to do for Him today.

Stepping stones

Reading: Psalm 139. 1-13

July 4

There is no creature hidden from His sight, but all things are naked and open to the eyes of Him to whom we must give account, Hebrews 4. 13

Have you ever played hide and seek with your friends? Was there ever a time when you found such a good hiding place that no one was able to find you no matter how hard they looked? Wasn't it great to hear your friends calling your name whilst you were well hidden out of sight knowing that you could never be discovered. Our first parents Adam and Eve tried to hide from God when they first sinned in the Garden of Eden. We can read about that in Genesis chapter 3 verse 8.

Of course you and I know that it is totally impossible to hide from God because He is a God who can see everything. That is what Psalm 139 is all about. The writer of this psalm tells us that no matter where we go or what we do God can see us and find us. Not only does God see us but He knows all about us. There is nothing that can be hidden from God! Whether we go into heaven or hell, into the depths of the sea or into the darkness of night God sees and knows everything.

Understanding that God knows everything about us and sees all that we do should make us very careful how we live. It will affect not only how we behave ourselves but also how we speak and where we go. We can hide things from our friends and even from our family but not from God. Our memory verse reminds us that nothing can be hidden from God and that one day we will have to answer to God for what we do. May this help us to be very careful how we live our lives.

Pray
Ask God for help to live your life knowing that He sees you, so that you will always try to avoid anything that will displease Him.

...through the Bible day by day

July 5

Reading: Psalm 139. 14-24

I will praise You, for I am fearfully and wonderfully made, Psalm 139. 14

You really are unique! There is nobody else quite like you in the whole world. You have around 60,000 miles of blood vessels in your body. The average person has over 100,000 hairs on their head. Messages travel from your brain throughout your body at about 170 miles per hour. If you live into old age your heart will have beaten over 3,000 million times and have pumped 48 million gallons of blood. That's not to mention the fact that you blink around 6,205,000 times each year and can sneeze at over 100 miles per hour. Wow! No wonder the writer of this psalm says, 'I am fearfully and wonderfully made'.

God the great creator made the human body in full working order when He created the first man Adam. How great and powerful is our God! However, God does not treat us as a builder does a house which he has built. Once he has sold it he has little further interest in it. Here the writer tells us God has a continuing interest and care for us. 'How precious also are Your thoughts to me, O God! How great is the sum of them!' verse 17. Even when Adam sinned God did not stop caring for His wonderful creation. He still longed that we might walk in the 'way everlasting' that leads to heaven. That's why God sent His Son the Lord Jesus allowing Him to die on a cross, suffering for our sins so that we could be forgiven and made fit for heaven.

We need to understand how serious our sin is, turn from it, and trust the Lord Jesus to save us. The God that made us loves us and longs to save us too.

Pray

Give thanks to God for His wonderful creation which you enjoy and for His constant love for you despite your sin.

Reading: **Proverbs 3. 1-10**

July 6

In all your ways acknowledge Him, and He shall direct your paths, Proverbs 3. 6

Do you enjoy reading? What are your favourite types of book? On the whole, boys like action or adventure stories and girls like stories about animals or even a love story. Maybe you like reading factual books about history or real life events. The Bible is a unique book that contains all of these types. In fact the Bible contains almost every type of story and event that you could imagine. God has put them there to teach and guide us as to how we should live for Him as believers.

King Solomon, who wrote the book of Proverbs, gives us advice on what our attitude should be to God's Word, the Bible. He tells us that we should always remember what God has written. 'Do not forget my law', he writes in verse 1. 'Write them on the tablet of your heart', he says in verse 3. If we try to memorize as much of the Bible as possible we will find it will help to guide us on a daily basis.

Pray

Lord, help me to memorize Your Word whilst I am still young, so that it will help to guide me in every event of my life.

The writer of Proverbs expects us to remember God's word but also to trust it and to trust God at all times. Look at verse 5, 'Trust in the Lord with all your heart, and lean not on your own understanding'. We need to remember that God's word is always right in what it teaches. The more we trust God and what He says the more we will be helped and guided in our Christian lives. It is, after all, through hearing the word of God that most of us were first saved, Romans 10. 17. Are we prepared to read God's word and trust it totally to guide us?

. . . through the Bible day by day

July 7

Reading: Proverbs 23. 15-26

My son, give me your heart, and let your eyes observe my ways, Proverbs 23. 26

Who controls your heart? Thinking about it, just what is your heart? In the Bible the heart means far more that just that 15cm by 10cm muscle that pumps 2,000 gallons of blood around your body each day. In God's word the heart speaks of your emotions (how you feel and react) as well as your will (what you want to do). Today we have read four things about the heart that, if obeyed will help us to avoid spiritual heart disease.

If we have a wise heart God will be happy, verse 15. To have a wise heart means that we need to think carefully about our thoughts and actions before we do anything. We are also told that we should not allow our hearts to envy sinners, verse 17. In other words we are not to look at what non-Christians have and want those things for ourselves. We are told to guide our hearts 'in the way', verse 19. This means that we should let God's word guide us in every decision that we need to make and not allow our own thoughts or ideas to control our lives.

Perhaps the most important of the four instructions given in this chapter of Proverbs is our verse for today where God says, 'Give me your heart, and let your eyes observe my ways'. God wants our hearts, our whole hearts and nothing but our hearts! What does this mean? It means that we'll make sure that everything we think, say, do, hear, and see will be what God wants. Have we given our wills totally over to God? If we have, God promises to guide us and help us.

Pray

Pray that the Lord will give you the help you need to allow Him to control every part of your life.

Stepping stones

Reading: Proverbs 4. 20-27

July 8

Whatever things are true ... noble ... just ... pure ... lovely, whatever things are of good report ... meditate on these things, Philippians 4. 8

What do you spend your spare time doing? Maybe you have an interest in sport, or in animals or perhaps you enjoy reading or listening to music? Do you like using the computer or riding a bike? King Solomon had tried everything at some time but found that every new thing he tried just made his life more empty and dull! He describes it all as 'vanity', or emptiness, Ecclesiastes chapter 2.

Pray
Ask the Lord to help you to be careful to think about only the things that will never lead you to sin.

How different are his words to what we have read today. God wants us to be wholly taken up with Him and His word. Therefore we must be very careful what we say, verse 24, what we see, verse 25 and where we go, verse 26. We will also be careful about what we do with any spare time that we have. There are certain things we may do which may not be wrong but do not encourage us to live for the Lord. The writer says, 'Ponder the path of your feet'. That means watch where our feet are leading us because as Christians it is so easy to go the wrong way and do the wrong thing. That is why the reading ended with, 'Remove your foot from evil' and began with, 'Pay attention to my words'. We must be so careful in our lives to avoid anything that is wrong and to do this we need the Bible to guide us.

In our memory verse today the great apostle Paul gives us some sound advice as to what we should be interested in without any fear of being connected with sin and evil. If we thought on these positive things more they would help us avoid the negative things that do not encourage us in living for God.

... through the Bible day by day

July 9

Reading: Proverbs 24. 30-34

As a door turns on its hinges, so does the lazy man on his bed, Proverbs 26. 14

Have you ever seen an overgrown garden where no one has bothered to cut the grass or do the weeding? Perhaps you know of a neglected house that has not been looked after where the paint is flaking off, the brickwork crumbling and the tiles broken? That's the idea King Solomon is trying to show us. This garden that the king saw belonged to a lazy man. The owner could not be bothered to get up and do any work in it as he preferred his sleep and rest to hard work.

We can all be lazy in one way or another at some time. Maybe we don't do our homework. Perhaps we can't be bothered to do our chores around the house. God does not want us to waste our time sleeping when we could be working for Him. Look how busy the Lord was when He was here on earth. No one was ever as busy as Him. Read Mark's Gospel chapter 1, verses 21 to 38. This chapter records one day in the life of the Lord. He taught, He healed, He cast out demons, He got up early to pray. The Lord was busy! Very busy! John writes that if everything the Lord had done was written down the world would not be big enough to contain all the books that would have to be written, John 21. 25.

There is plenty for us to do for the Lord. Each day as we pray and read the Bible we should ask, 'Lord what would You like me to do today?' The Lord will show us and help us in any task that He wants us to do for Him.

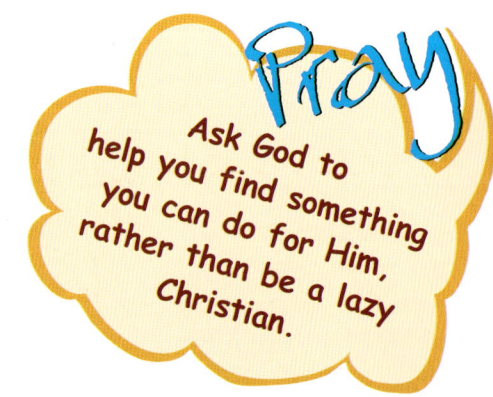

Pray

Ask God to help you find something you can do for Him, rather than be a lazy Christian.

Stepping stones

Reading: **Proverbs 6. 16-19**

July 10

I will set nothing wicked before my eyes; I hate the work of those who fall away,
Psalm 101. 3

Is there anything you really don't like? Some people hate certain foods. Perhaps there is something else that you really cannot stand to see or hear. God tells us of seven things that He does not like. In fact He says He hates them. What are they?

Pride is the first. Pride is thinking too much of ourselves or thinking that we are better than anyone else. God hates it! Telling lies, or not telling the truth, and being dishonest is another thing God hates. He expects Christians to be honest at all times.

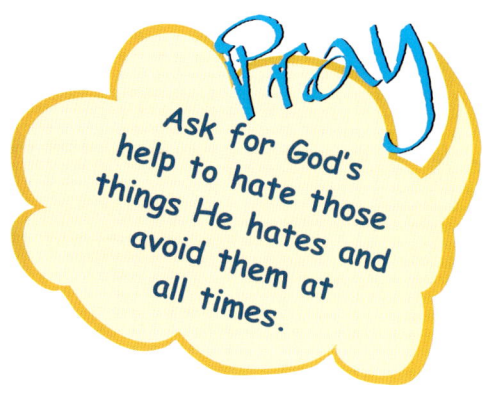

God hates murder too. Hopefully we will never kill anyone but perhaps we have said or thought, 'I could kill you'. Matthew chapter 5 verses 21 to 22 warn us about hate. Sometimes we imagine things that we know are wrong and it can be hard getting these thoughts out of our head. We must remember that God sees and knows everything and is willing to help us control our thoughts. Sometimes we know that what we are about to do is wrong but we still go ahead and do it anyway. Our feet run to mischief! Always ask, 'Would the Lord do this?' because that would help us avoid doing some of these things the Lord hates. Accusing someone falsely is not nice – deliberately telling lies so that we get others into trouble.

Lastly God says He hates those who cause trouble among brothers. These are people who deliberately cause trouble amongst other Christians perhaps by saying unkind things about them. We should always try to look for the best in each other.

If we could really understand how much God hates these seven sins we would avoid them in our lives and try to live in a way that pleases Him more.

> **Pray**
> Ask for God's help to hate those things He hates and avoid them at all times.

. . . through the Bible day by day

July 11

Reading: Proverbs 31. 10-31

He who finds a wife finds a good thing,
Proverbs 18. 22

Wow! What a wonderful lady we have described in this last chapter of Proverbs. Perhaps we could call her Super-mum! Not only is she a great mum to her children but a great wife to her husband as well. Just stop and think for a moment of what your mum does for you and the rest of your family each day. No doubt she will clean and tidy, wash and iron, do the shopping, run you on errands, prepare and cook the meals, read the Bible with you and pray with you as well as many other things she probably does for your dad! Have you ever stopped to thank her for doing all these things for you? More importantly have you ever stopped to thank God for your mum?

In this chapter of Proverbs we have a real role model of what the perfect mum and wife should be. She will always love her husband. Faithfulness to each other in marriage is something that most people in the world today are not too worried about. This model woman works hard for her husband and her family. She is wise in what she does with her money. She thinks of other needy people and tries to help them. She speaks only good, profitable and wholesome words. She works hard for her family to ensure that they have everything that they need. The result is that her children and her husband praise her and honour her.

Have a think today about all that your mother does for you and then thank her for it. You don't know what that might mean to your mum!

Pray
Thank God for your mother and all that she tries to do for you and the rest of the family.

Stepping stones

Reading: Luke 1. 5-25

July 12

When he came out, he could not speak to them; and they perceived that he had seen a vision in the temple, Luke 1. 22

Have you ever seen an angel? Almost certainly not, but Zacharias the priest saw an angel called Gabriel – and did not believe what the angel said! How about that! As a result Zacharias was told he would be unable to speak until the promise the angel brought had been fulfilled. Zacharias had to write things down in order to communicate with other people.

The angel spoke the first recorded words from heaven for four hundred years since the end of the Old Testament. What were they? 'Don't be afraid'. We know that if we trust God to take care of our problems and tell Him about them in prayer He will be with us and tell us, 'Don't be afraid', no matter how difficult they may be.

Zacharias and Elizabeth his wife had obviously at one time been praying for a baby. Sadly now they were old they had given up any hope of that prayer being answered. Then one day, as Zacharias was going about his usual job as a priest, God suddenly spoke to him through the angel who gave him the message that was to make him overjoyed. He was going to have a son after all and was told to name him John.

Poor Zacharias was so like us and did not believe what he was being told. He probably never expected that prayer to be answered anymore! It is good to know that every time we pray God does hear us. In His own time He can and will answer even in the most unexpected ways and at the most unusual times. It is good too to know that we can speak to God no matter where we are. Don't be afraid to take everything to the Lord in prayer.

Pray

Ask God to help you tell Him about everything in your life and give you the faith to trust Him to answer every one of your prayers.

... through the Bible day by day

July 13

Reading: Luke 1. 26-56

Mary said, 'Behold the maidservant of the Lord! Let it be to me according to your word', Luke 1. 38

Sometimes being a Christian is not easy and we must expect some opposition from our friends and even from our families. Mary must have had a shock when an angel visited her. Unlike Zacharias she believed what Gabriel told her about the baby boy that was going to be born to her. What a joy it must have been to hear that at last the Messiah God had promised was going to come into the world! What a thrill to know that He would be called 'the Son of the Highest'! And what a privilege for Mary to be told by the angel that she had been chosen to bear this child and bring Him into the world.

Pray

Ask for help from the Lord to make the right decisions that will please Him each time no matter what the final cost might be.

However, it was no easy thing for Mary to accept. She knew that some would accuse her of many wicked things that were not true. Mary was not married and in those days, unlike today, to have a baby without being married meant that you would be ignored and despised as well as whispered-about behind your back. In this brief meeting with the angel Gabriel Mary had to consider everything that would result if she accepted the privilege. What would Joseph think? How would he react? What would other family members think of her? What would the neighbours say about her?

After considering carefully all that might happen, Mary still said to Gabriel, 'Let it be to me according to your word'. It is always best to obey God in everything no matter what our friends or others might think and no matter how hard things may turn out. It is not easy but it is always best. Are we willing to obey God?

Stepping stones

Reading: **Matthew 1. 18-25**

July 14

Then Joseph, being aroused from sleep, did as the angel of the Lord commanded him and took to him his wife, Matthew 1. 24

Sometimes we can look at our lives and say, 'Life is just not fair. Why should this or that happen to me? Why did God allow that problem, that difficulty or that disaster to happen in my life?' Often we cannot answer these big and difficult questions. We have to look to God for the answers and for the courage to get through life despite the problems that He has allowed.

Perhaps Joseph felt a bit like that when he found out that Mary was expecting a baby that was not his! 'How will I cope? What should I do? It's not fair. Life was going so well. I was in love, expecting a wedding and looking forward to married life and now this happens'. Maybe these were some of the things Joseph was thinking about in verse 20. Just when everything was going well a disaster hit him and hit him hard. Joseph was not in a rush to make any decisions. He was taking his time about it. This was serious and needed serious thought.

Then it happened. A message came from heaven, an angelic vision! The baby was God's Son, the promised Saviour. Now Joseph had a real decision to make. Would he be willing to follow God, give the child the name he was instructed and accept the inevitable problems and difficulties that would go with such a decision? Joseph knew the answer and married Mary. If God is in a thing then nothing we do will be too much trouble as we try to obey Him.

Pray

It's important to obey God in everything, even when the results may upset your own plans and ambitions. Ask God for help to do that in your life.

... through the Bible day by day

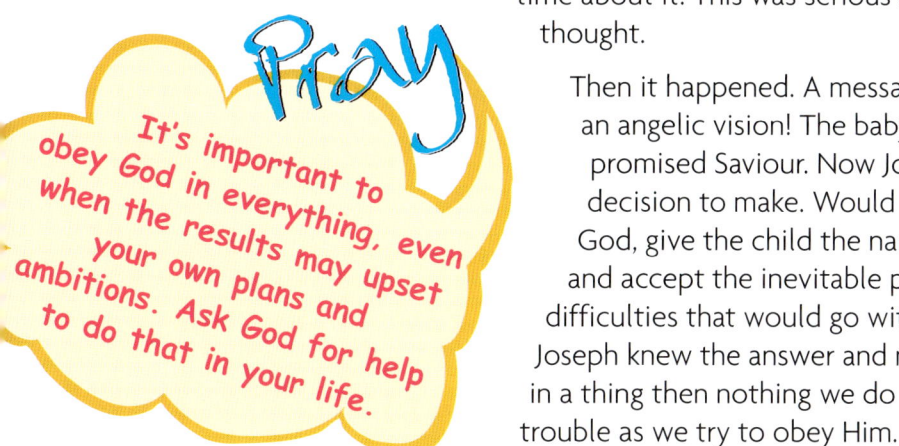

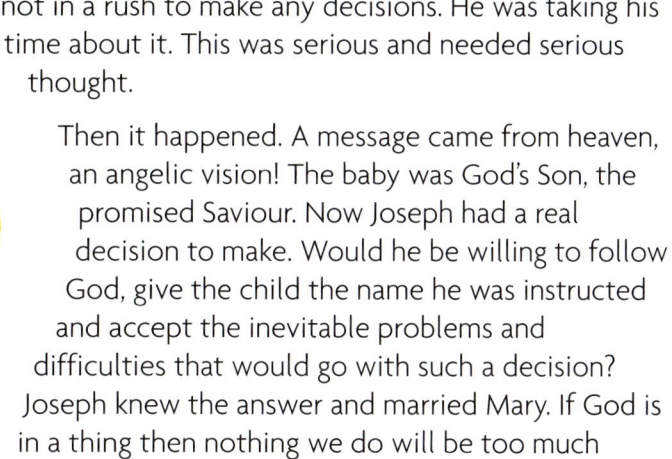

July 15

Reading: Luke 1. 57-80

You, child, will be called the prophet of the Highest; for you will go before the face of the Lord to prepare His ways,
Luke 1. 76

Have you ever tried to keep quiet just for one minute? How about a whole hour, a week or even a month? How long can you really keep quiet? Did you know that Zacharias had no choice but to keep quiet for over nine months? That takes some doing!

The reason Zacharias could not speak was that he had not believed the message he had received from the angel Gabriel. However, today we discover what Zacharias said after he had regained his speech. In fact what we have read is more of a song than a speech. He spoke about his son, whom he named John, and who would be the 'prophet of the Highest'. This child, who was later known as 'John the Baptist' would signal the arrival of the Lord Jesus who was the 'Son of the Highest'.

In olden days a man would go in front of an important person like a king or president announcing their arrival so that everyone knew who was coming. This person was called a forerunner. That is just what John the Baptist was – a person sent before the Lord Jesus to announce His arrival. Zacharias said about his own son John, 'You will go before the face of the Lord to prepare His ways'. John was sent to tell the people to get ready because the Lord was coming. When the Lord did come Zacharias said He would, 'Give knowledge of salvation to His people by the remission of their sins', verse 77.

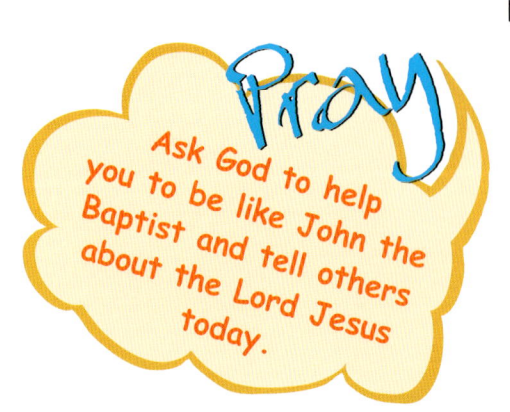

What a lovely person John had to tell the people about. We too can be like John the Baptist and tell others about the Lord Jesus. Are we willing?

Pray
Ask God to help you to be like John the Baptist and tell others about the Lord Jesus today.

Reading: Luke 2. 1-7

July 16

When the fullness of the time had come, God sent forth his Son, Galatians 4. 4

Caesar Augustus was a Roman Emperor who ruled over Israel. He decided that he wanted to know more about the people who lived in his empire so he ordered everyone to return to the place where they were born to register their backgrounds.

Joseph and Mary lived in Nazareth. They had to make a long and difficult journey to Bethlehem to obey Caesar's command. At that time Mary was expecting a baby and this would have been a tiring journey to make so close to the time when the baby was due to be born. To make matters worse, when they arrived in Bethlehem there was no room at the inn and they had to stay in the stable. Is your life so busy that you have no room for the Lord Jesus?

Stables look cute on Christmas cards but they are actually quite smelly and dirty places – not the ideal place to have a baby. Yet it was into these poor surroundings that God chose to send His Son. Why was the Lord Jesus born in a stable? He came to be the Saviour for the whole world, from the richest ruler to the poorest beggar. He had no special privileges when He became a human being. He loved us so much that He was prepared to leave the splendour of heaven so that we might be saved.

Why was the Lord Jesus born at this time when Joseph and Mary were far from home? God never makes mistakes. 'As for God, His way is perfect', 2 Samuel 22. 31. We read in Micah chapter 5 verse 2 that the Saviour had to be born in Bethlehem. This was all part of God's perfect plan of salvation. God has a perfect plan for each of our lives too.

Pray

Thank God for sending His Son into the world to be your Saviour. Ask God to help you to trust that He is in control and has a perfect plan for your life.

... through the Bible day by day

July 17

Reading: Luke 2. 8-20

There is no other name under heaven given among men by which we must be saved, Acts 4. 12

Out in the fields some shepherds were watching over their flocks of sheep. Shepherds would have been brave men, ready to defend their sheep from lions, bears and thieves. On this particular evening, however, they were terrified! An angel of the Lord had suddenly appeared and the glory of the Lord lit up the whole area around them. The angel had come to deliver a message of good news from God. He told the shepherds that in nearby Bethlehem a Saviour had been born who is Christ the Lord.

What actually is a saviour? Matthew chapter 1 verse 21 tells us that a saviour saves his people from their sins. Just think – the Son of God was born as a little baby so that He could become the Saviour of the world. Thirty-three years later He would suffer on the cross in our place so that we could be saved.

In the Old Testament the prophets told the Jews that God would send a Messiah, known as 'Christ', to be their king. The Jewish people probably imagined that this great person would be born in a palace, but, as so often happens, God had other plans. 'My thoughts are not your thoughts, nor are your ways My ways', Isaiah 55. 8.

The sky filled up with a host of angels who praised God. The shepherds decided to go immediately to Bethlehem to find the baby in the manger. Sure enough, they found everything just as the angel had said. Did they keep this a secret? No. They spread the message and praised and glorified God, Luke 2. 17. Everyone who heard the good news was amazed. If we have accepted Jesus as our Saviour, do we share the good news with others?

Pray
Thank God that the Lord Jesus came into the world to be your Saviour. Ask God to help you to share this good news with others.

Stepping stones

Reading: **Luke 2. 21-40**

July 18

My eyes have seen Your salvation,
Luke 2. 30

Joseph and Mary took baby Jesus to the temple in Jerusalem to present Him to God. While they were there they would have offered a sacrifice of two young pigeons or a pair of doves. In the temple they met two very special people, Simeon and Anna.

Simeon was a godly man who knew the Old Testament scriptures very well. He knew that the scriptures had promised that a Messiah was going to come. He had been eagerly watching and waiting to see the Messiah for himself because the Holy Spirit had told him that he would not die until he had seen this very special person. Finally the big moment had arrived and Simeon actually took Jesus in his arms, Luke 2. 28. Imagine how he must have felt as he looked down into the face of the Lord Jesus! He knew that this child would provide salvation for His own people the Jews and also for the rest of the world as well.

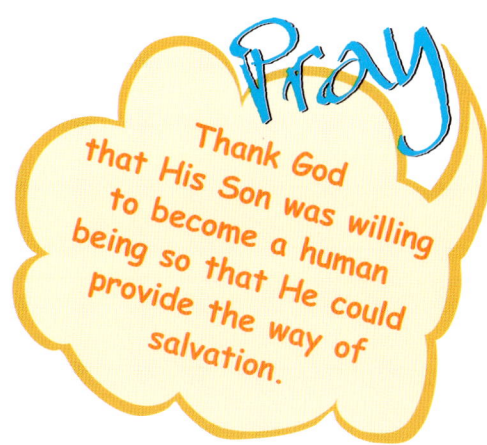

Anna was a very old lady who had been a widow most of her life. Luke chapter 2 verse 37 tells us that she never left the temple but worshipped there night and day. When Anna met Joseph and Mary with Jesus she also knew immediately that this baby was extra special. She gave thanks to God for sending His Son and, like the shepherds, she spread the good news.

Joseph and Mary must have often thought back to that day at the temple and watched the Lord Jesus with wonder as He grew up. It is amazing to think that the Son of God knows exactly what it is like to be someone of the same age as you.

Pray

Thank God that His Son was willing to become a human being so that He could provide the way of salvation.

... through the Bible day by day

July 19

Reading: Matthew 2. 1-12

At the name of Jesus every knee should bow, Philippians 2. 10

When Jesus was born God placed a new star in the sky. Wise men in the East knew that this was a sign that a king had been born. They wanted to worship this new king and so they set out to find him.

Where would such a king be born? The most obvious place seemed to be in the palace but when they arrived at the palace in Jerusalem no new baby king had been born there. King Herod was very disturbed to hear their news. He pretended that he wanted to worship this king too and asked the wise men to let him know where the child was. The wise men headed for Bethlehem and, to their delight, they saw the special star shining above the house where Jesus lived.

Pray
Thank God that Jesus can be Saviour and King of our lives. Praise God for how great and mighty He is.

Imagine the scene. Three very clever and important men find a young mother and baby. They bowed down and worshipped Jesus. Our verse for today tells us that one day everyone will bow and accept that Jesus is Lord. Have you accepted Jesus as your Saviour and Lord?

The wise men presented Jesus with gifts of gold, frankincense and myrrh. Why would they have given such strange gifts to a baby? Each gift had a special meaning. Gold is often linked with God. The Lord Jesus was the Son of God. Frankincense reminds us of purity. The Lord Jesus lived a perfect life. Myrrh is used at death and Jesus eventually died for our sins.

The wise men were warned in a dream not to report back to Herod and, now that they had achieved their goal of seeing the new king, they took a different route home. They had travelled far to see Jesus. Do we ever put ourselves out for Him?

Stepping stones

Reading: Matthew 2. 13-23

July 20

An angel of the Lord appeared to Joseph in a dream, saying, 'Arise, take the young Child and His mother, flee to Egypt, and stay there until I bring you word', Matthew 2. 13

After the wise men had left to go home the angel of the Lord appeared to Joseph in a dream telling him to take his little family to Egypt. God knew that Herod was not pleased at the idea that a baby had been born who might one day take his place as king. This must have been very frightening news for Mary and Joseph. No time was wasted because, even though it was the middle of the night, they got up and set off for Egypt.

Herod waited eagerly, expecting to hear news from the wise men. He was furious when he discovered that they had slipped home without letting him know where he could find Jesus. He was determined to get rid of this threat. He ordered that all baby boys who were two years old or younger, living in or near Bethlehem should be killed. Imagine being one of Herod's soldiers. What an awful order to have to carry out!

God knew exactly what Herod was up to and exactly what steps he would take. God is almighty and He is always in control. Proverbs chapter 21 verse 30 tells us that, 'There is no wisdom, no insight, no plan that can succeed against the Lord'. When we face difficult situations it is good to know that we can trust God to keep us safe and help us. We can pray as King David prayed, see Psalm 16. 1, 'Keep me safe, O God, for in You I take refuge'.

Eventually Herod died and the angel of the Lord appeared to Joseph again in a dream to let him know that it was now safe to return home, and the little family were able to go back home to live in Nazareth. How careful God was to keep His Son safe.

Pray
Thank God today that He watched over His Son and kept Him safe. Thank Him that He is always in control and can keep us safe, too.

...through the Bible day by day

July 21

Reading: Luke 2. 41-52

Children, obey your parents in all things, for this is well pleasing to the Lord,
Colossians 3. 20

Have you ever become separated from your parents or friends in a busy place? It can be a very frightening experience for everyone involved! When Jesus was twelve years old he went with his parents on their annual visit to Jerusalem to celebrate the Feast of the Passover. At the end of the first day's journey home Mary and Joseph must have been horrified to discover that Jesus was nowhere to be found. They had assumed that He was with His friends or other relatives. Jesus must have been left behind and their only solution was to turn around and go straight back to Jerusalem to find Him.

Where could Jesus be? No doubt they looked in lots of different places for Him. After three anxious days Mary and Joseph found Him at last. They must have been very glad to see that He was safe and well. Jesus was still in the temple where He had been sitting listening to the teachers of the law and asking them questions. Everybody was very impressed with Jesus because, even though He was only twelve years old, He had an amazing understanding of the scriptures and, of course, we know that is because He is the Son of God. The temple courts seemed like the most natural place for Him to want to be.

Pray
Thank God for giving you parents. Ask God to help you to be obedient to them.

Jesus returned to Nazareth with Joseph and Mary and He was obedient to them, Luke 2. 51. Isn't it just an amazing example to us that the Son of God should be obedient to them? As He grew up He was loved by those around Him and God was pleased with Him too. Obeying our parents is the right thing to do according to Ephesians chapter 6 verse 1. Such obedience always brings joy and is pleasing to God.

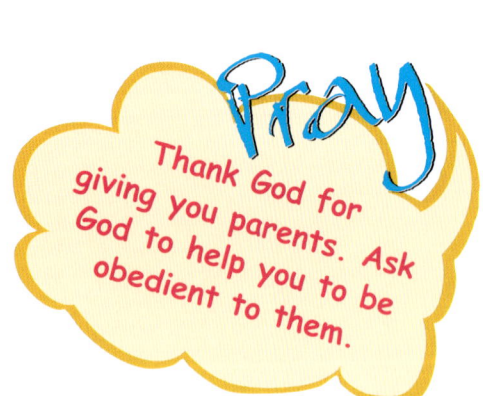

Reading: **Luke 3. 1-14**

July 22

He was not that Light, but was sent to bear witness of that Light, John 1. 8

A few months before the Lord Jesus was born, Mary's cousin Elizabeth had a baby boy who was called John. John's birth was quite a surprise to his parents as they were getting old. An angel had visited Zacharias, John's father, while he was in the temple and told him the good news. John was to have a special task. Luke chapter 1 verse 17 tells us he was to become a prophet like Elijah. A prophet is a messenger from God. God wanted His people to know that the coming of the Messiah was very close.

When he grew up, John moved about from place to place telling people to repent of their sins and to turn back to God. To show that they had repented of their sins, John baptized them by dipping them right under the water in the river, lakeside or even the sea. John encouraged the people to be kind to one another, to share their belongings with those who were in need and to stop cheating on one another. This was to show that they really had repented of their wrong-doing.

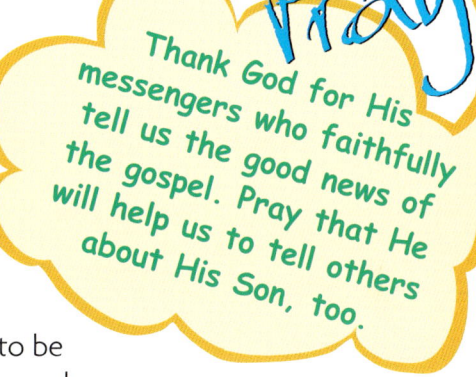

Pray
Thank God for His messengers who faithfully tell us the good news of the gospel. Pray that He will help us to tell others about His Son, too.

Some people must have listened to John and wondered if he could be the promised Messiah but John knew that this was not the case. Look again at today's verse. John's message from God was to tell the people to be ready for the arrival of the 'Light of the World'. One day soon Jesus will come back again. Are we ready for His return? Have we listened to the message of the Lord Jesus? Have we repented of our sins? Let us hope that we will all be ready and waiting for Him when He returns.

. . . through the Bible day by day

July 23

Reading: Matthew 3. 13-17

This is My beloved Son, in whom I am well pleased, Matthew 3. 17

John continued to preach his message and people continued to respond to his call to repent and be baptized. One day when he was preaching he noticed Jesus among the crowd. Jesus had travelled from Galilee to the Jordan river to find John. He wanted John to baptize Him too. John was so surprised. He tried to talk Jesus out of it. John felt very unworthy to baptize Jesus. He may have known that Jesus was the perfect Son of God. John felt that Jesus should be baptizing him rather than the other way around.

Up until this point in Jesus' life very few people actually knew who He really was. As the crowd watched Him walk into the Jordan river they must have thought that this baptism was just like any other but they were in for a big surprise! As Jesus came up out of the water, heaven opened up and the Spirit of God came down like a dove and rested on Jesus. At the same time God spoke in a loud voice from heaven letting everybody know exactly who had just been baptized. God announced to all that Jesus was His Son. God loved Him and He was very pleased with Him. Jesus' baptism was different from any other as Jesus was not confessing His sinfulness. God was showing everyone that this was the pure and spotless Son of God.

The secret was out and this was the moment when Jesus began His three years of preaching and teaching before He died on the cross for our sins. We are all sinners. Jesus died on the cross so that we can have our sins forgiven. Do we accept that we are sinners? Have we asked God to forgive our sins? He is willing and able to forgive.

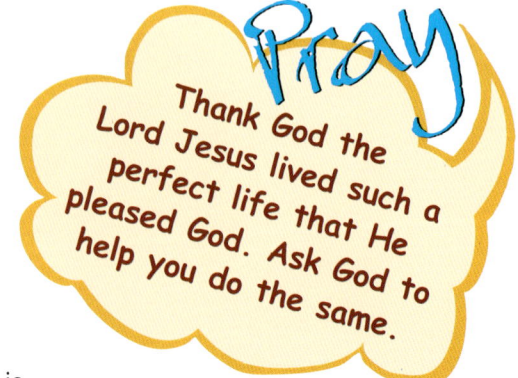

Pray

Thank God the Lord Jesus lived such a perfect life that He pleased God. Ask God to help you do the same.

Reading: Matthew 4. 1-11

July 24

We do not have a High Priest who cannot sympathize with our weaknesses, but was in all points tempted as we are, yet without sin,

Hebrews 4. 15

It had been a busy week and I hadn't learnt my spellings for the Friday test. What should I do? I could always copy. A little voice inside me whispered, 'Copy? That's cheating!'; 'Lots of people do it', I argued back. 'No one will ever know'.

Have you ever been in a similar situation where you were tempted to do something wrong? The temptation itself isn't a sin. Giving in to it is and it will lead you to sin. What are we to do?

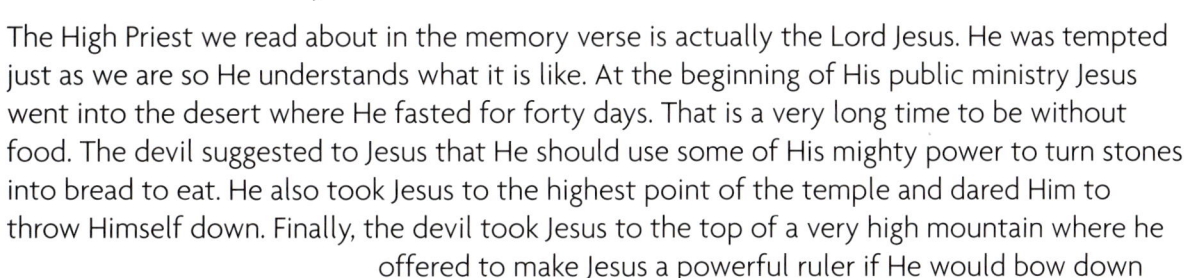

The High Priest we read about in the memory verse is actually the Lord Jesus. He was tempted just as we are so He understands what it is like. At the beginning of His public ministry Jesus went into the desert where He fasted for forty days. That is a very long time to be without food. The devil suggested to Jesus that He should use some of His mighty power to turn stones into bread to eat. He also took Jesus to the highest point of the temple and dared Him to throw Himself down. Finally, the devil took Jesus to the top of a very high mountain where he offered to make Jesus a powerful ruler if He would bow down and worship the devil.

Pray

Ask God to help you to resist temptation. Thank Him for the Lord Jesus who understands what it is like to be tempted.

How did the Lord Jesus deal with each of these tricky situations? In each case He answered the devil by quoting Bible verses and He was always able to resist the temptation. Jesus is able to understand what it is like to be tempted because He has been tempted. He does not understand what it is like to give in to temptation because He could not give in. When we are under pressure, however, He knows what that is like and sympathizes with us. Let us thank God that His Son knows and cares.

. . . through the Bible day by day

July 25

Reading: **John 1. 19-34**

He must increase, but I must decrease,
John 3. 30

While John was preaching and baptizing at Bethany the Jews from Jerusalem sent messengers to find out who he was. They wondered if John could possibly be the promised Messiah. John explained that he was not the Messiah but that his job was to announce the coming of the Messiah. John called the people to repent and prepare for His arrival.

Jewish religious rulers called Pharisees also questioned John. He was able to tell them that the Messiah was actually alive right at that very time. John described the Messiah as someone so great that he would feel unworthy even to untie the laces on His sandals – something even a slave could do.

The next day when John was preaching he saw Jesus coming towards him and he introduced Him to the crowd. How did John know that Jesus was the promised Messiah? God had told John that he would know who the Son of God was when he saw the Holy Spirit come down from heaven and rest on Him. John saw this happen the day he had baptized Jesus.

John really believed that Jesus was the most important person in the whole world. He was willing to step aside and let Jesus become the focus of attention. Today's verse tells us that John understood that Jesus must become greater than him and he, John, must become less important. Jesus must be the most important person in our lives today. Are we prepared to let Him take first place? Are we willing to fade into the background, as John was willing, so that Jesus becomes more important? It is not an easy thing for us to do but it is the right thing.

Pray

Thank God that Jesus wants to be your Saviour. Ask Him to help you make sure Jesus is also your Lord and has first place in your life.

Stepping stones

Reading: John 1. 35-43

July 26

And he brought him to Jesus, John 1. 42

The next day we find John still faithfully preaching. As Jesus passed by John once again proclaimed that He was the Lamb of God. Two of John's own disciples turned and started to follow Jesus. When Jesus realized that they were following Him He asked them what they wanted. They in turn asked Him where He was staying. They realized that Jesus was the promised Messiah and they wanted to be with Him to get to know Him better. When we put our trust in the Lord Jesus we also become His followers and we should have the same desire to be with Him as these two disciples.

Jesus invited them to come and see where He was staying. Jesus never turns away anyone who wants to follow Him. One of the disciples was called Andrew. When he left Jesus that evening he immediately went to find his brother Simon to tell him about Jesus. All Andrew said was, 'We have found the Messiah'. Andrew then brought Simon to Jesus. If we are Christians salvation is too good to keep secret. We might wonder about what we should say but God can use even a few simple words in a very powerful way.

When Jesus met Simon He gave him a new name, Cephas, which is translated as 'Peter' and means 'a stone'. Jesus knew that Simon had many faults but He also knew that in the future Simon would develop a faith that was as strong as a rock. God knows us inside out too. Psalm 139 verses 1 and 2 tell us that God knows every detail about our lives. He even knows our thoughts. Despite all our faults God wants us to follow Him and to bring others to Jesus.

Pray

Ask God to help you look for opportunities to tell others about Jesus and to give you the right words to say.

...through the Bible day by day

July 27

Reading: John 1. 43-51

He knew what was in man, John 2. 25

Jesus decided to head north to Bethsaida, which was a city on the shores of Lake Galilee. Jesus found another new disciple on the way. He was called Philip. He simply said to Philip, 'Follow me', and Philip did. The Lord Jesus wants each of us to follow Him too. Peter tells us that we should follow in the steps of the Lord Jesus, 1 Peter 2. 21. Are you following Jesus?

Philip was so excited about meeting Jesus that he went to find his friend Nathanael. Nathanael thought that Philip's news was a bit too good to be true. He was really unconvinced when he heard that Jesus came from Nazareth. He wondered if anything good could come from there because Nazareth wasn't the greatest place to live. People called it the despised city of Galilee. Philip didn't want to argue with Nathanael so he knew that the best thing to do was to introduce him to Jesus.

Pray

Ask God to help you remember that He knows you better than you even know yourself and that He is always with you.

Nathanael was really surprised when he met Jesus because Jesus knew all about him! Today's verse tells us that Jesus knew what Nathanael was like on the inside. As you know, at the end of every school year pupils get a school report. During the year, teachers get to know their pupils very well. You might think that your family knows you very well too but they will never know you as well as God does.

Jesus was also able to tell Nathanael that He had seen him sitting under a fig tree. The fig tree branches would have hung right down covering him completely. Yet we can never be hidden from God, Psalm 139. 7.

Now Nathanael was convinced! He had just seen two small examples of Christ's power and Jesus told him that he would see many greater things than these.

Reading: **John 2. 1-12**

July 28

Whatever He says to you, do it, John 2. 5

Have you ever been to a wedding? Perhaps you have been a bridesmaid or a page boy. Weddings are very exciting, happy family events. Jesus, His mother Mary and His disciples were invited to a wedding at Cana in Galilee.

During the wedding feast Mary noticed that the servants had run out of wine. How embarrassing that must have been for the master of the banquet! Mary told Jesus about the problem. Sometimes problems come into our lives too. Whether the problem is big or small the best thing to do is to bring it to Jesus by praying about it.

Mary turned to the servants and told them to do exactly what Jesus said. The servants obeyed Jesus' simple instructions. He told them to take six huge stone water jars and to fill them up to the top with water. He then told them to pour some of this water out of the jars and take it to the master of the banquet. The master of the banquet tasted the new wine and he was really impressed. He didn't know where it had come from. He called the bridegroom over to compliment him on the top quality wine being served late during the wedding feast. Normally the best wine was served at the beginning. This was the first miracle that Jesus did. The disciples were watching and this helped to strengthen their faith that He was the Son of God.

The servants did not argue or challenge Jesus' instructions. They did exactly as Jesus had commanded. We must be obedient to God's word too. Are you obedient? Are you willing to obey God's instructions to you, whatever they may be? Mary's words are very important for every true believer. Whatever Jesus says to you, do it.

Pray

Ask God to help you to be obedient to your parents and teachers and to help you with any problems that you are facing right now.

... through the Bible day by day

July 29

Reading: **John 2. 13-22**

His disciples remembered that it was written, 'Zeal for Your house has eaten Me up', John 2. 17

The temple courts were doing steady business. Men had brought cattle, sheep and doves to sell to those who needed an animal for a sacrifice in the temple. Jews from distant lands also came here to make sacrifices. They needed to change their money into the right currency to buy their sacrifice. Money-changers gathered here as well, but they didn't offer a very fair exchange rate and always made a very good profit.

It was close to Passover time and Jesus made His way up to the temple in Jerusalem. The temple was a very special place; it was the House of God. When Jesus walked into the outer area of the temple He was disgusted by what He saw. The steady selling of sacrifices and the moneychanging soon came to a halt. Jesus made a whip and used it to drive out the stallholders and to scatter the coins collected by the money-changers. What a commotion!

Why did Jesus act in this way? This was His Father's house, a holy place for worship. It was not a market or a place for stealing money! Jesus wanted the temple to be respected and used properly. He wanted the worship of God to be pure, so He cleared the temple courts.

The disciples watched in amazement. Today's verse tells us that they remembered part of Psalm 69 where the psalmist said that the Messiah would be totally focussed on the things of God. We need to be like Jesus by putting God first in our lives. Jesus tells us, 'Seek first the kingdom of God and His righteousness', Matthew 6. 33. Have we put God first in our lives? The Lord Jesus always put God first.

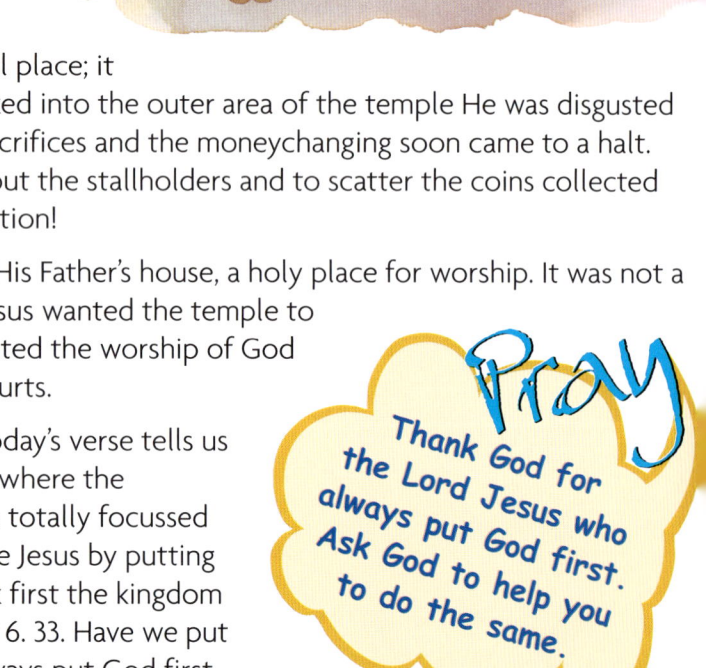

Pray

Thank God for the Lord Jesus who always put God first. Ask God to help you to do the same.

Stepping stones

Reading: John 3. 1-21

July 30

Do not marvel that I said to you, 'You must be born again', John 3. 7

Nicodemus was a teacher of the Jews. One night he decided to pay Jesus a visit. He accepted that Jesus had come from God. He realized that Jesus could not do the miracles He did without the power of God. The question remained – could Jesus possibly be the Messiah?

Jesus explained that Nicodemus could enter the kingdom of God. But Nicodemus would have to be born again first. Now Nicodemus was really confused! How could a grown man get back into his mother's womb and be born again? Jesus was not talking about being born in a physical way but in a spiritual way. Being born again means that a person's life is changed. If anyone is in Christ, he is a new creation; the old has gone, the new has come, 2 Corinthians 5. 17. When we are born again we become something completely new.

Pray

Thank God for providing a way for us to be born again through the Lord Jesus Christ.

Jesus reminded Nicodemus of something that had happened a long time before. The disobedient children of Israel had been bitten by snakes but God provided a way by which they could be healed. Moses placed a brass snake on a pole. If the people looked at the serpent they would be healed. The serpent of brass on a pole was a picture of Jesus who hung on a cross at Calvary. Every one of us has been bitten by sin. We are born again by believing that the Lord Jesus is our Saviour who was made sin for us. Whoever believes in Him receives the gift of eternal life. God's heart is full of love. He has provided a way for everyone to be born again.

There are only two groups of people in the world. There are those who are born again and those who are not. Into which group do we fall?

. . . through the Bible day by day

July 31

Reading: John 4. 1-42

God is Spirit, and those who worship Him must worship in spirit and truth,
John 4. 24

Jesus was travelling to Galilee. It was a long, hot journey. They passed through Samaria and about midday they came to a well. Jesus rested beside the well while the disciples headed into town to get some food. A Samaritan woman came to the well with her water pot. Jesus asked her to give Him a drink. She was surprised that He had spoken to her because Jews did not normally speak to Samaritans.

Jesus told her that she would be asking Him for living water if she knew who He was. The woman was confused because she could see that Jesus had no pot for collecting water. He explained that the living water He was offering would quench her thirst for ever. 'What a help that would be,' she thought. 'No more daily trips to the well!'

The water in the well is a picture of the pleasures that many people hope will satisfy them but never can. The living water speaks of the Holy Spirit and the Christian life. We will have total satisfaction when we give our lives to Christ.

The woman discovered that Jesus knew all about her sinful life so she changed the subject to talk about worship. God had given the Jews specific instructions about worship. Now that the Lord Jesus had come those Jewish ways were not necessary. God is not interested in outward ceremonies anymore. He wants us to come into His presence by faith and to worship from our hearts anywhere and at any time whether we are at home, in school or in a church building.

God is spirit. He is not limited to being in one place at one time and can be worshipped anywhere. Why not worship Him now!

Pray
Thank God that, because He is spirit and is everywhere, you can pray to Him anywhere. Worship God today for who He is.

Reading: John 4. 46-54

August 1

Whatever things you ask in prayer, believing, you will receive, Matthew 21. 22

It was a happy day when Jesus entered the little town of Cana. A joyful crowd had gathered. They were so pleased that Jesus was back in their town. One man, though, was very sad. His son was dying in the distant town of Capernaum. The man had a big decision to make. Would he leave his son and look for Jesus, or leave Jesus out and stay with his son? He made a wise choice. He went to look for Jesus. Many people have to make this same decision today. The choice is about who is to come first in their lives, Jesus or others.

Pray

Praise the Lord that His words have so much power. Ask Him to help you to rely more on His promises.

As the man approached Jesus the Lord knew all about him. Jesus knew the man was hesitating in his faith. He wanted to see a miracle before he would believe. The Lord once said, 'Those who have not seen and yet have believed' are happy, John 20. 29. It is always better simply to believe the promises of God.

The man didn't give up. He pleaded with Jesus, 'Come home with me, or my son will die'. The Lord Jesus replied, 'Go, your son lives!' Would the father believe and go home? It might seem impossible that a child could be healed over such a great distance but the Lord had said it and the man believed it. He went home.

When he arrived home his servants came with the great news, 'Your son is alive'. His heart was so happy! His son had been healed the very moment the Lord had spoken, just as Jesus had promised. The Lord hadn't needed to travel that long distance to heal the boy. His words have the same power as His hands. Do we believe His words have the same power today?

... through the Bible day by day

August 2

Reading: **Luke 4. 16-30**

He came to His own, and His own did not receive Him, John 1. 11

Jesus was back in the town of Nazareth. This was the town where He had grown up and learned to be a carpenter. He would be well known here. Perhaps He had even sold furniture to the people of this town!

The people, though, watched Jesus very carefully, as He entered their synagogue and began to read the Bible to them. As He read some verses everyone's eyes were fixed on Him. They listened to His wonderful words. They even said, 'No one has ever spoken like Him before'. It must have been a great experience to listen to Jesus that day.

When Jesus explained what the reading meant, their attitude to Him began to change. He was saying things they didn't like to hear. He revealed the evil they had in their hearts. No one likes to admit they have sin in their lives. The more Jesus spoke, the angrier the people became until they couldn't take it any more. 'Grab Him and throw Him out', they said. So they took Jesus and threw Him out of His home town, right out of Nazareth.

Their thoughts became even more wicked. 'We'll throw Jesus off this cliff and He will die'. Their plan was useless, however. No one can hold Jesus. He holds us instead! The Lord very simply walked right through the crowd and headed for another town. The people of that town would be willing to listen to His words. He would never go home again to Nazareth.

When the Lord Jesus speaks He always tells the truth. Sometimes this might even hurt us. We should remember, though, that His purpose in telling us the truth is to help us to become more like Himself. We should be grateful for that.

Pray

Thank God that Jesus is the Truth and only tells the truth. Ask Him to help you to be truthful today.

Stepping stones

Reading: Luke 5. 1-11

August 3

Peter answered and said to Him, 'See, we have left all and followed You', Matthew 19. 27

When Jesus visited the seaside a huge crowd followed Him. So many people wanted to hear Him that it was a very tight squeeze. There was hardly room for even Jesus to stand! The Lord saw some fishing boats. He could use them. If the fishermen pushed the boats out, He could sit on the edge of a boat and speak to the people. Everyone could then hear His words.

When Jesus had finished speaking He turned to the fishermen. 'Let your nets down to catch some fish', He said. Peter began to make excuses. 'We have been fishing all night, and we didn't catch anything'. Would he refuse to obey Jesus? No. Despite his reluctance he listened to the instruction of Jesus and they cast their net into the sea. Are we willing to obey the instructions of Jesus?

Jesus was right and it was the most amazing catch of their lives! As they pulled their net in, there were so many fish that it started to break. As they loaded the fish into the boats, the boats were so full that they began to sink!

When Peter stopped to think about all that had happened he felt very guilty. He had many sins and he stood before One who had no sins. He fell down right to Jesus' knees, and said, 'Leave me, I am a very sinful man'. None of us is good enough to stand before Jesus.

Jesus didn't leave Peter. Instead He gave Peter another challenge and said, 'Leave your nets, leave your family, leave your boat. Follow me'. What would Peter do? It was such a massive cost. Without hesitation, Peter left everything and began to follow Jesus. Today the Lord still says to us, 'Follow Me'. Are we ready to leave everything and follow Him?

Pray

Praise the Lord that He wants everyone to hear of Him. Ask Him to help you to follow Him more closely.

... through the Bible day by day

August 4

Reading: Mark 1. 21-28

I know who You are – the Holy One of God!
Mark 1. 24

A troubled man slipped into the silent synagogue. No one had noticed him. The people were busy concentrating on the words of Jesus. They were amazed at what Jesus said. His words were words of power. They were the words of God.

But the silence was broken as the man screamed out! Imagine how frightening it must have been to see this wild-looking man shouting at Jesus. Why was he shouting? The distressed man had demons living inside him and he was out of control! The demons knew exactly who Jesus was, the 'Holy One of God'. The people in the synagogue must have thought, 'What will Jesus do to the man? Will He argue with him or even send him home?'

The Lord Jesus didn't argue with the man. He had a different approach. He rebuked the demons. Remember, you mustn't argue with the devil. You have to reject him. The Lord commanded the demons to be silent and to come out of the man.

The demons wanted one last fight, so, as they left the man, they tried to destroy him. The devil never wants to help people. He only wants to destroy them. Even from his name we can see he is evil, vile (very nasty) and he makes people ill. These demons had to flee from the holy presence of Jesus. The troubled man was now a man at peace. Jesus had set him free.

The people in the synagogue were amazed. They had never seen anything like this before. God had been working in their little town. They could wait no longer. They just had to go out to tell others of the wonderful works of Jesus. Have we ever told anyone about Jesus?

Pray

Pray for God's strength to resist the devil. Ask for help to know when to run away from him.

Stepping stones

Reading: Mark 1. 40-45

August 5

If You are willing, You can make me clean, Mark 1. 40

In Bible days one disease was feared more than any other. It was the terrible disease of leprosy. A person with leprosy was called a leper. Lepers were sent to live outside their cities and would have to shout, 'Unclean!' if anyone came near them. No one would ever touch a leper in case he caught the disease. Lepers would be left to die with little company and few friends. A leper's life was very sad.

One day, one such leper began to approach the Lord Jesus. Perhaps he thought, 'Why sit and die when Jesus can heal me?' So the unclean man approached the Lord Jesus. The Bible says Jesus has 'no spot or blemish'. He is perfect.

The leper came very humbly and knelt down before the Lord. A leper couldn't be bold in the presence of such a wonderful man. Sadly, even today some people treat the Lord Jesus with no respect. As the leper knelt before Jesus he could wait no longer. He expressed his real desire. 'If you will, you can make me clean'. The man wanted to be healed from his leprosy more than anything. To ask the Lord Jesus to make you clean from sin is the most important thing a person can ever ask.

The Lord was filled with love for the leper. He *would* make the leper clean. Jesus stretched His hand forward and touched the man. Immediately the leprosy left him and he was completely healed. But the Lord remained perfectly clean. He can never be spoiled by our uncleanness.

That day the man returned home with great joy. He had come to the Lord as an unclean leper but returned home perfectly clean. He was so glad that he had met Jesus. Has meeting Jesus changed us?

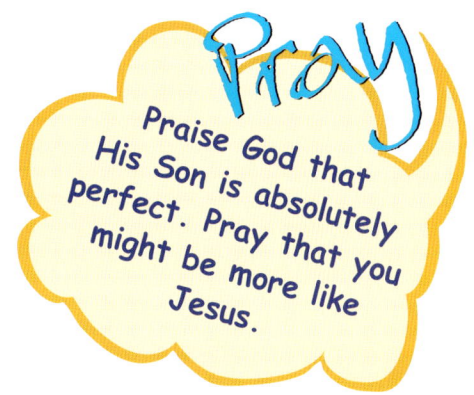

Pray

Praise God that His Son is absolutely perfect. Pray that you might be more like Jesus.

... through the Bible day by day

August 6

Reading: Mark 2. 1-12

'Who can forgive sins but God alone?'
Mark 2. 7

Jesus was back in Capernaum and this time He went into a house. One by one the people entered the house until it was so full they couldn't squeeze another person in. Outside the house, though, lay a man with no strength in his arms or legs. He was paralysed. He had wanted to meet Jesus but there seemed little possibility of this now. There was no room for him.

The paralysed man, thankfully, had four very helpful friends. They saw their friend's problem and had a great idea. 'We'll drop him through the roof'. In Capernaum the houses had flat roofs and stairs on the outside. They climbed the stairs and started to break open the roof. It would be very hard work carrying a full-sized adult up those steep stairs.

When the roof tiles were removed they lowered him slowly into the room. Their friend couldn't feel pain so they had to be careful not to break his bones. Jesus looked up and saw how great their faith was. Faith is fully trusting in the power and promises of God.

The Lord Jesus shocked the crowd by saying, 'Son, your sins are forgiven'. The man needed his sins forgiven, even more than he needed his body healed. Sadly, today many only think about their bodies and not about their souls. Many people in the crowd frowned. 'How could Jesus forgive sin?' they wondered.

Jesus spoke again to the man in the bed and said, 'Get up and walk'. The crowd wondered if he would fall over. Immediately, the man got up, picked up his bed and headed home. He had been healed! What wonderful things Jesus did!

The Bible clearly tells us that Jesus has power to forgive sins. Jesus still forgives sins today. Has He forgiven ours?

Pray

Thank the Lord that He knows your heart. Ask for help to trust in Him even more.

Reading: **Mark 2. 13-17**

August 7

I did not come to call the righteous, but sinners, to repentance, Mark 2. 17

No one wanted to speak to Matthew. He was a hated tax collector. In Bible days tax collectors took money from the people and gave it to the Romans. Some tax collectors even kept some of the money for themselves. One day, as Matthew was collecting taxes, Jesus walked by. The Lord had often spoken to large crowds. This time He wanted to speak to an individual. No one had guessed that Jesus would stop and speak to a tax collector.

When the Lord Jesus spoke, He said little but it meant a lot. His words had real power. He said, very simply, 'Follow Me', but those two words would change Matthew forever. Matthew stood up immediately, left his money behind and followed Jesus. He had just made the wisest choice as he began to follow the Saviour. Matthew must have set a great example because the Bible tells us that many tax collectors later followed Jesus. Would people follow the Lord Jesus because of our example?

The religious rulers were surprised that Jesus would meet with people they called 'sinners'. They even said that Jesus 'eats and drinks' with them! These rulers thought that they themselves were not sinners! But the Lord knew exactly how to answer them. He told them why He had come into this world. Jesus said, 'I came not to call the righteous (perfect) but sinners to repentance'. This was great news for the crowd of sinful people. They could be saved by turning to Jesus. For the rulers, though, this was very bad news. They could only be saved when they admitted that they were sinners. This was very hard for them to accept. Today, the Lord Jesus still only saves sinners! Those who think they are perfect will never come to Him.

Pray

Pray for help to follow Jesus. Ask God to show you what He wants you to do.

...through the Bible day by day

August 8

Reading: John 5. 1-18

Jesus answered them, 'My Father has been working until now, and I have been working', John 5. 17

A strange group of people were lying at the poolside. Some were blind, some were paralysed and others had terrible diseases. They weren't on holiday, sunbathing. They were waiting for a miracle at the pool of Bethesda. The Bible says that occasionally an angel would visit the pool. When the angel visited, the first person to enter the water would be healed. These people were hoping that they would be first into the pool.

One day the Lord Jesus came to Bethesda. His disciples were probably shocked at all the sad people that they saw that day. Sometimes, when we follow the Lord Jesus, He may ask us to go to places which we are scared to go to. Do you remember how scared a man called Jonah was?

The Lord looked over all the people. He knew exactly who He would speak to. Jesus had seen a man lying all alone, poor, helpless and paralysed. For thirty-eight years he had been unable to lift himself. No one had been willing to help him, but the Lord Jesus would.

As Jesus spoke to the paralysed man, He asked him a very simple question. 'Do you want to be made completely better?' The poor man said, 'I would love to be healed but no one is willing to help me into the pool'. Maybe he wondered if Jesus would help him into the water. The Lord had something even better to offer him. Jesus said, 'Take up your bed and walk'. After thirty-eight years lying in once place it might have seemed impossible but the man stood up straight away and began to walk. What a miracle! The impossible was made possible by Jesus. 'With God all things are possible', Matthew 19. 26.

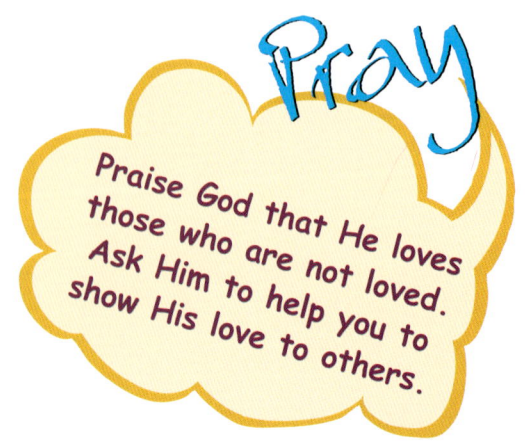

Pray

Praise God that He loves those who are not loved. Ask Him to help you to show His love to others.

Stepping stones

Reading: **Mark 3. 1-6**

August 9

He knew their thoughts, Luke 6. 8

A famous painting called the Mona Lisa hangs in the Louvre Museum in France. Many people have said that the eyes in the painting seem to follow you around. They seem to watch your every step.

When Jesus entered the synagogue some people watched His every step. They watched Him with hatred, not love. They watched Him and wondered, 'will He heal anyone today?' It was their special day called the Sabbath. No one did any work on the Sabbath. They wanted to catch Jesus working, though.

In the synagogue that day was a man with a shrivelled hand. He couldn't stretch it out or lift anything with it. Some rude people may have even stared at his hand. The Lord Jesus saw the man in his real distress. He looked first at the crowd, though. He looked right into their hearts. Their hearts were like stone, hard and without love. They had no love for the man and certainly no love for Him. The Lord was saddened that they had such hatred in their hearts.

Pray

Ask the Lord to help you to keep your eyes on Jesus. Praise Him that He does great and wonderful things.

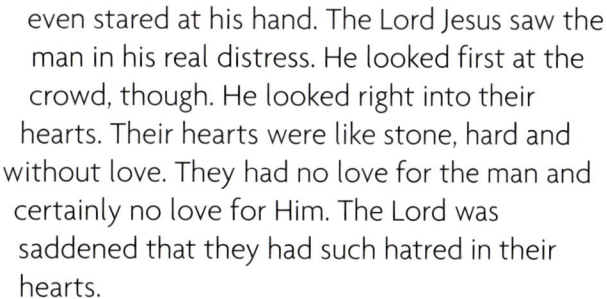

In front of the angry crowd Jesus spoke to the man. 'Stretch out your hand', He said. The troubled man reached out his hand. In the past he hadn't been able do this. He was amazed it was healed and it was just like his other hand.

The Lord Jesus had worked a miracle on the Sabbath day! The hostile crowd could no longer look at Jesus. They would only be happy if they never saw Him again. They quickly left the synagogue and started to plot how they might kill Jesus. That day they had made an important decision to reject the Saviour. What have we decided today? 'Today, if you will hear His voice, do not harden your hearts', Hebrews 4. 7.

. . . through the Bible day by day

August 10

Reading: Mark 3. 13-19

He appointed twelve, that they might be with Him and that He might send them out to preach, Mark 3. 14

Jesus loved to spend time in the mountains. Sometimes He prayed on a mountain. At other times He was alone with His followers on a mountain. Within a few years a mountain would be the place of His death. That mountain was called Golgotha, which means 'Skull Hill'.

One day He called twelve men to follow Him up into a mountain. They were a very unusual group of men but they were to become His disciples. One man called Matthew had worked for the Romans while Simon used to fight against the Romans! Some were fishermen and some were brothers. Sadly, one was a fake follower. Judas loved money rather than God.

On that mountain the Lord Jesus gave these disciples a very special work to do. They were to go out and tell others about Him. From this small beginning these eleven would eventually turn the world upside down! It seemed an impossible task. It was a task which could only be completed through the power that Jesus gave. Jesus gave them power to speak about Him to others. This is something that all Christians should be willing to do. He would also give them power to heal the sick. When people saw the sick healed many would follow the Saviour.

When the disciples left that mountain they would never be the same again. They had work to do for Jesus which they would do in God's power. How glad they were that they had followed the Lord into the mountain. Have you ever been alone with God? True followers of Jesus love to spend time with God alone in prayer. Find a quiet spot at home and make this a special place where you love to speak to God.

Pray

Ask the Lord to help you learn how important it is to spend time getting to know Him. Thank Him that you get to know Him through Bible-reading and praying.

Stepping stones

Reading: Matthew 5. 1-12

August 11

Godliness with contentment is great gain, 1 Timothy 6. 6

Have you ever wanted to be famous? Would you like people to read about you and talk about you? It might seem like great fun but it can be a very harmful thing. Fame has ruined many people. Fame seldom brings happiness.

Jesus never sought fame. Even when crowds followed Him, He often chose to be alone with His disciples. One day He left the crowds behind and climbed another mountain. It was time to be alone with His followers. Jesus wanted to teach them about true happiness.

Jesus tells His disciples how they can be happy in nine different ways. They can be happy when times are sad and things are difficult. They can be happy when others are at war and even when people despise their faith in God. Happiness is not found in having fame or money but in being humble, righteous and pure in heart. Happiness is found by those who look for peace and by those who show kindness. Happiness is found when you are persecuted for the name of Christ.

It might seem strange to be happy when people hate you, pick on you and say bad things about you. The Lord Jesus has promised us happiness even in these circumstances and His promises never fail. He has promised to fill the hungry and bring comfort to the sad. He will show us God if we have pure hearts. He gives rewards in heaven to those who are hated for speaking about Him.

Have you ever tried to live by these nine measures of happiness? True happiness will only come to those with Christ in their lives and His word in their hearts. This true happiness will last forever. Do we want fame or true happiness? The Lord tells us how to find it.

Pray

Thank the Lord for all the happiness He has given you. Ask Him to help you to spread His happiness to others.

... through the Bible day by day

August 12

Reading: Matthew 5. 13-20

You are the salt of the earth; but if the salt loses its flavour, how shall it be seasoned? It is then good for nothing but to be thrown out and trampled underfoot by men, Matthew 5.13

In the city of Dundee, Scotland, is the research ship *Discovery* which carried the famous Captain Scott to Antarctica. In the hold of the ship were vast quantities of salt. Salt was used to preserve food and to preserve wood. It was also used to give essential minerals to the sailors and enhance the taste of food. Salt is an amazing thing. It keeps things from going rotten and it improves the taste.

Pray: Ask the Lord for help to be kept pure for Him. Praise Him for the wonderful life that Jesus lived.

Jesus said Christians should be like salt. They can help preserve this world from evil and improve the earth by their godly lives. Every single Christian can have an effect on the people he or she meets. Sadly, some Christians are no longer salty! They have become just like the millions of non-Christians. They have lost their impact for God. Christians must live differently to be 'the salt of the earth'.

A few years ago the government suggested that too much salt was bad for your heart. Our family wanted to be healthy so we bought a low-salt product instead. It certainly looked like salt, but it didn't taste like salt. We soon returned to using real salt again! If we lose our saltiness for Christ, it will be impossible to be effective for Him.

The Lord Jesus expects Christians also to be like light, shining out for Him. What a difference it would make if every Christian shone brightly for Christ! Some people are ashamed to tell others about the Lord Jesus. Jesus would say that they are hiding their light.

Glow worms are often found hiding in caves. In the darkness of the cave they shine brightly. They attract other insects into the cave. Christians are to shine brightly for Christ, attracting others to Him. How are we shining today?

Stepping stones

Reading: Matthew 5. 21-47

August 13

From within, out of the heart of men, proceed evil thoughts, adulteries, fornications, murders, Mark 7. 21

Sometimes it seems easier to make enemies instead of friends. Some people can be very hard to love. It is easy to see what's wrong about other people and then despise them. It takes very little effort to hate instead of love.

The Lord Jesus taught that there is a far better way. 'Love your enemies'. Love those who say terrible things about you. Pray for those who just want to use you. Do good things to those who hate you. By obeying the words of Jesus we can show that we actually belong to God.

As Jesus travelled, He met some people who were full of anger. They were planning revenge and this attitude was ruining their lives. They even hated their own brothers. Despite their hatred these people attempted to worship God. Jesus taught that they needed to be at peace with their brother before God would accept their worship. Real love can overcome anger.

Then the Lord met some men who didn't like their wives. They wanted to be with other women instead of their own wives. Jesus taught that this was very sinful. Instead of looking at other women they had to learn to love their wives again. The Saviour also met people who were struggling to tell the truth. They always needed to prove that they were being honest by using God's name. If we love the Lord, everything we say should be true. People should be able to trust our words because they are always truthful.

The Lord Jesus showed the greatest example of love. He loved His enemies and died for them. Instead of remembering their hatred He said, 'Father, forgive them', Luke 23. 34. Can we obey His words and love our enemies?

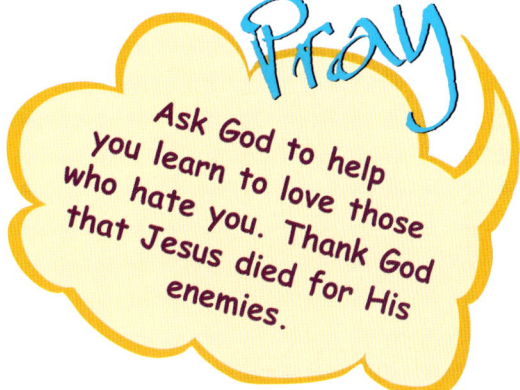

Pray

Ask God to help you learn to love those who hate you. Thank God that Jesus died for His enemies.

. . . through the Bible day by day

August 14

Reading: **Matthew 6. 1-18**

Do not do your charitable deeds before men, to be seen by them. Otherwise you have no reward from your Father in heaven, Matthew 6.1

An excited boy in his new clothes shouted, 'Look at me'. He wanted everyone to see him. A British politician in an important speech also said, 'Look at me'. He wanted everyone to consider his impressive record.

In Bible times, many people said, 'Look at me'. 'Look at me, when I am giving money away! Look at me, when I am praying! Look at me, when I am fasting (not eating food)!' Many people would have looked at them. Some would think that such devotion was evidence of their love for God. The Lord Jesus thought differently. He called such people hypocrites!

A hypocrite is someone who says one thing but actually does the opposite. These people gave the impression that they loved God. They actually loved to receive the praise of men. They hoped someone would see them praying in the street. This would convince others that they were holy. These hypocrites would have been far wiser to have kept these things secret. The Lord Jesus knew the true state of their sinful hearts.

Jesus taught that His followers should have three lovely secrets. These are secret giving, secret praying and secret fasting. When you give money away you shouldn't do it to get a reward from others. It should be a secret between you and God. God will reward you in heaven for this secret giving. Secret praying is about finding a place where you can get away from all distractions and pray to the Lord. He loves to hear what we really think. Secret fasting is when we don't eat for a short time because we would rather spend that time with God. Spending time with God in secret will lead to a wonderful reward. If you want a heavenly reward learn to keep a secret!

Pray

Ask God to help you to be generous in giving to Him and to people who need your help. Pray that He might help you to keep what you do for Him a secret.

Reading: **Matthew 6. 24-34**

August 15

Seek first the kingdom of God and His righteousness, and all these things shall be added to you, Matthew 6. 33

Do you ever worry? Some people worry about friends and some worry about money. Some people worry about what clothes to wear. Worrying might seem a natural thing to do but God doesn't want us to do it.

Every spring a large bird called an osprey flies from Africa to Scotland. Never once has it needed a person to feed it. God has always provided a glorious diet of fish to feast on. If God feeds birds we can be sure He will feed us. We don't need to worry about food.

Flowers are some of the most beautiful things that we can ever look at. They don't get their beauty through worry but by the wonderful hand of God. If God clothes flowers in beauty we know that He can clothe us.

There are many things that we might want in life but God supplies everything we really need. God knows what is best for us. Jesus taught that instead of worrying we should try to find God's will. God wants us to put Him and His standards first. We should try to live by the standards of the kingdom of God. The Bible tells stories about kings that worried instead of trusting in the Lord. Their kingdoms are now in ruins but God is still on His throne.

The Mr Men series of cartoon books has a character called Mr Worry. Mr Worry spent a very unhappy time worrying. God doesn't want us to copy him. He wants us to be a Mr Trust instead. Learning to trust in God is a precious lesson for us all. Trusting in God to provide our needs strengthens our faith in Him. We find real joy and happiness when God provides for our needs. Don't worry today. Trust God instead.

Pray

Thank God that He can give you everything you need. Pray that you will learn to trust God and not worry.

...through the Bible day by day

August 16

Reading: Matthew 7. 1-5

Judge nothing before the time, until the Lord comes, 1 Corinthians 4. 5

One day on a mountainside the Lord Jesus taught crowds of people. The words He spoke then are sometimes called the 'Sermon on the Mount'. As part of His message that day the Lord taught us that we should be more concerned about our own behaviour than the behaviour of others. We can often make a big fuss about the faults we see in other people and at the same time overlook our own failings.

To help us to understand this point the Lord spoke about someone trying to remove a speck of dust from another person's eye while they have a huge stick blocking their own eye. The first thing we need to do is realize we have a bigger problem than other people. Then we must move our own stick before we can even think about trying to remove someone else's speck.

It is easy to spot when someone else is being selfish, dishonest or mean but it's harder to notice when we are acting that way ourselves. To know what we look like we need to look in a mirror. By doing this we get to see ourselves as others see us. In the book of James chapter 1 verses 23 to 25 we are told that the Bible is like a mirror that helps us see the true reflection of our behaviour. By reading the Bible we learn what the Lord Jesus was like and how we should behave. Then we can compare this with our own actions.

When we see ourselves in the light of God's word we will be less quick to judge others. This means we can concentrate on removing the stick from our own eyes and living a life pleasing to God who is the ultimate judge.

Pray

Thank God He is a patient judge. Ask God for help to see your own faults and for His help to remove them.

Reading: **Matthew 7. 7-14**

August 17

Ask in faith, with no doubting, James 1. 6

God is ready and willing to open the door and answer our prayers. There is however a condition attached to this. It is that we have to seek before we can find and knock before the door opens.

Someone has said that the only prayers that are never answered are the ones that are never prayed. While it is important to pray, it is just as important when we pray to ask in faith. 'Whatever things you ask in prayer, believing you will receive', Matthew 21. 22. That simply means we must have confidence that God will answer our prayer in accordance with His will.

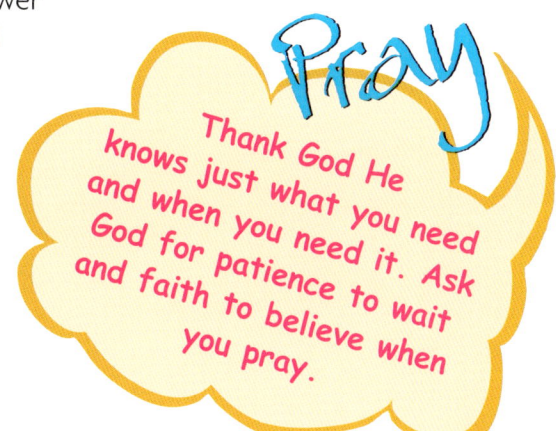

Why is it then that we don't always get what we want? Does it mean God hasn't answered our prayers? No, it just means the answer is 'No', or 'Not now'. Sometimes when our parents refuse to give us something we think they don't care. However, the opposite is actually the case. They refuse because they love us and know that what we are asking for will not do us good.

In our reading the Lord says that our parents know what is best for us although they are imperfect. Our perfect Father in heaven will know even more how to give us good things when we ask Him. If we ask for something good He is not going to give us something bad. If we ask for something bad He'll give us something better instead. 'Your Father knows the things you have need of before you ask Him', Matthew 6. 8. So let us be sure God will always do what is best and let us 'ask in faith with no doubting', James 1. 6.

Pray

Thank God He knows just what you need and when you need it. Ask God for patience to wait and faith to believe when you pray.

...through the Bible day by day

August 18

Reading: Matthew 7. 15-29

Not everyone who says to me, 'Lord, Lord', shall enter the kingdom of heaven, but he who does the will of My Father in heaven,
Matthew 7. 21

The song, 'The wise man built his house upon the rock' followed by the verse, 'The foolish man built his house upon the sand' is an old favourite at Sunday schools and children's meetings. Sometimes it is sung with an extra verse added which goes like this, 'So build your life on the Lord Jesus Christ and the blessings will come down'.

Some people think that when you trust the Lord as your Saviour and become a Christian, life will be easy and that somehow we will escape the hard times which everyone else goes through. This is not true. We all have to face storms and difficult times just like everyone else. The difference is we don't have to go through them just like everyone else because we have our Lord to turn to. He is the rock that we can lean on.

Our lives may be shaken but He never moves. He is the same yesterday, today and forever and He will never leave us nor forsake us.

Of course the Lord is not there for us in troubled times only. We should try to find Him every day, even when things are going well. Our reading today teaches us to build our whole life on Him and not on unreliable things that will let us down when troubles come. We can depend on Him for today, for tomorrow and forever.

So let's try to do as our text above suggests and not just pay Him lip service by calling Him 'Lord', but do God's will by building our lives on Him.

Pray
Thank God that He is a rock you can depend on through good times and bad. Ask God for help to build your life on His Word.

Stepping stones

Reading: Luke 7. 1-10

August 19

Lord, do not trouble Yourself, for I am not worthy that You should enter under my roof, Luke 7. 6

My dictionary's definition of 'humble' is when you are 'not proud or not believing you are important'. To everyone else this Roman centurion was very important because he had the authority to tell others what to do. Yet he knew he was not good enough even to be in the presence of the Lord Jesus.

Other people thought the centurion was worthy of the Lord's help because he loved the nation of the Jews and helped them build a synagogue. We also know he was compassionate because he cared for his sick servant. As well as these things he showed great faith in the Lord. Yet none of this made him worthy of the Lord's help and he knew it.

John the Baptist felt he was not worthy enough to untie the Lord's sandals and this important centurion felt he was not worthy enough for the Lord to enter his house. How did the Lord respond? He responded in grace and healed the centurion's servant anyway. That means He showed a kindness that was not deserved. 'God resists the proud, but gives grace to the humble', James 4. 6.

This story is a great example of God's grace to sinners in sending His Son. We were worthy of nothing except punishment for our sin so it is amazing that 'while we were still sinners, Christ died for us', Romans 5. 8.

This Roman centurion is also a great example of how to be humble and have faith in Christ. We should not only see ourselves unworthy before God but also learn to show humility to each other. 'In lowliness of mind let each esteem others better than himself', Philippians 2. 3. Are we humble enough to do that?

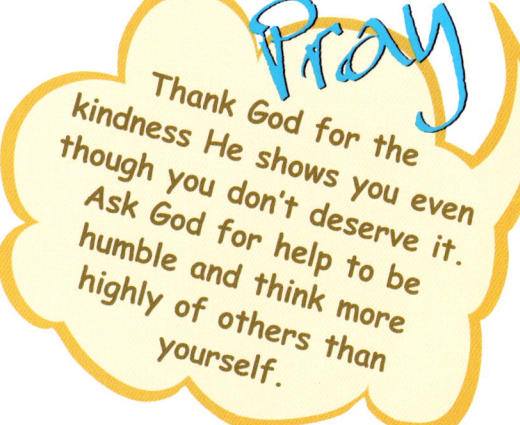

Pray
Thank God for the kindness He shows you even though you don't deserve it. Ask God for help to be humble and think more highly of others than yourself.

...through the Bible day by day

August 20

Reading: **Luke 7. 11-17**

He who was dead sat up, and began to speak, Luke 7. 15

The Lord and His disciples went into a city called Nain and came across a very sad procession. A woman who had already had her heart broken once when her husband died was grieving again because of the death of her only son.

When the Lord saw her He was very sorry for her. He was sensitive to the woman's feelings. The Bible tells us we should be considerate of how people are feeling. We need to learn to weep with those people who weep and rejoice with those who rejoice.

The Lord stopped the coffin the lad was on and told him to get up. Dead people can't hear, let alone get up, but when the Lord commands even the dead have to obey. So 'he who was dead sat up'! The Lord then reunited the son with his mother and so mended her broken heart. The Lord Jesus stood up in the temple one day and told people some of the things He had come to do. He said He was come to preach good news to the poor, to repair the sight of the blind and to heal the brokenhearted. He can still heal broken hearts today.

Sin brought disease and death into the world and sin breaks hearts because of the sadness it brings. The Lord Jesus Christ died for our sins and will take them away if we will trust Him as our Lord and Saviour. Happy is the person who trusts in the Lord. The song 'Happiness is to know the Saviour' sums it up well when it says, 'Real joy is mine, no matter if the tear drops start. I've found the secret — it's Jesus in my heart'. Do we know this secret?

Pray
Thank God we have examples of how the Lord Jesus Christ is so caring and compassionate. Ask God to help you to be caring and compassionate too.

Stepping stones

Reading: Luke 7. 18-35

August 21

Tell John the things you have seen and heard: that the blind see, the lame walk, the lepers are cleansed, the deaf hear, the dead are raised, the poor have the gospel preached to them, Luke 7. 22

At one time John the Baptist had no doubts who the Lord Jesus was and why He had come. John had once seen the Lord walking beside the river Jordan and had called out, 'Behold! The Lamb of God who takes away the sin of the world', John 1. 29. Now, however, John is in prison, not because he had committed any crime, but simply because he had pointed out that King Herod was doing wrong. Doubts start to creep into John's mind now. He may have been thinking, If Jesus really is the Promised One, I shouldn't be in prison. Sometimes, like John, it's harder to believe in the Lord Jesus than at other times. Then it is important to remember that although we may change the Lord never does. He is the same yesterday, today and forever. Jesus still encourages us to cast all our care upon Him because He cares for us.

> **Pray**
> Thank God for the greatness of His Son, the Lord Jesus Christ. Ask God to remove any doubts and for help to appreciate more and more His wonderful Son.

If we ever doubt, we can take John's example and look again at the Lord. John was stuck in prison so he sent his disciples to Jesus. We can't see Jesus for ourselves either but we can read about Him in the Bible. His miracles remind us that He really is the Son of God, John 5. 36.

Nicodemus said, 'We know that You are a teacher come from God; for no one can do these signs that You do unless God is with him', John 3. 2. How we behave also shows people who we are. 'By this all will know that you are My disciples, if you have love for one another', John 13. 35.

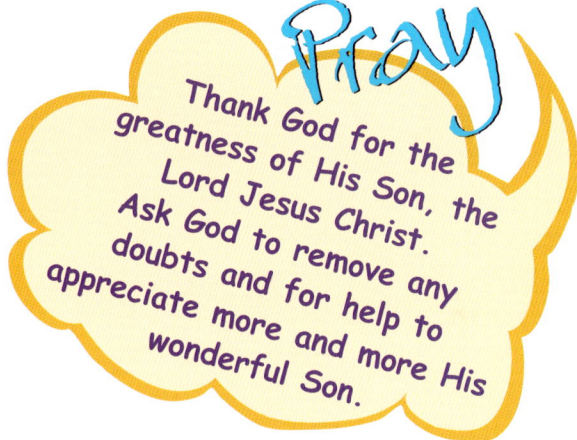

. . . through the Bible day by day

August 22

Reading: **Luke 7. 36-50**

Her sins, which are many, are forgiven, for she loved much. But to whom little is forgiven, the same loves little, Luke 7. 47

Pray

Thank God that forgiveness of sins is available to all through believing in the Lord Jesus Christ. Ask God that He might help you to be more grateful to him.

The Lord was having a meal at Simon the Pharisee's house when a gate crasher came in. It was a woman well known for being openly sinful. She had come to show her love and appreciation for the Lord. Although she hadn't been specifically invited to the meal the Lord had given an open invitation to all who were weary and heavy laden with sin to come to Him and He would give them rest.

Simon, in whose house the meal was being served, was very put out by the woman's interruption. He could not understand what she did nor did he understand why the Lord would have anything to do with a woman like this. So the Lord explained by telling a story about two debtors. One owed fifty pence the other five hundred but neither could pay his debt. The creditor, who gave them the money, kindly forgave them both their debt. 'So', the Lord asked Simon. 'Which one would be the most grateful?' Simon answered, 'The one who owed the most and had the most forgiven'. He had given the right answer.

The Lord went on to explain that this woman had shown such great appreciation of Him because, although she had such a debt of sin, she had been completely forgiven. In fact the Lord told her plainly that her sins had been forgiven and because of her faith in Him she was saved. The parable was a strong hint to Simon that, as he had shown no gratitude whatsoever to Jesus, he had not yet known any forgiveness. What a challenge to those of us who know the forgiveness of the Lord! What can we do for Him today to show our gratitude, love and appreciation of what He has done for us?

Stepping stones

Reading: **Mark 3. 19-27**

August 23

If a house is divided against itself, that house cannot stand, Mark 3. 25

The saying, 'United we stand, divided we fall' is so true in many different situations. The Lord Jesus said that it was true of a kingdom and also of a household. It can also be seen in sport especially in team games. I remember playing football and seeing the opposition start to blame each other for mistakes, bicker and then fall out. When that happened we knew it wouldn't be long until our team was winning. As long as we played like a team and were united (not necessarily like Manchester United) as one man we would win.

The Lord said that unity is very important in a household. When families stick together and work as a team a lot more can be achieved. Whatever battles come along can be faced together. Difficulties seem much smaller and can be dealt with far more quickly when there is unity in a household. However, when there is disharmony and when we are too busy fighting among ourselves the enemy gains an advantage. If we are distracted by each other we forget about the danger Satan poses to our families each and every day. When families are united they are at their strongest but when disunited they are at their weakest.

The Lord told a parable in today's reading about how a strong man's house can't be spoiled unless the strong man is first tied up. Once he is tied up his house can be spoiled. If we become tied up quarrelling with one another we will then be in no position to defend against any attack from Satan and are in danger of having our family spoiled. So remember, 'United we stand, divided we fall'!

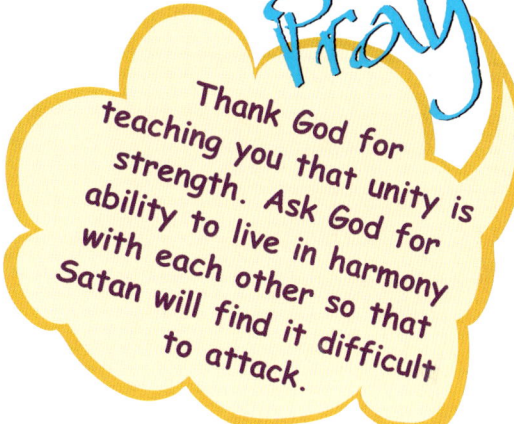

Pray

Thank God for teaching you that unity is strength. Ask God for ability to live in harmony with each other so that Satan will find it difficult to attack.

. . . through the Bible day by day

August 24

Reading: Matthew 12. 46-50

He is not ashamed to call them brethren, Hebrews 2. 11

One of the favourite celebrations of the year has to be a birthday. The tremendous thing for Christians is that we have two birthdays. Birthday number one is when we were born into this world and became a member of our natural family. We celebrate that birthday once a year. For Christians their second birthday is the day that they trust Christ as their Saviour, receive eternal life and are born into God's family. This is called being born again. Each Christian surely must celebrate the wonder of this every single day, not just once a year. An adapted version of the Happy Birthday song says 'Happy birthday to you, only one will not do, take Christ as your Saviour and then you'll have two'.

Not only does the Bible teach us that Christians have two birthdays. It also says they have two families. The Lord Jesus tells us in today's Bible reading that those who do the will of His Father are His brothers and sisters. Believers in the Lord Jesus Christ have God as their Father and so all other believers are their brothers and sisters too – brothers and sisters in the Lord.

One of the most wonderful things about being in God's family is that, regardless of age, colour or nationality, there is a special bond of love for the Lord and a special affection that Christians have for each other. Many times Christians find they have more in common with other Christians they have just met than with non-Christians they have known for years.

The Lord Jesus is not ashamed to call believers His brothers and sisters. Our challenge is that we should not be ashamed to be known as believers in the Lord Jesus nor be unwilling to do what His Father in heaven wants us to do.

Pray

Thank God He is a kind Father and that we have so many Christian brothers and sisters to love. Ask God for help not to be ashamed of the Lord Jesus.

Reading: Matthew 13. 1-23

August 25

I planted, Apollos watered; but God gave the increase, 1 Corinthians 3. 6

When sowing a seed, the ground the seed falls into needs to be good ground because its condition will determine how well the seed will grow. The Lord Jesus uses this parable to show how God's word can be planted as a seed and then bear fruit in someone's heart.

Four types of ground are described. The first ground the seed landed on was hard and the birds came and snatched the seed away. Unfortunately, some people's hearts can be stubborn and won't let God's word in. Then Satan snatches it away. The Bible warns us not to harden our hearts, Hebrews 4. 7.

The second type of ground had rock underneath the shallow soil so the seed could not put down roots. This is a picture of what happens when God's word has some effect in making a person interested but it does not lead to them being saved. Then, when problems and difficulties come, they give up. Let us make sure we are saved and continue to live for God as we should.

In the third type of ground the seed seems to grow for a while but then weeds grow up stronger and thicker and choke the growth. Some people seem to receive God's word well and show signs of life. Later, however, other things become more interesting and important and these other things win. True faith in Christ should overcome the world.

God wants us to have hearts like the last piece of ground, good, soft, fertile ground, producing fruit for His pleasure. Are we prepared to listen to and develop what the Bible teaches? Let's not allow anything to get in the way or distract us from receiving God's word and obeying it. Then we will surely 'grow in grace', 2 Peter 3. 18.

Pray

Thank God for His Word, the Bible, and for those who sow the good news about His Son, the Lord Jesus Christ. Ask God for help to sow this seed.

. . . through the Bible day by day

August 26

Reading: Mark 4. 35-43

Who can this be, that even the wind and the sea obey Him! Mark 4. 41

'Why are you so fearful? How is it you have no faith?' These are the questions the Lord Jesus asked those sailing with Him in the boat. Perhaps He will ask them of us.

Obviously, the reason for their fear and lack of faith was that they didn't truly appreciate the wonderful person of the Lord Jesus. If they had understood who He was they would have had no need to doubt or fear, for He is the Son of God, the Creator of the universe, including the wind and the waves.

Picture the scene, waves lashing over the side, the boat filling with water, shipwreck and death very close. Yet the Lord Jesus is the calm in the storm, fully at peace, lying fast asleep. The men can't understand it and they wake Him up with some of the saddest words recorded in the Bible. 'Do You not care that we perish?'

What a question to ask the Saviour of the world! Of course He cares. The very reason He was in the world was because He cared that we were perishing. 'For God so loved the world that He gave His only begotten Son, that whoever believes in Him should not perish but have everlasting life', John 3. 16. Can we think of a more horrific word in the English language than this word 'perish'?

Faith in the Lord Jesus for salvation means we need not be afraid about the next life, about eternity. There will be no perishing for us – after all we have everlasting life which cannot be taken away from us. However, we must also trust in Him every single day so that we might know His peace through the troubles of life that we may soon have to face.

Pray
Thank God that the Lord Jesus willingly came to die for us that we might never perish. Ask God to help you not to say words that would grieve Him.

Stepping stones

Reading: Mark 5.1-20

August 27

They began to plead with Him to depart from their region, Mark 5. 17

Transformers are fantastic toys that start as robots but with skilful twists transform into a car, a boat or a plane. The man in today's reading goes through an amazing transformation by the power of the Lord Jesus.

When the Lord Jesus arrived on shore He was greeted by this deranged man. We are told the man was mad because he was possessed by demons. He ran about the mountains and graves with no clothes on, cutting himself with stones. People had tried to tame him and even tied him in chains. But their efforts were futile.

Could the Lord Jesus help this seemingly hopeless case? Of course He could. With God all things are possible. The Lord got rid of the man's problem by expelling the unclean spirits. They then possessed a herd of terrified pigs which ran over the cliff and fell into the sea. The pig-herders ran to tell everyone what had happened. When everyone came to see for themselves, they saw the man sitting at Jesus' feet clothed and sane.

The great transformer of mankind had done it again. The good news is that He still transforms people today. All who trust Him receive forgiveness of sins and the power to win the fight against sin every day.

The people in the city rejected Christ and asked Him to leave. How tragic was that! What about the man? He wanted to go with the Lord but the Lord had a special task for him. He was to go and tell his friends about what the Lord had done for him. What a privilege for the man. May we have the same courage to tell our friends about what our Saviour has done for us, even if they still reject Him.

Pray

Ask God for help to tell your friends the great things the Lord has done for you. Thank God that all can be saved, no matter how bad they may be.

. . . through the Bible day by day

August 28

Reading: Mark 5. 25-34

His disciples said to Him, 'You see the multitude thronging You, and You say, "Who touched me?"', Mark 5. 31

Here is another seemingly hopeless case for the Lord to deal with. For twelve years this poor woman had been ill, seeing doctor after doctor and spending all her money trying to find a cure. The unfortunate thing was that, instead of getting better, she grew worse. With nowhere else to go and no one else to turn to she reached out in faith to the Saviour, the Lord Jesus. She was healed not because she touched His clothes but because of her faith in Him.

She must have been on her knees or even lower because when she reached out to Him all she could get hold of was the hem of His clothes, the part that would have touched the ground as He walked. Unfortunately, some people like this woman wait until they are in despair and can't get any lower before reaching out to the Lord. There is no need to wait that long. He is always ready and willing to save those who come to Him.

The Lord knew who had touched Him. He asked, 'Who touched my clothes?' so that she could own up publicly that she had been ill and was now healed. The Lord does not want those who have known His saving power to hide it but to be open about it.

It may be that we, like this woman, would do so in fear and trembling but the Lord will give us the peace and the help as He did her. A song I once heard seems to sum up the lesson from today's reading:

'Just reach out and He'll reach in,

Take your broken heart and make it whole again.

It doesn't matter who you are or where you've been,

Just reach out and He'll reach in'.

Pray

Thank God for the wonderful examples we have of the love and compassion of the Lord. Ask God for help to tell out fearlessly His good news of Christ.

Reading: **Mark 5. 21-43**

August 29

As soon as Jesus heard the word that was spoken, He said to the ruler of the synagogue, 'Do not be afraid; only believe',
Mark 5. 36

The Lord Jesus once cured a mad man whom no one could control and He also healed a woman whom no doctor could cure. Surely, however, this was the most hopeless of all cases. The little girl's dad, Jairus, would have thought all hope had gone when they came from his house to tell him not to trouble the Master any more because his little girl was dead. Jairus' heart would have sunk into despair. Surely no words could bring comfort or hope to the poor father except for the words of the Saviour, 'Don't be afraid, only believe'.

Jairus had to put his trust in the Lord as they went to the house where the little girl lay. When the Lord saw her He said she was only sleeping. All the mourners laughed out loud because they knew she was dead. They were right. She was dead, but the Lord called it sleep because it was only temporary. She would not be dead for long. When believers in the Lord die the Bible also calls them those 'who sleep in Jesus'. This death is only temporary until the Lord comes again to take those believers that have died and those believers that are still alive when He returns, to be with Him forever.

Pray

We have such a great and mighty God who is all powerful. Ask God for help to suffer patiently when others laugh at you for being a Christian.

The Lord took the little girl by the hand and told her to get up. Immediately she got up and walked. Can you imagine the joy and amazement of her mum and dad when they saw their twelve-year-old daughter, who had been dead, get up again?

There were those who laughed at the Lord while He was on the earth and sadly there are those who mock Christians today. Christians, however, are on the side of the One who has proved He has power over death.

. . . through the Bible day by day

August 30

Reading: Matthew 14. 1-12

His disciples came and took away the body and buried it, and went and told Jesus, Matthew 14. 12

Pray

Thank God for making it clear that you may have to suffer for being a Christian. Ask God for help to stand up for what is right.

A young boy was overjoyed to be picked for his local football team but was very unhappy and disappointed to discover his coach was cheating as he was playing boys in the team that were too old for the under-fourteens league. When he spoke to the coach and told him it was wrong the lad was dropped from the team. Sadly, standing up for what is right will often cost us a lot. It may mean we will be unpopular with those who are doing wrong and benefitting from it.

John the Baptist was standing up for God's word against the most powerful man in the country, the king. It must have taken a lot of courage to stand before the king and the others in his palace and point out to the king that the way he was living was an offence to God. John would know that the king would have a great influence over those who looked up to him. They may have thought that if it was all right for the king to go against God's word it was all right for them too.

John was a God-fearing and a God-honouring man. The Bible tells us it is important to pray for our government and all those in a position of authority. This is so that we may lead a quiet and peaceful life, 1 Timothy 2. 2. Sometimes, however, we may have to speak up. John died for his courage and stand against wickedness. Many Christians over the years have also suffered for their faith and some are still suffering today. May we have John's courage to do what is right even though it may cost us something. Remember that our ultimate reward will come from the King of Kings.

Stepping stones

Reading: **John 6. 66-71**

August 31

There is a lad here who has five barley loaves and two small fish, but what are they among so many? John 6. 9

Have you ever had to share your picnic lunch with someone else? Or perhaps you had a packet of sweets that you had to share around. It's not too hard a thing to do if you have some of it yourself. But just imagine how you would feel if some grown-ups came to you and asked you to give away *all* your lunch, as this boy did!

Many years ago I arrived late and sat at the back of a prayer meeting. An old gentleman got up to his feet and read this story. He did not know I was there. 'There is a lad in this assembly, too, called Ian', he said. 'All he has is five loaves and two fish. But if he would only give that to the Lord, there will be enough to feed many people'.

I have never forgotten what he said. Did he mean that I literally had bread and fish in my pocket? No. He meant that I had just a little ability to teach God's Word. He meant that what little ability I may have had would not have helped many people unless God blessed it. But if I gave my little gift to God, He could use it to help many.

This is true of any one of us, of course. It doesn't matter if we haven't got much to give the Lord. Five bread rolls and two small fish was all this young boy had. But he gave it all to Jesus and Jesus multiplied it in a wonderful way. Maybe you don't have much to give God. But He can take a little and make it a lot if we give it to Him.

Did He take my 'five loaves and two fish' and feed many people with it? I think so. He can take yours, too.

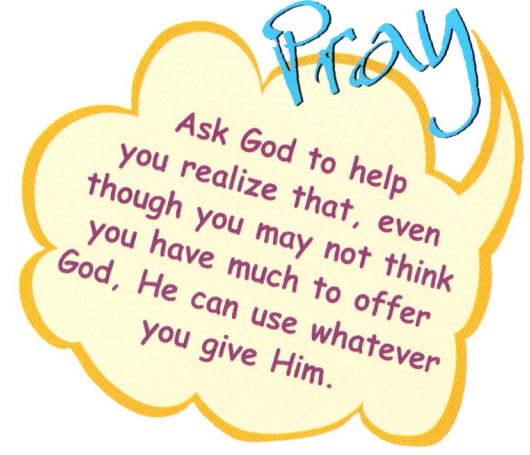

Pray

Ask God to help you realize that, even though you may not think you have much to offer God, He can use whatever you give Him.

...through the Bible day by day

September 1

Reading: Matthew 14. 22-33

According to your faith let it be to you,
Matthew 9. 29

Can you imagine how Peter was feeling when he was walking on the water? He must have been terrified as he heard the wind howling and felt the sea beneath his feet. One minute he had been safe in the boat, and now he was on the open wave. Why had he been crazy enough to think he wanted to walk on the water to Jesus?

Have you ever been terrified?

Life is full of frightening things like thunder and lightning, darkness and even spiders! Perhaps you are scared of other people who bully you and are nasty. New experiences, like starting a new school, can be very frightening. Many people even live with the fear of illness or death. How can we feel safe and secure in a world that is so full of fear?

Do you remember Peter? He was safe as long as he kept his eyes on Jesus but he started to sink when he looked at the waves. The same is true for us. It is very important for us to keep our eyes on Jesus. We do this by reading about Him, thinking about Him, speaking to Him in prayer and praising Him. We should also remember how much He loves us and how much He has done for us by dying on the cross. If we do this our eyes will be on Him and we will know that He is right beside us keeping us safe.

Pray
Ask God to help you whenever you are afraid. Thank Him for promising to be near you.

If we 'look around' at our difficulties and fears we will start to doubt God and His word. We may even stop trusting Him the way we used to and 'sink' into unbelief. Let's make sure that today, whatever happens, we won't look around at the 'storms' but we will keep our eyes fixed on Jesus.

Reading: John 6. 22-59

September 2

Jesus said to them, 'I am the bread of life. He who comes to Me shall never hunger, and he who believes in Me shall never thirst', John 6. 35

I once had a fridge magnet that said, 'Some people eat to live and other people live to eat!' It's true. Some of us are not interested in food but we still have to eat up those vegetables to grow strong! Some of us *love* food and like nothing better than trying out new foods and new places to eat.

God has made our bodies, and food is the 'fuel' that runs them. He kindly provides this food for us every day. In the Old Testament He fed the children of Israel with manna and in the New Testament the Lord Jesus fed over five thousand people with just five loaves and two fish.

But did you know there is something even more important than the food we eat? It is the *spiritual* food we need for our souls. In John chapter 6 verse 27 the Lord Jesus spoke about 'food which endures to everlasting life'. Our lives have a spiritual side which also has to be 'fed' and cared for. This spiritual part of us is even more important than our bodies.

So where do we get spiritual food? Jesus answers this Himself in our memory verse when He says, '*I am the bread of life. He who comes to Me shall never hunger*'. This means that when we believe in Him we no longer feel empty but satisfied.

He also said, '*He who eats this bread will live forever*', John 6. 58. This means by trusting the Lord Jesus we will have everlasting life with Him in heaven.

It's wonderful to feel full after a lovely meal. But it's so much better to know that the Lord Jesus is all we need to satisfy our spiritual hunger pains!

Pray

Thank God at every mealtime for the food He has given you. Give thanks also for Jesus, the bread of life, who will satisfy you and give you everlasting life.

... through the Bible day by day

September 3

READING: Matthew 16. 13-20

Simon Peter answered and said, 'You are the Christ, the Son of the living God', Matthew 16. 16

Peter was a great disciple of the Lord Jesus. He had so many questions to ask, but this time Jesus had a question to ask him; 'Who do you say that I am?'

Other people had thought Jesus was John the Baptist, Elijah or Jeremiah but the Lord wanted to know what His disciples thought. Peter was the first one to jump in with his answer. 'You are the Christ, the Son of the living God', he said boldly. And he was right! What a wonderful reply he had given but only because God Himself had told him the answer! Matthew 16. 17.

Jesus was pleased with Peter's answer, then He said a very strange thing. 'You are Peter, and on this rock I will build My church'. Here is a little Greek lesson to help you see what Jesus meant.

He said, 'You are *Peter*', which means, 'You are a *little stone* (petros)'. Then He said, 'on this *rock* I will build My church' and the word 'rock' is 'petra' which means a very big stone like a foundation boulder in a house. Some people say that the Lord Jesus was going to build His church on Peter, the 'little stone', but this is not so. He was going to build His church on the great cornerstone fact that Jesus Christ is the Son of God! What a foundation boulder that truth is; that Jesus Christ was no ordinary man but was the Son of God.

Now that's a truth that is powerful and solid and secure enough to build a mighty church on . . . and He's still building and there's nothing Satan can do about it!

Pray

Ask God to help you be strong in your belief that Jesus Christ is the Son of God.

Stepping stones

Reading: Matthew 16. 21-23

September 4

Do not . . . give place to the devil,
Ephesians 4. 26-27

Pray
Ask God to help you to be a careful Christian. Ask Him to make you strong when Satan tries to bring you down.

Have you ever been excited that everything in your life is going well? Have you ever felt pleased that your behaviour has been very good? Have you ever smiled to yourself when you think how much you are pleasing the Lord Jesus?

This is how Peter must have felt after he had stated that Jesus was the Son of God, and Jesus had called him, 'Blessed', Matthew 16. 17. What a good day this had been for him. He had been used by God!

Were you surprised to read that just a short time later Jesus had to turn to Peter and say, 'Get behind Me, *Satan*'? What had gone wrong? Jesus had explained to his disciples that He was on His way to Jerusalem to suffer and die. Peter couldn't cope with this idea and said, 'This shall not happen to You', Matthew 16. 22. Now the Lord Jesus had to give Peter a row as he had said something very wrong.

Have you ever had that feeling, when your sunny day suddenly becomes very cloudy? Have you ever done something bad just after you have been *so* good? This happens to all of us, and it's because Satan likes to bring us down and spoil our lives. He wants us to do wrong instead of right. He waits till we are being careless, then he makes us fall.

Let's learn the lesson from Peter, that we must always be careful, especially after we have done something very good. And let's make sure that we are used by God and not Satan!

. . . through the Bible day by day

September 5

Reading: John 6. 66-71

Lord, to whom shall we go? You have the words of eternal life, John 6. 68

Pray

Thank God that the Lord Jesus is the way to eternal life. Ask Him to help you follow Him, even when others turn away.

It's time to tell you a secret! I once lay thinking in bed at night. I was thinking about what I had learned in Sunday School. I had been a Christian since I was young, but now I was having doubts. Was there a God out there? Did God's Son come to earth? Was there a Heaven and Hell? Was I really saved? None of my friends at school believed and I began to wonder if I was crazy!

Then this story from John chapter 6 verses 66-71 came into my head. I remembered that lots of people had followed Jesus and said they believed in Him. Then many of them left and would not follow Him any more. I pictured the Lord Jesus sadly turning to His twelve disciples and saying, 'Do you also want to go away?' At that moment I felt as if the Lord Jesus was saying these words to me. Was I going to stop following Him? Immediately the words of Peter came into my mind, 'Lord, to whom shall we go? You have the words of eternal life'. It became clear. Who else did I have? Who else explains how this world was formed? Who else tells us where we came from and where we are going? Who else explains why we are the way we are? And who else loved us enough to die for us?

I remember crying in my bed and thanking God for reminding me of this story. Even if my friends didn't believe I *would*, as Jesus is the only One who can give eternal life. I am much older now but I still hold on to that verse if the doubts come. Why don't you do the same?

Reading: Matthew 17. 1-8

September 6

We made known to you the power and coming of our Lord Jesus Christ, and were eyewitnesses of His majesty,
2 Peter 1. 16

Do you have a good imagination? When I read the historical events of the Bible I like to try to imagine what it was *really* like to have been there. Let's try and do this for the story in today's reading.

It would have been an ordinary day for Peter, James and John but Jesus was going to show them something they would never forget! Can you imagine the four of them climbing up the high mountain? At the top the Lord Jesus was 'transfigured' before them. This means His appearance was dramatically changed.

Imagine how He must have looked. His face was shining as bright as the sun! On a sunny day you can't even look at the sun. It is too bright and would hurt your eyes. This is how bright Jesus' face was. Think of His clothes becoming as white as the light. Then a cloud came right over them and the voice of God said out loud, 'This is My beloved Son'. Can you imagine how amazed the disciples were? They had only seen the Lord Jesus as a humble man in ordinary clothes. Now the glory of God is seen shining from Him. This was a tiny glimpse of the majesty of the Son of God before He came to Earth.

This also helps us realize how awesome He is now in heaven. One day we will all see Him like this. Some people will be terrified as they never trusted in Him but those of us who believed will share in His glory! Today may have started as an ordinary day for you, but this could be the day when we look upon the glory of our wonderful Lord Jesus.

Pray
Praise God that one day we will look upon a glorious Lord Jesus Christ and share in His glory!

...through the Bible day by day

September 7

Reading: Matthew 17. 24-27

You know the grace of our Lord Jesus Christ, that though He was rich, yet for your sakes He became poor,
2 Corinthians 8. 9

'I want it and I want it *now*!' I heard a little boy screaming this in a shop one day. His mum explained he didn't need it and she didn't have the money for it but, guess what – he got it!

Sometimes we are all like that. We want something and we want it now but we don't have the money for it. Maybe we resent this and wish we were richer!

It might help us to remember that when the Lord Jesus was here on earth He was poor. He wasn't born in a hospital, He didn't own a home and He had very little money or possessions. Even the tomb He was buried in was borrowed.

In today's Bible reading we learn that Jesus was asked to pay a tax towards the upkeep of the temple. Notice how He didn't go into His purse or wallet and pay. He probably didn't have the money.

I love the way the money was found. Jesus showed that He was the Creator. He knew that there was a fish in the sea nearby that had exactly the right amount of money in its mouth. He then made the fish swim right up to Peter's hook and bite it. Amazing! So now Peter and Jesus could pay the temple tax. This teaches us that Jesus used His money to pay what He owed and to help others. We should follow His example. Our money is not for us to get, get, get. We should be willing to share. And if we feel that we aren't quite rich enough, let's stop being discontented and remember our blessed Lord was poor and that it was 'for *your* sakes He became poor'!

Pray

Thank God that Jesus was willing to become poor for us. Ask Him to help you be contented with whatever you have.

Reading: Matthew 18. 1-7

September 8

Let the little children come to Me, and do not forbid them; for of such is the kingdom of God, Mark 10. 14

We had such a great time at Funland recently. It's a large indoor play centre; perfect for a rainy day in the summer holidays! There are things to climb on and things to crawl under and every kind of fun activity for a little child (and even those not so little!). I watched as my friend's adorable little boy stood at the top of a large slide. He wanted to go down it but he wasn't sure. He waited till his mum stood at the bottom with her arms outstretched. Then he threw himself down the slide, straight into the safety of her hands! He enjoyed it so much. He was able to enjoy it because he was trusting in someone much bigger and stronger than himself to keep him safe.

In Matthew chapter 18 the Lord Jesus said we have to become like little children. This doesn't mean we have to use a dummy and start crawling about again! It means we have to trust in someone who is much bigger and stronger than us. That *Someone* is the Lord Jesus Christ. He wants us to come to Him and completely trust Him to take us to heaven. This means we have to be humble and admit we can't do it ourselves. He wants us to trust Him for everything in our lives. Every problem we have we can bring to Him, no matter how large or small. This means we have to be like a little child who trusts without questioning.

Whatever age we are doesn't matter. If we want to be in heaven and if we want the Lord Jesus to guide us through life we have to have faith that trusts just like a little child does.

Pray
The Lord Jesus loved, and still loves, children. Ask God for help to have faith like a little child.

...through the Bible day by day

September 9

Reading: Matthew 18. 15-22

Be kind to one another, tenderhearted, forgiving one another, even as God in Christ forgave you, Ephesians 4. 32

Pray

Thank God that your many sins have been forgiven. Ask for help to forgive others.

What does it mean to 'forgive'? I looked up the word in the dictionary and it means 'to stop feeling angry towards someone who has done wrong to you', or to 'let someone off if they owe you a debt'.

Can you think of someone who has done something wrong to you or who owes you something? I'm sure you can. Very often in our lives we will feel wronged or hurt. Maybe someone at school was nasty to us, or broke up a friendship, or let us down badly. This makes us feel hurt, angry and resentful.

How does the Bible tell us we should deal with this? Should we cry and feel sorry for ourselves? Should we fight back and be just as nasty to them? Or should we talk about it to everyone who will listen to our side of the story? The answer to all of these is NO!

Jesus teaches us that first we should explain to the person who has offended us what he or she has done wrong. Then we must forgive him. This means we should stop feeling angry towards him and let him off for what he has done.

That is a *very* hard thing for us to do. We would rather hold on to our bitterness and think bad things about that person! The truth is, that by holding on to bitterness the only person we are hurting is ourselves.

Let's just do what Jesus said and forgive seventy times seven, in other words, over and over again.

If you think you can't do that, take a minute to think how much Christ has forgiven you!

Reading: Luke 9. 57-62

September 10

I also count all things loss for the excellence of the knowledge of Christ Jesus my Lord, for whom I have suffered the loss of all things, and count them as rubbish, Philippians 3. 8

When I was young we used to play a game called 'Follow the Leader'. We all got into a line and the person at the front was the leader. As we moved around the playground everyone had to follow the leader and copy what he or she did. Following Jesus is a bit like that too. He is our leader and we are behind Him, walking in His steps and trying to be like Him.

That is a very easy thing to say, but we learn in our Bible reading today that there is a cost to following the Lord Jesus. We read about three people who wanted to follow the Lord. Jesus had to make clear to them the true cost of being a disciple. He showed them that to follow Him His disciples might have to give up certain things like their homes, their belongings and even certain aspects of family life. They would no longer be living for themselves. He would have first place in their lives. He also said if they started to follow Him they must never look back.

This is a very challenging lesson. If we are saved and can say, 'I follow Jesus', we must understand it will cost us everything. We must be willing to give things up that will come between Him and us. We must be willing to use our possessions for His work even if that means we will never be rich. We must be prepared to give our whole selves to Him.

How wonderful it would be if we were like the apostle Paul and counted everything else as 'loss' so that we could know Christ, be like Christ and follow in His steps!

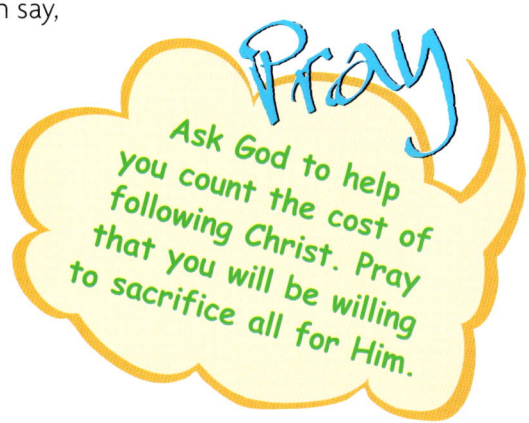

Pray

Ask God to help you count the cost of following Christ. Pray that you will be willing to sacrifice all for Him.

...through the Bible day by day

September 11

Reading: John 7. 37-52

So there was a division among the people because of Him, John 7. 43

Pray

Thank God that you know who Christ is. Ask Him to help you to be strong when others speak against Him.

If you are a Christian then you understand who Christ is. You believe that He is the Son of God and you know that He is the Messiah sent to the Jews. You accept that He is the only Saviour of the world.

Many people, however, do not understand who Christ is. Some will accept that He was a good man and maybe even a prophet. Most will not accept His claim to be the only way to heaven and it is no longer 'politically correct' to state this fact.

We must understand that our friends at school will not think the same about the Lord Jesus as we do. Even when Jesus lived here opinion was divided about Him.

When He made the appeal on the last day of the Feast of Tabernacles to come to Him and believe in Him there was a mixed reaction. Some people said He must be the prophet or even the Messiah. Others showed their ignorance of His background by saying the Messiah wouldn't come from Galilee but Bethlehem! The chief priests, rulers and Pharisees were definite that none of them had ever believed on Him.

There was a split in the crowd over what they thought about Jesus. The same is true today. If you were to talk about the Lord Jesus to your friends there would be many different opinions about Him, and not all would be positive.

It is good for us to be prepared for this. We should understand that other people do not love the Lord as we do. We should accept this, but do not let it move us in our conviction that He is indeed the Messiah, the Son of God and the only Saviour of the world.

Stepping stones

Reading: John 8. 1-11

September 12

For such a High Priest was fitting for us, who is holy, harmless, undefiled, separate from sinners, Hebrews 7. 26

'People in glass houses shouldn't throw stones'. This is a famous proverb that reminds us that we shouldn't criticize other people for faults that we also have. We are very quick to spot the bad points in other people and often fail to notice that we are just as bad ourselves.

The scribes and Pharisees were like this. They had found a woman committing adultery and they wanted to stone her to death. They brought her to Jesus in the temple and tried to trick Him by asking what He thought should be done to her.

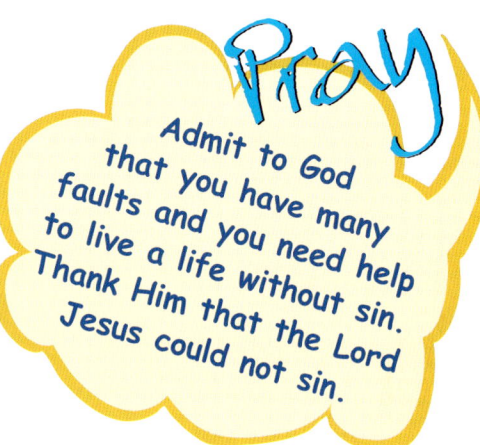

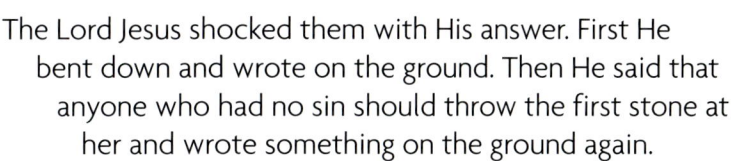

Pray
Admit to God that you have many faults and you need help to live a life without sin. Thank Him that the Lord Jesus could not sin.

The Lord Jesus shocked them with His answer. First He bent down and wrote on the ground. Then He said that anyone who had no sin should throw the first stone at her and wrote something on the ground again. Maybe He was giving them time to think. Did you notice what they did? From the oldest to the youngest they left and not a stone was thrown. They knew they were just as sinful as her.

Did you notice the one person who was left standing there? It was the Lord Jesus. He stayed because He was the only one who was absolutely perfect and He had never done one single sin. He could have stoned her but instead He did not condemn her but told her to go and stop sinning.

Let's learn to look at ourselves and correct our own faults instead of criticizing others. And let's ask the perfect, sinless Man called Jesus to help us do this.

. . . through the Bible day by day

September 13

Reading: **John 8. 12-24**

Jesus spoke to them again, saying, 'I am the light of the world. He who follows Me shall not walk in darkness, but have the light of life', John 8. 12

Pray

Thank God for Jesus, the light of the world. Thank Him for delivering us from darkness. Ask God's help to walk in His light.

Everyone has a favourite place. Mine is Corbiere on the island of Jersey in the English Channel. At Corbiere there is a lighthouse which stands on rocks overlooking the sea. If the tide is out you can walk right out to the lighthouse. If you've never been, you should go one day.

The lighthouse does a very important job. It must shine out a bright light to sailors to keep them away from dangerous rocks and to show them the way. If there was no light a boat could get lost in the darkness and may hit rocks and sink.

This world is a place of spiritual darkness because of sin. Many people have lost their way and are in danger of ruining their lives. Many are under the judgement of God.

So what is our hope in this stormy life? It is found in the One who said, 'I am the light of the world'. Christ is our light. He shows the way and saves us from danger. He has promised that we do not have to walk in darkness but can have 'the light of life'.

This is a wonderful promise but note what we have to do. We have to 'follow'. This word has the idea of giving yourself completely to the One you follow. If we follow Christ we will be able to see our way and we will be no longer in danger. We can be sure He will lead us in life and will take us safely to heaven.

So the next time you see a lighthouse think of the blessed Lord Jesus Christ, give thanks you are safe, and walk in His marvellous light!

Reading: **John 9. 1-12**

September 14

One thing I know: that though I was blind, now I see, John 9. 25

Have you ever tried to imagine being blind? I used to close my eyes to feel what it was like but I quickly opened them again. It was always a relief to see the light streaming in and to look at everything beautiful around me.

This poor blind man couldn't do that. He had *never* seen a single thing. He didn't know what a flower or a bird or even his own family looked like! All he could do was beg for food.

One day all that changed. He met Jesus! How amazing it is to read how Jesus made clay from the dust and put it on his eyes. Some people think He might have been making him new eyes. Whatever happened, one thing was clear – this man who had been born blind could now see! Such a thing had never been heard of before. What a difference Jesus made!

Pray

Thank God if you have eyes to see all the beauty around you. Ask Him to give you spiritual sight that sees things from God's point of view.

The same is true today. We were born spiritually blind. This means that we couldn't see things as God sees them. We couldn't see how to do right. We couldn't see God's eternal plan. We couldn't understand God's Word and we would never see heaven because of our sin.

The good news is that the Lord Jesus can cure our spiritual blindness. He can make us see our sin. He can make us see the purposes of God and help us understand His Word. He can take us to see heaven.

To have our eyes opened we must believe. The blind man believed and went and washed his eyes in the pool of Siloam. Let's have the faith to believe in our Lord Jesus and know that one day we will *see* His face!

. . . through the Bible day by day

September 15

Reading: **John 10. 1-10**

I am the door. If anyone enters by Me, he will be saved, and will go in and out and find pasture, John 10. 9

Maybe you are reading this but you are not a Christian. Maybe you have never put your trust in the Lord Jesus Christ. Maybe you have not had your sins forgiven. You know that you are not going to heaven. Let's think about this beautiful part of the Bible and find out how you can be saved.

In Israel, where Jesus lived, shepherds would lead their flocks of sheep to find grass to eat. At night the sheep would be placed safely in a fold and often the shepherd would lie across the opening to form a door. In doing this he was protecting his sheep from thieves and wild animals. He was keeping them safe. Any sheep that was on the wrong side of the door was in great danger.

The Lord Jesus calls Himself the Door. This means that He is our way to safety. In our sins we are in danger of the judgement of God. We can't go to heaven as no sin is allowed there. If we died we could never be saved.

But the Lord Jesus loved us so much He came all the way down from heaven and died on a cross to take the punishment for our sins. Now He offers a way to be saved. If we trust in Him and ask Him to be our Saviour He will take away our sins. This means the judgement of God is no longer upon us and we are safe – just like the sheep in the fold!

But it's up to you. The door has two sides – inside and outside. Trust the Lord Jesus today and make sure you are on the inside.

Pray

If you have not yet become a Christian, ask Jesus into your life to be your Lord and Saviour. Thank God for sending His wonderful Son to die for us on the cross.

Reading: **John 10. 11-18**

September 16

My sheep hear My voice, and I know them, and they follow Me, John 10. 27

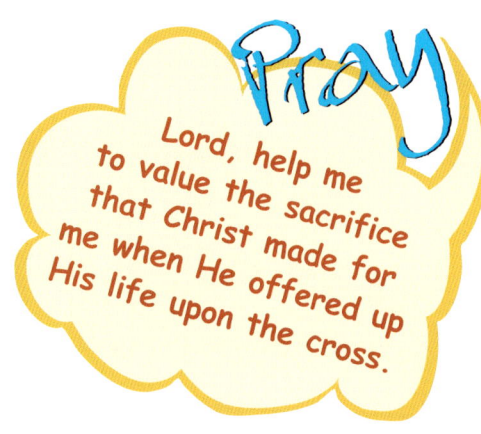

Pray

Lord, help me to value the sacrifice that Christ made for me when He offered up His life upon the cross.

Young Kate enjoyed her life on the remote hill farm. Her father was a shepherd and her mother worked as a school secretary. Sadly, Kate became very ill. Both of her kidneys had stopped working and the only thing that was keeping her alive was the dialysis machine on the hospital ward. She needed a kidney transplant. Tests showed that both her father and mother were suitable donors. So the surgeons removed one of her father's kidneys and transplanted it into the daughter.

The operation was a success. However, after ten years, that kidney failed, and it was then that the mother offered one of her kidneys. That operation too was a success, and thanks to the selfless attitude of her parents, Kate is now managing to lead a fairly normal life.

I am sure we are amazed at the tremendous sacrifice of the mother and father. What they did was worthy of the highest praise. I am also sure that the father wouldn't have made the same sacrifice for one of his sheep! And he certainly would not have given *his life*; not even for a whole flock of sheep! The sheep would have been left to perish.

How touching it is then to hear the Lord say, 'I am the good shepherd. The good shepherd gives His life for the sheep'. When God looks down upon mankind, He sees us all as sheep. 'All we like sheep have gone astray; we have turned, every one, to his own way', Isaiah 53. 6. We humans are the sheep for whom 'the good shepherd' gave His life. Do we appreciate the amazing sacrifice He made for us?

. . . through the Bible day by day

September 17

Reading: Luke 10. 25-37

Just as you want men to do to you, you also do to them, Luke 6. 31

Over today's story we could write the title, **'The Two Comings'**.

The First Coming: A 'certain man', who was most probably Jewish, was travelling from Jerusalem to Jericho. Jerusalem is 800 metres above sea level and Jericho is 258 metres below sea level, making it the lowest city on earth. Jericho was also a city that was cursed, Joshua 6. 26. So here we have a man who was on a downward journey, heading for the city of the curse, when all of a sudden he was attacked and left 'half dead'. This is a clear picture of the human race today as it turns its back on God and heads carelessly downhill towards destruction from God. This man was in *big* trouble! Sadly the two religious men failed to help. But then 'a certain Samaritan' suddenly appeared on the scene. If the victim's eyes had been open, the sight of the Samaritan must have caused his heart to sink, because the Jews and the Samaritans were bitter enemies. Surely he would get no help from this man! However, this Samaritan was different. Taking pity on him, 'he *came* where he was', and dressed the man's wounds. This is a picture of the *first coming* of Jesus, the Saviour, who *came* down to earth to save sinners.

The Second Coming: Having brought the Jew to an inn, the Samaritan took care of him. Before heading off the following day, he promised the innkeeper, 'When *I come again*, I will repay you'. The Lord Jesus also left His disciples with a precious promise, 'I *will* come again', John 14. 3. This is His *second coming*. How we look forward to seeing Him, who saved us when we were in trouble and has cared for us ever since!

Pray
Thank the Lord for the certain hope that one day He will return to take His people to the glory and splendour of heaven.

Stepping stones

Reading: Luke 10. 38-42

September 18

But one thing is needed, and Mary has chosen that good part, which will not be taken away from her, Luke 10. 42

The pages of our Bible contain many verses which give sound advice. A verse in the Old Testament asks, 'Can a man take fire to his bosom and his clothes not be burned?' Proverbs 6. 27. The answer to this question is obviously, 'No!' The New Testament puts the same truth in a slightly different way. 'Do not be deceived: 'Evil company corrupts good habits', 1 Corinthians 15. 33. In other words, be careful what sort of company you keep. Bad company leads to bad behaviour. That's why the psalmist could say blessed is the man who does not sit 'in the seat of the scornful', because scornful people, people who mock others, are bad company, and bad company leads to bad conduct. A clear example of this can be seen in the life of Peter. He sat at the fire warming himself in the company of those who had arrested his Lord. He was sitting with the 'scornful'. This really was *bad* company! It wasn't long before he 'began to curse and swear'.

Mary of Bethany sat at Jesus' feet and heard His word. She was in the best of company! She was not sitting with the scornful. She was at the feet of the Saviour listening carefully. She had chosen 'that good part'. Good company leads to good behaviour. We see this to be true when we meet Mary at a later date. At great personal cost, she took a pound of very expensive perfume and anointed the Lord. She was perhaps the only one who understood from His teaching that He was soon to die. She wanted to anoint His body before He was buried.

The lesson for us today is simply this; look for the Lord's company and be careful when choosing your friends!

Pray
Lord, help me to want to look for Your fellowship and the friendship of those who love You.

. . . through the Bible day by day

September 19

Reading: Luke 14. 16-24

They all with one accord began to make excuses, Luke 14. 18

Excuses! Excuses! Excuses! We've all made excuses at sometime. Some excuses are pathetic. There was the teenage golfer who, on the final hole before lunch, looked up at his friend and said, 'Ken, you know I'm so religious that when I saw my mother was ill this morning I didn't go to church'.

What about today's reading? Imagine how disappointed the master must have been when those invited to his grand supper began to make excuses. The master of the feast is like God who, at great personal cost – the death of His Son upon the cross – invites sinners to come in faith to Him so that they can feast in heaven. Many people these days show no interest in accepting this generous offer of salvation and respond with all sorts of excuses. Here are three of them:

Pray

Lord, I pray for those who hear the gospel. May they not make excuses, but may they come to trust the Saviour.

(1) 'I'm too young. I'll wait until I'm older'. But how do you know you will get older? The Bible says, 'Remember *now* your Creator in the days of your youth', and 'Do not boast about tomorrow, for you do not know what a day may bring forth'. For many people, tomorrow never came!

(2) 'I'm too busy'. We meet a busy farmer in the New Testament who said this. His crops had made him rich and he looked forward to many years of success. What a dreadful shock he got when God told him he would die that night. 'Fool! This night your soul will be required of you', God said.

(3) 'God is a God of love. He will allow everyone into heaven'. Those who make this excuse should read Revelation chapter 20 verse 15, 'And anyone not found written in the Book of Life was cast into the lake of fire'. Whatever you do, don't make excuses to God.

Stepping stones

Reading: Luke 15. 1-7

September 20

The Son of Man has come to seek and to save that which was lost, Luke 19. 10

The parable of the lost sheep is a simple story that even the youngest child can understand. However, beneath the surface details of the story, there are four great Bible truths to be discovered in the four groups of people we meet.

The ninety-nine sheep are a picture of people who feel they have *no* need to repent. They do not see themselves as sinners, even though God has said in His word, 'there is no one who does not sin', 1 Kings 8. 46. They stick out their chests and say with pride, 'God, I thank You that I am not like the rest of men'. A Christian was about to put a gospel tract through a door when he spotted a note on the window. It said, 'Before you knock my door, please note: I don't want double glazing and I don't want God to save me'.

The Shepherd is Jesus, the Lord of Glory, who left His throne above and came into this hostile world 'to seek and to save that which was lost'. How sweet to read the words 'until he finds it'. This Shepherd would never turn back, would never give up, until He could lay down His life for that lost sheep upon the cross!

The lost sheep is the 'one sinner who repents'. He, or she, sees his sin clearly, and understands the pressing need for a Shepherd-Saviour. He trusts in the Lord.

His friends and neighbours represent the angels who, on seeing a sinner accept the salvation of God participate in the joy that reaches up from earth to heaven itself! How good it is to know the Shepherd came to search for us and how right it is to be pleased when we, and others, are found by Him.

Pray

Thank You, Lord, that You were willing to endure the extreme and awful sufferings of the cross for such an undeserving sinner as me!

. . . through the Bible day by day

September 21

Reading: Luke 15. 8-10

When she has found it, she calls her friends and her neighbours together, saying, 'Rejoice with me, for I have found the piece which I lost', Luke 15. 9

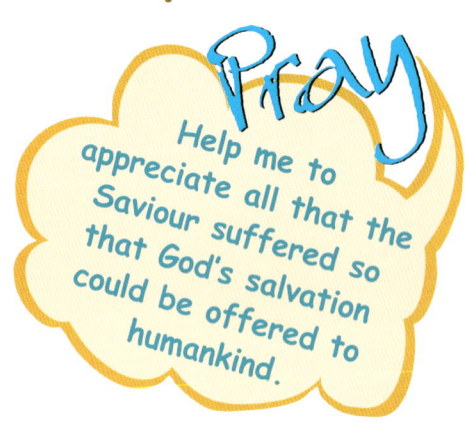

Pray
Help me to appreciate all that the Saviour suffered so that God's salvation could be offered to humankind.

I am sure we have all lost things at home before. How annoying it can be when what we want appears to have vanished into thin air. We waste so much time hunting high and low for it.

The lady in today's parable owned ten silver pieces. They were actually Greek coins known as 'drachmas'. Having lost one of them, she set out with great determination to find it. She uses two objects to help her with her search, a brush to sweep the house and a lamp. The brush deals with the *dirt* and the lamp deals with the *darkness*.

The Lord uses this parable to explain the great truth 'this Man receives sinners'. However, before sinners can be received, the serious matter of sin must be dealt with in a way that honours God's righteous and holy character. Sin cannot be overlooked. It can't be just 'swept under the carpet'. It must be 'put away' in a right way. That's why the Son of God came. He had 'come to seek and to save that which was lost', Luke 19. 10, and that 'seeking' brought Him eventually to the cross!

Remember how the woman searched in the *darkness* and *dirt* to find the lost coin. Well, the Son of God, too, experienced the *darkness* and *dirt* at the cross. 'When the sixth hour had come, there was darkness over the whole land until the ninth hour', Mark 15. 33. As for the dirt, well that was our filthy sins which He 'bore in His own body on the tree', 1 Peter 2. 24. How wonderful that the Saviour went to such lengths to seek and to save us!

266　　　　　　　　　　　　　　　　　　　　　　　Stepping stones

Reading: Luke 15. 11-24

September 22

For this my son was dead and is alive again; he was lost, and is found, Luke 15. 24

Life is full of *ups* and *downs*, but the son who left home and squandered his inheritance could have said, 'Life is made of *SEVEN UPS*!'

SPLIT UP — He was the youngest son who thought that happiness and excitement could be found far away from home. So he decided to split up with his father and leave, but not before he'd said, selfishly, 'Give me!'

SPENT UP — The wild and self-centred life style he adopted eventually left him penniless and friendless. When he found he had no money he found he had no friends.

FED UP — The only work he could get was looking after pigs. This 'far country' wasn't such a nice place after all. Turning his back on his father had only brought him to the pig trough. With despair in his heart and hunger in his belly, he must have been incredibly *fed up*!

WOKEN UP — Thoughts of home flashed through his mind. He remembered the kindness of his father and his heart was stirred. In that very moment he *woke up*, came to his senses and said, 'I shall return to my father'. However, this time he was not going to say, *'Give me'*, but, *'Make me!'*

OWNING UP — As the father covered him with kisses, the son *owned up* and confessed, 'I have sinned against heaven and before you'.

DRESSED UP — He certainly got more than he bargained for. The shoes, the ring and the best clothes his father gave him saw him *dressed up* and ready to live in his father's house.

RAISED UP — His father was overjoyed and was heard to say, 'It's just as if he was *raised up* from out of death!' This story shows us how, when we return to God, we will always find Him waiting for us.

Pray: Help me to see that true happiness and contentment can only be found in friendship and fellowship with God my Father.

. . . through the Bible day by day

September 23

Reading: John 11. 17-45

Jesus said to her, 'I am the resurrection and the life. He who believes in Me, though he may die, he shall live',
John 11. 25

Two sisters, Martha and Mary, looked for the Lord's help to heal their brother Lazarus. Strangely, when Jesus 'heard that he was sick, He stayed two more days in the place where He was'. Onlookers might have thought that the Lord was uncaring and indifferent to the concerns of the sisters. However, such thinking was wrong, for His timing is always perfect. We know He could have healed Lazarus without making the long journey to Bethany. After all, He had already done something similar when He healed the nobleman's son from a long distance, John 4. 46-54. Had the Lord travelled immediately to Bethany, they would not have witnessed His glorious power in raising Lazarus from four days of death, and they certainly would not have witnessed His silent tears which showed His love, verse 36.

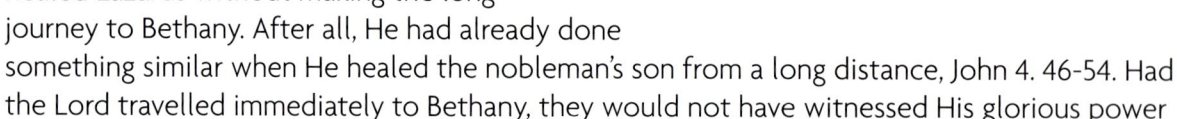

A Christian, while having a hearing test at hospital, asked the young doctor if dead people could hear. The doctor was surprised by this unusual question and replied with a definite, 'No!' He was even more surprised when the Christian said, 'There is *one* man all dead people can hear!' Keen to know the answer to this conundrum, the doctor asked, 'And who might that person be?' With delight the Christian declared, 'That man is Jesus', and proceeded to quote John chapter 5 verses 28 and 29, 'For the hour is coming in which *ALL* who are in the graves will *HEAR* His voice and come forth'. Today's story proves that dead men can hear, and must respond to His voice! 'Lazarus, come forth!'

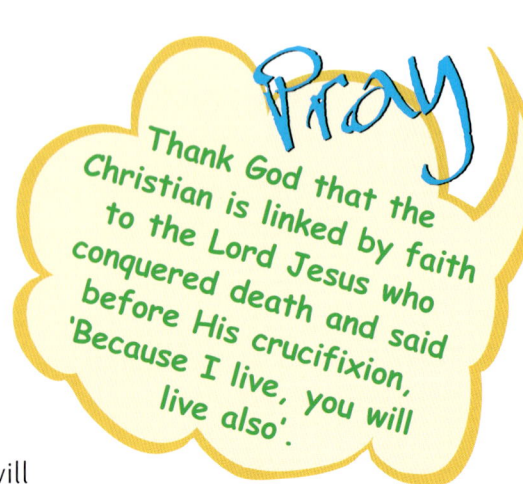

Pray
Thank God that the Christian is linked by faith to the Lord Jesus who conquered death and said before His crucifixion, 'Because I live, you will live also'.

Reading: John 11. 45-54

September 24

It is expedient for us that one man should die for the people, and not that the whole nation should perish, John 11. 50

I am sure when travelling into town we have all seen the massive hoardings along the roadside advertising various things such as the latest luxury cars and sunny holiday destinations. They are so big it's almost impossible not to miss the bold messages they are giving out. The many mighty miracles that the Lord performed were just like those advertising boards but the bold message they declared was, 'JESUS IS THE SON OF GOD. HE IS THE PROMISED MESSIAH'.

When the Jewish leader, Nicodemus, saw the miracles, he understood their unmistakeable message, for he said to the Lord, 'We know that You are . . . come from God; for no one can do these signs that You do unless God is with him', John 3. 2. We might be tempted to think that anybody who saw just one of the Lord's miracles would have been so impressed they would have believed in him instantly. Sadly today's story shows that this is not the case! Many of the Jews believed on Him, verse 45. However, verse 46 says, 'Some of them went away to the Pharisees and told them the things Jesus did . . . then, from that day on, they plotted to put Him to death'.

It's not unusual these days to hear some say, 'If I could see Jesus with my own eyes then I would definitely believe'. You can say to such a person, 'Seeing is no guarantee you'd believe in Him'. Some of those who actually saw Lazarus brought back to life were so blind they couldn't read the message of the miracle and they became partners in crime with those who planned to murder the Lord. How blind the human heart can be!

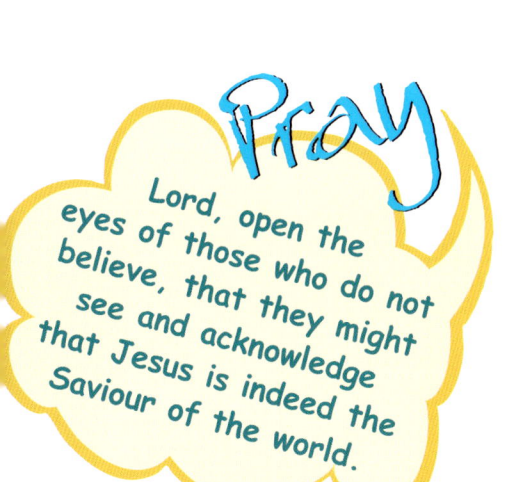

Pray

Lord, open the eyes of those who do not believe, that they might see and acknowledge that Jesus is indeed the Saviour of the world.

. . . through the Bible day by day

September 25

Reading: Luke 16. 19-31

Not many wise according to the flesh, not many mighty, not many noble, are called, 1 Corinthians 1. 26

Pray

Give me a wise heart so that I will understand that the things which are seen won't last forever, but the things which are not seen are eternal.

Today we meet two men so very different to one another. One was noted for his wealth, which allowed him to dress in the latest fashionable clothing and live a life of ease. This nameless man was happy and thousands would be jealous of his life-style. The other person was a pitiful specimen of humanity, a poor, starving, sore-covered beggar named Lazarus, whose only friends appeared to be the dogs which licked his sores. Which of these two men would you like to be?

Before making a hasty decision, pause a while and think about the following. Reading the story carefully we discover that the beggar had two things the rich man did not have. He obviously had *faith*, for the Bible tells us, 'Without faith it is impossible to please God'. He must also have repented and having repented he would know 'the forgiveness of sins'.

It should be no surprise to us that the beggar died first, but eventually the rich man died too. 'What man can live and not see death?', Psalm 89. 48. As far as these two men are concerned, death changed everything. Learn from this four important lessons. (1) Death isn't the end. Both men continued to exist. (2) The rich man is never called rich after he died! 'For we brought nothing into this world, and it is certain we can carry nothing out', 1 Timothy 6. 7. (3) Death leads to two possible places. One is the place of blissful comfort where poor Lazarus went, and the other is the place of fiery torment. (4) The rich man will never escape the awful destination of his choosing! From *the dead* comes this warning for *the living!*

Now answer the question: Which of these two men would you rather be?

Reading: **Luke 17. 11-19**

September 26

Oh give thanks to the LORD, for He is good: for His mercy endures for ever,
Psalm 107. 1

Leprosy is one of the oldest diseases known to men. It attacks the nerve endings, particularly in the hands, feet and face, causing horrible deformities and blindness. Because the nerves are damaged the sufferer feels no pain. Imagine picking up a hot pan or stepping onto a sharp nail and not feeling anything!

In Bible times lepers were forced to live away from people, separated from friends and family. When others approached they were obliged to shout out a warning, 'Unclean! Unclean!' Worst of all was the fact that lepers knew the disease would eventually kill them.

Pray

Lord, help me constantly to open my mouth in gratitude and praise because, 'It is good to give thanks to the LORD'.

As the Saviour approached a village He was greeted by the grim sight of ten lepers, all standing at a distance and all showing the marks and deformities of this incurable disease. Instead of shouting out the prescribed, haunting call, 'Unclean! Unclean', however, they threw themselves upon the compassion of the Lord and cried out, 'Jesus, Master, have mercy on us!' The Lord graciously responded to their appeal and as they left Him they were cleansed.

Imagine their joy and delight as they discovered they were now free from this horrible disease. No longer separated from others! No longer unclean! Surely this dramatic miracle would cause all ten to respond with willing praise and gratitude! Sadly only *one*, and he a despised Samaritan, returned to thank the Lord. One can almost hear the deep disappointment in the Lord's voice as He asks, 'Didn't I cleanse ten? Where are the other nine?'

It is a sad fact that the majority of people today have little time for God and are ignorant of what He has done for them. Let us not be like them, but thank God for His goodness to us.

. . . through the Bible day by day

September 27

Reading: Matthew 19. 13-15

Jesus said, 'Let the little children come to Me, and do not forbid them; for of such is the kingdom of heaven',

Matthew 19. 14

The vast majority of parents wish only the very best for their children. Some would do anything and make great personal sacrifices to ensure their children get the best start in life. They want to expose them to what is good, honourable and wholesome. They are probably aware of the saying, *'Children are like wet cement: Whatever falls on them makes an impression'*. In today's reading we meet such parents. They were keen to bring their young ones into contact with the Son of God so He could 'put His hands on them, and pray'. They wanted the very best for their children and knew where to get it. The harsh criticism of the disciples is over-ruled by the Lord, who said, 'Let the little children come to Me, and do not forbid them'. He will never turn away any child who comes to Him!

A well-known preacher had just finished weeks of gospel preaching. A friend asked him, 'Did anyone get saved?' The preacher answered, 'Yes! Two and a half!' This unusual reply caused the friend to ask, 'Oh, you mean, two adults and one child'. The preacher said, 'No! Two children and one adult!' 'What do you mean by that?' asked the enquirer. The evangelist answered, 'When children get saved they have their *whole* lives to live for the Lord. However, with adults, a large slice of their life has already passed!'

To get married in England a person has to be at least 16. To drive a car, one needs to be 17. How wonderful to know that there are no restrictive age limits for children coming to Christ. Children, come to Christ in your early years. Become like wet cement and let Him make lasting impressions on you.

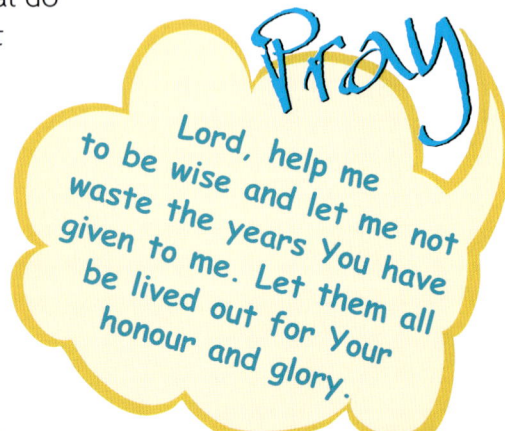

Pray

Lord, help me to be wise and let me not waste the years You have given to me. Let them all be lived out for Your honour and glory.

Reading: Matthew 19. 18-30

September 28

How hard it is for those who have riches to enter the kingdom of God! Luke 18. 24

We know that the man who came to see the Lord on this occasion had many things going for him. He was a ruler, he was very rich and he was young. He could buy whatever he wanted. Money was no problem because his bank account was bursting. However, there was one thing he desperately wanted and he was so keen to get it that he *ran* and fell at the Saviour's feet asking, 'What good thing shall I do that I may have *eternal life*?'

Sadly he refused to listen to what the Lord said and in doing so he made four mistakes. (1) He forgot that youth doesn't last. He's dead now! (2) He turned his nose up at 'treasure in heaven'. (3) He turned his back on eternal life. (4) He was blinded by the false security of riches on earth but when he died left it *all* behind.

Pray

Help me, in the excitement of youth, to give God my Creator, the first place in my life.

Imagine you are standing on top of England's highest mountain, Scafell Pike, and the cloudless summer sky is tinged with orange and red from the warm rays of the setting sun. You are surrounded on every side by views that are so stunningly beautiful they take your breath away. In your pocket you have two small pennies. What would you think if someone said it was possible for those two pennies to block out that beautiful view? Impossible! you might say. How can two tiny pennies take this sublime scene away? Easy! All you have to do is to hold each penny as close to your eyeballs as possible and they will blot out the view completely! Sadly the young ruler allowed his puny riches to wipe out the wonderful view and opportunity of eternal life and treasures in heaven! Let us be careful not do the same.

September 29

Reading: Luke 18. 35-43

'What do you want Me to do for you?' He said, 'Lord, that I may receive my sight',
Luke 18. 41

Being blind must be one of the most awful things that could happen to anyone. A blind person would have little idea of colour, space and beauty. Imagine being locked into a never-ending world of darkness. How dreadful it must be!

The blind man in today's story was in such a condition. His name was Bartimaeus and being unable to work he was forced to beg. Bartimaeus must have heard of the great miracles that the Lord had done and no doubt he lived in the hope that one day this Jesus would come to Jericho.

Imagine the intense excitement he felt as the people shouted out, 'Jesus of Nazareth is passing by'. His heart must have been pounding with increased hope. The moment he had dreamed of and longed for had actually come! Yet when he did call out to the Lord he didn't shout, 'Jesus of Nazareth have mercy on me'. Instead he shouted, 'Jesus, Son of David'. This simply means that Bartimaeus knew Jesus was the Messiah King that God had promised to send into the world. So although he was blind, he could *see* something that the crowds couldn't!

> **Pray**
> Ask God to open the 'eyes of your heart' so that you can see and know a little bit more of the glory of the Lord Jesus.

As Bartimaeus called out the crowds became angry with him and insisted he keep quiet. This placed him on the horns of a dilemma. What should he do? If he called out he'd annoy the people; if he didn't Jesus would be gone. I don't think he thought too long about the issue. He sensed the opportunity must be grasped *immediately* because 'Jesus of Nazareth was *passing* by'. Indeed the Lord never returned to Jericho, and it is solemn to think that had Bartimaeus listened to the crowds he would have died blind! As Bartimaeus did, we should call on God now.

Reading: **Luke 19. 1-10**

September 30

The Son of man has come to seek and to save that which was lost, Luke 19. 10

The open-air preacher was boldly preaching the gospel to the small crowd that had gathered. He emphasized that the many miracles done by Jesus were startling evidence that He really was the Son of God. One of the crowd started to heckle the preacher and shouted, 'Surely you don't believe that Jesus turned water into wine! How could you possibly believe that?' The preacher was unshaken by this outburst and said, 'Let me tell you, He also turns beer into furniture!' What did he mean?

Before his conversion the preacher had been an alcoholic. Virtually every penny he earned he spent on beer. This meant that his wife struggled to bring up their sons in a home that was full of old, threadbare furniture that was falling apart. The man's life was a real mess! One day, however, after hearing the gospel he was wonderfully converted and delivered from the iron grip of alcohol. Money that normally he spent on beer was now spent on his wife and children and he even bought a new sofa for their living room. 'You see', said the preacher, 'I speak from deep personal experience. Jesus really does turn beer into furniture!'

The preacher's conversion shows the wonderful power of God to change lives for the better. The taxman Zacchaeus experienced the same transforming power when he got saved the day the Lord came to Jericho. Such was the change in his life he said, 'Lord, I will give half my property to the poor. And if I have cheated anybody I will pay him back four times as much'. The conversion of Zacchaeus confirms the great Bible truth, 'If anyone is in Christ, he is a new creation; old things have passed away; behold, all things have become new', 2 Corinthians 5. 17.

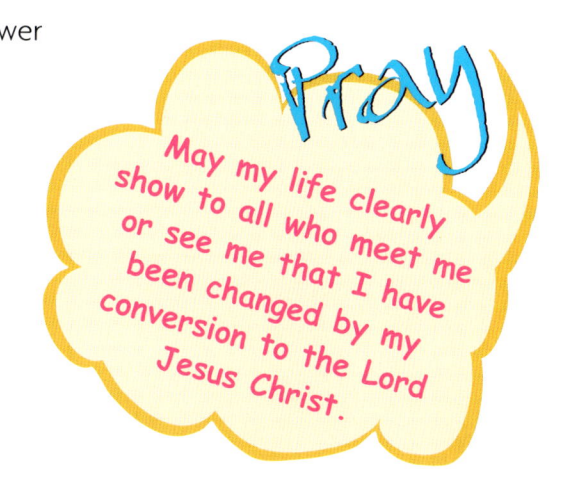

Pray

May my life clearly show to all who meet me or see me that I have been changed by my conversion to the Lord Jesus Christ.

... through the Bible day by day

October 1

Reading: **Matthew 21. 1-9**

Behold, your King is coming to you; He is just and having salvation, lowly and riding on a donkey, Zechariah 9. 9

Pray

Pray that you might know what it is to be a true and obedient follower of the Lord Jesus Christ.

It must have been a surprise to the owner of the ass and the colt when the disciples arrived and led the animals away. Jesus had told the disciples where to go, what to do and what to say. When the owner asked what they were doing the disciples replied, 'The Lord needs them'.

Luke tells us that no one had sat on the colt before so it would have been very difficult to ride. Do you think the man followed to see what would happen? If he did he would have been surprised to see that, despite the crowd and the noise, the colt remained calm. It was as though he knew the One riding him was very special.

The crowd also thought that Jesus was someone special because they shouted, 'Blessed is He who comes in the name of the Lord!' Most of the people would have gone to the synagogue where the scriptures were taught. They would remember these words had been written long ago by the prophet Zechariah. This is our memory verse but they had probably learned it too and remembered that their king would ride into Jerusalem on a colt.

This story could have had a happy ending had the people meant what they said and accepted Jesus as their king. But some days later the Jews arrested Jesus. The Roman governor questioned Him and told the people Jesus was not guilty and should be set free. The same people who had welcomed Jesus shouted out, this time, 'We will not have this man to reign over us!'

It is important to make sure we are true followers of the Lord Jesus. Many people know a lot about Him but like the people in our story sadly never really trust Him personally. Let's make sure we do.

Reading: Matthew 21. 33-41

October 2

Still having one son, his beloved, he also sent him to them last, saying, 'They will respect my son', Mark 12. 6

The man preparing his vineyard was rich and important. He planted it with good vines, protected it with hedges and dug out places to produce and store wine. It was so good that we might think he was preparing it for himself. His plan, however, was to let it out to his neighbours so that he could share the fruit with them. The neighbours must have been pleased and thought the owner a very kind man.

The picture changes, however, when the owner of the vineyard goes away. At harvest time he sends his servants to collect his share of the fruit. The men looking after the vineyard turned out to be evil men. They refused to give the owner his share, stoned and beat his servants and even killed one of them! When more servants were sent they treated them in the same way. In an act of extreme kindness the owner finally sent his son to them. They even killed his son because they wanted the vineyard for themselves as well as the fruit!

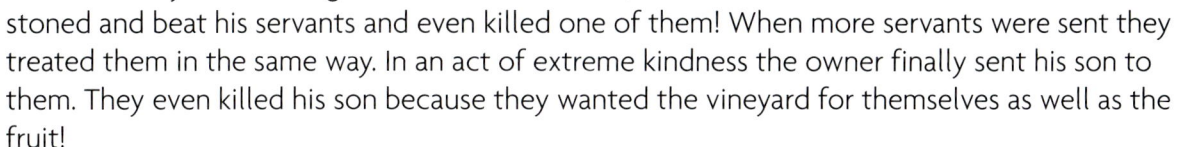

In this story Jesus was really explaining God's kindness to His people, the Jews. He had wanted to share His kingdom with them but they rejected Him. They behaved like the men in the story and put Him to death on a cross. By dying in this way, Jesus showed even greater kindness and bore God's judgement for the sin of the whole world. His kindness now extends beyond the Jewish people to us all. If we confess our sins, repent and thank Him for dying for those sins upon the cross, we will be born into His kingdom. We will become His true children and one day will live with Him in His eternal kingdom in heaven.

Pray

Pray that you might learn more about the kindness and love of the Lord Jesus and that you might want to tell others about His love.

... through the Bible day by day

October 3

Reading: Matthew 23. 29-39

How often I wanted to gather your children together, as a hen gathers her chicks under her wings, but you were not willing! Matthew 23. 37

Our reading today is linked with the parable of the kind man and his vineyard. The men who cared for the vineyard, you may remember, were wicked men and rejected the owner's kindness. This story explains the sadness the owner of the vineyard felt over the way he had been treated.

One day Jesus looked down upon the city of Jerusalem from the Mount of Olives. As He saw the city and thought about the people He began to cry. He longed to provide shelter for them in the same way that a hen provides shelter for her chicks when she sees danger approaching. Long ago God chose the Jews to be His people and promised them a Messiah or King who would lead and care for them. He also promised to bless them if they would obey Him.

The Lord Jesus was God's fulfilment of that promise. He wept over the people because they rejected His great love and kindness. They also rejected His laws and He knew what would be the awful consequences of their decision. How strong and wonderful His love for them must have been! He did not forsake them but went on to provide that shelter for them and the whole world by suffering for sin on the cross. He knew fully what that suffering would be like but in love He thought of them and not of Himself.

It was the people who caused Jesus to weep and sorrow. We must always remember that the things we do affect others and can make them happy or sad. God watches over us as His children and He, too, can be grieved or pleased with the way we behave.

Pray

Pray that God might show you that your behaviour can make the Lord Jesus sad. Ask Him to help you to want to do the things that please Him.

Stepping stones

Reading: **Matthew 25. 1-13**

October 4

Watch therefore, for you know neither the day nor the hour in which the Son of Man is coming, Matthew 25. 13

The time of the marriage and the celebration feast for this Jewish wedding had arrived. The bride waited for the bridegroom in her father's house with ten of her unmarried friends. When the bridegroom arrived her friends would be expected to go out to greet him with brightly burning lanterns and then bring him into the house.

The bridegroom arrived later than expected and the ten friends had fallen asleep. They were woken up at midnight by a loud shout – 'The bridegroom is arriving: go out to meet him!' The ten quickly set about trimming the wicks in their lanterns but five of them were horrified to find they had not brought enough oil with them and their lamps were going out. The other five could not help them because that would have made them short of oil too. The five that had no oil hurried off to the bazaar, woke up the shopkeeper and begged him to sell them some oil. By the time they returned the bridegroom had arrived and the door was closed. Despite their knocking they were not allowed in. More than that, the bridegroom said that he did not even know them! They had been found out because they were not really the true friends of the bridegroom and his bride.

Pray

Lord God, help me to live to please the Lord Jesus and wait and watch every day for His return.

When Jesus ascended back to heaven an angel said He would return again to the Mount of Olives to His people the Jews. Before that day He will come to the sky to take true believers to Him, 1 Thessalonians 4. We have not been told the exact time so we must expect Him at any time and live in a way that shows we are His followers and, like true friends, look forward to meeting Him. We must be ready when He comes!

October 5

Reading: Matthew 25. 14-30

Well done, good and faithful servant; you were faithful over a few things, I will make you ruler over many things. Enter into the joy of your lord', Matthew 25. 21

Pray

Help me humbly to recognize the talents You have given me. May I be Your good and faithful servant.

The rich man decided to travel to a far country and asked three servants to look after his business while he was away. He gave them valuable 'talents' according to their abilities. To one servant he gave five talents, to another two and to a third only one. He expected them to use these talents to make him more money. Two of the servants began trading and working immediately. They felt honoured to be entrusted with their master's business. The third servant took a different view and preferred to do other things with his time. He thought the master was hard and unreasonable so he dug a hole in the ground and buried his one talent.

When their master returned the first servant gave him ten talents and the second gave him four. They had worked hard while he was away and had doubled what he had given them. The master was pleased. He congratulated them, promised them greater responsibilities and blessed them.

The servant who had received only one talent was only able to return what he had been given and had to own up to what he had thought and said. His master was not pleased, took his one talent from him and put him out of the house. He had shown he was not a true servant.

The Lord Jesus is now in heaven but He will return one day. He has given talents to all believers and expects us to use them for Him while He is away. Each talent is of great value to Him but we must remember, the greater our talents the greater our responsibilities. When He returns He will reward us according to our faithfulness. Do you think He will be pleased with what we have done for Him?

Reading: John 12. 1-11

October 6

Mary took a pound of very costly oil of spikenard, anointed the feet of Jesus, and wiped his feet with her hair. And the house was filled with the fragrance of the oil, John 12. 3

The Lord Jesus was enjoying an evening meal with friends at Bethany. It was held in the home of Simon whom Jesus had cured of leprosy, Matthew 26. 6. Mary, Martha and Lazarus were there together with the disciples.

Jesus would soon make His last journey from Bethany to Jerusalem to die on the cross. Mary knew this and remembered how Jesus had shown His love for them by raising their brother Lazarus from the dead. She also remembered sitting at Jesus' feet and listening in amazement to His teaching. She wanted to show how much she loved Him so she took her most treasured possession, some special, expensive perfume, broke the alabaster container and poured the perfume over Jesus' feet. As she wiped His feet with her hair, everyone knew what she had done because the house was filled with the fragrance of the perfume.

Pray
Deepen my love for the Lord Jesus so that all can see it. May it bring others to Him.

Judas, the disciple who would later betray Jesus and was a thief, thought the perfume should have been sold and the money (the equivalent of a year's wages) should have been given to the poor. Mary, however, was sure that Jesus would understand. She was right. He told everyone there that she had done it in preparation for His burial. She understood, in a way that the others had not, that His death on Calvary would be for them.

The more we learn about the Lord Jesus from speaking to Him in prayer and from reading His word the more we become aware of His great love for us. He loves each of us and this should stimulate our personal love for Him. Mary could not hide her love for the Lord and neither should we. It shows in what we do and say and attracts others to Him and to His love.

...through the Bible day by day

October 7

Reading: John 13. 1-16

There was also a dispute among them, as to which of them should be considered the greatest, Luke 22. 24

Jesus loved His disciples deeply and wanted to eat the final Passover supper with them before going on alone to the cross. The disciples seemed unaware of how He was feeling. They spent time arguing over which of them would be the greatest in God's kingdom instead. Jesus explained that true greatness is seen only when we humbly help others.

On entering the room, the disciples walked past the water and towel provided for the servant to wash the feet of the guests as they arrived. There was no servant there this evening and the disciples thought themselves far too important to serve in this way. So Jesus Himself took the towel, poured water into a bowl and washed the disciples' feet.

Peter was embarrassed by what had happened and refused at first to allow Jesus to wash his feet. Jesus explained that those who were not washed had no part with Him. Peter then asked Jesus to wash his hands and head as well as his feet. Jesus' reply is very important: 'He who is bathed needs only to wash his feet!' We were washed from the guilt of our sin once and forever when we trusted the Lord Jesus as Saviour. Daily contact with sin, which we cannot avoid while we live on earth, can still make us dirty. By washing their feet only, and not bathing them, Jesus showed us we need to keep ourselves clean. Daily reading of God's word, the Bible, cleans from the 'dirtiness' of sin. Paul also tells us about 'the washing of water by the word', Ephesians 5. 26.

Pray
Help me to want to keep away from sin. Help me to be so clean and pure that I can serve the Lord Jesus faithfully and humbly.

Most people see greatness only in physical strength which comes with boasting and arrogance. God says greatness is to be shown in humble service done by true believers who are cleansed through God's word. Are we clean?

Reading: John 13. 18-30

October 8

'What are you willing to give me if I deliver him to you?' And they counted out to him thirty pieces of silver, Matthew 26. 15

Judas Iscariot was one of twelve men Jesus chose to be His disciples. He appeared no different from the others and they even trusted him to look after their money.

We do not know why Judas chose to follow Jesus. Iscariot means 'man from Cherioth' and suggests he was the only southerner amongst the twelve. He knew the way the Romans dominated the Jews. Perhaps he thought that Jesus, as Messiah, would soon defeat the Romans, set up His kingdom and give Judas, as one of the twelve, a position of high authority. As time passed he saw this would not be and that Jesus and His kingdom would be rejected. He thought he could make some money by betraying Jesus to the Jewish leaders. He betrayed Jesus for thirty pieces of silver – the price one would pay for a common slave!

Jesus knew Judas' thoughts and our reading today shows one of the opportunities Jesus gave him to repent. Jesus told the group as they gathered in the upper room that one of them would betray Him. Several asked, 'Is it I?' But John asked, 'Lord, who is it?' Jesus said it was the one to whom He would offer a piece of food. Jesus offered the piece to Judas and said to him, 'What you do, do quickly!' Judas suddenly realized that Jesus knew of his plans and that He was giving him an opportunity to change his mind. Judas refused and went out into the night. The darkness was not only outside but also inside Judas' mind and heart.

The Bible shows us the truth even when it is not very pleasant. In this way we learn about sin and how to avoid it. Judas afterwards realized his mistake but never truly repented. How sad.

Pray

Lord, You know all my thoughts and the reasons why I do what I do. Help me to live and walk in the light of the truth of Your Word.

...through the Bible day by day

October 9

Reading: Matthew 26. 31-35

The Lord said, 'Simon, Simon! Indeed, Satan has asked for you, that he may sift you as wheat', Luke 22. 31

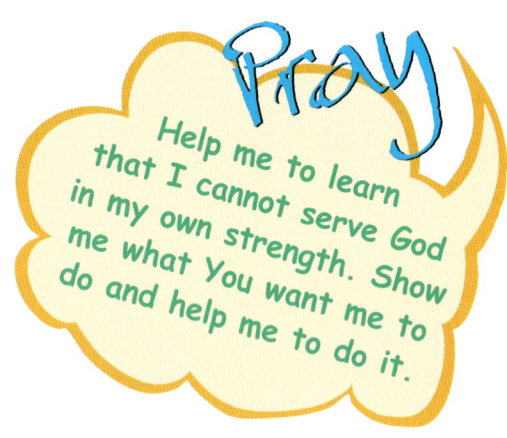

Pray

Help me to learn that I cannot serve God in my own strength. Show me what You want me to do and help me to do it.

Peter, with the other disciples, lived and travelled with Jesus for three years. They saw the miracles He did and listened as He taught the people. Many ordinary people accepted the teaching but most of the religious leaders rejected it and hated Jesus for what He said. Jesus explained to His disciples that He and His kingdom would be rejected and the Jews would crucify Him but He would be raised from the dead.

This troubled Peter deeply and he made up his mind to be an even more faithful follower of the Lord Jesus. This was good but Peter's mistake was that he thought he could do it in his own way and in his own strength. God would later use Peter in a wonderful way when he preached to the very Jews who crucified the Lord Jesus. In the meantime there were some hard lessons Peter had to learn before he was ready for God to use him. Peter said he would never desert the Lord Jesus and would even die for Him. But before a new day dawned he had denied knowing Jesus to a young servant girl in a most cowardly way.

We can only serve God effectively when He prepares and equips us for what He wants us to do for Him. To rely upon our own strength and ability only leads to failure. Jesus had said that the events surrounding His death and resurrection would cause the disciples to be shaken about like wheat is shaken during the threshing process, Luke 22. 31-32. He also said specifically to Peter, 'I have prayed for you'! This must have been an encouragement to Peter. It should encourage us as we serve Him in our day to know that He prays for us too.

Stepping stones

Reading: 1 Corinthians 11. 23-26

October 10

He took bread, gave thanks and broke it, and gave it to them, saying, 'This is My body which is given for you; do this in remembrance of Me', Luke 22. 19

As Jesus' death drew closer, He taught His disciples things that would help them overcome their sadness. He told them they would see Him after His resurrection. He said He would not desert them when He finally returned to heaven but would send them the Holy Spirit. The Holy Spirit would live in them permanently, comfort them and help them understand more fully what He had taught them. In this way He would continue to be with them and they would never be alone.

At the final Passover supper in the upper room He asked them to do something to show their love for Him. He asked them to meet together on the first day of each week to remember Him by breaking bread together and drinking wine from a cup. In other places in the Bible this is called the Lord's Supper. Paul was reminding Corinthian believers about this in our reading today. The bread and wine have no special powers but are simply reminders of who Jesus is and what He has done for us. The bread speaks of His sinless body and life; the wine of the price He paid that we might be saved.

When we truly love someone we want to tell them how we feel! Our love for the Lord Jesus is special to Him and the Lord's Supper gives us an opportunity to tell Him of our love. He receives this as worship but we must always remember that true worship is more than just words. The sincerity of what we say must be shown in the way we live for Him each day. How precious the thought of this supper must have been to the Lord Jesus in that He spoke about it on the night He was betrayed, just before He died! Is it precious to us?

Pray

Pray that you might live in a way that pleases the Lord Jesus. Only then can you tell Him of your real love and give Him true worship.

...through the Bible day by day

October 11

Reading: John 14. 1-9

Father, I desire that they also whom You gave Me be with Me where I am, that they may behold My glory, John 17. 24

The disciples were sad and perplexed at the thought of Jesus leaving them. 'How could One as great and powerful as He allow this to happen?' Jesus answers their question in a way that gave them immediate comfort and assurance about the future.

He was leaving to return to His Father in heaven where He would prepare a place for them. Jesus could do this because it was His Father's house and He was God's Son. He was sinless and so there was no doubt He was fit for heaven. The disciple's suitability for heaven was a different matter, though. They had failed, quarrelled amongst themselves and sinned in many ways. It was necessary for Him first to go to the cross where He would bear God's judgement upon sin and make it possible for their sins to be forgiven. Only those whose sins have been forgiven can enter heaven.

We can draw comfort from a promise only if we have confidence in the person making it. Jesus told the disciples that in seeing Him they were actually seeing God His Father. When Jesus said He was the 'way' to the Father and would prepare that way for them it was actually God who was speaking to them. It was certainty over this that gave them immediate comfort and made them sure of joy in the future.

God's words and purposes have not changed. Jesus' words are God's words. His love for us is the same as His love for the disciples. Jesus is still the way to God and the source of comfort for those who repent and trust Him. He is the *only* way. No one can come to the Father unless it is through Him. He has made the way. We must come through Him.

Pray

Help me to appreciate the importance of the things the Lord Jesus taught. His words are words of love which can be relied upon at all times.

286

Stepping stones

Reading: **John 14. 14-31**

October 12

This is the love of God, that we keep His commandments. And His commandments are not burdensome,

1 John 5. 3

Pray

Lord Jesus, help me to show my love for You by what I do, not by what I say. Help me to be happy to obey Your Word.

The Lord Jesus loved and cared for His disciples and He wanted them to respond to His love. Other people would not see Him again after His death but He would show Himself to the disciples. They would be eye-witnesses of His resurrection and tell others about it, along with the things Jesus had taught them. This would be the gospel that would be preached to the whole world.

The disciples had been dependent upon Jesus' presence with them. How could they do this great work without Him? He promised He would not leave them on their own but would send them the Comforter, the Holy Spirit. He, too, is God and would stay and live in them. The Holy Spirit would give them power as well as comfort and help them remember all the things Jesus had taught them. Through Him, in Jesus' name, they could pray to the Father and He would answer in a way that would bless them and make His kingdom grow.

In these ways Jesus showed His love for the disciples. His earnest desire, as He went on alone to the cross, was that they should love Him in return. True love could be shown only in obedience to what He had taught them. Jesus says to them, 'If you love Me you will keep My commandments'.

These words of the Lord Jesus apply to us too. God loves us as those who have trusted the Lord Jesus for salvation and the Holy Spirit lives in us. We are uniquely blessed in our day in that we have the complete word of God in our Bible. Let's read it and show our love for God by doing what it, and He, tells us to do.

. . . through the Bible day by day

October 13

Reading: John 15. 1-14

I am the vine, you are the branches. He who abides in Me, and I in him, bears much fruit: for without Me you can do nothing. John 15. 5

The vine was first used as a picture of the Jewish nation. The disciples were Jews and knew the history of God's people. They were like branches of a vine and could only be fruitful whilst they drew their strength from the vine. God, like a gardener, cared for that vine but had to prune it to make it more fruitful. Jesus takes this picture and applies it to those who believe in Him.

Pray

Lord, please give me the strength to be obedient and fruitful for You. Help me to show Your love and know Your joy.

God is glorified when we are obedient to His word and bear spiritual fruit. Jesus was always obedient to His Father and is the perfect example. We often fall short of this and He has to lead us through experiences that are sometimes painful. This helps our spiritual growth and is like the pruning of a vine. God does this in love that we might bear *'much fruit'*. If we ignore or defy God's word we are like dead branches that cannot bear fruit and He might have to take us away from the work He wants us to do for Him. If, however, we have truly trusted Him, we can never be separated from the salvation received from Him.

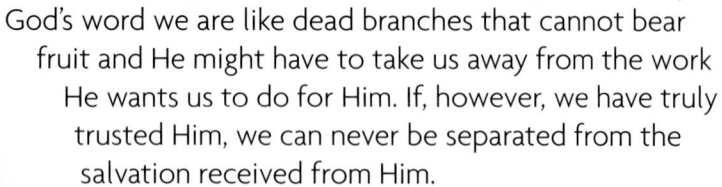

Jesus tells us that one very precious fruit is seen when we show love to one another as He has shown love to us. When this love is at its highest we will even be prepared to lay down our lives for each other. Jesus showed this love when He gave His life on the cross when we were His enemies.

We should be keen to live a life that is fruitful for God even though we know we fall short of the highest standard. Our reward, even when we fail, is to know the fullness of His joy when He calls us His friends!

Stepping stones

Reading: Mark 14. 32-42

October 14

When He had offered up prayers and supplications, with vehement cries and tears to Him who was able to save Him from death, and was heard because of His godly fear, Hebrews 5. 7

The Lord Jesus shared many experiences with His disciples but they could not go with Him as He went to the cross. They followed Him into the Garden of Gethsemane and He allowed three of them – Peter, James and John – to glimpse His anguish of soul. But He was alone when He poured out His heart in prayers and tears to His Father. Jesus knew exactly how He would feel when He would suffer for sin. As He thought of it He sweat great drops of blood falling to the ground, Luke 22.44

His words show us that He knew how deeply He would suffer on the cross and why He had to bear it alone. He asked Peter, James and John to watch and pray. Twice He returned to them and found them asleep. Their physical weariness was greater than their understanding of what Jesus was about to suffer. At that very moment Roman soldiers were approaching and one of the disciples was about to betray Him. Despite their brave words the rest were about to desert Him and run away. None of the disciples could help Him.

Pray
Lord Jesus, we thank You for enduring such suffering for us so that our sins can be forgiven.

Salvation was only possible through One who was sinless bearing the sin of others. The Lord Jesus is the only Person to lead a sinless life on the earth since sin entered the world. There was and is no sin in Him. He did not and could not commit sin because He was God. It was He alone, and in great loneliness, who could go to the cross and bring us salvation.

Our reading today has shown us something of what our salvation cost the Lord Jesus and why no other could provide it or share in it. He must have loved us deeply to suffer in this way. Do we love Him deeply in return?

. . . through the Bible day by day

October 15

Reading: Mark 14. 43-50

Jesus said to him, 'Judas, are you betraying the Son of Man with a kiss?'
Luke 22. 48

Pray

Lord Jesus, help me to read and follow the examples contained in Your Word.

Judas Iscariot betrayed Jesus when he led a mob to capture Him in the Garden of Gethsemane. Jesus knew that Judas would do this and that he was a thief. All Judas ever wanted was the best for himself. Despite this Jesus loved him and treated him no differently from the other disciples. Judas was sent out to heal and preach as the others were and Jesus even trusted Judas to look after their money.

Judas believed Jesus was the Messiah and hoped to hold high office when Jesus set up His kingdom. He was disappointed when Jesus taught them that the Jews would reject His kingdom and He would die on a cross. Judas thought he could do best for himself by betraying Jesus for thirty pieces of silver. Later he realized the terrible mistake he had made but he never really repented. In the end he killed himself and the money was used to buy a burial ground for his body.

God in His word does not hide difficult truths from us. This sad incident is recorded to teach and guide us. The Lord Jesus, in love, has done so much for us but we can sometimes be lured away from Him by things that happen to us and by circumstances in the world around us. Like Judas, though not with such serious consequences, we can forget or betray the Lord Jesus by giving priority to things that are not as important. We can betray Him for an unsuitable friendship, for fame, for promotion in our jobs as well as for financial gain. May God help us to consider examples like Judas in His word as we make important decisions about our lives. We may not sell the Lord for money, but do we sell Him for anything else?

Reading: Matthew 26. 57-75

October 16

The Lord turned and looked at Peter. Then Peter remembered the word of the Lord, how He had said to Him, 'Before the cock crows, you will deny Me three times', Luke 22. 61

It was cold out in the courtyard. Peter moved closer to the fire. He hoped that no-one would notice him. He wanted to see what would happen to Jesus. After Jesus had been arrested in the garden of Gethsemane all the other disciples had disappeared. They were afraid. It was dangerous now to be linked with Jesus.

Although it was the middle of the night, the soldiers had taken the Lord straight to the High Priest's house. The Jewish leaders didn't want to waste any time. They wanted to get rid of this trouble-maker. But they had a problem. There was nobody who could find a good reason for putting Jesus to death. However, when Jesus said He was the Son of God that was enough for the High Priest and the other leaders. He must die!

Jesus would not defend Himself. His disciples had left Him. He stood alone. Peter wasn't far away but he was afraid. He knew very well that the Jewish leaders would be looking out for him. When the soldiers had arrested Jesus, Peter had used his sword against the High Priest's servant and cut off his ear. Jesus had healed him but Peter was a marked man.

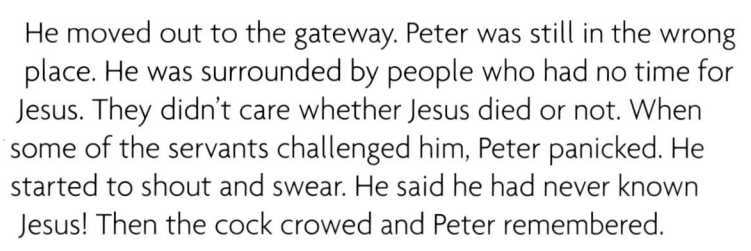

He moved out to the gateway. Peter was still in the wrong place. He was surrounded by people who had no time for Jesus. They didn't care whether Jesus died or not. When some of the servants challenged him, Peter panicked. He started to shout and swear. He said he had never known Jesus! Then the cock crowed and Peter remembered.

It's easy for us to deny the Lord, like Peter. We can deny Him by the places we visit and the friends we have, by the way we speak and the words we use. Let's be careful!

Pray

Ask God to help you to behave and speak in such a way that will show others that you follow Jesus.

...through the Bible day by day

October 17

Reading: John 18. 28-38

Jesus answered, 'My kingdom is not of this world', John 18. 36

Pilate was the Roman governor in charge of Jerusalem. It was not an easy job. The Jews were always making trouble. Now they wanted him to make a decision about one of their prisoners. They wanted Him executed. Pilate found the Jewish leaders difficult to deal with. Why were they so determined that this man Jesus should die? Pilate tried hard to shift the decision back to the Jewish court, but they were too clever. They told him they had no power to put anyone to death. Only the Romans, who were ruling the country, could do that.

Pilate needed to find out exactly what was going on. So he questioned Jesus himself. Pilate was sure that Jesus had done nothing wrong. But if Jesus really was a king, He would be an enemy of the Roman emperor. He would have to be executed.

Jesus explained that He had a kingdom but it was not one that belonged to this world. For Pilate, this was hard to understand. He was part of the mighty Roman Empire. Kingdoms meant armies, cities, people and power. Jesus spoke about a spiritual kingdom, something you couldn't see. But it was a real kingdom. Its power came from God. Its people were those who believed the words of Jesus. He spoke the truth.

Pilate had never before met anyone like Jesus. He said you could believe everything He said. But Pilate was afraid. He understood that to become part of Jesus' kingdom would mean an end to his life as a governor. That was too big a price to pay. Jesus teaches us to value those things which belong to His kingdom, things which we cannot see, but which will last forever, like truth, love, kindness, joy, obedience and peace. What do we value most?

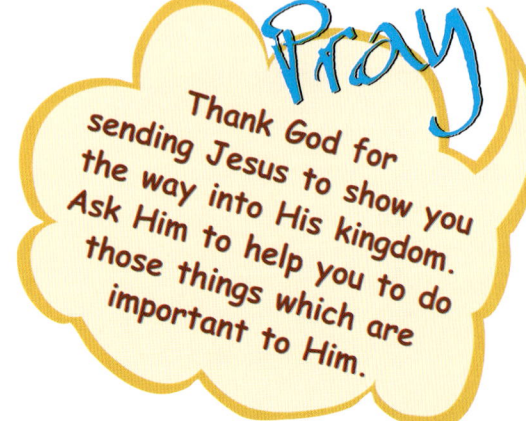

Pray

Thank God for sending Jesus to show you the way into His kingdom. Ask Him to help you to do those things which are important to Him.

Reading: Luke 23. 3-12

October 18

He questioned Him with many words, but He answered him nothing, Luke 23. 9

Herod was a man who loved showing off. He was a king in Israel but he had no real authority. Power belonged to the Romans. When Pilate sent Jesus to him, however, he was really pleased. It seemed that the Romans needed his help after all.

Pilate hoped that Herod would sort out his problem about Jesus. Herod hoped that Jesus would do some miracles for him. Perhaps he could put on a show for his friends!

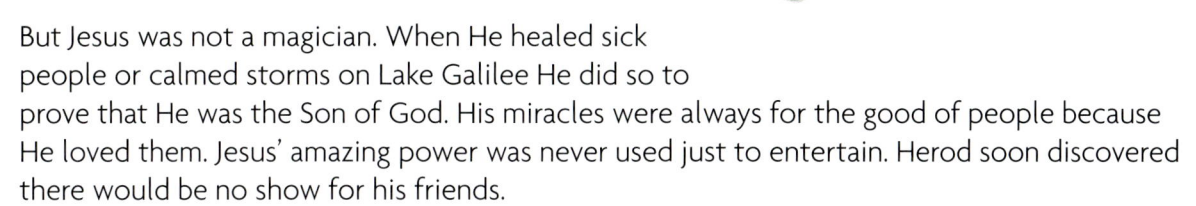

But Jesus was not a magician. When He healed sick people or calmed storms on Lake Galilee He did so to prove that He was the Son of God. His miracles were always for the good of people because He loved them. Jesus' amazing power was never used just to entertain. Herod soon discovered there would be no show for his friends.

Jesus knew exactly what the king was thinking. 'Let's have some fun. Let's see this man do some clever tricks'. Jesus didn't even bother to speak to him. He knew that Herod was not interested in God's kingdom. Herod only cared about himself and what people thought of him.

Because Jesus ignored him Herod felt insulted and angry. He was glad he had the excuse to make fun of Jesus. They would have their entertainment after all. The soldiers dressed Jesus up as a king and sent Him back to Pilate. Let Him die!

Jesus knows what is in the minds of everyone. It may be difficult to know how to answer when people are unkind to us. Sometimes it is better not to say anything at all. Jesus will help us to behave in ways which will please Him, if we ask Him. And He understands when people are unkind too.

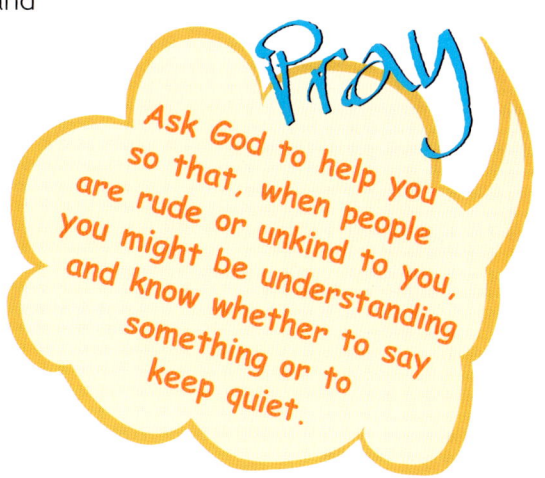

Pray

Ask God to help you so that, when people are rude or unkind to you, you might be understanding and know whether to say something or to keep quiet.

...through the Bible day by day

October 19

Reading: Matthew 27. 19

God may speak in one way, or in another, yet man does not perceive it. In a dream, in a vision of the night, when deep sleep falls upon men, while slumbering on their beds, Job 33. 14-15

It had been a terrible night for Pilate's wife. She had been hearing all about Jesus and His trial. She knew that her husband was responsible for what would happen to Him. But to dream about it all? And it had been so clear, so vivid. She was frightened, very frightened.

Outside the Governor's house was the judgement seat where Pilate sat before all the people. He was the judge and Jesus stood before him. But who was the real prisoner? Who was on trial that day? Was it Jesus or Pilate?

Once again Pilate asked Jesus if He was the King of the Jews. His reply was simply, 'It is as you say'. This was not what Pilate wanted to hear. How could he release this man who refused to defend Himself? This trial was becoming more and more difficult to handle. What was he going to do?

And then came the message from Pilate's wife. But it was much more than a message. It was an appeal for the release of Jesus. It was a command to Pilate to have nothing more to do with 'this innocent man'. His wife had probably never made any comment on Pilate's work as governor before. Why should she in this case?

God was giving Pilate another opportunity to make the right decision. To make an impression on him, God sent this dream to his wife. Perhaps she had heard the teachings of Jesus. Her mind was certainly open to hear God's voice. It was sad that Pilate did not listen to his wife's appeal. It was God's will that Jesus should die, but Pilate need not have been responsible for His death.

Today God speaks to us through His Word, the Bible. Are we listening to Him? Do *we* pay attention to His warnings?

Pray

Thank God that you have His Word, the Bible, in your own language to guide and help you every day.

Reading: Matthew 27. 15-17, 20-21

October 20

As for me and my house, we will serve the Lord, Joshua 24. 15

Pray: Ask God to help you make the right choices in everything you do.

Barabbas was well known in Israel. He had led a rebellion, he had robbed and murdered. Yet when the people were offered a choice between Barabbas and Jesus they chose the robber. What had happened?

Just a few days before His trial, Jesus had ridden into Jerusalem on a donkey. The people had given Him a great welcome. Many saw Him as Israel's king – the Messiah, which means 'Anointed One'. The whole city was excited. Everyone wondered what would happen next.

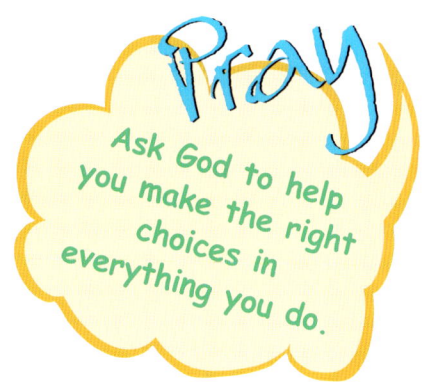

But it was not what they had expected. Jesus had been arrested and was on trial for His life. Behind it all were the chief priests and leaders. They were His enemies and had been watching Him for a long time. They knew this could be the moment to get rid of Jesus. This was their plan.

There were crowds of people in Jerusalem. People had come from all over Israel for the feast of the Passover. It was the day when a well-known prisoner would be set free. But this year Pilate would give the people a choice! The leaders moved amongst the crowds. They made sure that the people chose Barabbas.

It was only a few days since they had called for Jesus to be their king. Now the people believed the lies of their leaders. They had forgotten the miracles and words of Jesus. Their love and respect had turned to hatred. They rejected Him and chose a murderer.

Those that we choose to have around us will always influence us in one way or another. Our friends and activities, the books we read, the television we watch – how do these affect us? What will help and what will spoil our lives for Jesus? Choices are so important. Think about them very carefully!

... through the Bible day by day

October 21

Reading: **Mark 15. 20-39**

Him, being delivered by the determined purpose and foreknowledge of God, you have taken by lawless hands, have crucified, and put to death, Acts 2. 23

Jesus was worn down by His trial and suffering. At some stage He was too weak even to carry His cross. Now He faced a long and painful death. The mixture of wine and myrrh would have dulled the pain but He would not drink it. Jesus needed to have a clear mind.

People around the cross made fun of Him. 'Save Yourself!' they shouted. How could He? Jesus would never come down from the cross. He had come to save the world. The sin of men and women from Adam until the end of the world was laid on Jesus that day. God was punishing Him instead of us. To become our Saviour, He had to die.

Pray

Thank Jesus for going to the cross. Ask God to help you never to forget what Jesus did for you there, because He loved you.

It was a terrible moment when Jesus cried out to God, 'Why have you turned away from Me?' Never before had He been separated from His God. But God is absolutely pure and holy. He cannot look upon sin. He had to turn away from the sight of His own Son and leave Him to suffer alone.

The crowds at the cross looked upon Jesus as just another criminal. He deserved to die. But one man, a Roman soldier, saw Him differently. He had never watched a man die like this one. Jesus had even forgiven those who had driven the nails into His hands and feet. He was convinced that Jesus was the Son of God.

When Jesus died, the thick curtain in the temple was torn in two. Jesus had made it possible for sinners to go into the holy presence of God. Our sins can be forgiven.

The cross tells us everything we need to know about the love of Jesus. He allowed wicked men to crucify Him. His death was the price of our salvation. But He was willing to pay because He loves us so much.

Reading: **Matthew 27. 57-66**

October 22

They made His grave with the wicked – but with the rich at His death, Isaiah 53. 9

Joseph had to move quickly to get the body of Jesus. After crucifixion criminals were buried in a common grave. This would be somewhere unknown and outside the city. But Joseph wanted to give Jesus a decent burial.

It needed courage for Joseph to go to Pilate. Up till now, no one had known that he was a follower of Jesus. He was well known in the city. He was a rich man and was one of the Jewish leaders. But now everyone would know that he was a disciple. Joseph was showing respect for the body of Jesus. He was even using his own new tomb for the burial.

The chief priests were not happy about this and still had their worries, especially about something Jesus had said. 'After three days I will rise'. They demanded that the tomb was sealed and guarded. They were taking no chances. His disciples could come and steal the body. Worse still, they might make up a story about a resurrection.

A chapter in the Old Testament – Isaiah 53 – tells us about the life and death of Jesus. It was written many years before He was born. But it describes the sufferings and death of Jesus very clearly. 'He was a Man of sorrows . . . He was despised . . . for He was cut off from the land of the living . . . they made His grave with the wicked but with the rich at His death'. Joseph of Arimathea fulfilled the words of the prophet when, as a rich man, he gave his tomb to Jesus.

Joseph's gift to Jesus was more than a new tomb. He gave Him love and honour. He came out into the open as a follower of Jesus. By showing respect for the name and the words of Jesus we too can show others that we follow Him.

Pray
Ask God to give you the courage to show others you respect the name of Jesus.

. . . through the Bible day by day

October 23

Reading: Matthew 28. 1-10

He is not here, but is risen! Remember how He spoke to you when He was still in Galilee, Luke 24. 6

It was just beginning to get light when Mary Magdalene and her friend arrived at the tomb. They had come to wash and anoint the body of Jesus. But they were worried. The women knew that the tomb was sealed. There were soldiers standing guard. There was a large and heavy stone across the entrance. How would they get in?

As they came closer to the tomb they saw that their problems had been solved. The great stone was rolled away and the guards were unconscious. And no wonder! An angel, a messenger from God, was sitting on the stone.

The angel came with the greatest message ever sent by God, but first of all, he calmed the women. 'Don't be afraid. I know who you're looking for, Jesus, who was crucified'. Mary and her friend were going to be messengers themselves. They needed to listen carefully. They needed to look inside the tomb.

The stone had been rolled away, but not to let Jesus out. He was raised already. The stone was removed so that people could see that the tomb was empty. Jesus had told His disciples that He would come back from the dead. He always keeps His promises. The women hurried away with their wonderful news. They had stayed near the cross until Jesus had died. They had watched while He was put in the tomb. They had been faithful to the end. Now they were at the beginning of something new. They were the first to see Him alive, to hear His voice, to tell His disciples, 'He is risen'.

Like Mary and her friend we have problems and challenges in our lives. Remember, God knows all about them. He wants us to trust Him with our concerns. Bring them to Him. Don't be afraid!

Pray

Thank God that Jesus is alive today and is with you all the time. Ask Him to help you to trust Him whenever you need Him.

Reading: Luke 24. 13-35

October 24

Their eyes were restrained, so that they did not know Him, Luke 24. 16

It was a long walk from Jerusalem to Emmaus. But Cleopas and his friend hardly noticed the miles. They were too busy talking. What had the women said? Jesus was alive and they had seen angels at His tomb! But like the other disciples, Cleopas found it hard to believe their story. Jesus was dead. There was no doubt about that. He could not have been the promised king, the Messiah. Now their land would never be free from the rule of Rome. The way home seemed longer now, the road full of dust and stones.

> **Pray**
> Thank God that although you cannot see Jesus, He knows all about you and He understands just how you feel. Ask God to help you recognize that Jesus is with you.

Then quite suddenly, a man joined them. It was no one they recognized. He seemed to know nothing about what had been happening in Jerusalem. So they told him about Jesus and all their hopes and disappointments. Then they discovered that the man knew all about the Messiah. He took Cleopas and his friend through the books of the Old Testament and showed them why the Messiah had to suffer and die. It was all part of God's plan after all.

The friends forgot about the long, dusty road. They felt hopeful again. Who was this man? They wanted to hear more. Perhaps he would stay overnight with them.

As they sat down together in the home, the stranger gave thanks for the meal. Immediately the two friends recognized Him. It was Jesus! And then He was gone, as silently as He had appeared.

We have our disappointments too. But like Cleopas we can share them with Jesus. Friends may let us down. Things don't always work out as we'd like them to. Sometimes we fail no matter how hard we try. We cannot see Him but Jesus is always near us even though we don't always know that. Let's ask Him to make Himself real to us today.

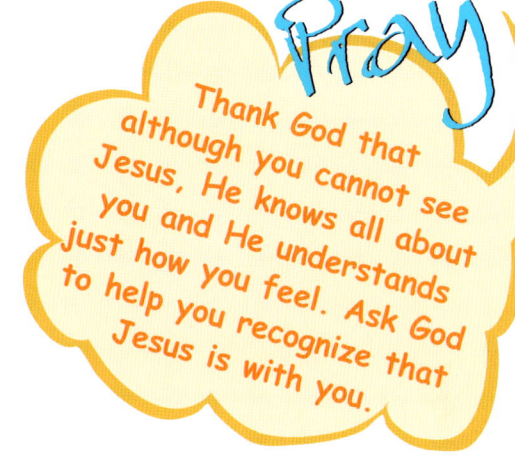

... through the Bible day by day

October 25

Reading: **John 20. 19-31**

Thomas answered and said to Him, 'My Lord and my God!' John 20. 28

It was resurrection day, in the evening. The disciples were together and they were afraid. They had made sure that the door was locked securely. But locked doors were no problem for Jesus. Suddenly He stood in front of them. The disciples were frightened and happy at the same time when they saw the Lord. Was this really Jesus or was it His spirit?

Jesus knew what they were thinking and how frightened they were. He told them not to be afraid. He showed them His hands and His feet. The nail prints were there – the marks of His crucifixion. This really was Jesus. This was not a ghost. This was the man they had known before His death.

It was a pity that Thomas had missed seeing the Lord. Now he had lots of doubts and demands. He wanted proof. He refused to take the disciples' word that Jesus was alive. But, when he saw the Lord, Thomas changed his mind. Just the very sight and sound of Jesus was enough. How could he have doubted? He stood before Jesus ashamed of himself and his words.

Jesus understood Thomas' doubts. He wasn't angry with him. He knew that His disciple just wanted to be sure and He was willing to let Thomas do what he had asked. 'Reach your finger here, and look at My hands'. Jesus is always patient and kind. He will help us even when we struggle to believe and trust Him.

But Jesus reminded His disciples that to believe on Him *without* seeing Him is so much better. It shows that we trust His word and believe His promises. We were not there to see Him and hear Him, and we have never touched Him. But we do believe in Him, don't we?

Pray
Thank God for all His promises in the Bible. Pray that God will show you promises which will become special to you in your life.

Stepping stones

Reading: John 21. 3-17

October 26

I have prayed for you, that your faith should not fail; and when you have returned to Me, strengthen your brethren, Luke 22. 32

Tired and disappointed, the disciples were pulling in their fishing net. It was empty even after a whole night out on the lake. It was Peter who had decided to go fishing. He wanted something to do. He was still thinking of the time when he had denied the Lord.

A man standing on the beach shouted across the water and told them where to fish. The disciples did as the man said. What a surprise! A net so full of fish they had to drag it in.

John recognized it was the Lord but it was Peter who got to Him first. He needed to see the Lord and put things right. But Jesus is never in a hurry. He wanted the disciples to have a rest and some breakfast. The fire was warm and comforting. The fish and the bread smelled good to the tired and hungry men. Jesus knows that food and rest are necessary for our health and strength. He took time to provide it for His disciples.

Pray
Thank God for His special gifts which keep you healthy in mind and body – for food and rest and for His love and forgiveness.

After the meal Jesus spoke to Peter. He didn't want him to hold on to the shame he still felt because of his failure. It was time for Peter to start again. It was time for the other disciples to see that Peter, their leader, was forgiven.

Jesus asked Peter three times if he loved Him. 'Look after My sheep', said Jesus. He was saying to His disciple, 'Care for the people who will become my followers'. There was still important work for Peter to do.

We all let the Lord down in one way or another. We must never be afraid to come to Him for forgiveness. He will always forgive us as long as we really mean what we say. But we have to learn to accept others who have failed, too.

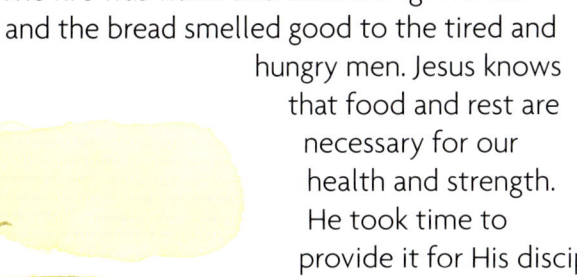

... through the Bible day by day

October 27

Reading: Acts 1. 1-11

This same Jesus, who was taken up from you into heaven, will so come in like manner as you saw Him go into heaven, Acts 1. 11

It had been a wonderful six weeks for the disciples, spending time with the Lord. They treasured every moment of His company. They would remember everything He said. Now it was time to say goodbye.

But before Jesus left the disciples He had something important to tell them. It was not time yet for Him to become king and reign in Jerusalem. That was still in the future. No one but God knew how long they would have to wait. Jesus told the disciples to stay in Jerusalem. In a few days the Holy Spirit would come. He would live in each believer and help them in their work for the Lord. It would be as though Jesus Himself was with them, guiding and encouraging. What a promise!

As He spoke to them Jesus was taken up into heaven. It seemed that invisible hands were lifting Him up through the clouds. And then He was gone out of their sight. The men went on looking. They wanted just one more glimpse of the Lord.

Jesus did not leave His disciples without giving them something very special. It was another promise, sent through an angel. He would come again – down through the clouds from heaven. And He would be the same as He had always been, Jesus, the Man of Galilee, their Lord and Saviour.

Jesus is still in heaven. We don't know how much longer we have to wait for His return. But we have His promise to encourage us. One day He will come again to bring peace to our world. While we wait for Jesus to come back we have His Holy Spirit. He helps us to live in ways which please the Lord and show others that we love Him.

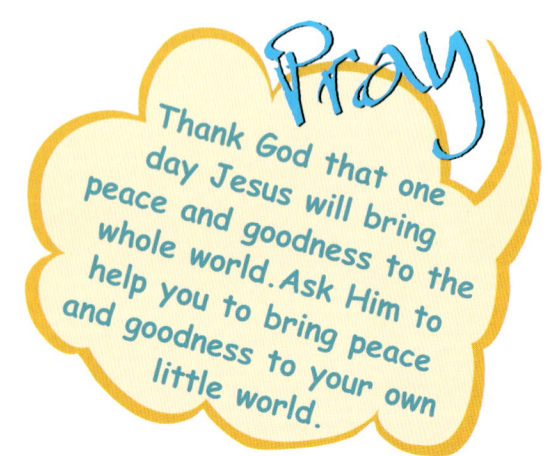

Pray

Thank God that one day Jesus will bring peace and goodness to the whole world. Ask Him to help you to bring peace and goodness to your own little world.

Reading: Acts 2. 1-14, 21-24, 37-42

October 28

The Lord added to the church daily those who were being saved, Acts 2. 47

Crowds filled the city of Jerusalem. Pentecost was one of the special feast days in the Jewish calendar. Jews from many other countries came to share in the celebrations. But that year would be different. God had a wonderful surprise in store for the city.

The disciples had obeyed the Lord. They were waiting in Jerusalem for the gift of the Holy Spirit. But how exactly would He come? His arrival was beyond anything they could ever have imagined. The sound of a strong wind filled the house. Tongues of fire rested on each disciple. All the disciples began to speak in other languages. The Holy Spirit was giving them the ability to preach to everyone that day, no matter where they came from.

Peter took the lead and stood up before the crowds. He felt no fear. It was time for him to speak. His words were powerful and went deep down into the hearts and minds of the people. They felt ashamed and frightened as they thought about what they had done to Jesus. He is God's Son and they had crucified Him! What could they do to show they were sorry?

Pray
Ask God to give you the right words to speak. Ask the Holy Spirit to make Jesus real and special when you talk to your friends about Him.

Many people were forgiven that day. Their lives turned around and they became followers of Jesus. Peter had done the preaching but the Holy Spirit had changed people's understanding of Jesus. They knew Him now as God's promised Messiah. They asked God to forgive them. They showed their change of heart by being baptized. As new disciples, they joined with other believers for prayer and teaching.

Three thousand people! We may not see such great crowds becoming Christians today. But remember – the Holy Spirit still has the power to change people's lives. And just one person who comes to Jesus for forgiveness is precious to God.

. . . through the Bible day by day

October 29

Reading: Acts 3. 1-22

Repent therefore and be converted, that your sins may be blotted out, so that times of refreshing may come from the presence of the Lord, Acts 3. 19

It seemed to the people who went up to the temple that the man had been there for years. He had never walked. He had to be carried to the gate. He had such a sad life and no future. Every day, all he could do was hope. Perhaps someone would feel kind and give him a few pence.

Then one day a miracle happened. He was healed! He could walk, he could jump. He shouted and sang. Not sad any longer, he kept close to this man called Peter. He was someone special!

Crowds began to gather around. They wanted to find out exactly what had happened. Peter was ready for them. It was most important that the people understood that the disciples had not healed the man. It was the power of the risen Lord Jesus. Peter spoke very plainly about the death of Jesus. It had to have happened, so that people's sins could be forgiven. But they need not have shouted for Barabbas and turned away from Jesus. God knew that they had not understood that Jesus was His Son. He would forgive them. But they must repent and believe that Jesus was God's promised king, the Messiah.

To repent means much more than to be sorry. It means to turn around and face the other way. We all need to face the right way – God's way. We all need to admit that we do and say wrong things and ask for God's forgiveness. When we say to God, 'I'm sorry. I want to live for Jesus. Help me to turn from my ways to your ways', God will forgive us.

The man who was healed certainly knew that something wonderful had happened to him. Forgiveness is just like that!

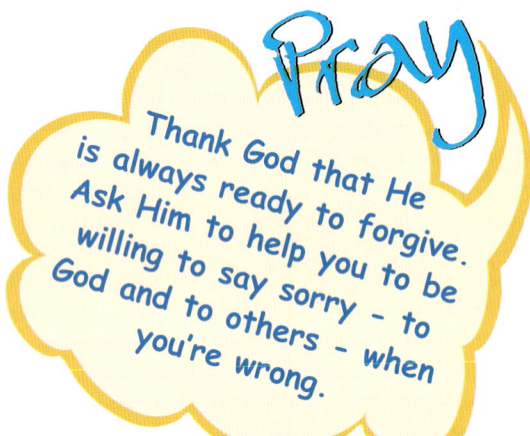

Pray

Thank God that He is always ready to forgive. Ask Him to help you to be willing to say sorry – to God and to others – when you're wrong.

Stepping stones

Reading: **Acts 6. 8-15; 7. 52-60**

October 30

Then he knelt down and cried with a loud voice, 'Lord, do not charge them with this sin'. And when he had said this he fell asleep, Acts 7. 60

Jerusalem had never known anything like it before. More and more people were becoming disciples of Jesus. But many were poor and needed looking after. Seven reliable and responsible men were chosen to organize their care. One of them was called Stephen. God had given him special gifts. He could do wonderful miracles and he was a powerful preacher.

It wasn't long before the leaders of an important synagogue heard about him. They didn't agree with his teachings about Jesus and argued with him. They were clever men but the Holy Spirit gave Stephen wisdom in everything he said. The Jewish leaders gave up in disgust. They would have to think of other ways to stop him preaching.

They found men who were willing to tell lies about Stephen. They twisted his words. They made sure that other leaders began to have doubts about him. It was just like the trial of Jesus. Would it end in the same way? Even when faced with hatred and lies, Stephen didn't seem to be afraid. Calm and clear-minded, he was ready to speak. He looked as though he was in the presence of God.

Stephen told his accusers that the nation of Israel had always behaved in the same way. They killed God's prophets because they didn't like what they said about the nation and their sins. Finally they killed Jesus, His Son. That was enough! Outside the city great stones were flung at Stephen. It was a terrible death. But just like Jesus he asked God to forgive those who were killing him.

A young man stood near and watched him die. What was he thinking? One day, he too would sacrifice his life because of his love for Jesus. What an example Stephen proved to be, both in his life and in his death.

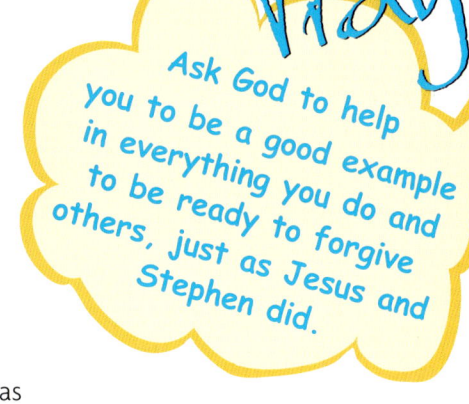

Pray

Ask God to help you to be a good example in everything you do and to be ready to forgive others, just as Jesus and Stephen did.

. . . through the Bible day by day

October 31

Reading: Acts 8. 26-40

Then Philip opened his mouth, and beginning at this Scripture, preached Jesus to him, Acts 8. 35

The chariot moved swiftly along the desert road. It was a long journey home, but the man in the chariot had something to read. He was a very important person who looked after the Queen of Ethiopia's great wealth. He was usually counting money or writing letters, but not today. He was busy reading a book by a Hebrew prophet called Isaiah.

This man from Ethiopia was happy to make the long journey to Jerusalem and back. Every year he came to worship the God of the nation of Israel. He knew that their God was different from the gods of the other nations. The eunuch was keen to find out more about Him. The way to do that, he knew, was to read the Hebrew Bible.

But the eunuch was sad as he read the prophet's words. He found them hard to understand. Who was this person who suffered without saying a word? Why did no one speak up for him? Why was he killed?

At that moment a man appeared at the side of the chariot. He offered to help the eunuch. It seemed that God had sent him. There in the chariot, Philip explained that Isaiah was writing about Jesus, God's Son. He told him that Jesus had been God's Lamb. He was sacrificed for the sin of the whole world, not just for the Jews. This was such good news! It was just as though a light had shone in the heart and mind of the eunuch. Isaiah's words were all about Jesus. He felt so happy. Jesus had died for *him*, *his* sins could be forgiven! Jesus loved *him*.

Isaiah's words are for each one of us too. Jesus loves you and died for you. He wants to be your Saviour and Friend.

Pray

Thank God for the Bible and for those who can explain it. Ask Him for help to make sure you read it every day and learn more about Jesus.

Stepping stones

Reading: Acts 9. 1-22

November 1

Go, for he is a chosen vessel of Mine to bear My name before Gentiles, kings, and the children of Israel, Acts 9. 15

The disciples in Damascus were scared. They had heard that Saul was on his way to the city. Everyone knew what he was like. He did not believe that Jesus was the Son of God. He was determined to get rid of every follower of Jesus. No wonder the believers were frightened.

Saul was an angry man and it showed, even as he rode to Damascus. Nothing and no one was going to stop him destroying this new religion. All the followers of Jesus, 'the Way', deserved prison, punishment or death. He was the man who would put an end to it all. And he was sure he was doing the right thing. But the Lord showed Saul that he was wrong. There on the road to Damascus, Saul's life was changed. It was changed forever.

The light from heaven was so bright! Now it was Saul's turn to be frightened. He knew straight away that it was the Lord who was speaking to him. This was Jesus. This was the One he hated and wanted to destroy! Was he making a terrible mistake?

The Lord knew just what Saul was thinking and what he should do. He needed time by himself. When he arrived in Damascus, in darkness, without food or drink, the Lord spoke to him. It was only for three days, but it was enough. Ananias could not believe that Saul was such a changed man. But in spite of his fears, he went to see him. He found that God could change even a man like Saul. God had a wonderful plan for Saul's life.

No one is beyond God's love and power. We may think some people cannot be saved because of the way they are. God *can* save them. We must keep on praying.

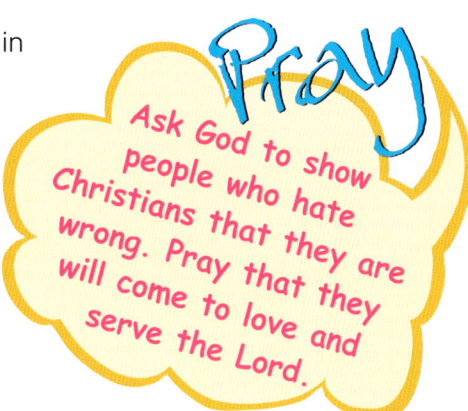

Pray

Ask God to show people who hate Christians that they are wrong. Pray that they will come to love and serve the Lord.

...through the Bible day by day

November 2

Reading: Acts 11. 1-18

There is neither Jew nor Greek, there is neither slave nor free, there is neither male nor female; for you are all one in Christ Jesus, Galatians 3. 28

The leaders in Jerusalem could hardly believe it! Peter, a Jew, had gone to a Gentile's house and had a meal. Peter would have some explaining to do. Jewish people would never eat a meal with a Gentile, a non-Jew. Gentiles often ate food, such as pork, which was forbidden to Jews. It was no wonder the leaders were so shocked.

Peter realized he had upset his friends. He made sure he told them the whole story. He'd had a very strange dream about eating animals, but they were animals which Jewish people were not allowed to eat. A voice from heaven told him to kill them and eat them. Peter was horrified. He told the Lord that he would never do such a thing. He'd never eaten any unclean meat! Then God told him that He had made the meat clean. Peter could eat it now. This strange dream was repeated three times. Whatever did it mean? Whatever was God teaching him? Peter soon found out.

Pray

Thank God for His love to all people. Thank Him that Jesus' sacrifice is enough for every person in the world to be saved.

While he had been dreaming, three men had come to the house. Their master, a Roman centurion, wanted to know more about Jesus. Now Peter understood. God had been telling him that the Saviour was for everyone, Jew and Gentile. The Gentiles needed to hear about Jesus too. If it meant going into their houses and having a meal with them, that was fine.

It was a very special moment. As Peter finished telling his story, the room went silent. Everyone present had learned that at the cross there is no difference between Jew and Gentile. God does not have favourites. We have all sinned and need forgiveness. The good news about Jesus is for all people. What a wonderful Saviour we have!

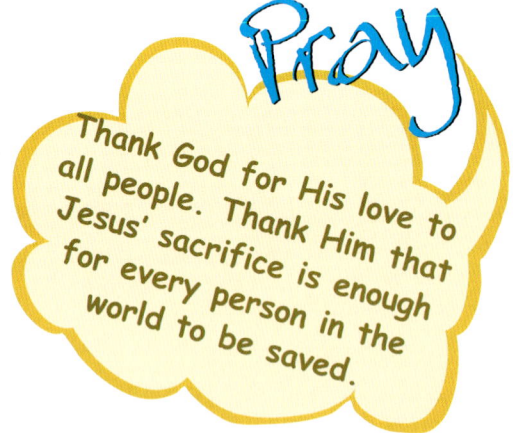

Reading: **Acts 12. 1-17**

November 3

Remember my chains, Colossians 4. 18

It was the middle of the night but people were still praying. James had been executed. Peter was in prison. Herod and the Jewish leaders were determined to destroy all the followers of Jesus. Peter was to go on trial in the morning. Herod wanted to show everyone that he was an important and powerful king. But the Christians believed that God was more powerful than Herod. They prayed that God would give Peter courage.

Pray

Thank God for the brave Christians who live in dangerous countries but still preach the gospel. Ask Him to keep them and their families safe.

Herod made sure that his prisoner could not escape. Peter was in chains and guarded by four soldiers. Every three hours the guard was changed. The soldiers needed to keep awake. Herod would kill them if Peter got out of prison.

But Peter knew that Herod and his soldiers could not do what God did not want them to do. He was safe in God's hands. So he went to sleep. In Mary's house, his friends stayed awake and prayed for him.

Peter really thought he was dreaming. Had an angel come to rescue him? His chains fell to the ground. What a noise! But no one else woke up even when the great iron doors of the prison swung open. Suddenly, he was free. Peter knew now that it was God who had taken him out of prison and danger. He went through the silent streets to Mary's house. What an answer to prayer! It was a miracle. The believers were so excited when they saw him. The Lord had delivered Peter. Peter still had a lot to do for the church.

Even today, many people are in danger because they believe in Jesus. Some are put in prison, and others are being killed for their faith. Some have to leave their families and friends. Like the believers in Mary's house, we need to keep praying for them.

... through the Bible day by day

November 4

Reading: Acts 13. 1-3

Go therefore and make disciples of all the nations, baptizing them in the name of the Father and of the Son and of the Holy Spirit, Matthew 28. 19

Antioch in Syria was a large and important city. Many Christians had gone there to live. It was too dangerous for them to stay in Jerusalem. Of course, when they arrived, they started telling people about Jesus. They told both Jews and Gentiles. Many of them believed and came together to worship and pray. This was all very exciting. Wonderful things were happening in towns and cities outside of Israel.

The church in Jerusalem sent a man called Barnabas to Antioch. He was excited to discover how much God was doing in the city. The church was growing. But the believers needed someone to teach them. They needed to be shown how to live the Christian life.

Barnabas knew just the man for the job. It was his friend Saul. Barnabas had helped Saul after Saul became a Christian. Now he asked Saul to help him teach the church in Antioch. They were together there for a whole year.

But God had something else for them to do. One day, the leaders in Antioch were having a special time of prayer. They knew that Jesus had told His disciples to go to *all* nations and preach the gospel. While they were praying, God told them He had chosen Saul and Barnabas for this work. They would begin the great task of taking the good news about Jesus into all the world. It would not be easy. Hard times were ahead. But Saul and Barnabas, the first missionaries, were willing to go.

Everyone can share the gospel about Jesus with friends and neighbours. But God asks some men and women to leave their homes and friends. He asks them to take the gospel to countries and people far away. Perhaps one day, He might ask you to go. Would you be willing?

> **Pray**
> Ask God to help those who leave home to go to other countries to preach about the Lord. Ask Him to help their families too, when they say goodbye.

Reading: **Acts 14. 19-26**

November 5

We had the sentence of death in ourselves, that we should not trust in ourselves but in God who raises the dead, 2 Corinthians 1. 9

It was a terrible moment for the disciples. Paul's body was being dragged out of the city. He must be dead. No one could still be alive after such a battering. Had God taken Paul away to heaven already?

No, He had not! Paul was still with them. He was alive, able to walk and talk. Sorrow and fear turned to joy. God had worked a miracle and protected him. They all went back into the city. There was work still to be done.

When Paul had become a Christian, God had told him that his life would be hard and dangerous. Many people would be filled with hatred against him and his news about Jesus. When they left the church in Antioch, Paul and Barnabas had gone to Cyprus. Then they went north to another city called Antioch. It was here that their troubles had started. The whole city wanted to hear Paul preach. Many Gentiles believed. They were so happy to learn about the true and living God and His Son Jesus. Idols had done nothing for them. But many of the Jews in Antioch did not believe and were not happy. They stirred up the leaders of the city. Paul and Barnabas had to leave.

Pray

Thank God for the men and women who sacrificed their lives because they were willing to tell people about Jesus. Help us not to forget them.

It was the same story wherever they went. Many Jews and Gentiles became followers of Jesus. But there were others who hated the two men and did their best to get rid of them. The disciples were brave men. They even went back to the cities where they had been ill-treated! They loved and served the Lord. They wanted to help the new believers. Whatever the cost, they would obey the Lord. He had died for them. They were ready to die for Him. Would we be willing to do the same?

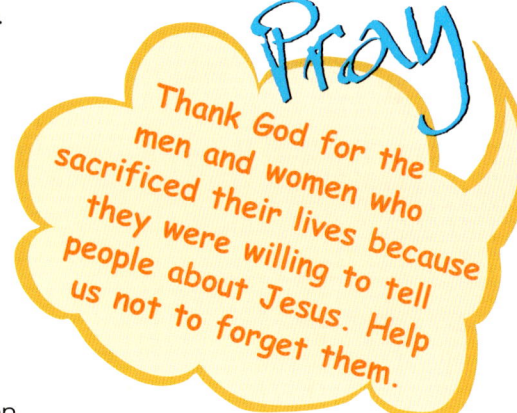

. . . through the Bible day by day

November 6

Reading: **Acts 16. 16-34**

They departed from the presence of the council, rejoicing that they were counted worthy to suffer shame for His name,

Acts 5. 41

Pray

Ask God to comfort you when life is difficult and you don't feel like singing. Then others will see that you have a God who is always there to help.

The prisoners wondered what was happening. It was midnight and they could hear voices. People were singing — not shouting. They were actually singing! No one had ever sung in prison before. They listened more carefully. Prisoners were singing to God! In between the songs men prayed. They were thanking God for His help and guidance. They even thanked God for their sufferings!

Who were these men who sang and prayed? They had been flogged and flung into the darkest and dirtiest cell. And yet they were singing about Jesus and His love. They didn't seem worried about themselves. Paul and Silas didn't enjoy being in prison. They wanted to be outside on the streets. They had come to tell people about Jesus. But they believed that God had a plan for them, even in prison. While they waited they would sing about the Saviour. They would sing loud enough for the prisoners to hear.

And God did have a plan! But it was not at all what Paul and Silas had imagined. Suddenly the ground creaked and groaned. The heavy prison doors flew open. The jailer was ready to kill himself. All his prisoners would escape. But no one moved.

It was Paul who sorted everyone out. His back was bleeding and sore, his feet were bruised and painful. But he told the jailer how he and his family could be saved. Their lives, their eternal lives, were more important to Paul than his sufferings.

Sometimes God's plans for us are not what we would like. We need to trust Him, like Paul and Silas did, especially in the difficult times. It may be hard to sing, but we can pray. The Lord will always help us and who knows what good things can come out of our hard times.

Reading: **Acts 17. 16, 22-34**

November 7

He has appointed a day on which He will judge the world in righteousness by the Man whom He has ordained, Acts 17. 31

Athens was a beautiful city. While Paul was waiting for his friends he had time to look around. But the buildings and altars made him feel sad. He was sad because the gods of the Athenians were not real gods. They had names and altars but the stories about them were just fairy tales. The gods were all imaginary.

The people of Athens had heard about Paul. He was always ready to talk to people. They wondered if this 'Jesus' was a new god. But they didn't understand what being raised from the dead was all about. They asked Paul to explain.

Paul knew that the men he was talking to were very clever. They thought a lot about life and the future. Was there life after death? What would happen at the end of time? Paul thought carefully about what he would say. The Athenians knew nothing about the Bible. But Paul remembered seeing an altar dedicated to 'the unknown god'. He would tell them about the *true and living* God, the one that everyone can know.

The Athenians listened quietly. Paul told them they needed to ask the real God to forgive their sins. They heard about God's plan for the future of this world, about a time when all wrongs will be put right. God has even set a date for it and He has chosen the Man (the Lord Jesus) to be the ruler and judge. But then Paul said that this man had been raised from the dead by God. That was too much for clever men to take in. They laughed and walked away.

But a few people believed. Many people still walk away from Jesus. They find it hard to believe He will come again. We need to keep praying for them. God still loves them.

Pray

Remind us that Jesus is coming again. Help us to thank Him that He will put right all the wrong things in this world. He will be our King and our Saviour.

...through the Bible day by day

November 8

Reading: **Acts 19. 11-20**

Many of those who had practised magic brought their books together and burned them in the sight of all, Acts 19. 19

It was a huge bonfire. People were burning books in a public square in the city. They were books about magic and were very expensive. Something unexpected must have happened. Ephesus was famous for its magicians. Some of them delivered people from demon possession. They would use a name or a strange word and hope that the magic would work.

Then a family of magicians heard that the name of Jesus had special powers. Paul had been living in Ephesus for two years. He spoke about the Lord in synagogues and colleges. He also healed people and cast out demons. But this had nothing to do with magic. The Bible says that it was God who worked unusual miracles through Paul's handkerchiefs and aprons. Paul was a tent maker as well as being a preacher and teacher. It was heavy work. He needed cloths to wipe away the sweat from his face. He needed aprons to protect his clothes. But there were no magical powers in them.

Sceva and his sons, however, saw a way to earn a lot more money. If they used the name of Jesus lots of people would come to them for healing. But their plan went terribly wrong. They used His name without knowing Him as their Saviour. They were not believers and the demons knew they were cheats. And so did the whole city after Sceva and his sons were attacked by an evil spirit.

Many magicians and sorcerers saw that the power of God was greater than the power of their spells. They believed in God and, instead of selling their spells to others, burned them. They lost a fortune when they did that. Following Jesus means that we may have to change our lives and lose a lot. But God's ways are always best.

Pray
Ask God to show us the things we need to change in our lives. We should thank Him that His ways are always best for us.

Reading: Acts 20. 6-12

November 9

On the first day of the week, when the disciples came together to break bread, Paul, ready to depart the next day, spoke to them, Acts 20. 7

Paul was in a hurry to get back to Jerusalem. The boat from Troas sailed in the morning. But he wanted to speak to his friends before he left. It was a Sunday evening, the first day of the week. Sunday is a special day for Christians. On that day, Jesus was raised from the dead. Before He died, Jesus had asked His disciples to remember Him. He showed them how. They were to share bread and wine with each other. This would remind them of His death on the cross. Even now, every Sunday, Christians come together to share the bread and the wine. Together, we think about the Lord Jesus.

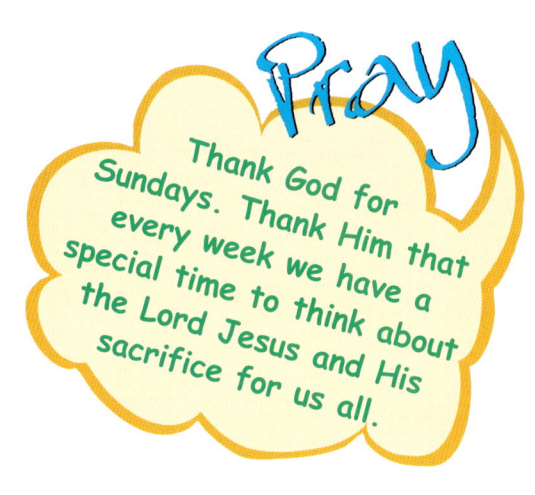

Pray

Thank God for Sundays. Thank Him that every week we have a special time to think about the Lord Jesus and His sacrifice for us all.

That evening in Troas, before they shared the bread and wine, Paul spoke to the church. He knew he might never see his friends again. There was so much he wanted to teach them. He forgot the time. The lamps were lit. The room was warm. Some, like Eutychus, were sitting on window sills. It was not a safe place to sit, especially if you were very tired!

It was a terrible shock when the young man fell out of the window. It was such a long way to the ground. Everyone was sure he must be dead. Paul went straight down to see what he could do. He put his arms around Eutychus, who started to breathe again. What a relief! Paul had been busy teaching a room full of people. But caring for just one person was important to him as well.

The meeting went on until morning. Paul had taken the bread, drunk the wine and remembered the Saviour with his friends. He just loved to be with those who belonged to Jesus. It was a very special time for them all. Is it special for us?

. . . through the Bible day by day

November 10

Reading: Acts 21. 27-36; 23. 10-11

From now on let no one trouble me, for I bear in my body the marks of the Lord Jesus, Galatians 6. 17

What must it be like to have a whole city wanting to kill you? The people of Jerusalem were so angry. They accused Paul of taking someone who wasn't a Jew into the temple. This was a lie, but the Jews didn't care. They were determined to kill Paul. Nothing was going to stop them. They would beat him to death.

It must have been terrifying for Paul. Imagine being right in the middle of a crowd of angry people. He could see their faces, full of hatred. He could hear their voices shouting, 'Away with him'. He could feel their fists and sticks beating against his body. He could hardly breathe.

In no time at all, Roman soldiers came running to the temple. They would protect Paul. It wasn't God's time for Paul to die. But even the tough Roman soldiers had a hard job. The crowds were out to get Paul.

Paul later wrote a letter to the believers in Galatia. He thought about those frightening days in Jerusalem. He remembered the pain he felt when his body was beaten. He remembered his sadness because the people refused to listen to him. Jesus had been through suffering like that. Paul was His servant. He knew he had to suffer too.

Paul had to stay in prison in Jerusalem for a long time. The army commander didn't know what to do with him. But the Lord had not forgotten Paul. There in prison, Jesus came to cheer Paul up. He knew how much Paul wanted to visit Rome. He knew how much Paul wanted to preach the gospel there. Jesus promised him he would go!

The Lord knows all about us. We may not see Him, but He's always by our side. He promised He would never leave us. He's our Friend as well as our Saviour.

Pray

Today we remember that Jesus is always with us. He stands by us and He knows the plan He has for our lives. We are special to Him.

Stepping stones

Reading: Acts 26, 1-6, 27-32

November 11

I would to God that not only you, but also all who hear me today, might become both almost and altogether such as I am, except for these chains, Acts 26. 29

Festus, the Roman governor, had visitors. King Agrippa and Queen Berenice had come to stay. Festus was glad to see Agrippa. He was hoping that the king would be able to help him. Festus could not understand the fuss the Jews were making about Paul. Agrippa was not Roman. He was a local man. Perhaps he would understand. The problem was that the Jews wanted Paul to be executed. Festus hadn't thought he deserved it, but Paul had asked to go to Caesar for trial. Festus needed some advice from the king about what to write to Caesar.

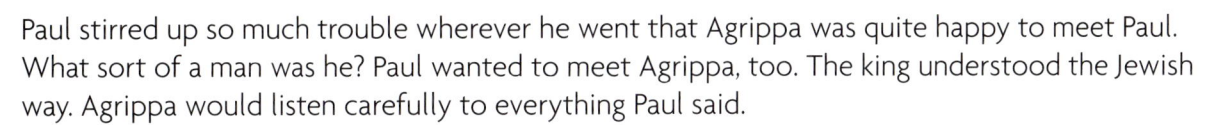

Paul stirred up so much trouble wherever he went that Agrippa was quite happy to meet Paul. What sort of a man was he? Paul wanted to meet Agrippa, too. The king understood the Jewish way. Agrippa would listen carefully to everything Paul said.

Paul introduced himself. He was a Jew who had kept Jewish religious laws all his life, he said. But when he met Jesus his life changed. God had promised He would send the nation of Israel a saviour, which is what they had hoped for. But when Jesus came, the people had rejected Him. Paul had been trying hard to show them that Jesus was their Saviour. But they had no time for Jesus or for Paul.

Agrippa listened carefully. He knew the prophets had talked about the coming of God's king. But this Jesus had come to save His people from their sins and Agrippa wasn't interested in that. Paul pleaded with him. 'I am in chains,' he said, 'But I wish you were like me'. How could Paul be better off than a king? Paul's sins were forgiven and he had eternal life. It's better to be a prisoner and have peace with God than to be a king without it. Wouldn't you agree?

Pray

Pray for those who like to hear about Jesus, but who don't want to have Him as their Saviour. Pray that they change their minds and come to know Him.

. . . through the Bible day by day

November 12

Reading: **Acts 28. 1-16**

All the saints greet you, but especially those who are of Caesar's household,
Philippians 4. 22

It was a wonderful welcome. The Christians in Rome couldn't wait to see Paul. They came out from the city to meet him. When Paul saw his friends coming, he felt strong again. He thanked God for their welcome. Paul was a great preacher and teacher, but God knew that he needed friends. Some of them were important and rich. Others were poor or even slaves. Paul loved them all. He was always so thankful for what they did for him and for others. He knew he could not manage without them.

After speaking to Festus and King Agrippa, Paul and some of his friends had started on their journey to Italy. And what a journey that had been! The voyage had been difficult from the beginning. Winds and waves had whipped up into a massive storm. Sailors had struggled to control the ship and keep it from the rocks. In the end, everyone had jumped into the sea. They managed to reach dry land in whatever way they could. No one from the ship had drowned. It had been such a relief to be safe on the island. Even there Paul made friends! He was always ready to help. Sometimes it was just gathering a few sticks. No job was too small for Paul.

After all those adventures Paul was glad to arrive in Rome. That great city was the capital of the most powerful empire in the world. But God wanted Paul to speak about the greatest person in the world – the Lord Jesus. God had kept His promise and brought Paul safely to Rome. Now His servant would make sure that he told as many people as possible about the Saviour, right on Caesar's doorstep and even in Caesar's palace. Nothing is too hard for God!

Pray

Thank God for all your friends. Pray that you may be helpful and kind to them and to people that you don't know very well.

Reading: **Philemon**

November 13

If he has wronged you or owes anything, put that on my account, Philemon 18

Pray

Pray that, as Jesus was always ready to forgive, we will be like Him and forgive others too. And help us to be ready to say, 'I'm sorry', when we need to.

The slave Onesimus had run away from his master Philemon. That was a wrong thing to do. He knew he deserved to be punished. So he went to Rome. It was a big city. No one would find him there. But God knew exactly where he was. You can never hide from God.

Although Paul was a prisoner in Rome he was allowed to live in a house. He had many visitors. Some were not Christians and he told them about the Saviour. One visitor who listened and believed was Onesimus. He became like a son to Paul. He loved being with him. He was always ready to help Paul in any way he could. But they both knew there was something wrong which had to be put right. Onesimus had to go back to Philemon.

Paul knew Philemon very well. Philemon had become a Christian and Paul had worked with him. He was a good man. Paul decided to write to Philemon about his slave. If Onesimus returned to his master, he could have been executed for running away. So Paul thought very carefully about what to say in his letter.

He was sure that God had sent Onesimus to him, and he told Philemon that he would miss his care and his help. So Paul asked his friend Philemon to forgive Onesimus. God had forgiven Onesimus' sins. He was now, like his master Philemon, a member of God's family. Onesimus was coming back to put things right with Philemon.

It's not always easy, when we've done something wrong, to say, 'I'm sorry'. It can also be very hard to say, 'I forgive you'. It's not always easy to try to put things right. But God will help us, if we are willing. Are we?

. . . through the Bible day by day

November 14

Reading: Romans 1. 16-17

I, if I am lifted up from the earth, will draw all peoples to Myself, John 12. 32

Do you ever feel embarrassed about talking about the Lord Jesus? Maybe your friends make fun of Him and don't understand about Him dying on the cross. They may make jokes about Him or just ignore Him and pretend He doesn't exist.

We shouldn't be ashamed to share our faith with others and show people that we love God. God loved us so much that He sent His only Son for us. You know how sinful we are and how much God hates sin. He is so holy that He cannot excuse sin. This means our sin separates us from God. It comes between us and God. As He is so holy and just, He must punish sin. So the Lord Jesus took our punishment and died for us on the cross. He took our sin upon Himself and bore our punishment so that, through faith in Him, we can become close to God. This is the good news our friends and everyone in the world needs to hear. Through this the Holy Spirit will draw people to God.

Pray

Ask God to help you to be brave, and not to be ashamed, when you have the opportunity to tell others about Jesus.

Have you ever experimented with a magnet? When you put a magnet near to a paperclip the paperclip can't help being drawn to the magnet. The attraction of the magnet is so great that the paperclip can't help clinging to it. People all over the world are being drawn to the Lord Jesus because of what He did for sinners on the cross. The great love and mercy He showed by giving His life for us on the cross can attract people to Him. So let's never be ashamed to tell people we know about the good news of Jesus because what we say can draw them to Him.

Reading: **Romans 5. 6-11**

November 15

We love Him because He first loved us,
1 John 4. 19

These words remind us that, when we were weak and helpless and could do nothing to save ourselves, someone needed to come and rescue us.

I remember two boys who were out playing when they heard a whimpering noise. They followed the sound and it led them to a big, green bin. When they opened the lid and peered into the darkness, they could just make out a little animal. The smell was terrible and there were flies everywhere. One of the boys climbed up and managed to reach down to the bottom of the bin. He groped around and eventually found a little puppy. It was very dirty and very scared. The boys lifted it from the bin and took it home. The bathed it, fed it, and looked after it. That puppy became a much-loved pet.

What the boys did for the puppy is like what God did for us, but He did much more than that. God found us when we were spiritually dirty, lost and trapped in our sin. He reached down to rescue us. He sent His perfect Son to save us while we were still sinners. This is just amazing love. God loved us when there was nothing loveable about us and He sent Jesus to die for us, not because we were good enough, but simply because He loved us.

The Lord Jesus came down from heaven, which is a wonderful place of happiness and peace. He came to earth where He felt hungry, thirsty, tired and sad. Jesus came willingly, even though men mocked Him, beat Him and hurt Him. Then He died for us.

Pray

Thank God that He loved you long before you loved Him. Ask Him to give you the confidence to trust in His love, even when you don't feel worthy of it.

If you ever feel uncertain of God's love for you, remember that He loved you before you turned to Him and before you believed in Him. Remember, too, that He gave His very best for you.

. . . through the Bible day by day

November 16

Reading: Romans 8. 14-17

Go to My brethren and say to them, 'I am ascending to My Father and your Father, and to My God and your God',

John 20. 17

It is a happy day in the life of a family when a child is born. The excited parents are thrilled! They look at their baby, the tiny ears, the little nose, the shape of the eyes, the colour of the hair, searching for features that resemble them. The day of the birth is a day of great joy but there are days of hard work ahead. They know they will need to provide for the child, to protect and nurture, to teach and guide, to correct and discipline.

It is also a happy day when someone is born into God's family. In fact it makes all heaven rejoice, Luke 15. 7. Have you ever become a child of God? This is what the Lord Jesus was speaking about when He told Nicodemus, 'You must be born again', John 3. 7. We aren't God's children naturally and we don't become God's children gradually. Whenever someone receives Christ as their Lord and Saviour, God brings them into His family and becomes their Father, John 1. 12. Since God is our Father it means He provides for us and as today's passage shows, His children will share all that He has forever!

As our Father He loves and cares for us individually. A man may have several children but each one of them is special to him. In the same way there are millions in the family of God but every one of them is special to Him, including you! Isn't it wonderful to know that God is always watching over us and He is there to help us in all that we do?

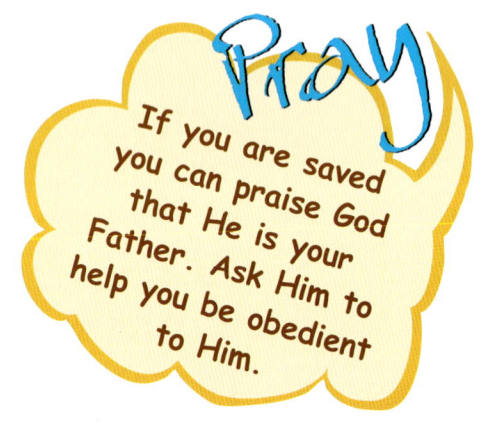

> **Pray**
> If you are saved you can praise God that He is your Father. Ask Him to help you be obedient to Him.

Reading: Romans 10. 8-15

November 17

Nor is there salvation in any other, for there is no other name under heaven given among men by which we must be save, Acts 4. 12

Have you ever been so excited about something that you were almost bursting to tell people about it? Maybe you got a special present for your birthday that you couldn't wait to show to your friends. Perhaps you met someone famous and you wanted everyone to know. When we are excited about something it isn't difficult to talk about it. Why then is it so difficult to talk to our friends about the Lord? Is it not a wonderful thing to have met Him? Has He not given us the greatest gift anyone could ever have, Romans 6. 23? How come we are so slow to tell others? There is one big reason – FEAR! 'What if people laugh?' 'What if my friends tell me to go away?' 'What if . . .' 'What if . . .'

It is because people are afraid that many don't witness, but here are some reasons why you should:

Do it for the Lord – the Lord has done so much for you, is it too much for you to tell others about Him? When we think of what He suffered for us it makes our excuses seem a bit feeble doesn't it?

Do it for others – those friends at school need to be saved and he or she will never be saved unless they hear the gospel, Romans 10. 14. It's awful to be on the broad road to hell – tell them about the One who can save them!

Do it for yourself – there is no greater joy than telling others about the Lord. It may be scary but when you do it you will be so glad.

Remember, there is nothing more important and nothing more wonderful than salvation – so don't keep it to yourself!

Pray
Ask God for the opportunity, courage and wisdom to tell others about the Lord.

. . . through the Bible day by day

November 18

Reading: **Romans 13. 1-7**

Honour all people. Love the brotherhood. Fear God. Honour the king, 1 Peter 2. 17

'You have no right to tell me what to do!' Perhaps you have heard an angry outburst like this. It can sometimes be heard in the classroom shouted at the teacher. It can sometimes be heard in the bedroom shouted at a parent. It can sometimes be heard in the workplace shouted at the boss. It seems that there are a lot of people who think that no one should be allowed to tell anyone what to do. We need to make sure we don't have that attitude. We all agree that God has the right to tell us what to do but don't forget that He has given others that responsibility as well. Our reading focuses on the government of the country but parents and teachers are other examples of people whom we must obey.

Pray
Pray that God will help you to be submissive to those who have the right to tell you what to do.

Satan was the first to rebel. He rebelled against God's rule and anytime we see rebellion against authority today we can be sure he is involved – it has his fingerprints on it!

The Bible tells us that there is only one situation in which it is right not to obey those in authority and that is when it would mean disobeying God. In those circumstances we can say, 'We ought to obey God rather than men', Acts 5. 29. This is the only time when disobedience is allowed. But remember, rudeness and bad manners are never allowed – always show respect and courtesy.

This world is marked by rebellion against authority. God hated rebellion when the devil did it and He still hates it now. We have an opportunity to please God and be a witness to others by our attitude and obedience. Don't follow the devil's example. Follow the Bible – don't be a rebel!

Stepping stones

Reading: Romans 13. 8-10

November 19

Owe no one anything except to love one another, for he who loves another has fulfilled the law, Romans 13. 8

As Christians it is wonderful to remember that the massive debt we owed to God because of our sin was paid by Christ at Calvary and we are forgiven. We could have never paid that debt, but thank the Lord that He did! However, we do need to be careful that we pay all the other debts that we owe and that we don't expect others to bail us out.

Are you always asking friends to lend you money because you have spent all yours? If the answer is yes, then there are two things you need to do:

- Make sure you pay back all that you owe, quickly! The Bible says, 'The wicked borrows and does not repay', Psalm 37. 21.

- Be more responsible with your money so that you don't have to borrow from others.

- Christians should not be scroungers. It is dishonouring to the Lord. We should be known as givers, not takers.

- There are a couple of things that the Bible tells us we do owe. Our passage today tells us that we have a debt to others to love them. Think about that person in your class who doesn't seem to have any friends or the person who is nasty and annoying. The Bible says you owe them love.

Pray
Ask God to show you if there are any debts that you need to repay. Ask Him to help you to remember to buy only what you can afford.

In Romans chapter 1 verse 14 Paul says he is a debtor to all to preach the gospel to them. Have you told your friends about the Lord? Are you a witness to others? Remember – it's a debt you have to pay!

Loving others and witnessing to others are two debts we will never be able to pay off fully but make sure that they are the only debts you owe. Then spend your life paying those debts as much as you can.

. . . through the Bible day by day

November 20

Reading: 1 Corinthians 6. 19-20

If anyone loves Me, he will keep My word; and My Father will love him, and We will come to him, and make Our home with him, John 14. 23

One of the great things about being a Christian is knowing that we will live with the Lord in heaven forever but maybe we don't think so much about the fact that the Lord lives with us here on earth now. Our reading tells us that the Holy Spirit lives within us – your body is God's house!

It wasn't cheap for God to make your body His house. 'You are bought with a price', and that price was the death of Christ. This means that we do not have the right to do whatever we want with our bodies. They belong to Him and just as your parents make the rules for their house so God has made the rules for what you are allowed to do with your body.

Home is the place where we enjoy the company of family. That is one reason why the Spirit of God lives within each Christian. He has come to help us speak to God in prayer and hear God speak to us through the Bible. Have you been enjoying God's company lately?

> **Pray**
> Remember that your body belongs to God. Present it to Him today and ask Him to use you.

Every house has locks to stop people sneaking in to do damage or to steal. We need to remember that sin is always trying to break into our lives to damage us and rob us of joy. Have you checked the locks on the doors and windows of your body? What about your eyes? Are sinful things getting into your mind through the things you watch and read? What about your ears? Are sinful thoughts and words sneaking into your mind through the music you listen to or the conversations you take part in?

Remember – your body belongs to God. He wants you to look after it to keep it clean and use it for Him. It's His house!

Stepping stones

Reading: **1 Corinthians 12. 1-18**

November 21

God has set the members, each one of them, in the body just as He pleased,
1 Corinthians 12. 18

The human body is a wonderful thing but have you ever wondered exactly what each part is for? What about your little toes? Maybe you don't give them too much thought but do we really need them? Could we not get by all right with four toes on each foot? If you think you could then you should talk to a friend of mine who had his little toe taken off in an accident. He never realized how valuable that little toe was until he lost it. He now suffers severe back pain because his body is not properly supported. The loss of that one little member affected the rest of his body. My friend is looking forward to the rapture when he will have ten toes again instead of nine!

God has given every Christian a spiritual gift to help others. Each Christian in the local assembly is like a part of the body and we all have our part to play. Some think that being a great preacher is the most important gift, but remember the most important parts of the body are those that people don't see. Not too many people ever see your little toe but without it the body suffers. No one has ever seen your heart but I'm sure you agree it is quite important!

The point is, every part of the body has something to do, and if one part isn't working then the whole body suffers. God doesn't want you to try to copy others. He only wants you to do what He has enabled you to do. If you aren't a great preacher don't worry. You still have vital work to do for God. Every part of the body is important – even that little toe!

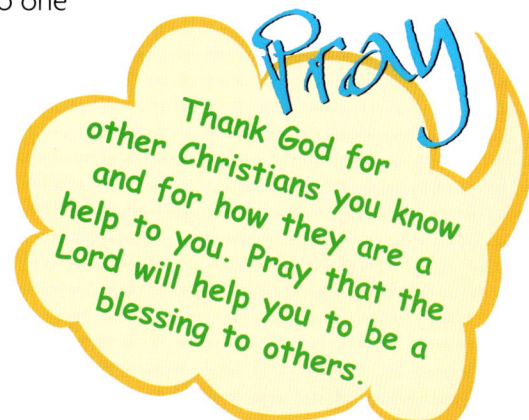

Pray
Thank God for other Christians you know and for how they are a help to you. Pray that the Lord will help you to be a blessing to others.

... through the Bible day by day

November 22

Reading: 1 Corinthians 13

Love never fails, 1 Corinthians 13. 8

Pray
Thank God for His love for you and ask Him to help you love others in the same way.

What does it mean to love someone? Sometimes we have the idea that loving someone just means really liking them, or that your heart goes all fluttery when you are with them. But is that what God expects of us when He commands us to love others? Maybe you know some very nasty people and you can't make yourself like them. What are you supposed to do?

The answer is *'love them!'* When God tells us to love others He is telling us to do them good no matter how they behave and even if it costs us. It actually has nothing to do with feelings.

God did not wait until He saw good in us before He loved us. This world was in rebellion against Him but He determined to do us good anyway even though it meant giving His Son to die for us. That's how God loved us.

Can you see now how God wants you to love others? You can do it by praying for people and witnessing to them, by being helpful and friendly, kind and generous. Look around you and if you see a need then do what you can to meet it. You can start in your own home and show your family that you love them. But don't stop there. God wants you to show love to everyone, even to those who aren't very loving to you. Isn't that what God did?

It's easy to say, 'I love you', but it's not so easy to show it. But then God never said it would be easy. In fact sometimes it can be very costly. Remember the greatest example of all – 'For God so loved the world that He gave His only begotten Son', John 3. 16.

328

Stepping stones

Reading: 1 Corinthians 15. 50-58

November 23

O Death, where is your sting? O Hades (grave), where is your victory?
1 Corinthians 15. 55

Did you sleep well last night? Have you had a good breakfast today? I hope so. It is very important to look after your body because it's the only one you've got! But no matter how much we might care for our bodies, no matter how strong and healthy we try to make them, we cannot change the fact that our bodies are dying. Older people will tell you that there are things they could do when they were your age that they cannot do now.

Why? Because their bodies have aged and won't let them. Then comes the sad day when the body dies. We know that the spirit goes to heaven, but the body is laid in the grave. Death has finally won – or has it?

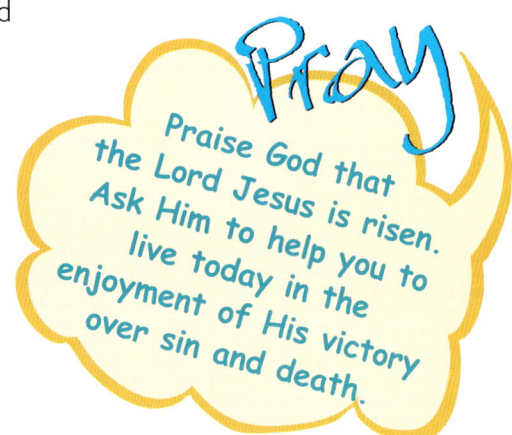

Pray
Praise God that the Lord Jesus is risen. Ask Him to help you to live today in the enjoyment of His victory over sin and death.

They thought that when they took the body of the Lord Jesus down from the cross and laid it in the tomb. Death had won! But three days later they realized that death had actually been defeated. The tomb was empty and Christ was risen. He was victorious and because of His resurrection we don't need to fear death anymore. He has broken its power and can undo its damage. When the Lord comes to take Christians to heaven the body of every believer who has died will be raised and every living believer will be changed. We will all have bodies that will never get old or sick or tired ever again!

Look after your body but don't be overprotective of it. Use it for God and keep remembering that you'll be getting a free upgrade to a better one very soon, maybe even today!

November 24

Reading: 2 Corinthians 9. 1-8

God loves a cheerful giver, 2 Corinthians 9. 7

God is the greatest giver in the universe. Every day He gives life, health, food and shelter to billions in the world. But the greatest gift He ever gave was His only Son. We don't need to give anything for us to be saved. We simply need to take the gift of salvation that God is offering us. But once a person is saved God expects them to be givers. He wants us to give our time and energy to Him for His use and He also wants us to give our money.

You have a decision to make about what you are going to do with the money you get as you grow older. You can either use it for yourself or you can use it for the Lord and for others. You can either spend it on something for this world or you can make it count for eternity. The choice is yours. There are so many people in need and so many ways that we can help.

Perhaps you think that you can't really make a difference because you don't have much money. But don't forget the story about the poor widow in Mark chapter 12 verses 41-44. She only had two mites but she gave them both to God and the Lord said that she threw into the collection box more than anyone else.

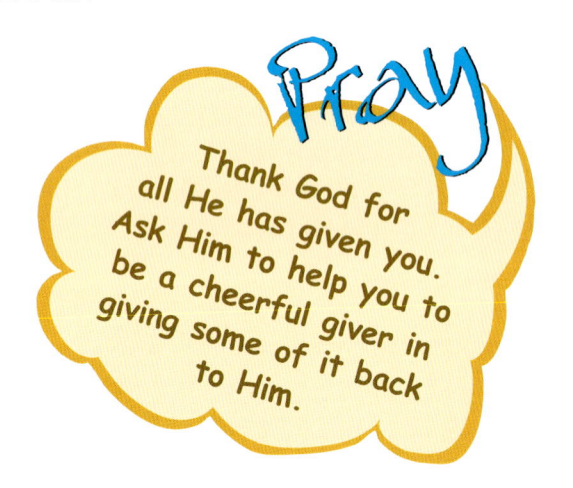

Pray: Thank God for all He has given you. Ask Him to help you to be a cheerful giver in giving some of it back to Him.

If you give to God then He will pay you back, not in the currency of this world but in the currency of heaven. Everything we spend for the Lord and give to Him will be appreciated by Him and rewarded in heaven. Never be afraid to sacrifice and give to the Lord. It pays off in the long run. That widow would tell you that if she could. Do we give enough to God?

Reading: **Galatians 5. 22-23**

November 25

By their fruits you will know them,
Matthew 7. 20

Five portions of fruit or vegetable a day! That's what the nutrition experts tell us we need to eat if we want to be healthy. God tells us that a healthy Christian actually produces fruit – but nine portions a day! The Bible calls it the fruit of the Spirit because we could never produce it naturally. Only by relying on the power of the Spirit of God, who dwells in every Christian, can this fruit be produced.

As you think about these nine portions of fruit do you think others can see them in your life? If we are honest we would admit that there are times when the fruit is dried up, or the branches are bare. Why would this be? Perhaps you are allowing sinful things in your thoughts and actions. Sin will only produce ugly weeds and prevent the growth of any fruit. Maybe you aren't spending time with God each day in prayer and reading the Bible. Without these things your soul will dry up and lack the essential nutrients that will produce fruit. Personal witness and fellowship with other Christians are other things that will help in the growth of these portions of fruit. By letting the Spirit of God control our lives (that means living in obedience to all of scripture) we will begin to see this fruit being brought forth in our lives more and more.

Can you imagine walking through a desert and then coming across a tree whose branches are loaded with ripe, refreshing fruit? It would certainly get your attention wouldn't it? That really is what God wants His children to be in this world. Fruitful in a fruitless wilderness.

Five portions of fruit for the body, nine portions of fruit for the soul. How many portions can others get from your life?

Pray
Think about how many of the nine aspects of the fruit of the Spirit can be seen in your life. Ask God for special help for those ones you are struggling with.

... through the Bible day by day

November 26

Reading: Ephesians 4. 25-32

Be kind to one another, tenderhearted, forgiving one another, even as God in Christ forgave you, Ephesians 4. 32

Mephibosheth could have been one of David's enemies. His grandfather had hunted and hounded David for years. Now David was king. It was normal practice in those times for a new king to kill all descendants of the previous king to ensure they would not try to take the throne again. David asked if any of Saul's family were living, not because he wanted to kill them, but because he wanted to show 'the kindness of God' to them. Mephibosheth was found and brought trembling before the king, thinking that the end had come. But David took him into his own home and treated him like one of his own sons. He showed the kindness of God!

The Bible says that before we were saved we were 'enemies of God'. Yet God loved us and offered us forgiveness, friendship and a place in His family through the death and resurrection of the Lord Jesus. When David showed kindness to someone who was his enemy he was copying God. God expects the same behaviour from you and me.

You may know some people whom you really can't stand. Or maybe you are feeling really fed up with someone in your family or class. Perhaps you want to ignore them, be cheeky to them or hurt them. Do you know what God wants you to do? He wants you to show His kindness to them. You may be thinking, 'But they don't deserve it!' Did you deserve God's kindness? David's question is one that we should ask ourselves today. 'Is there not still someone to whom I may show the kindness of God?' see 2 Samuel 9. 1. It shouldn't be too hard to find someone.

Pray

Give God thanks for His kindness and forgiveness to you. Ask Him to give you a tender heart. Pray for help to show His kindness to others today.

Stepping stones

Reading: **Ephesians 6. 1-4**

November 27

'Honour your father and mother' which is the first commandment with promise,
Ephesians 6. 2

Do you ever find yourself getting annoyed when your parents ask you to do things around the house? No doubt you do what they ask but do you argue and complain a bit? Do you do what they say with a 'tut', a long face and in the quickest way possible? That doesn't actually fulfil the commandment in our reading today, 'Honour your father and mother'. Honouring them means more than just doing what they say. Honouring them means doing what they say, when they say it and with the right attitude. Does that sound impossible? Well, here are a few things to keep in mind when you feel like that:

Pray

Be thankful to God for your parents. Pray for a good attitude towards them and try to honour them today.

Think about how much your parents do for you. You maybe don't realize it, but your parents spend a lot of time and money looking after you. You'll never hear them complain about it. They do it because they love you. If they do so much for you is it too hard for you to do the few things they ask you to do?

It is a commandment of God. If He says it, we should do it.

Disobedience to parents is something that God highlights time and again as a most serious sin, Romans 1. 30; 2 Timothy 3. 2.

Obedience to parents is well-pleasing to the Lord, Colossians 3. 20. Would you not like to please the Lord who has done so much for you?

There are good reasons for honouring our parents. So the next time you are given a chore to do, wipe the scowl off your face, replace it with a smile and do it with a willing heart. You'll please your parents, you'll please the Lord, and you'll even find some pleasure in it yourself!

. . . through the Bible day by day

November 28

Reading: Ephesians 6. 5-9

Whatever you do, do it heartily, as to the Lord and not to men, Colossians 3. 23

When I was at school our head-teacher told us that while we had the uniform on we were representing the school. This was meant to remind us to behave when we were on our way to and from school, not just when we were in school. We could all do with being reminded that if we are saved then we are representing the Lord Jesus. We don't wear a uniform but we carry His Name. We are Christians and we don't get any time off!

If we represent Christ then it is important that we do our best in all things. Being lazy or half-hearted reflects badly on the Lord. But today's Bible reading tells us that we are not just to work hard when people are watching, but when we are not being watched as well. We are to remember that all that we do should be for the Lord and therefore we should do our best for Him.

I don't imagine you would put your pen down and start chatting to the person sitting next to you in class when the teacher is watching you. But if the teacher leaves the room don't forget that the Lord is still watching! When you do your homework do you scribble it down as fast as you can and say, 'It will do', so you can go out and play? Would you not be a bit more careful if you were giving that homework to God?

It is a wonderful thing to remember that we can please the Lord even in the everyday things of life, like schoolwork and household chores just by giving them our best. So check your work one more time, take a little bit longer, and remember, you are a servant of Christ. He deserves our best!

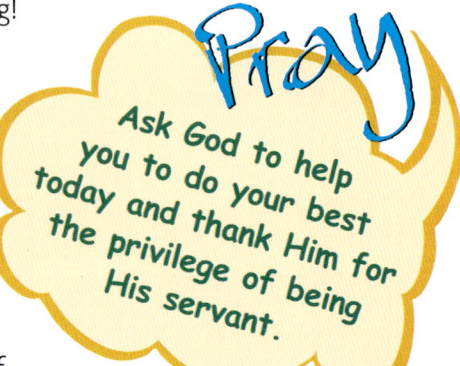

Pray

Ask God to help you to do your best today and thank Him for the privilege of being His servant.

Reading: **Philippians 4. 4-9**

November 29

Keep your heart with all diligence, for out of it spring the issues of life,
Proverbs 4. 23

You are in a battle – right now! Who is it with? The devil and all his forces. What's it for? Your mind. The devil wants to penetrate and pollute your mind with his poisonous ideas and images. He has lots of different techniques. He floods the world with notions that are anti-God; he fills the media with immorality and uncleanness; he distracts our focus onto things that are of no value. No matter what his tactics are, his aim is the same – to get our minds off God and all that is good. The devil knows that we will never be any use to God unless our minds are focussed and free from clutter.

Pray

Ask God to help you to be disciplined and not think about things that are impure. Gather some good thoughts together that you can think on during the day.

Has the enemy managed to make an advance into your mind? What do you spend your time watching, listening to, thinking about? Maybe we need to root out the enemy's agents and take our thoughts captive to the obedience of Christ, 2 Corinthians 10. 5.

But it is difficult isn't it? Our thoughts are so quick and quiet and without even noticing we suddenly find ourselves thinking about things we shouldn't be thinking about! How can we have a mind that pleases God? Our reading gives two major strategies:

Think about *good* things. I don't think it is possible to think about two things at once. So if you start the day with a Bible verse in your mind or a thought about the Lord, you can chew it over at those times when your mind doesn't have to be on your schoolwork, etc.

Pray, pray, pray. By prayer we build up a fortress around our minds and that makes it more difficult for sinful thoughts to invade.

The battle is on. Don't give the devil an inch. Keep your mind pure for God.

. . . through the Bible day by day

November 30

Reading: Colossians 3. 1-4

Where your treasure is, there your heart will be also, Matthew 6. 21

I'm glad this world isn't all there is. When I think of the sorrow, sin, pain and tears that are so common on earth it makes me glad to know there is a world where none of these things will ever enter. What a wonderful place heaven will be!

Some people have the idea it will be a boring place with not much to do. But the Bible tells us it is a place of great activity, constant joy, unbroken peace, complete harmony, sinless perfection, glorious light and so much more. I'm looking forward to it! But I'm looking forward to it most of all because the Lord Jesus is there. It is because He has saved me that I'll be there and I'm looking forward to seeing Him. Are you going there?

The Bible also tells us that heaven is a place of reward. This doesn't mean that getting there is a reward. Getting there is a gift. But the Lord will graciously reward us in heaven for whatever we did for Him on earth. The rewards He gives are rewards that will bring us eternal enjoyment and will bring Christ eternal glory. So it makes sense to seek as much as possible.

The apostle Paul gave up position and riches in this world because he was living for the world to come. Demas gave up Christian service to enjoy this present world, 2 Timothy 4. 10. Those two men died almost 2,000 years ago and both are in heaven. Which one made the right choice? Do you think the apostle Paul wishes he had lived more for himself or do you think that Demas is glad he lived for his own comfort? You know the answer so which of the two will you copy? Don't make the mistake Demas made.

Pray

If you are saved thank God that there is a home for you in heaven. Ask God to help you live for eternity today.

Stepping stones

Reading: **Colossians 3. 8-14**

December 1

Love one another as I have loved you,
John 15. 12

Lots of things make people different. Some people are cleverer than others or are richer or have better jobs. In New Testament times some Christians were poor slaves but others were rich slave-owners. Some of them were Jews but others were not Jews, they were Gentiles.

Some people only want to know you if you are the right kind of person for them – if you are rich enough or important enough. That's not how Christians should think! In today's reading Paul tells us that once a person becomes a Christian these kinds of differences shouldn't matter anymore. The only thing that should matter is that we love and belong to the Lord Jesus. That is what 'Christ is all and in all' means.

But a Christian will be different from people who are not Christians. When a person becomes a Christian it's as if they become a new person inside. Instead of liking to sin they want to be holy, like the Lord Jesus. Some people can be very unkind but when they become a Christian they become kind people. Others might use bad language but after they became a Christian this changes. The change may not seem so great on the outside if you become a Christian when you are young but the change inside is just as real. As you get older the change will become obvious to others.

One way in which we are different is that we will love other Christians. Some Christians may hurt our feelings but because we love the Lord Jesus we will forgive them as the Lord has forgiven us. After all, it cost the Lord Jesus His life upon the cross in order to forgive us so it could never cost us too much to forgive others, could it?

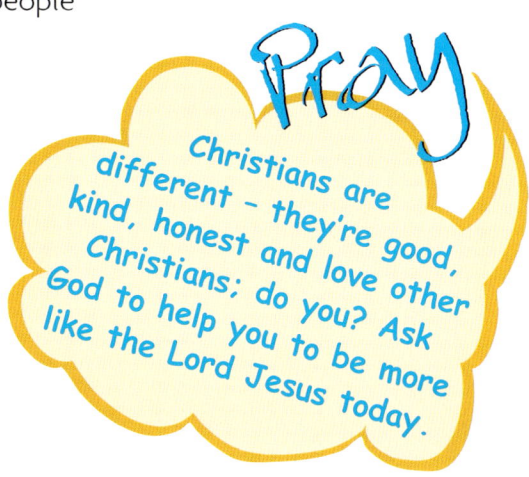

> **Pray**
> Christians are different – they're good, kind, honest and love other Christians; do you? Ask God to help you to be more like the Lord Jesus today.

... through the Bible day by day

December 2

Reading: Colossians 3. 15-25

Whatever you do in word or deed, do all in the name of the Lord Jesus,

Colossians 3. 17

Families are very important. One of the first things God did after He made the world was to give Adam a wife, Eve, so that they could love and look after each other as husband and wife. God knew this was the best way for men and women to be happy. Husbands should love and care for their wives. Wives should love and obey their husbands. God intended that children should share in the love and happiness of their parents. This is what families are all about. Sometimes this isn't the case which is very sad.

When we're children we need to be loved and looked after because we don't always know how to look after ourselves. Our parents need to teach us what is right and wrong to prepare us for the time when we are grown up. This is something that God requires and expects our parents to do. That's why the Bible tells us that we should 'obey our parents in all things'. One of the ten commandments given to Moses was that we should 'honour our father and mother'. Another reason we should be glad to do this is because 'this is well pleasing unto the Lord'.

Keeping families together in happiness isn't always easy. But Christians have a secret weapon from God to help us in every circumstance. It's the Bible. If we read it, it will keep us and our family close to God. That's why our reading says, 'Let the word of Christ (the Bible) dwell in you richly'. That's why we should read it every day – whether we are a mum, a dad or a child. And that's why godly parents will want to read the Bible and pray together with their family every day.

Pray

Thank God for His Son the Lord Jesus. Make sure to thank Him, too, for parents and children, for brothers and sisters.

Stepping stones

Reading: 1 Thessalonians 4. 13-18

December 3

I will come again and receive you to Myself; that where I am, there you may be also, John 14. 3

We look forward to lots of things – holidays, presents and lots more. But Christians should look forward to one thing above everything else and that is being in heaven with the Lord Jesus. Paul once even described this as being 'far better' than remaining in the world!

Heaven is a place where the Lord Jesus Christ is. Because He is there, there will be no more sin, no more crying, no more pain and no more sadness in heaven. Sometimes we're sad because someone we love has died. But if the person who died was a Christian then they are 'with Christ' which is far better for them. Although they are not 'with us' anymore, if we are Christians then one day we know that we will be 'with them' again, in heaven with the Lord.

Not everyone will die. One day the Lord Jesus is going to come back to take believing people with Him into heaven. Not everyone will go, only those who are true Christians. When He comes again all Christians who have died will be raised from their graves and they, with the Christians who are alive at the time, will be 'caught up together' to be with Christ in heaven. No wonder the Bible says, 'comfort one another with these words'.

The Lord Jesus says that He will come quickly, in 'the twinkling of an eye'. He could come back any time, maybe even today! This is the Christian's great hope no matter what else makes us sad. That's why Paul once said that Christians are 'looking for the Saviour, the Lord Jesus Christ'. Are we? Let's make sure we are ready today!

Pray
Ask God to help you to remember Jesus is coming again. Pray for help to be ready in case He comes today.

. . . through the Bible day by day

December 4

Reading: 1 Timothy 2. 1-8

I exhort first of all that supplications, prayers, intercessions, and giving of thanks be made for all men, 1 Timothy 2. 1

Imagine you were asked to take part in a survey to find out what you and lots of other people thought they needed most of all. Many people would think they needed more money or more holidays. Our reading tells us about one thing everyone needs and that is 'to be saved'. Not many people think they need to be saved but God tells us that we all do.

If you've ever been lost you'll know it can be very frightening. One minute you're enjoying yourself walking along a beach or looking around a shop and then suddenly you realize you're lost. Perhaps you didn't realize it at first and so you were quite happy. If you think about it, though, you were lost even before you realized it. You were only happy because you didn't know you were lost.

> **Pray**
> God gave His Son to be our Saviour. Pray today that you can tell someone else about Him.

That's just like lots of people in our imaginary survey. Because they don't realize that they are separated from God they are quite happy. Sometimes, when we are lost, we can be in great danger without knowing it. We are all separated from God because of our sin, which means we are in great danger. The Bible tells us that God is angry with the sinner.

When we are lost we need someone to come and find us to bring us back home again. The Lord Jesus came into the world to find us. He 'gave Himself a ransom for all' by dying on the cross in order to be punished for sin. If we ask Him to, He will save us and bring us back to God. Then once we are saved we can pray for others to be saved too. Even kings, queens, presidents and prime ministers need this more than anything else. You do, too.

Stepping stones

Reading: 1 Timothy 6. 6-16

December 5

Godliness with contentment is great gain, 1 Timothy 6. 6

One day God asked King Solomon what he wanted most. He didn't ask to be famous or successful. Instead he asked God to make him wise so that he would know what he should do to please Him. Sometime later someone came to visit Solomon and when they left they told him that, 'the half has not been told me' of all his wealth. Although he didn't ask for it God made him the most successful king of his day. Everyone spoke of his glory.

What would you have asked for? When he died Solomon had to leave all that he had behind. If all he had asked for was to be rich or famous he would have had nothing left. In our reading we are told to long for 'righteousness, godliness, faith, love, patience'. These are the things that please God. These are the things that will last forever. These are the things that bring real joy and happiness to us if we are Christians. If all we want is something selfish we might become very sad instead and miss out on what God really wants for us in our lives. God might make us rich just like He did Solomon but we shouldn't want this more than we want to please God. Our reading warns us that 'the love of money is the root of all evil'.

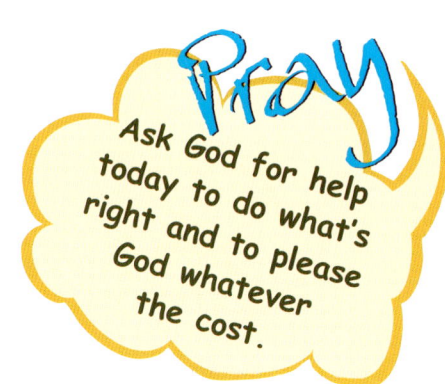

One day the Lord Jesus will be revealed to the world as the 'only Potentate, the King of kings'. What will matter then is not what we have done for ourselves, but what we have done for God.

Pray
Ask God for help today to do what's right and to please God whatever the cost.

. . . through the Bible day by day

December 6

Reading: 2 Timothy 1. 15-18

A friend loves at all times, Proverbs 17. 17

Who would you want to be your friend? Sometimes it's nice to have friends who are popular so we can be in the right crowd. But would you want to be the friend of a man who had lost his importance, had lost his freedom and had lost his friends? The apostle Paul had lost all of these. He lost his importance to the world the day he became a Christian. He lost his freedom when the Romans threw him into prison because he preached the Lord Jesus. He lost lots of his new Christian friends because they became afraid of what might happen to them if they stayed close to him. Being a Christian can cost you a lot!

So it must have been very hard for Paul when he was in prison. He was an old man now and chained on both sides to two Roman soldiers. He must have been uncomfortable and very lonely. After all the places he had visited and all the people he had helped it seems that no one wanted to help him now. No one was even sure where he was being held prisoner.

There was one man who did care. His name was Onesiphorus and he searched hard until he found where Paul was. Imagine how Paul must have felt when he saw his old friend! What mattered was that someone cared enough to find him. We don't know how long Onesiphorus stayed but we can guess that he and Paul talked about the Lord Jesus and about heaven, because Paul was looking forward to going there so much.

Real friends are those who stick with us even when things are difficult and who know and love the Lord Jesus and talk to us about Him. What sort of friend are you?

Pray
Be a real friend; pray for someone today who needs your help and try to talk to them about the Lord Jesus.

Reading: **2 Timothy 3. 1-5**

December 7

The preaching of the cross is . . . the power of God unto salvation,
1 Corinthians 1. 18

Sometimes it's hard to be a Christian because other people make it difficult for us to live as Christians should. It was hard back in the day when Paul wrote his letter to Timothy. It may get worse before the Lord Jesus comes back to take Christians to heaven. People can be very selfish. They often put what's good for them before what's good for everyone else. They are 'lovers of themselves'. Some people are proud, boasting about what they are and what they have. Some children are disobedient to their parents and are out of control. Other people are violent and dishonest and many people love pleasure more than they love God. Some of these people even like to 'go to church' but their lives are no different to others. Although they look as though they are godly they don't know the power of God in their lives. They only have 'a form of godliness'.

If you are a Christian you should make sure that you are not like this. The Bible says that the gospel 'is the power of God unto salvation'. In other words, if you have received the Lord Jesus as your Saviour, He will give you the power to live a different kind of life. Instead, you can live as Jesus did being kind, patient, always obedient to God and submissive to your parents. Paul lived like that. He could say, 'Christ lives in me'! Find people who are like this and be like them. It is possible, though, that if you become friends with people like those described in our reading, you might be encouraged to become like them instead. Paul told Timothy to keep away from such people. So should we.

Pray

Remember you're different! Ask God to help you live as Jesus did. Remember others are watching you.

. . . through the Bible day by day

December 8

Reading: 2 Timothy 3. 14-17

From childhood you have known the Holy Scriptures, which are able to make you wise for salvation through faith which is in Christ Jesus, 2 Timothy 3. 15

Did you know that more copies of the Bible have been sold than any other book? It's true; it's the world's bestseller ever! It's been written over thousands of years by many people. Some of those who wrote it were kings, others were fishermen, some were students and others were shepherds. But it never contradicts itself. It's full of history and prophecy about the future, of songs and poems, letters and genealogies. But it's all about the same person, the Lord Jesus. When He was on earth the Lord Jesus taught 'from all the scriptures the things concerning Himself'. But what makes the Bible so different from any other book? It's inspired by God; that means that every one of its authors wrote as they were told to by the Spirit of God. The Bible tells us that God cannot lie, so we can be sure that His word, the Bible, is all true in what it teaches. That's why it's different!

Pray
Ask God to teach you how important it is to read your Bible today and every day. Pray for help to understand it.

We will find out about a lot of things in the Bible. The ancient history of the Pharaohs, the empires of the Greeks and Romans and more. We'll find out great scientific facts and read beautiful literature about war and peace, romance and adventure. The greatest thing we will find in the Bible, however, is salvation. It will show us how to be saved, by receiving the Lord Jesus as our Saviour.

Once we become Christians we should read it every day. Reading it will be like eating and drinking – it will help us to grow and become healthy Christians. It will be like a light to show us the way to go. It will wash away the sinful things that we see and hear all around us. If we read it, we'll become more like the Lord Jesus every day!

Stepping stones

Reading: Hebrews 4. 14-16

December 9

Let us therefore come boldly to the throne of grace, that we may obtain mercy and find grace to help in time of need, Hebrews 4. 16

If you had lived with the children of Israel long ago, you would have seen someone who was different from everyone else. You could easily have found him because he wore special clothes coloured in blue, purple and scarlet red and he had a bell attached to his clothes which meant that you could hear him as he walked about. This was a good idea because he was the person you needed to find if you had any problems; he would listen to you and try to help you. He was called 'the high priest'.

Christians today have a high priest. The Bible calls him our 'great high priest', because He's the Lord Jesus. Sometimes, in Israel, the high priest might not really understand your problems or how you felt. Our great high priest is not like this. Our reading today tells us that Jesus has been 'tempted in all points as we are'. This means that when He lived here He had the same problems as we do, so He can sympathize with us. But one important way in which the Lord Jesus is very different is that He has no sin. Israel's high priests were all sinners just like us. This meant that before they could ask God to forgive the sins of other people they had to be forgiven for their own sins. But the Lord Jesus is God, so He can't sin; our reading says that He was 'apart from sin'.

Today you might be worried about something. It might be to do with your friends or school, with bullying or tests or something else. Remember, because He is God there is nothing too difficult for Him to help us with. This means that when we pray we can ask Him for whatever we need.

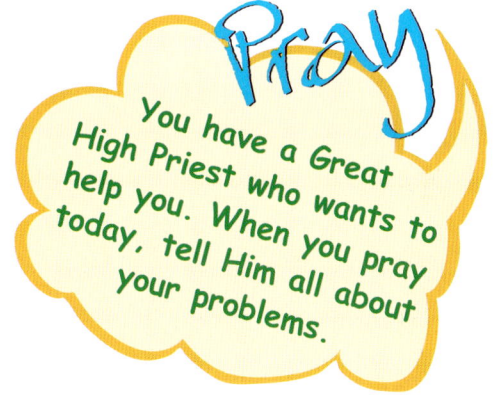

Pray

You have a Great High Priest who wants to help you. When you pray today, tell Him all about your problems.

... through the Bible day by day

December 10

Reading: Hebrews 5. 7-10

If anyone desires to come after Me, let him deny himself, and take up his cross, and follow Me, Matthew 16. 24

If you were watching a great artist like Van Gogh you might be amazed at his skill and spellbound as you watched him bring to life on canvas whatever he was painting. But even though he made no mistakes as you watched him, you wouldn't be able to appreciate the perfection of his painting until the great artist had added his final touches and the picture was finished. Only then, when the last of the many brush strokes had been added, could you really see just how perfect the completed painting was.

Pray: Ask for help to become more like the Lord Jesus and to do whatever He would have done.

The Lord Jesus was always perfect; He was God so He must have been. But before He was born in Bethlehem He never knew what it was like to grow up as a child, to become a teenager or to experience all the things that we do. That's why He became like us, so that He could understand how we feel and help us. When He was here He was lonely, despised, rejected, even laughed at. He was hungry, thirsty, tired. He cried, too, and was sad. He knew what it was like to be misunderstood and accused of things He hadn't done. He also knew what it was like to lose friends. He even knew what it was like to die! Now that He has done all of these things, we can look at Him and fully appreciate just how perfect He is.

The Lord Jesus came into the world and experienced all these things because he was obedient to His Father. Sometimes being obedient can be hard but our reading today tells us that the Lord gives salvation to those 'that obey Him'. Once you become a Christian you will want to obey the Lord in whatever He asks. How will we obey Him today?

Reading: **Hebrews 11. 23-29**

December 11

What things were gain to me, these I have counted loss for Christ,
Philippians 3. 7

Have you ever dreamt about living in a palace? Moses lived in one but he hadn't always. His parents were slaves in Egypt, his first crib was made out of mud and slime and his people, the Israelites, were beaten every day by their cruel Egyptian taskmasters. One day, though, everything changed. An Egyptian princess took him to live in the palace and he became like her son. He had the best of everything, the nicest clothes, plenty of food, and, just imagine, servants to fetch whatever he wanted!

Pray
If you have to make a choice today, ask God for help to make the choice that puts Him first.

You might think that nothing could have been better for Moses; but Moses wasn't happy. Outside the palace his family and friends, God's people, were still very poor. What's more, they were still being used as slaves by the Egyptians. Moses wanted them to be free.

One day he made his choice. He fought some of the Egyptians that were bullying one of the Israelites and then he ran away. He didn't want to live like a prince in the palace when his family and friends were treated as slaves. He decided that he loved God and His people more than he loved all the pleasures he enjoyed in the palace.

After he left the luxury of the palace Moses lived most of the rest of his life in the desert! But God used him to help his people. He became one of the world's greatest leaders and by God's help he delivered the Israelites out of their slavery. What would you have done? God can use you too, if you let Him.

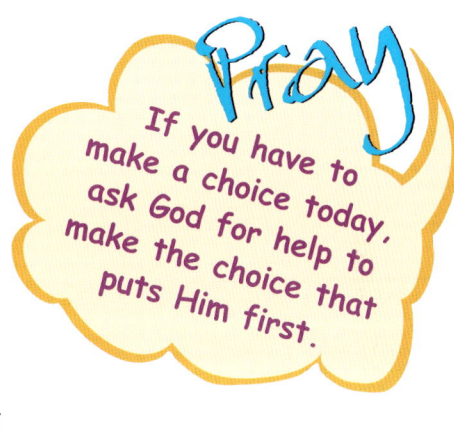

. . . through the Bible day by day

December 12

Reading: Hebrews 11. 32 - 12. 3

Since we are surrounded by so great a cloud of witnesses . . . let us run with endurance the race that is set before us, Hebrews 12. 1

How would you like to be famous? Lots of celebrities are famous for their money or their sport and others just for their looks. Some are soon forgotten. In our reading we learn about some of the Bible's celebrities – they're great because they did great things for God and what they did is never forgotten by Him.

Some of these heroes of the faith were great soldiers and leaders who conquered kingdoms and won great battles. Some of them had great escapes and others tamed wild animals. They were famous in the world they lived in. People wanted to be like them.

But then there were 'others'. We don't know their names and they weren't famous in the world they lived in. They were persecuted because of their faith in God. Some of them were thrown into prison. Some were even killed. Can you remember some of the ways they died? Others were mocked and laughed at. Some lost everything they had and wandered about in deserts and mountains, in dens and caves, dressed only in the skins of animals – sheep and goats. They weren't glamorous at all but they gave up everything for God. We might not know their names but God knows all about each of them. In different parts of the world even today some Christians are being persecuted. God knows all about them too.

Then there are 'others', who were 'tempted'. It might not seem very much to us, but God thinks it is. We might be tempted today to do something we know is wrong, to tell a lie or maybe to cheat or steal or even worse. It's easy to give in; it's much harder not to. By not giving in we too could be some of heaven's heroes.

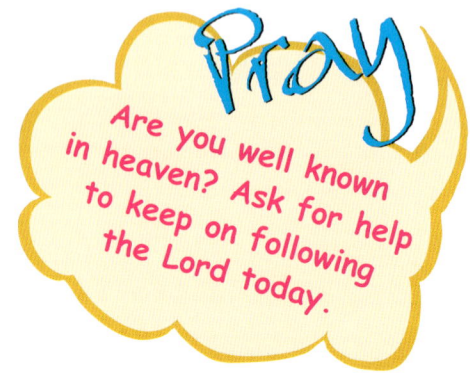

Pray
Are you well known in heaven? Ask for help to keep on following the Lord today.

Stepping stones

Reading: **James 1. 1-7**

December 13

Casting all your care upon Him, for He cares for you, 1 Peter 5. 7

Tests! Who likes them? Do you enjoy revising for 'Sats' or exams, or waiting to know if you've passed? But did you know that the Bible is a survivor's guide to tests? In fact, the Bible tells you how you can be joyful about tests – imagine that!

We're used to all sorts of tests in numeracy, maths, literacy, English and lots more. The tests God sends us are tests of faith and they can come in different ways too. The Christians James was writing to had been chased away from their homes and 'scattered abroad' because they loved and obeyed the Lord Jesus. You might be tested because of this too. But tests can also come through illness or loneliness, sadness and even sometimes by being given what we want. God doesn't test us to find out how much we know, like at school. Instead the tests He sends are to prove to us how real our faith is and whether we will be loyal to Him.

And wouldn't tests be so much easier if the teacher gave us the answer book as well as the questions! Well, God doesn't always give us the answers to the questions we face in life either but He does promise to help us in our tests. In fact our reading tells us that we can ask God for wisdom and He'll give it to us generously. In other words He'll give us all the help we could ever possibly need. You see, God wants us to pass these tests. And if we endure and pass them, these tests will surely make us become more perfectly like Jesus Himself. That's why we should be joyful and thankful for them.

Pray
When things are difficult ask God for His help. You can be sure that nothing is too hard for Him.

. . . through the Bible day by day

December 14

Reading: James 3. 1-12

Let your speech always be with grace,
Colossians 4. 6

Two boys were helping on the farm during the summer holiday. The farmer had harvested his crop and the heavy work of carting the straw bales back to the barn was complete. Before ploughing the field, he asked the boys to help him burn the stubble left behind. This was the work the boys had been waiting for. Lighting the fire was the work of a moment, and soon they were gleefully spreading the burning straw so that within minutes the field was alight. Later, and sure that the fire was dying out, the boys left to go home, but soon came rushing back. Rekindled by the wind the fire had jumped the trench that surrounded the field and spread to the railway embankment. The boys were scared and ran to the farmhouse for help but nothing could be done except to wait until the fire had burnt itself out, leaving destruction behind it. Starting the fire was easy but controlling it proved impossible.

James used this kind of example to teach us how much damage words can do. Our tongues might be small but they can cause BIG trouble! Can you remember a time when you've been hurt by what someone has said? A wise person knows how important it is to be careful what they say. We can pretend to be nice, but if we say things which are nasty or spiteful, untrue or impure, it shows that we really are not.

People said of the Lord Jesus 'never man spoke like this man'. In another place the Bible says that, as people listened, they wondered at the gracious words that came out of His mouth. Is that what they say when they listen to us?

Pray

When you go out today, remember that someone else is listening to all that you say. Ask God for help to say the right things.

Stepping stones

Reading: James 4. 13-15

December 15

My times are in Your hand, Psalm 31. 15

Making plans is fun. We all enjoy looking forward to things – holidays, birthdays or something else. Some people love making lists of all the things they need to do. Some of us just daydream about what we'd rather be doing. But one thing's certain; none of us actually knows what we will be doing. So many things can happen that might change our plans.

Sometimes people talk as if things just happen by chance or luck, as if nobody's in control. If something nice happens it's 'good luck' and if not it's just 'bad luck'. People can be afraid of what might happen. They try to find out the future by paying money to have their fortunes told. Other people think the position of the stars in the sky can tell them what will happen, so they 'read their stars' in magazines. But the Christian doesn't need to do any of these things. Why? Because we know that the Lord is in control of everything and that nothing can happen that He doesn't allow. One day Jesus told His disciples that even a single sparrow couldn't fall to the ground without God knowing all about it. Imagine how many sparrows there are! And He said we are of more value than many sparrows. In fact, Jesus said that God even knows the number of hairs on our heads. Imagine that!

Because the Lord controls everything, we shouldn't plan to do anything without remembering that it can only happen 'if the Lord will'. Our reading tells us that He even decides how long our lives will be. Don't forget to pray for help to keep God in your plans today.

Pray: Ask God to help you trust the One who made the world and knows all about its inhabitants. Ask Him to give you peace in remembering that He knows the future, too.

... through the Bible day by day

351

December 16

Reading: James 5. 16-18

Whatever things were written before were written for our learning, that we through the patience and comfort of the Scriptures might have hope, Romans 15. 4

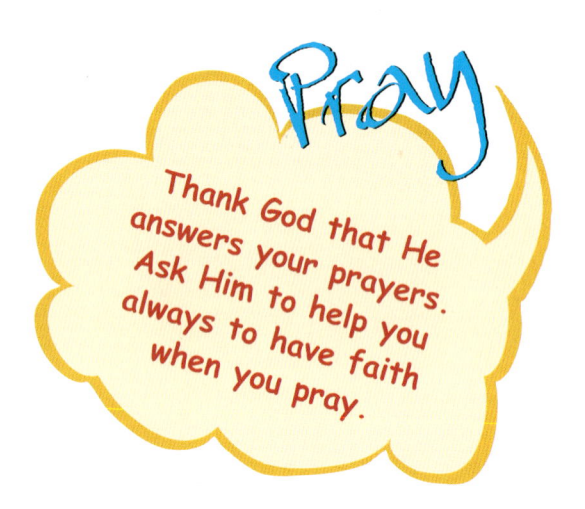

Pray

Thank God that He answers your prayers. Ask Him to help you always to have faith when you pray.

Imagine living in a country where it hasn't rained for three-and-a-half years! Most of us live where it doesn't go three-and-a-half days without raining. Elijah lived in Israel where they had a wicked king called Ahab. Ahab did not pray to God. In fact, he ignored God and worshipped a false god called Baal. So Elijah prayed that God would not send rain and for three-and-a-half years the country was punished for Ahab's sin. During those years of drought Elijah prayed many times and God answered in wonderful ways. God always made sure Elijah had something to eat and drink. A widow was kind to Elijah. When her son died, Elijah prayed and God brought him back to life.

Elijah was determined to show that his God was the true God. He set a challenge for the priests of Baal. They were to build two altars, put sacrifices on them but not to add fire. The priests prayed to Baal and Elijah prayed to God for fire to be sent onto the sacrifice. It's not surprising that nothing came from Baal, but God sent fire from heaven. No one could doubt the power of the true God now. Then Elijah prayed and asked God to send rain again. He did.

Elijah was just an ordinary person like you and me. Because he was righteous his prayers were powerful and God answered them. If we want God to answer our prayers we must believe He is able to, and we must be righteous, too. The Lord Jesus told His disciples that if they had faith and didn't doubt they could ask God to move a mountain and He would! He said, 'Whatever things you ask in prayer, believing, you will receive', Matt. 21. 22. Do we believe that?

Stepping stones

Reading: **1 Peter 3. 1-9**

December 17

As for me and my house, we will serve the Lord, Joshua 24. 15

'Happy the home where Jesus' name
　　Is sweet to every ear;
Where children early lisp His fame
　　And parents hold Him dear'.

This verse hangs on my wall and I love it! It reminds me how important it is that the whole family loves God and lives for Him.

I have a friend who was saved as a young girl. She is the only person in her house who is a Christian. It is difficult for her as she has no encouragement at home to live for God. She cannot understand why every young person who is being brought up in a home with Christian parents is not very grateful for that privilege. I know sometimes it is easy to take it for granted but let's determine to thank God every day for our Christian home, if we have one.

Pray

If your parents are Christians thank God for that. If not, ask God to help you live in such a way that your parents can see Christ in you.

Peter teaches every family member who is a believer in the Lord Jesus how they should live. If you hope to be married some day this is how to be a good wife or husband. A wife has to be submissive to her husband. She has to understand that true beauty is not about how she looks. True beauty is seen in how she lives. She must 'do good'. She must not show off with her clothes and jewellery. And a husband has to be understanding towards his wife and honour her.

Most importantly we ALL have to be compassionate, loving and polite to each other. Now that would make for a happy home! God is wise when He gives us directions for life. If we obey Him we will be truly happy. It would be good if we could all make an early resolution to show love and kindness to our Mum, Dad, brothers and sisters. After all, God commands us to!

. . . through the Bible day by day

December 18

Reading: 2 Peter 3. 1-9

The Lord is not slack concerning His promise, as some count slackness, but is longsuffering toward us, not willing that any should perish but that all should come to repentance, 2 Peter 3. 9

When I was young my Mum would sometimes leave my sister and me with a babysitter. This was fine with me but my sister hated it. She wailed when Mum left and if she thought Mum was away too long she wailed some more. Reminders of the fact Mum had promised she was coming back would not console her. I couldn't understand it because Mum didn't break her promises!

Sometimes we can be a bit like my sister. We might think the Lord Jesus has been away such a long time He won't be coming back. No matter what anyone tells you, He is coming back! How can I be so sure? The Lord Jesus told His disciples in John chapter 14 verse 3, 'I will come again and receive you unto Myself'. God made many other promises about the Lord Jesus and everyone has been kept. We can be sure this is a promise He will keep too.

It took Noah 120 years to build the ark. God was giving the people plenty of time to believe the message of coming judgement and get into the ark. They didn't get in and as a result they died in the great flood.

The Lord Jesus is coming back to take away Christians. After that the world will be judged. Just because He has been away for over 2000 years doesn't mean God's promise won't be kept. Maybe He hasn't come back yet because you haven't repented and had your sins forgiven. Maybe you're praying for someone to be saved and He is leaving time for that to happen. God knows best and His Son *will* return at the right time. The many years He has been away shows us how gracious God is in giving us time to repent. Don't be too late.

Pray

Thank God that He has given you time to repent and turn to Him. Ask Him to give you faith to keep believing that His Word will be done.

Stepping stones

Reading: 1 John 1. 1-7

December 19

This is the condemnation, that the light has come into the world, and men loved darkness rather than light, because their deeds were evil, John 3. 19

Have you ever lifted a big stone in the garden and watched the beetles run away? What do you think they're running from? I think they are running from the light because it makes them feel exposed and vulnerable. The Bible tells us that people who haven't asked God to forgive their sins and believed in the Lord Jesus are like that. God is light and when He shines His light on people's lives they feel exposed and can see how sinful they are. They feel vulnerable thinking about the judgement of God. That's why they try to stay away from the things of God and prefer the darkness of their sins.

Christians should not feel like that. We should always want to live in the light of God. To do that, we need to keep reading our Bibles and praying. This keeps us close to God because we are listening to Him talk to us through His Word and we are talking to Him in prayer. We will not want to sin if God's light is shining in our lives. When you go into a dark room and turn on the light the darkness disappears and everything is bright. When you put the light off again the darkness comes back. Darkness and light can't be in the same room at the same time.

In the Bible 'light' speaks to us of truth and holiness and 'darkness' speaks of lies and sin. Light and darkness can't both be in your life. Either you have God's light and don't want to sin or you want to keep on sinning. Then it's obvious you are not a Christian. If you are a Christian you will want to be like the Lord Jesus who is the light and who has nothing to do with darkness.

Pray

Thank God that you can have fellowship with Him because your sins are forgiven. Ask Him to help you always walk in His light.

. . . through the Bible day by day

December 20

Reading: 1 John 1. 8 – 2. 6

If we confess our sins, He is faithful and just to forgive us our sins and to cleanse us from all unrighteousness,
1 John 1. 9

When I was young I accidentally broke a special ornament of my mum's. I was playing with a ball in the living room - definitely against the house rules! I hid the broken pieces and for a few days lived in fear of being found out. Eventually I couldn't live with my guilty conscience any longer and confessed to mum what had happened. She could see how sorry I was and despite being disappointed in me she forgave me. The relief was incredible and I felt so much better.

Christians should never sin deliberately. Sometimes we find ourselves sinning despite our best intentions not to. What a disappointment this is to God! His Son died to free us from the power of sin yet here we are straying away from Him and sinning. If we sin, what should we do? Certainly not try to cover it up like I did with the broken ornament. If we sin we must confess it to God right away. You might wonder why we have to tell God something He already knows. God wants us to own up to it and admit that we know we have done wrong. If we do that God has promised He will forgive us.

When the Lord Jesus took the punishment for our sins it wasn't just for the sins we committed before we were saved. It was for every single sin we commit through our whole lives. Because God is satisfied with His Son's sacrifice at Calvary, He can forgive us and still be just.

So, how can we keep from sinning? It's by staying close to God through reading the Bible and praying. The more aware we are of God's presence with us the less likely we are to sin.

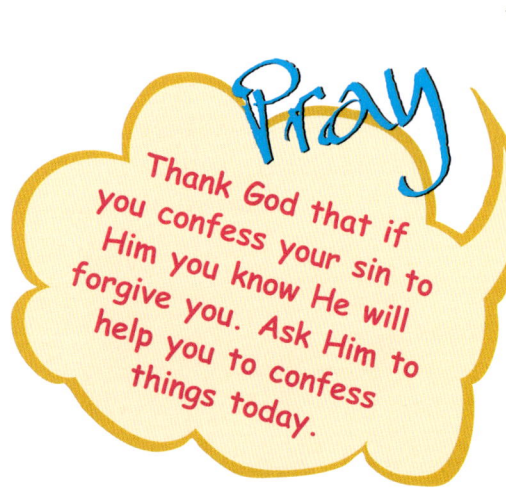

Pray
Thank God that if you confess your sin to Him you know He will forgive you. Ask Him to help you to confess things today.

Stepping stones

Reading: 1 John 2. 12-17

December 21

Do not be conformed to this world, but be transformed by the renewing of your mind, that you may prove what is that good and acceptable and perfect will of God, Romans 12. 2

When I was a child I made models of Disney characters. I poured a gooey mixture into the moulds and when it hardened the models came out looking exactly like Snow White and the seven dwarves. I painted them and they looked great. Maybe you've seen this done or perhaps you've seen a jelly made in a mould. In our memory verse today the words 'don't be conformed to this world' mean 'don't let the world put you into its mould'. People who are not Christians don't like us living for God and they try to make us exactly like them. Satan wants to ruin our lives for God by tempting us to love sinful things. The Bible tells us that our lives must be different because God has changed us from the inside.

John warns us that we must not 'love the world or the things of the world'. What does he mean? Unbelievers love things that are anti-God and go against His commandments. They make sinful things allowable and want sin to look good in their songs, books and films. John is very blunt – anyone who loves things that go against God cannot be a Christian. That means if I am a Christian I shouldn't listen to songs that make sin sound like a good thing, I shouldn't watch anything that shows people doing sinful things and I shouldn't read anything that goes against what God tells me is right. If I do love these things maybe it's time I made sure I am really saved.

There seems little point in spending time and effort on things that are going to be destroyed. The Bible tells us the things of the world will be destroyed soon and it is only the things of God that are worthwhile and will last forever.

Pray: Praise God if you are saved and ask Him to save you if you are not. Ask Him to keep you from loving sinful things.

... through the Bible day by day

December 22

Reading: 1 John 4. 7-21

By this all will know that you are My disciples, if you have love for one another, John 13. 35

Have you ever heard the saying 'actions speak louder than words'? Sometimes it can be easy to say things but harder to prove we mean what we say by what we do.

In the upper room the Lord Jesus told His disciples that He loved them. Just hours later He showed them how much He loved them when He went to the cross and took the punishment for sin.

I have a CD with a song on it called 'Loving God, Loving Each Other'. It tells the story of what the Lord Jesus said to His disciples, John 13. After He told them He loved them He gave them a new commandment. He said, 'A new commandment I give to you, that you love one another; as I have loved you, that you also love one another', John 13. 34. Sometimes we can find it easy to say 'I'm a Christian, I love the Lord Jesus'. How can we prove that we do love Him? The Lord Jesus tells us how. 'He who has My commandments and keeps them, it is he who loves Me', John 14. 21. His commandment is that we love one another. If we truly love the Lord Jesus we will love our fellow Christians.

How can I show that love? Perhaps by praying for them, being kind, visiting them if they're sick, helping them, not talking about them behind their back, forgiving them quickly if they've wronged us. I'm sure you can think of some more.

When we think of the great love that God showed us surely it can't be too hard to pass some of that love on to others in His family. We can't say we love God if we don't love each other.

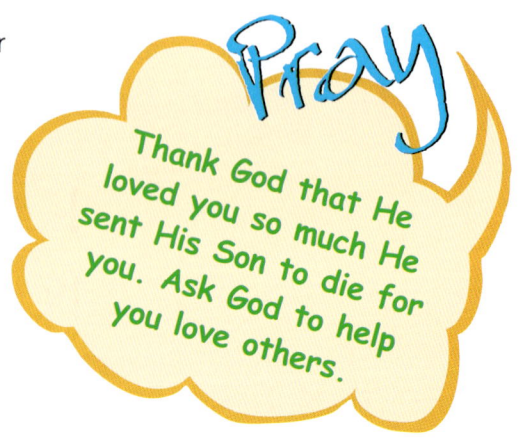

Pray

Thank God that He loved you so much He sent His Son to die for you. Ask God to help you love others.

Stepping stones

Reading: Jude 24-25

December 23

Kept by the power of God through faith for salvation ready to be revealed in the last time, 1 Peter 1. 5

My grandparents live by the sea and when I was a child I loved to go for a walk along the promenade. My favourite thing was to walk on the sea wall. I was only allowed to do this as long as I promised to hold my dad's hand. It was too dangerous otherwise. On the other side of the wall there was a long drop into the sea.

Our heavenly Father knows that we face dangers in our Christian life and promises to help us. Satan tempts us to sin and if we are relying on ourselves, we will never be able to resist the temptation. Our life for God is like a path and the temptations are like boulders. Without someone to hold onto, you would trip and fall. When I was on the sea wall I was only safe if I held on tightly to my dad's hand. How can we stay close to God and hold on to Him? By speaking to Him every day in prayer and listening to Him speak to us through the Bible. In Psalm 119 verse 105 we read 'Your word is a lamp to my feet and a light to my path'. It keeps us safe from the dangers Satan puts before us to make us fall.

Sometimes on our walk I thought about letting go of dad's hand. I decided not to because the risk of getting hurt was too great. If we don't stay close to God we risk sinning and hurting ourselves and others around about.

God is always close to us. Jude tells us He is able to keep us from falling into sin. We must work at staying close to Him and letting Him keep us safe.

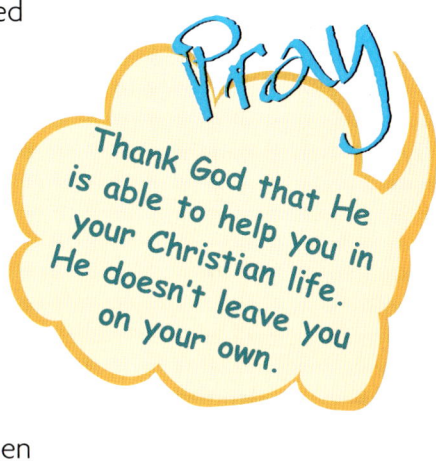

Pray

Thank God that He is able to help you in your Christian life. He doesn't leave you on your own.

...through the Bible day by day

December 24

Reading: **Revelation 1. 9-20**

Come up here, and I will show you things which must take place after this,
Revelation 4. 1

I would love to go to London and visit Buckingham Palace. I have seen pictures of what it is like and I would really like to see the beautiful furnishings and rooms for myself. I am quite sure, however, that if I do make it to Buckingham Palace, I won't be invited to go and see the Queen. John was not only invited into heaven but he met the King of kings!

It must have been wonderful to see the Lord Jesus and to hear what He had to say. The Lord Jesus told John things that would happen in the future. He asked him to write them down so that others could learn about them too. John was so overwhelmed with the awesomeness of the Lord Jesus that he fell down as if he were dead. But the Lord Jesus Himself told John not to be afraid.

Although John was given a special treat in seeing the Lord Jesus before John went to heaven, everyone who has their sins forgiven will one day be there and will see the Lord Jesus. We won't just see Him from a distance but we shall actually see His face, Revelation 22. 4. That will be amazing – to see the face of the Man that loved us enough to die for us and take the punishment for our sins.

We must be very careful as we live our lives on earth that we live in such a way that we won't be ashamed to look the Lord in the face one day. We must live close to Him so that when we hear His voice speaking to us He will be able to say to us, 'Well done, good and faithful servant'. How amazing that will be!

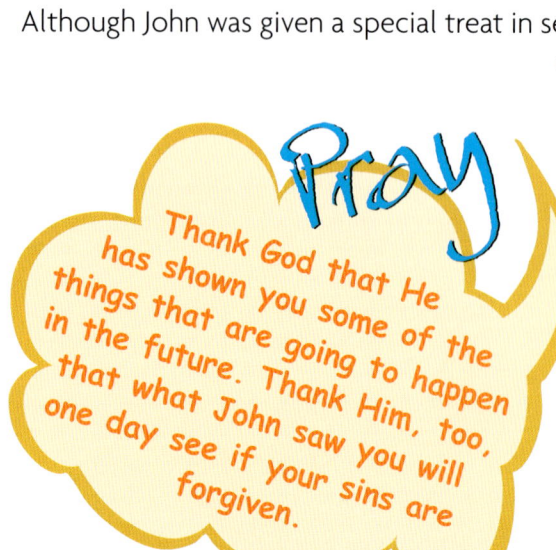

Pray

Thank God that He has shown you some of the things that are going to happen in the future. Thank Him, too, that what John saw you will one day see if your sins are forgiven.

Stepping stones

Reading: **Revelation 4**

December 25

You are worthy, O Lord, to receive glory and honour and power; for You created all things, and by Your will they exist and were created, Revelation 4. 11

A boy from my town once won a singing competition on the TV. Suddenly he was the best known person in the town. Posters of him appeared all over the place and people were wearing T-shirts with his face on the front. When he came home for a visit everyone wanted to see him and his house was mobbed. You would have thought he was a great hero.

Unlike this boy, God is mostly ignored by people in the world and no one wants anything to do with Him. Because people can't see Him they ignore Him. But in heaven He is rightly worshipped and praised.

You might be wondering what He has done to deserve this praise and worship. The song they sing in heaven tells us. He is the One who is holy. This means that He is perfect and there is no sin in Him at all. He has never done anything wrong! He is also almighty. He can do whatever He wants and no one has the power to stop Him. He also lives forever and ever. He is the One who does not change, Malachi 3. 6. That means His love will always be the same, His holiness will never change and His power will never get weaker. He is also the One who created all things. 'In the beginning God created the heavens and the earth', Genesis 1. 1. And He is the One who gives us all life. We exist because He has made us.

When John heard this wonderful song of praise to God upon the throne, he saw all in heaven fall down and worship God. It is our privilege to praise and worship this wonderful God now, and to look forward one day to praising Him in heaven. How awesome that will be!

Pray

Thank God that you can praise and worship the One who is worthy of all honour because of what He has done in creation and at Calvary.

. . . through the Bible day by day

December 26

READING: Revelation 5

You are worthy to take the scroll, and to open its seals; for You were slain, and have redeemed us to God by Your blood out of every tribe and tongue and people and nation, Revelation 5. 9

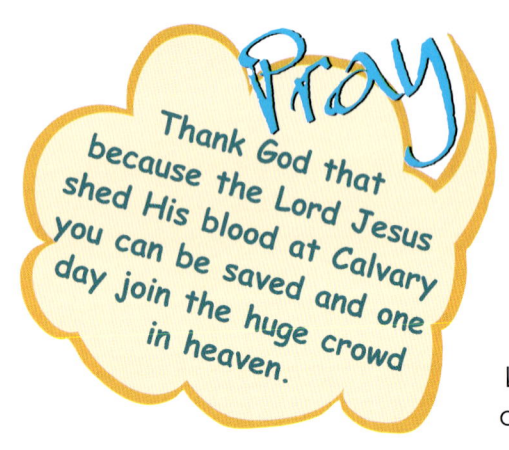

Pray

Thank God that because the Lord Jesus shed His blood at Calvary you can be saved and one day join the huge crowd in heaven.

John was sad because there seemed to be no one good enough to open a very special book that God held in His hand. As John cried he was comforted when he was told that someone had been found who was worthy to open the book. This One was called 'the Lion of the tribe of Judah'. That is a very powerful name and John turned to see who this person was. What he saw was a surprise to him, because there, before the throne of God, stood a Lamb looking as if it had just been killed. It was, of course, the Lord Jesus.

How can someone be described as a Lion and a Lamb?

The Lord Jesus is like a Lion because He is God and therefore all-powerful. He created the world and keeps it in place. He is, at the moment, 'upholding all things by the word of His power', Hebrews 1. 3. It is wonderful to think that One so powerful was once 'found in appearance as a man . . . and became obedient to the point of death, even the death of the cross', Philippians 2. 8. And that is why He is called a Lamb. John called Him the Lamb of God who would be sacrificed to take away the sin of the world.

In Old Testament times the Israelites had to shed the blood of a lamb to save the lives of their first-born children. That was a picture of what the Lord Jesus would do for us. He shed His blood and took the punishment for sin at Calvary. If we ask Him to forgive us He will and one day we will see Him in heaven, where we will join billions of others who will all sing the same song. I can't wait. Can you?

Stepping stones

Reading: Revelation 6. 1-4; 8. 1-6; 15. 1-7

December 27

Alas! For that day is great, so that none is like it; and it is the time of Jacob's trouble, but he shall be saved out of it, Jeremiah 30. 7

Sometimes in the Bible we read things that are not nice to think about and not easy to understand. The chapters we read today can be a bit like that. As we read them we have to remember that God is fair in all He does and would never punish anyone who doesn't deserve to be punished.

God will send dreadful judgements on the world in the last days. As each seal is opened, each trumpet blown and each bowl emptied more and more terrible things happen on earth. Some are plagues like the ones the Egyptians received when Moses freed the children of Israel. There will be wars, famine, disease, cosmic disturbance, earthquakes and horrendous suffering. You may have read in the newspapers about famine and war but this will be far worse than anyone has ever seen before.

The whole world will be affected but the nation of Israel will suffer even more. They will become the hate-target for all the other armies. A terrible man will pretend to be their friend then turn against them and persecute them. Unless they worship him he will starve them, hunt them and ultimately kill them. Some will choose to worship this 'Beast' as he is called but many will be martyrs and will die to stay faithful to God.

It is very solemn to think of the consequences of rejecting God's offer of salvation. He sent His Son to take the punishment we deserve but we have to accept this special gift and thank God for it. If you have done this then thank God that He has promised that before any of these terrible things happen in the world the Lord Jesus will come back to the air and take all true believers to heaven where we will be safe.

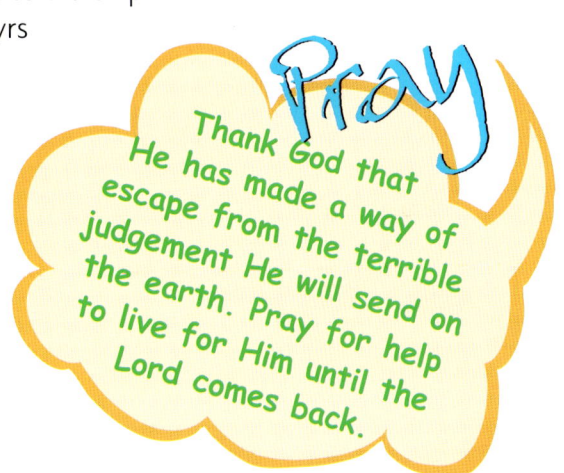

Pray

Thank God that He has made a way of escape from the terrible judgement He will send on the earth. Pray for help to live for Him until the Lord comes back.

. . . through the Bible day by day

December 28

Reading: **Revelation 19. 11-21**

It is a righteous thing with God . . . to give you who are troubled rest with us when the Lord Jesus is revealed from heaven with His mighty angels, 2 Thessalonians 1. 6-7

Pray

Thank God that He doesn't ask any of us to put up with more than we can bear. Ask Him to help you in difficult situations.

I remember at playtime in school one day a small boy was surrounded by bullies. They were hitting and kicking him, sure that they wouldn't be caught because the teacher was out at a staff meeting. Suddenly, without warning, the teacher marched into the mob. He rescued the poor boy and removed the bullies to be punished. What a shock they got – the teacher's meeting had finished early and he unexpectedly returned!

This incident reminds me of what is going to happen to the land of Israel in the future. After all the Christians have been taken to heaven by the Lord Jesus, the armies of the world will surround that land. They will seem to be defeated and unable to defend themselves. Without warning the Lord Jesus will appear. He will destroy the armies of the world and save the people of Israel from certain death. The Lord Jesus will set up His kingdom and reign in peace for 1000 years.

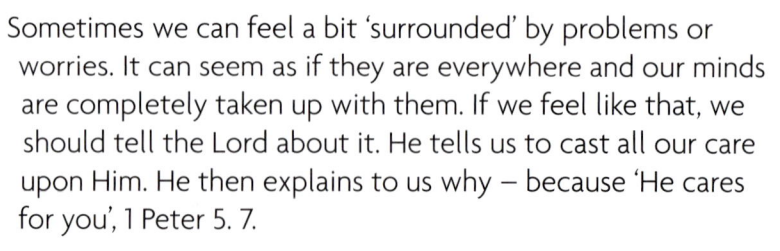

Sometimes we can feel a bit 'surrounded' by problems or worries. It can seem as if they are everywhere and our minds are completely taken up with them. If we feel like that, we should tell the Lord about it. He tells us to cast all our care upon Him. He then explains to us why – because 'He cares for you', 1 Peter 5. 7.

It is important to speak to God about our trials and troubles. He will not allow us to go through more than we can handle. 'God is faithful, who will not allow you to be tested beyond what you are able', 1 Corinthians 10. 13. He is always ready to listen when we come to Him and will always give us the strength we ask for in times of trouble or testing.

Stepping stones

Reading: Revelation 20. 1-10

December 29

Woe to the inhabitants of the earth and the sea! For the devil has come down to you, having great wrath, because he knows he has a short time, Revelation 12. 12

During the First World War something special happened between the German and British soldiers. On Christmas Day one year a cease-fire had been called. There was fighting until Christmas Eve and then all fell silent. Each side could hear the other singing Christmas carols and their hearts were warmed. On Christmas Day a British soldier climbed out of his trench and called to the German soldiers that he'd like to meet them. Some brave Germans came out and then more came from both sides.

Before too long a game of football had started between the men! For a short time they were friends and there was peace.

Unfortunately, it couldn't last. The cease-fire finished at midnight and the fighting began again. Millions of men were killed over the next four years of war. The world has never really known lasting peace.

God has a great plan for this world and it includes lasting peace. While Satan is around there can never be peace but God will deal with him to ensure His plan comes to pass. After the Lord Jesus returns to save Israel from the armies of the world Satan will be thrown into the lake of fire, never to be released. God will judge those who followed Satan and the world will at last know eternal peace.

Each of us has a decision to make. We have to decide whose side we are going to be on. Satan cannot bring us peace and is going to be defeated. God will give us peace now and forever. Just now it might feel like everyone is against the Christians and want nothing to do with God. One day, however, the Lord Jesus will reign over the whole world in peace. Trust the Lord Jesus now and be on the winning side!

Pray: Thank God that despite the unrest in the world today He has a plan that will bring peace. Thank Him, if you are a Christian, that His plan includes you.

...through the Bible day by day

December 30

Reading: Revelation 20. 11-15

It is appointed for men to die once, but after this the judgment, Hebrews 9. 27

There was once a judge who lived by the sea. He knew its dangers and volunteered to help on the life boat. One day he was called out. Along with the rest of the crew he raced to help a boat in trouble. They didn't know the boat was stolen. The thieves didn't realize they were in danger and sailed onto treacherous rocks. Just before they sank the life boat came along side and the judge helped pull them to safety. The two thieves were handed over to the police and came to court to be charged for their crimes. The judge who sentenced them to prison was the same man who had saved them from certain death. One day he was their saviour, then became their judge.

If you have never trusted the Lord Jesus and had your sins forgiven He is longing to save you. The Bible warns us, however, that 'now is the accepted time, now is the day of salvation'. If you die before you repent, or the Lord Jesus comes back for His people, your opportunity will be gone forever. God has a register in heaven called the book of life. When you trust in the Lord Jesus to save you from your sins God writes your name in that book. One day the book will be opened and God will look for your name. If your name is not found in it you will be punished forever for your sins. The Lord Jesus will be sitting on a great white throne as your Judge and will sentence you to everlasting death.

Today He wants to be your Saviour and waits for you to ask Him to save you. If you don't, one day He will have to be your Judge.

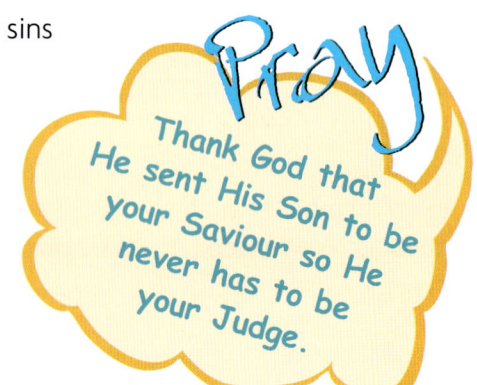

Pray
Thank God that He sent His Son to be your Saviour so He never has to be your Judge.

Reading: Revelation 22. 1-5

December 31

God will wipe away every tear from their eyes; there shall be no more death, nor sorrow, nor crying. There shall be no more pain, for the former things have passed away, Revelation 21. 4

I love to read and I'll tell you a secret about me and books. When I start a new book I just have to have a quick look at the back page to see if it has a happy ending or not. Sometimes I don't even read a book if the ending is sad.

I am so glad the Bible has a happy ending. In the last book of the Bible God outlines the future for Christians. It says that we will be in a place where there is no more curse. When this world was newly created Adam and Eve lived in the garden of Eden and everything was perfect – until they sinned. After that the world and mankind were cursed. There was illness, dying, sadness, weeds, cruelty and every kind of sin.

After the judgement at the great white throne, God will make a new heaven and a new earth, which will not be cursed. That means that there will be no sadness, no illness, no dying, no pain, no darkness and no sin. More importantly we will be with God and 'God Himself will be with' us, Revelation 21. 3. What a beautiful description of heaven God gives us.

We must remember that all this is only for those who have accepted they are sinners and taken the Lord Jesus as their Saviour. For those of us that are already Christians we should surely be spreading this good news of God's happy ending. It would be terrible if someone we love doesn't see this beautiful new earth and new heaven because we didn't tell them about God's plan of salvation. It's a plan that God started to work out in the very first book of the Bible and God finishes in the very last. What a great God we have!

Pray

Thank God that He has planned a happy ending for those who believe on Him. Pray that God will give you the courage to share the good news with others.

...through the Bible day by day

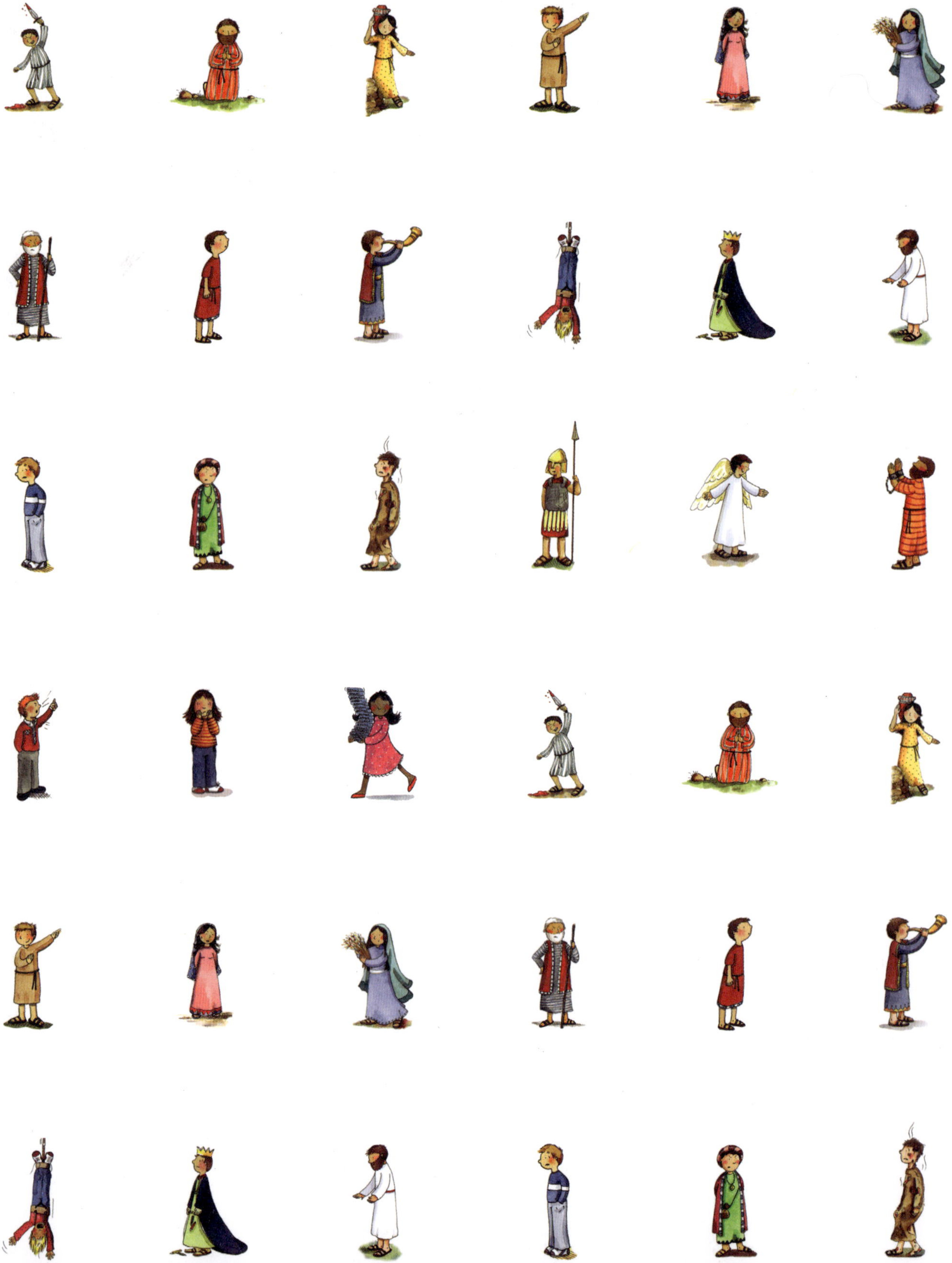